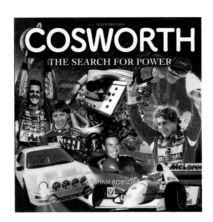

SIXTH EDITION

COSWORTH
THE SEARCH FOR POWER

GRAHAM ROBSON

Other great books from Veloce:

Essential Buyer's Guide Series
Alfa Romeo Alfasud – All saloon models from 1971 to 1983 & Sprint models from 1976 to 1989 (Metcalfe)
Alfa Romeo Giulia GT Coupé (Booker)
Alfa Romeo Giulia Spider (Booker)
Audi TT (Davies)
Austin Seven (Barker)
Big Healeys (Trummel)
BMW E21 3 Series (1975-1983) (Cook & Wylie)
BMW E30 3 Series (1981 to 1994) (Hosier)
BMW GS (Henshaw)
BMW X5 (Saunders)
Citroën 2CV (Paxton)
Citroën ID & DS (Heilig)
Cobra Replicas (Ayre)
Corvette C2 Sting Ray 1963-1967 (Falconer)
Choosing, Using & Maintaining Your Electric Bicycle (Henshaw)
Fiat 500 & 600 (Bobbitt)
Ford Capri (Paxton)
Ford Escort Mk1 & Mk2 (Williamson)
Ford Model T – All models 1909 to 1927 (Barker)
Ford Mustang – First Generation 1964 to 1973 (Cook)
Ford Mustang – Fifth generation/S197 (Cook)
Ford RS Cosworth Sierra & Escort (Williamson)
Hillman Imp – All models of the Hillman Imp, Sunbeam Stiletto, Singer Chamois, Hillman Husky & Commer Imp 1963 to 1976 (Morgan)
Jaguar E-Type 3.8 & 4.2-litre (Crespin)
Jaguar E-type V12 5.3-litre (Crespin)
Jaguar Mark 1 & 2 (All models including Daimler 2.5-litre V8) 1955 to 1969 (Thorley)
Jaguar S-Type – 1999 to 2007 (Thorley)
Jaguar X-Type – 2001 to 2009 (Thorley)
Jaguar XJ-S (Crespin)
Jaguar XJ6, XJ8 & XJR (Thorley)
Jaguar XK 120, 140 & 150 (Thorley)
Jaguar XK8 & XKR (1996-2005) (Thorley)
Jaguar/Daimler XJ 1994-2003 (Crespin)
Jaguar/Daimler XJ40 (Crespin)
Jaguar/Daimler XJ6, XJ12 & Sovereign (Crespin)
Land Rover Series I, II & IIA (Thurman)
Land Rover Series III (Thurman)
Lotus Seven replicas & Caterham 7: 1973-2013 (Hawkins)
Mazda MX-5 Miata (Mk1 1989-97 & Mk2 98-2001) (Crook)
Mazda RX-8 All models 2003 to 2012 (Parish)
Mercedes Benz Pagoda 230SL, 250SL & 280SL roadsters & coupès (Bass)
Mercedes-Benz 190 All 190 models (W201 series) 1982 to 1993 (Parish)
Mercedes-Benz 280-560SL & SLC (Bass)
Mercedes-Benz SL R129 Series (Parish)
Mercedes-Benz W123 All models 1976 to 1986 (Parish)
Mercedes-Benz W124 – All models 1984-1997 (Zoporowski)
MG Midget & A-H Sprite (Horler)
MG TD, TF & TF1500 (Jones)
MGA 1955-1962 (Crosier)
MGB & MGB GT (Williams)
MGF & MG TF (Hawkins)
Mini (Paxton)
Morris Minor & 1000 (Newell)
New Mini (Collins)
Peugeot 205 GTI (Blackburn)
Porsche 911 (964) (Streather)
Porsche 911 (993) (Streather)
Porsche 911 (996) (Streather)
Porsche 911 (997) Model years 2004 to 2009 (Streather)
Porsche 911 (997) Second generation models 2009 to 2012 (Streather)
Porsche 911 Carrera 3.2 (Streather)
Porsche 911 SC (Streather)
Porsche 924 – All models 1976 to 1988 (Hodgkins)
Porsche 928 (Hemmings)
Porsche 930 Turbo & 911 (930) Turbo (Streather)
Porsche 944 (Higgins)
Porsche 986 Boxster (Streather)
Porsche 987 Boxster & Cayman (Streather)
Rolls-Royce Silver Shadow & Bentley T-Series (Bobbitt)
Subaru Impreza (Hobbs)
Sunbeam Alpine (Barker)
Triumph Herald & Vitesse (Davies)
Triumph Spitfire & GT6 (Baugues)
Triumph Stag (Mort)
Triumph TR6 (Williams)
Triumph TR7 & TR8 (Williams)
Volvo 700/900 Series (Beavis)
VW Beetle (Cservenka & Copping)
VW Bus (Cservenka & Copping)
VW Golf GTI (Cservenka & Copping)

Rally Giants Series
Audi Quattro (Robson)
Austin Healey 100-6 & 3000 (Robson)
Fiat 131 Abarth (Robson)
Ford Escort MkI (Robson)
Ford Escort RS Cosworth & World Rally Car (Robson)
Ford Escort RS1800 (Robson)
Lancia Delta 4WD/Integrale (Robson)
Lancia Stratos (Robson)
Mini Cooper/Mini Cooper S (Robson)
Peugeot 205 T16 (Robson)
Saab 96 & V4 (Robson)
Subaru Impreza (Robson)
Toyota Celica GT4 (Robson)

Biographies
A Chequered Life – Graham Warner and the Chequered Flag (Hesletine)
A Life Awheel – The 'auto' biography of W de Forte (Skelton)
Amédée Gordini ... a true racing legend (Smith)
André Lefebvre, and the cars he created at Voisin and Citroën (Beck)
Chris Carter at Large – Stories from a lifetime in motorcycle racing (Carter & Skelton)
Cliff Allison, The Official Biography of – From the Fells to Ferrari (Gauld)
Edward Turner – The Man Behind the Motorcycles (Clew)
Driven by Desire – The Desiré Wilson Story
First Principles – The Official Biography of Keith Duckworth (Burr)
Inspired to Design – F1 cars, Indycars & racing tyres: the autobiography of Nigel Bennett (Bennett)
Jack Sears, The Official Biography of – Gentleman Jack (Gauld)
Jim Redman – 6 Times World Motorcycle Champion: The Autobiography (Redman)
John Chatham – 'Mr Big Healey' – The Official Biography (Burr)
The Lee Noble Story (Wilkins)
Mason's Motoring Mayhem – Tony Mason's hectic life in motorsport and television (Mason)
Raymond Mays' Magnificent Obsession (Apps)
Pat Moss Carlsson Story, The – Harnessing Horsepower (Turner)
'Sox' – Gary Hocking – the forgotten World Motorcycle Champion (Hughes)
Tony Robinson – The biography of a race mechanic (Wagstaff)
Virgil Exner – Visioneer: The Official Biography of Virgil M Exner Designer Extraordinaire (Grist)

General
11/2-litre GP Racing 1961-1965 (Whitelock)
AC Two-litre Saloons & Buckland Sportscars (Archibald)
Alfa Romeo 155/156/147 Competition Touring Cars (Collins)
Alfa Romeo Giulia Coupé GT & GTA (Tipler)
Alfa Romeo Montreal – The dream car that came true (Taylor)
Alfa Romeo Montreal – The Essential Companion (Classic Reprint of 500 copies) (Taylor)
Alfa Tipo 33 (McDonough & Collins)
Alpine & Renault – The Development of the Revolutionary Turbo F1 Car 1968 to 1979 (Smith)
Alpine & Renault – The Sports Prototypes 1963 to 1969 (Smith)
Alpine & Renault – The Sports Prototypes 1973 to 1978 (Smith)
Anatomy of the Classic Mini (Huthert & Ely)
Anatomy of the Works Minis (Moylan)
Armstrong-Siddeley (Smith)
Art Deco and British Car Design (Down)
Autodrome (Collins & Ireland)
Autodrome 2 (Collins & Ireland)
Automotive A-Z, Lane's Dictionary of Automotive Terms (Lane)
Automotive Mascots (Kay & Springate)
Bahamas Speed Weeks, The (O'Neil)
Bentley Continental, Corniche and Azure (Bennett)
Bentley MkVI, Rolls-Royce Silver Wraith, Dawn & Cloud/ Bentley R & S-Series (Nutland)
Bluebird CN7 (Stevens)
BMC Competitions Department Secrets (Turner, Chambers & Browning)
BMW 5-Series (Cranswick)
BMW Z-Cars (Taylor)
BMW – The Power of M (Vivian)
British at Indianapolis, The (Wagstaff)
British Cars, The Complete Catalogue of, 1895-1975 (Culshaw & Horrobin)
BRM – A Mechanic's Tale (Salmon)
BRM V16 (Ludvigsen)
Bugatti Type 40 (Price)
Bugatti 46/50 Updated Edition (Price & Arbey)
Bugatti T44 & T49 (Price & Arbey)
Bugatti 57 2nd Edition (Price)
Bugatti Type 57 Grand Prix – A Celebration (Tomlinson)
Caravan, Improve & Modify Your (Porter)
Caravans, The Illustrated History 1919-1959 (Jenkinson)
Caravans, The Illustrated History From 1960 (Jenkinson)
Carrera Panamericana, La (Tipler)
Car-tastrophes – 80 automotive atrocities from the past 20 years (Honest John, Fowler)
Chrysler 300 – America's Most Powerful Car 2nd Edition (Ackerson)
Chrysler PT Cruiser (Ackerson)
Citroën DS (Bobbitt)
Classic British Car Electrical Systems (Astley)
Cobra – The Real Thing! (Legate)
Competition Car Aerodynamics 3rd Edition (McBeath)
Competition Car Composites A Practical Handbook (Revised 2nd Edition) (McBeath)
Concept Cars, How to illustrate and design (Dewey)
Cortina – Ford's Bestseller (Robson)
Cosworth – The Search for Power (6th edition) (Robson)
Coventry Climax Racing Engines (Hammill)
Daily Mirror 1970 World Cup Rally 40, The (Robson)
Daimler SP250 New Edition (Long)
Datsun Fairlady Roadster to 280ZX – The Z-Car Story (Long)
Dino – The V6 Ferrari (Long)
Dodge Challenger & Plymouth Barracuda (Grist)
Dodge Charger – Enduring Thunder (Ackerson)
Dodge Dynamite! (Grist)
Dorset from the Sea – The Jurassic Coast from Lyme Regis to Old Harry Rocks photographed from its best viewpoint (also Souvenir Edition) (Belasco)
Draw & Paint Cars – How to (Gardiner)
Drive on the Wild Side, A – 20 Extreme Driving Adventures From Around the World (Weaver)
Dune Buggy, Building A – The Essential Manual (Shakespeare)
Dune Buggy Files (Hale)
Dune Buggy Handbook (Hale)
East German Motor Vehicles in Pictures (Suhr/Weinreich)
Fast Ladies – Female Racing Drivers 1888 to 1970 (Bouzanquet)
Fate of the Sleeping Beauties, The (op de Weegh/Hottendorff/ op de Weegh)
Ferrari 288 GTO, The Book of the (Sackey)
Ferrari 333 SP (O'Neil)
Fiat & Abarth 124 Spider & Coupé (Tipler)
Fiat & Abarth 500 & 600 – 2nd Edition (Bobbitt)
Fiats, Great Small (Ward)
Ford Cleveland 335-Series V8 engine 1970 to 1982 – The Essential Source Book (Hammill)
Ford F100/F150 Pick-up 1948-1996 (Ackerson)
Ford F150 Pick-up 1997-2005 (Ackerson)
Ford GT – Then, and Now (Streather)
Ford GT40 (Legate)
Ford Midsize Muscle – Fairlane, Torino & Ranchero (Cranswick)
Ford Model Y (Roberts)
Ford Small Block V8 Racing Engines 1962-1970 – The Essential Source Book (Hammill)
Ford Thunderbird From 1954, The Book of the (Long)
Formula 5000 Motor Racing, Back then ... and back now (Lawson)
Forza Minardi! (Vigar)
France: the essential guide for car enthusiasts – 200 things for the car enthusiast to see and do (Parish)
Grand Prix Ferrari – The Years of Enzo Ferrari's Power, 1948-1980 (Pritchard)
Grand Prix Ford – DFV-powered Formula 1 Cars (Robson)
GT – The World's Best GT Cars 1953-73 (Dawson)
Hillclimbing & Sprinting – The Essential Manual (Short & Wilkinson)
Honda NSX (Long)
Inside the Rolls-Royce & Bentley Styling Department – 1971 to 2001 (Hull)
Intermeccanica – The Story of the Prancing Bull (McCredie & Reisner)
Jaguar, The Rise of (Price)
Jaguar XJ 220 – The Inside Story (Moreton)
Jaguar XJ-S, The Book of the (Long)
Jeep CJ (Ackerson)
Jeep Wrangler (Ackerson)
The Jowett Jupiter – The car that leaped to fame (Nankivell)
Karmann-Ghia Coupé & Convertible (Bobbitt)
Kris Meeke – Intercontinental Rally Challenge Champion (McBride)
Lamborghini Miura Bible, The (Sackey)
Lamborghini Urraco, The Book of the (Landsem)
Lancia 037 (Collins)
Lancia Delta HF Integrale (Blaettel & Wagner)
Land Rover Series III Reborn (Porter)
Land Rover, The Half-ton Military (Cook)
Lea-Francis Story, The (Price)
Le Mans Panoramic (Ireland)
Lexus Story, The (Long)
Little book of microcars, the (Quellin)
Little book of smart, the – New Edition (Jackson)
Lola – The Illustrated History (1957-1977) (Starkey)
Lola – All the Sports Racing & Single-seater Racing Cars 1978-1997 (Starkey)
Lola T70 – The Racing History & Individual Chassis Record – 4th Edition (Starkey)
Lotus 18 Colin Chapman's U-turn (Whitelock)
Lotus 49 (Oliver)
Maserati 250F In Focus (Pritchard)
Mazda MX-5/Miata 1.6 Enthusiast's Workshop Manual (Grainger & Shoemark)
Mazda MX-5/Miata 1.8 Enthusiast's Workshop Manual (Grainger & Shoemark)
Mazda MX-5 Miata, The book of the – The 'Mk1' NA-series 1988 to 1997 (Long)
Mazda MX-5 Miata Roadster (Long)
Mazda Rotary-engined Cars (Cranswick)
Maximum Mini (Booij)
Meet the English (Bowie)
Mercedes-Benz SL – R230 series 2001 to 2011 (Long)
Mercedes-Benz SL – W113-series 1963-1971 (Long)
Mercedes-Benz SL & SLC – 107-series 1971-1989 (Long)
Mercedes-Benz SLK – R170 series 1996-2004 (Long)
Mercedes-Benz SLK – R171 series 2004-2011 (Long)
Mercedes-Benz W123-series – All models 1976 to 1986 (Long)
Mercedes G-Wagen (Long)
MGA (Price Williams)
MGB & MGB GT– Expert Guide (Auto-doc Series) (Williams)
MGB Electrical Systems Updated & Revised Edition (Astley)
Micro Caravans (Jenkinson)
Micro Trucks (Mort)
Microcars at Large! (Quellin)
Mini Cooper – The Real Thing! (Tipler)
Mini Minor to Asia Minor (West)
Mitsubishi Lancer Evo, The Road Car & WRC Story (Long)
Montlhéry, The Story of the Paris Autodrome (Boddy)
Morgan Maverick (Lawrence)
Morgan 3 Wheeler – back to the future!, The (Dron)
Morris Minor, 60 Years on the Road (Newell)
Moto Guzzi Sport & Le Mans Bible, The (Falloon)
Motor Movies – The Posters! (Veysey)
Motor Racing – Reflections of a Lost Era (Carter)
Motor Racing – The Pursuit of Victory 1930-1962 (Carter)
Motor Racing – The Pursuit of Victory 1963-1972 (Wyatt/Sears)
Motor Racing Heroes – The Stories of 100 Greats (Newman)
Motorhomes, The Illustrated History (Jenkinson)
Motorsport In colour, 1950s (Wainwright)
MV Agusta Fours, The book of the classic (Falloon)
N.A.R.T. – A concise history of the North American Racing Team 1957 to 1983 (O'Neil)
Nissan 300ZX & 350Z – The Z-Car Story (Long)
Nissan GT-R Supercar: Born to race (Gorodji)
The Norton Commando Bible – All models 1968 to 1978 (Henshaw)
Nothing Runs – Misadventures in the Classic, Collectable & Exotic Car Biz (Slutsky)
Off-Road Giants! (Volume 1) – Heroes of 1960s Motorcycle Sport (Westlake)
Off-Road Giants! (Volume 2) – Heroes of 1960s Motorcycle Sport (Westlake)
Off-Road Giants! (volume 3) – Heroes of 1960s Motorcycle Sport (Westlake)
Pass the Theory and Practical Driving Tests (Gibson & Hoole)
Peking to Paris 2007 (Young)
Pontiac Firebird – New 3rd Edition (Cranswick)
Porsche Boxster (Long)
Porsche 356 (2nd Edition) (Long)
Porsche 908 (Födisch, Neßhöver, Rossbach, Schwarz & Rossbach)
Porsche 911 Carrera – The Last of the Evolution (Corlett)
Porsche 911R, RS & RSR, 4th Edition (Starkey)
Porsche 911, The Book of the (Long)
Porsche 911 – The Definitive History 2004-2012 (Long)
Porsche – The Racing 914s (Smith)
Porsche 911SC 'Super Carrera' – The Essential Companion (Streather)
Porsche 914 & 914-6: The Definitive History of the Road & Competition Cars (Long)
Porsche 924 (Long)
The Porsche 924 Carreras – evolution to excellence (Smith)
Porsche 928 (Long)
Porsche 944 (Long)
Porsche 964, 993 & 996 Data Plate Code Breaker (Streather)
Porsche 993 'King Of Porsche' – The Essential Companion (Streather)
Porsche 996 'Supreme Porsche' – The Essential Companion (Streather)
Porsche 997 2004-2012 – Porsche Excellence (Streather)
Porsche Racing Cars – 1953 to 1975 (Long)
Porsche Racing Cars – 1976 to 2005 (Long)
Porsche – The Rally Story (Meredith)
Porsche: Three Generations of Genius (Meredith)
Preston Tucker & Others (Linde)
RAC Rally Action! (Gardiner)
RACING COLOURS – MOTOR RACING COMPOSITIONS 1908-2009 (Newman)
Racing Line – British motorcycle racing in the golden age of the big single (Guntrip)
Rallye Sport Fords: The Inside Story (Moreton)
Renewable Energy Home Handbook, The (Porter)
Roads with a View – England's greatest views and how to find them by road (Corfield)
Rolls-Royce Silver Shadow/Bentley T Series Corniche & Camargue – Revised & Enlarged Edition (Bobbitt)
Rolls-Royce Silver Spirit, Silver Spur & Bentley Mulsanne 2nd Edition (Bobbitt)
Rootes Cars of the 50s, 60s & 70s – Hillman, Humber, Singer, Sunbeam & Talbot (Rowe)
Rover P4 (Bobbitt)
Runways & Racers (O'Neil)
Russian Motor Vehicles – Soviet Limousines 1930-2003 (Kelly)
Russian Motor Vehicles – The Czarist Period 1784 to 1917 (Kelly)
RX-7 – Mazda's Rotary Engine Sportscar (Updated & Revised New Edition) (Long)
Singer Story: Cars, Commercial Vehicles, Bicycles & Motorcycle (Atkinson)
Sleeping Beauties USA – abandoned classic cars & trucks (Marek)
SM – Citroën's Maserati-engined Supercar (Long & Claverol)
Speedway – Auto racing's ghost tracks (Collins & Ireland)
Sprite Caravans, The Story of (Jenkinson)
Standard Motor Company, The Book of the (Robson)
Steve Hole's Kit Car Cornucopia – Cars, Companies, Stories, Facts & Figures: the UK's kit car scene since 1949 (Hole)
Subaru Impreza: The Road Car And WRC Story (Long)
Supercar, How to Build your own (Thompson)
Tales from the Toolbox (Oliver)
Tatra – The Legacy of Hans Ledwinka, Updated & Enlarged Collector's Edition of 1500 copies (Margolius & Henry)
Taxi! The Story of the 'London' Taxicab (Bobbitt)
To Boldly Go – twenty six vehicle designs that dared to be different (Hull)
Toleman Story, The (Hilton)
Toyota Celica & Supra, The Book of Toyota's Sports Coupés (Long)
Toyota MR2 Coupés & Spyders (Long)
Triumph TR6 (Kimberley)
Two Summers – The Mercedes-Benz W196R Racing Car (Ackerson)
TWR Story, The – Group A (Hughes & Scott)
Unraced (Collins)
Volkswagen Bus Book, The (Bobbitt)
Volkswagen Bus or Van to Camper, How to Convert (Porter)
Volkswagens of the World (Glen)
VW Beetle Cabriolet – The full story of the convertible Beetle (Bobbitt)
VW Beetle – The Car of the 20th Century (Copping)
VW Bus – 40 Years of Splitties, Bays & Wedges (Copping)
VW Bus Book, The (Bobbitt)
VW Golf: Five Generations of Fun (Copping & Cservenka)
VW – The Air-cooled Era (Copping)
VW T5 Camper Conversion Manual (Porter)
VW Campers (Copping)
Volkswagen Type 3, The book of the – Concept, Design, International Production Models & Development (Glen)
You & Your Jaguar XK8/XKR – Buying, Enjoying, Maintaining, Modifying – New Edition (Thorley)
Which Oil? – Choosing the right oils & greases for your antique, vintage, veteran, classic or collector car (Michell)
Works Minis, The Last (Purves & Brenchley)
Works Rally Mechanic (Moylan)

Veloce Publishing's other imprints:

Hubble & Hattie BATTLE CRY!

eBooks and Apps:

Also available ... eBook Download now from www.digital.veloce.co.uk

Also available ... Apps Download now from www.digital.veloce.co.uk

For post publication news, updates and amendments relating to this book please scan the QR code above or visit www.veloce.co.uk/books/V4895

www.veloce.co.uk

First published in April 2017 by Veloce Publishing Limited, Veloce House, Parkway Farm Business Park, Middle Farm Way, Poundbury, Dorchester DT1 3AR, England. Fax 01305 250479 / e-mail info@veloce.co.uk / web www.veloce.co.uk or www.velocebooks.com. ISBN: 978-1-845848-95-8; UPC: 6-36847-04895-2

© 2017 Graham Robson and Veloce Publishing. All rights reserved. With the exception of quoting brief passages for the purpose of review, no part of this publication may be recorded, reproduced or transmitted by any means, including photocopying, without the written permission of Veloce Publishing Ltd. Throughout this book logos, model names and designations, etc, have been used for the purposes of identification, illustration and decoration. Such names are the property of the trademark holder as this is not an official publication. Readers with ideas for automotive books, or books on other transport or related hobby subjects, are invited to write to the editorial director of Veloce Publishing at the above address.

British Library Cataloguing in Publication Data – A catalogue record for this book is available from the British Library. Typesetting, design and page make-up all by Veloce Publishing Ltd on Apple Mac. Printed in India by Replika Press.

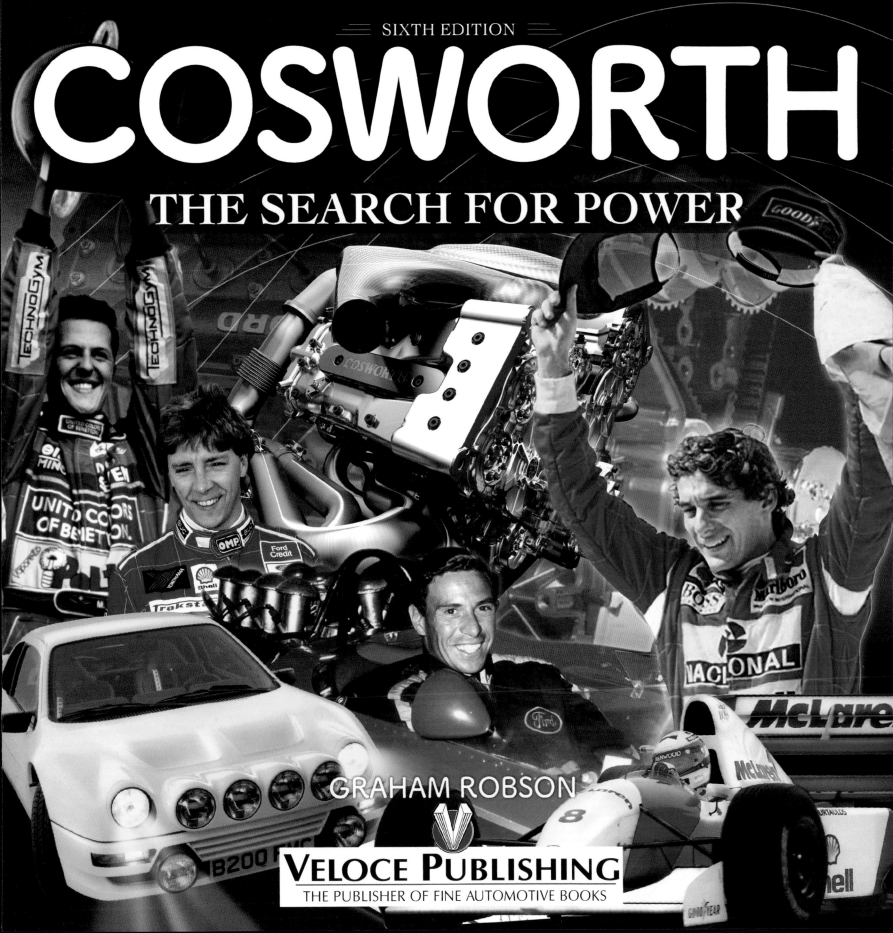

SIXTH EDITION

COSWORTH

THE SEARCH FOR POWER

GRAHAM ROBSON

VELOCE PUBLISHING
THE PUBLISHER OF FINE AUTOMOTIVE BOOKS

CONTENTS

ACKNOWLEDGEMENTS

Assembling all the stories for this book, and finding the illustrations, has meant begging help from many people. Over the years, and on many occasions, all were busy, all had better things to do than to reminisce about the past, but they all willingly spared the time. In particular I must thank: Keith Duckworth and Gill, for their endless patience; Mike Costin, Keith's co-founder of Cosworth; Walter Hayes; Mike Kranefuss; Stuart Turner; Mike Moreton; Steve Parker, Harry Calton and Steve Woolmington of Ford; Stuart Banks; Ian Brisco; Richard Bulman; Brendon Connor; John Dickens; Jack Field; Bernard Ferguson; John and Valerie Given; Geoff Goddard (the engine designer, not the photographer); Matthew Grant; Bob Graves; Mike Hall; Nick Hayes; Mark Hunt; Kevin Kalkhoven; Annys Kirk; Steve Madincea; Rob Oldaker; Mark Parish; Hal Reisiger; Ben Rood; Dick Scammell; Bob Smith; Trudi Syevens; Frank Sumner; Pio Szyjanowicz; Geoff Tupman; Malcolm Tyrrell; Rob White; Bruce Wood and Chris Woodwark; all of Cosworth; Charles Bolton; Sarah Frankham; David Godber and Mike Richards of Cosworth Technology; Roy Bacon; Graham Dale-Jones;

John Dunn; Robin Herd; Brian Hart, and Ray Hutton.

Cosworth and Ford, in particular, provided many of the pictures, with Claire Adams, Valerie Given, Kelly Powell, Denise Proctor, Steve Clark, Jim Fowler, Dave Hill and Sheila Knapman digging out real treasures for me to use.

In addition I also want to thank Paddy Baker of *Insight* magazine, Ian Bamsey, John Blunsden, Norman Burr, Paul Davies of PDPR, John Evans of Mercedes-Benz, Geoff Goddard (the photographer, not the engine designer!), Maurice Hamilton, Ralph Hardwick, Richard Langworth, Leo Levine, Dan Margulies, Andrew Duerden and Ken Moyes of Vauxhall-Opel, Frank Peiler of Publications International, Nick Perry, David Phipps, Stewart Grand Prix, and Eoin Young for providing extra illustrations.

Companies House, in Cardiff, provided many of the financial details, with Cosworth's company secretary, Frank Sumner, filling in the gaps.

My grateful thanks to everyone.

Graham Robson

Publishers Note
We appreciate that a number of the images in this book are of relatively poor quality. However, we hope that the reader will appreciate that such images have had to be included because of their rarity and historical importance.

INTRODUCTION

Keith Duckworth founded Cosworth in 1958, and was its guiding genius for the next 30 years ...

... and throughout his life he was interested in new machinery, and how it could make his precious pieces of engineering correctly.

The original edition of this book, I hope, was as close to the full story of Cosworth's 30 years as anyone would be able to write, but, since then, the company has expanded, changed, been bought and sold – and a lot has happened along the way. Originally, I had been looking forward for years to tackling the job, but it took a great deal of time to persuade Keith Duckworth to get involved, for there always seemed to be something more pressing to occupy his amazing intellect.

Cosworth's original co-operation as a company was assured, I think, when it realised that a book written without its help would have to rely on recycled information; might be missing great chunks of history, and might be inaccurate in so many ways. The breakthrough came, I am sure, when Keith decided to retire from the business he had founded, and could actually spare me some time to discuss the earlier days. Not only did I spend many hours persuading Keith to stop lecturing me about my own (and the journalist profession's) technical shortcomings, and to talk into my tape recorder, but I also managed to corner most of the important personalities who had contributed to the growth of Cosworth since 1958.

I first met Keith Duckworth and Mike Costin in 1965. The occasion was social – one of those fascinating *Autocar* 'Thursday Club' dinners in Warwickshire, where top engineers got together, secrets were swapped, and everything said was *strictly* off the record – and both were in their element. Here was a stage on which Keith, in particular, could give a performance. Here was the place where everyone could polish their aphorisms, savour the latest industry scandal, and float some often outrageous engineering theories.

I noticed, right away, that Keith and Mike clearly liked each other enormously, and enjoyed these occasions, but that they had different characters.

Both were relaxed and affable with their peers, and both were delighted to gossip about cars, engines, and motorsport in general. Mike, on the one hand, would ease his way out of any conversations, or controversies, which he didn't enjoy. Keith, however, used to fasten on them, and pursue them – like a dog after a rabbit – and follow an argument to the end. It was on occasions like this that the wagging finger would come into play, the facial expression might become somewhat belligerent, and the voice volume would gradually increase.

Over the years I realised that Keith simply would not put up with those he succinctly called "bloody idiots," and I was flattered that he never cast me off as one of them. Two of Keith's most chilling remarks were to call something "fundamentally unsound," and

There was always much fun to be had at Cosworth, where Mike Costin (left) and Keith Duckworth enjoyed each other's company for 40 years.

future of his business. There have been several such arguments since.

All this, and much more, made me realise that Keith, Mike, and Cosworth, which they had founded, were quite exceptional, and one day I vowed to write a complete story of the company. When the time came, Keith, Mike, and their Cosworth colleagues, could not have been more helpful.

Right away, I decided that this book should not be just a number-crunching, nuts-and-bolts, power-outputs and average-speeds product. After all those years, I thought, there must be many personal stories to be told, many secret files to be prised open, with successes to be balanced against failures, policies to be weighed against practicalities, and people to be matched to machinery.

That original book, I hope, was as much about 'why' as about 'what.' Why did Keith discard aero-engine work for motorsport? Why did he link up with Mike? Why did he move the Cosworth business from London to Northampton? Why did he dabble with transmissions, helicopters and motorcycle engines? Why did he sell out in 1980? And why did he walk away from the business in 1988?

I think I have asked all the questions, and I hope I got all the honest answers. It is a fascinating story …

Graham Robson, 1989

to be heard to say of unlikeable people: "Well, he's not one of us, is he?"

I shall never forget the expressions that flashed across his face when, at a VIP's lunch at Silverstone one day in about 1970, a so-called eminent technical director of one of Britain's largest car-making concerns expressed the opinion that an overhead-camshaft valve gear was not justified on a road car, but invited Keith to convince him otherwise. That man, whose products were always boring, may never know how close he was to being bawled out …

There was also an occasion, some years later, when Keith and I ducked out of a particularly boring new-product launch, and made for the hotel coffee-shop instead. But Keith was never very good at killing time. Having settled down placidly behind a large pot of tea, he beamed at me, came to the alert, pointed like a gun dog, and said: "Right, let's have an argument, I'm just in the mood for a good argument!" The subject, that afternoon, was the technical consultancy business, why he didn't think the time was ripe for Cosworth to 'do a Porsche,' and his own thoughts about the

But that was not the end of the beginning. To my delight, there seemed to be a continuous demand for the story of Cosworth's ongoing development, so in 2003 I was privileged to update it all yet again. This was what I had to say at the time:

Introduction to the fifth edition

Cosworth never marks time. In the years since this book was originally written, Keith Duckworth and Mike Costin have retired, and the company has expanded considerably. Many of the personalities have changed, while more and yet more remarkable new engines have appeared.

Not only has there been worldwide success in Formula 1 and CART/Champcar racing, but these achievements have been matched by victories at world level in touring car racing, and in rallying. Significantly, a number of universally praised road-car engines have also been produced.

Even though the financial control of the company changed hands several times in the 1980s and 1990s, its reputation for technical excellence was never once in doubt. Along the way the business expanded mightily, for, from the 1970s onwards, Cosworth's unique ability to produce world-beating and reliable power was applied to engines for road cars.

When Cosworth was put up for sale by Vickers, in 1998, the famous (then 40-year-old) concern was immediately split into two entirely different operations. Audi bought the road-car side of the business, naming it Cosworth Technology, while Cosworth Racing – always the most glamorous side of the business – was absorbed by Ford, and soon inserted into that company's prestigious Premier Performance Division.

As the new century opened, the two companies drifted firmly apart, although some technical links were retained. As expected, much of the work being done by Cosworth Technology was, and remains, confidential, and eventually the business was sold to the German concern of Mahle.

Cosworth Racing's work, on the other hand, was often in the public eye, for it was still much involved in the media-glamorous sport of Formula 1 racing.

Under Ford's tutelage, Cosworth Racing has already had an exciting time. It looks likely to be in the spotlight of Ford's motorsport operations for many years to come and the prospects for the future are enthralling.

Graham Robson, 2003

Introduction to the totally updated sixth edition

As the 50th anniversary of the birth of Cosworth's world-famous DFV engine drew closer (for the record, that anniversary came around in April 2017), the idea of producing a totally updated story of the company and its still-developing life took shape. Not only that, but modern technology allowed many more colour illustrations to be displayed than ever before.

In the meantime, the company once again changed hands, by settling into the safe keeping of two North America-based enthusiasts, Jerry Forsythe and Kevin Kalkhoven, in 2004, and because of their generosity and the open way in which they did business, I finally got the chance to talk freely (rather than guardedly) about the most recent developments in the Cosworth company.

By bringing the Cosworth story up to date, I have been able to describe the growing importance of the electronic activities for which the company is now justly famous, and to describe the way in which the business has been re-aligned, on the way to restarting the total assembly of engines for high-performance road cars. I have also been able to give (and be given) a tantalising glimpse of the way that the company has expanded, and will further expand, into the US and Asian markets.

So is this the complete Cosworth story? Yes, up to the present – but there will, I am sure, be a lot more to come!

Graham Robson, 2017

FOREWORD

Along with his long-established business associate Jerry Forsythe, Kevin Kalkhoven had been closely linked with Cosworth for many years in the 1990s because of the cars he raced in the CART, then Champcar, series. Along with Jerry Forsythe, he took control of Cosworth at the end of 2004, when he bought the business from Ford.

Along with my partner, Jerry Forsythe, the two of us are delighted to see that Graham Robson has updated his detailed history of Cosworth: the company we acquired in 2004. When that opportunity came, I don't think that many people realised how important Cosworth was to us, as team owners in the North American Champcar race series, and what a business and sporting tragedy it would be if we no longer had access to this icon of the highest quality of British engineering.

Although Jerry and I realised that we would be taking control of a multi-faceted operation, it was some time before we could re-align the company to the realities of the new century. Along the way we have reshaped the business, not only by rationalising our motor racing operations, but by expanding our OEM (Original Equipment Manufacturer) links with the world's motor industry.

While staying strictly within the bounds of commercial confidentiality (and, believe me, we have had to be very firm with him on this!), in his most recent researches, interviews and descriptions of Cosworth's modern activities, Graham has been able to spell out just how far Cosworth has now set up high-performance programmes concerning not only engines, but also sophisticated electronic equipment, with major car manufacturers, world-famous motor racing operations, and significant start-up manufacturers. At Northampton and, shortly, in Michigan, USA, we have state-of-the-art, high-tech, versatile machining facilities, too, which are, I can tell you, the envy of rivals all over the world.

Accordingly, it still gives me enormous pleasure to see that a company which started life in 1958 with just two men involved, went on to become a dominant part of the world's motor racing establishment, and later undertook the complete manufacture of engines in significant quantities, is still vibrantly in operation, making new products, using processes that its founders would have been proud of.

Cosworth has never been a company to boast about its achievements – and today, maybe, I am guilty of prolonging that tradition, but we are nevertheless proud of what has often been achieved, and I can assure everyone that we have every intention of breaking new ground, and introducing astonishing new products, in the future.

Although Cosworth is not in the Formula 1 engine business right now, it is still happy to note that it pulled out while its engines were acknowledged as the most powerful of the bunch. It may not be in the business of building complete road-car engines as I write these words but, believe me, we have the technology, and the ambition of getting back into that field in the future. We are so proud of the way our legendary DFV engine has transformed F1 during its lifetime, and we have just recently celebrated the 50th anniversary of its birth.

On the other hand, this latest edition of Graham's book makes it clear that Cosworth is not only thriving, and is demonstrably proud of itself, but is currently building new OEM-serving premises in North America and in the Far East. By the time this book comes around for another very welcome update, there may (will – I hope) be a lot more to tell.

Kevin Kalkhoven, Chairman,
Cosworth

1: KEITH DUCKWORTH AND MIKE COSTIN – THE FOUNDERS

"It is a fundamental that I should understand what I am doing, and that is what turns me on ..."

Genius may be born, and develop, in unexpected places. Would any motoring enthusiast really have expected the founders of Cosworth to be, respectively, the second son of a Lancashire weaving shed owner, and the third son of a fashionable marbler and grainer who lived in North Harrow?

Real life, however, is often much more complicated than fiction – and never as romantic. Although Keith Duckworth was probably the world's most famous race engine designer, and Mike Costin is renowned as the practical and resourceful engineer who always underpinned the growth of Cosworth, neither had an engineering background in the family. So much for heredity ...

This, at least, is not a story of rags to riches, for both families were comfortably off, if not actually wealthy. In neither case is there a story of 'how I rose above the bare-foot holes-in-trousers stage, and look how well I have done today.' Even so, it was fascinating to listen to Keith and Mike talking about their early days, in the 1930s:

"I was born in August 1933, at Blackburn, in Lancashire" Keith recalled, "the second of two sons. My father, Frank Duckworth, was the owner of a weaving shed, who also sold cloth on the Manchester Cotton Exchange. My mother was the daughter of a blacksmith, and she then took a diploma in domestic science. She was the very first lady demonstrator of cookers in the Blackburn electricity showrooms.

"My father was an enthusiastic wood-worker, and a rebuilder of cars in his spare time. His father had died when he was only twelve, so he'd had a fairly hard, and a fairly poor, upbringing. But he managed to go to night school, and he also traded in motorcycles. Fairly early on, then, he was running a motorcycle, and my mother even managed to do some racing across Southport sands on a motorcycle and sidecar."

Mike Costin, on the other hand, was a Londoner – not an East Ender, though that was where his father and mother met:

"Father and mother nominally came from East London, where they met." Mike recalled, "They got married at the end of the 1914-1918 war, and moved to a house in North Harrow."

Henry John Costin had been born in Hammersmith, and was always the dominant figure in the marriage.

"He was a very straightforward character, with very strong views, and his educational background was utterly straightforward – he had no higher education of any sort.

"Very quickly, I think, he decided he'd like to join the Army for an interesting life. He went on to do all sorts of things in the services – he was a rifleman in the Rifle Brigade, then a Corporal PT instructor, he was in the Army right up to the end of the 1914-18 War (he was one of the lucky ones), ending up as a Battery Sergeant Major in the Artillery.

"After the war, he still didn't have a trade of any sort, so he set himself up in business, from nothing, as a marbler and grainer. He just found that he'd got a bit of a bent for it. From about 1920, to 1939, he built up a very distinguished clientele.

"There were four children by the marriage – Frank, Eric, myself, and Mary. Frank was born in 1920, while I was born in 1929."

Mike's eldest brother, Frank Costin, would later go on to make his own distinguished career as an aerodynamicist (his shapes for various Lotus sports cars, and for the Vanwall F1 car made him famous), and later as an idiosyncratic designer of sports cars, including the early Marcos models. At this stage there was no more than a hint at future links with motor cars, and engines, for either future partner:

"My father became a Riley fan," Keith Duckworth said, "and we had a succession of Rileys. By the beginning of the war we had gone to live in Wilpshire, just north of Blackburn. Going out through our back gate, I found myself on the first fairway of Wilpshire golf course.

"My elder brother was Brian. There's absolutely no connection between his career and the kind of things I've done. He went to Leeds University after doing his National Service, where he became an officer in the Gunners, then he got a degree in Textile Engineering. After spending time selling papermakers' felts, as a technical representative, all round the world, he ended up running a string of launderettes in and around Blackburn."

"There was no engineering in the Costin family, as such" said Mike. "However, I was interested in engines and engineering from the time I had my first bike – a push-bike, that is. I was always taking that bike to bits, then putting it back together. Even when I was about three, they tell me, my little two-wheeler bike (I never had a three-wheeler) had an old sparking plug wired on to the front tube. I got my leg pulled a lot about this."

When Keith was born, the Duckworth business was very successful, not only for weaving and selling the cotton, but for trading on the Manchester Cotton Exchange. By the time Keith Duckworth's father died, in 1944, his business, Oak Street Manufacturing, was well set, and the Duckworth family was comfortably off. Keith not only insisted that his father was "very competent" (close acquaintances of the dynamic Duckworth realise that, to him, 'competence' – along with 'brightness' – is a real virtue, and a term of professional recognition), but gleefully pointed out that "... he wasn't a Mason, either!". When war broke out, the Duckworth family had a Riley Kestrel 16hp, complete with hemi-headed 2½-litre engine, and a Riley Adelphi 1½-litre as well:

"Father liked his Rileys, they had fine engines. He once tried an Alvis, but it required too much warming up. He went about a mile down the road with the engine coughing and fighting," (I think he said 'fighting' ...), "came home, said 'This is no good, I'm taking it back,' and that was the end of the Alvis, so we stayed faithful to the Riley."

At first, Keith attended a convent in Blackburn (there were only about seven boys there at the time), but soon his brother went off to Giggleswick School. Keith later went to a small private school in Blackburn, with about 70 pupils, but from 1942 he joined his brother at Giggleswick, as a boarder.

Giggleswick was, and still is, a much-respected public school, set in the folds of hills close to Settle in Yorkshire. Later made more famous to TV addicts as being the school where Russell Harty taught before becoming a show business personality, it was a very happy location for a growing boy to move towards manhood:

"I boarded at Giggleswick from 1942 to 1950. I played a lot of rugger, but couldn't stand cricket."

[Perhaps that explains why, when in later life Keith was invited to visit his old school he travelled by helicopter, landed it on the cricket pitch, and was politely asked to remove it so that the Old Boy's match could take place!] "By the time I was 18 years old I was quite good at drinking beer. I was a fat sod, a prop, second row, or hooker. I hooked for the school for a time.

[At this point in an interview, Keith exploded into typical rumbustious gales of laughter: "A hooker, yes, a hooker! You'll have to be careful if you're going to sell this book in America ... !"]

Even when he was a schoolboy the reputation for independence, deep thought, and – at times – sheer chin-jutting stubbornness, was developing fast. "I trace my first demonstration of independence of thought to Giggleswick, when I was 14. Everyone else was to be confirmed, into the Church of England. This meant that you had to say The Creed – 'I believe,' and all that. I read this through, and said that I was sorry, but it would be grossly hypocritical for me to say that I believed, at my age. It all sounded grossly unlikely.

"Pandemonium. I had to go to see the Padre, the housemaster, then the headmaster, to explain myself, and I never was confirmed.

"It was the first time that I actually went on my own analysis of a situation, and came to my own conclusions." This approach to life led to all sorts of difficulties for the growing boy, especially where discipline was expected:

"When I was at school, I always held out, and tried to get an explanation of things. I used to get my arse tanned [which, in Lancashire dialect means 'backside spanked!'] – now I know there was a war on, but I thought that to try to produce leather while it was still on the living animal was a bit unfair!

"I had similar problems in the RAF, but compared with school the discipline and the food was so much better that I almost found it to be a holiday."

Mike Costin was the individual who first guided Lotus to respectability in the 1950s, founded Cosworth in conjunction with Keith Duckworth in 1958, joined full-time in 1962, and remained with the company until his final retirement in 1990.

MIKE COSTIN'S OFFICIAL BIOGRAPHY LOOKS LIKE THIS:

COSTIN, Michael Charles. Co-Founder and past-Chairman, Cosworth Engineering Ltd, St James Mill Road, Northampton NN5 5JJ. Born: July 10 1929. Education: Salvatorian College, Harrow Weald; engineering apprenticeship, de Havilland Aircraft Co, Hatfield; licensed aircraft engineer 1950. Career: 1953-1955 Design Draughtsman, de Havilland. 1953-1956 Lotus Engineering, part-time and full-time. 1956-1962 Technical Director, Lotus Cars. 1962 took up appointment with Cosworth. Became Chairman in 1988. Retired in 1991.

BUT that isn't enough. I also ought to add:

Long-time 'king' mechanic, talented racing car driver, practical design and development genius, flying enthusiast (gliders and light aircraft), and irreplaceable 'sheet anchor' to every Cosworth project conceived in the first 30 years. Not even this summary, however, can catch the sheer down-to-earth, practical, engineering ability which superbly matched and balanced everything produced by Keith Duckworth's design talents all along the way.

KEITH DUCKWORTH'S OFFICIAL BIOGRAPHY LOOKS LIKE THIS:

DUCKWORTH, David Keith. Honorary Life President, Co-Founder and past-Chairman, Cosworth Engineering Ltd, St James Mill Road, Northampton NN5 5JJ. Born: 1933. Education: Giggleswick School, Yorkshire, and Imperial College, London. Career: 1957-1958, transmission development engineer with Lotus. Founded Cosworth Engineering in 1958, with Mike Costin. Chairman and chief engineer of Cosworth until 1988. Member of main board of UEI plc. Retired from executive management of Cosworth in 1989. Died 2005.

BUT that isn't enough, not by any means. This must also be added:

Engineering design genius, inventing the world's most successful Formula 1 engine. Workaholic, frustrated helicopter pilot, successful businessman, the inspiration behind every Cosworth project until mid-1980s. Multi-talented, super-confident, deep-thinking, forthright, stubborn, often combative, dismissive of fools, gregarious in company, but dangerous in argument, unbeatable in analysis of engineering problems and possibilities, a one-off in every respect.

From an early age Keith had been a keen model builder. Even though there was a war on, he remembers building the odd Frog kit, and making model aeroplanes from "spills and bog paper, rubber bands and all sorts of odds and ends." He also had a Bassett-Lowke stationary steam engine and boiler, which used meths burners to raise the steam.

The Duckworth family home was a solid, but unpretentious 1930s-style three-bedroom type, "nothing special," but at least it had a workshop of a most unusual type. Just before he died, Duckworth senior saw that his younger son was keen on engineering and model making, so he bought up an old Myford lathe, a vertical drill, and a grinder, and set up the workshop in the old air-raid shelter, which had been added to the back of the house.

"We'd had a window knocked into it, he had just wired it up, and he had just put the machines into the workshop when he died," Keith remembers.

After that, with Keith and his elder brother still at boarding school, and the war still on, the cotton exchange business stopped immediately, while the weaving shed had to be run by a manager.

"Eventually we sold off that business. I wasn't interested in running it, neither was my brother Brian. Father had already decided that cotton wasn't going to be a goer in England after the war, because of cheap imports from India and elsewhere ... he was right, wasn't he?"

Keith rapidly built up his modelling and engineering expertise. Having inherited his workshop at the age of eleven, where no-one in the family knew how to work the machine tools, he became a self-taught operator, made bits and pieces for model steam engines, then, after the war, he began flying powered model aircraft.

"I had a great stack of miniature engines, petrol and diesel, and when I was 16 I built my first radio-controlled equipment, from plans in Aeromodeller."

Already, therefore, he was on his way to becoming the 'whiz-kid from Wilpshire.' He got a name for sorting out electrical wiring problems, for repairing electric sewing machines, and other mechanisms:

"I once won a bet with my uncle by being able to switch on an electric blanket at two miles range, by radio-controlled equipment."

All the time, the teenage Duckworth was teaching himself about engineering, for he had started making parts for his engines and steam boilers, had bought many measuring instruments and tools, and reckoned he had done all the "compulsory filing and graunching" by the time he left school.

As soon as he was 16 years old, he bought a motorcycle, paying out £25 for a side-valve 250cc BSA, so old that it still had a hand, rather than a foot, gear change:

"It wasn't a runner at the time, but I refurbished the engine, putting in new valves and guides. We weren't allowed to ride motorbikes at school, but as I had fairly long holidays from Giggleswick, I could have the bike at home, and play with it then."

By 1950, School Certificate and A-Level examinations were over, and National Service was looming on the horizon:

"I had done reasonably well in exams, ['reasonably' is another well-known Duckworth buzz-word which, being roughly translated, means 'very good, but maybe I'd better not boast too much about this' ...], taking A-Levels in Maths, Physics and Chemistry, while I did extra Latin, in case I wanted to go on to Oxford or Cambridge.

"I decided I was keen on flying, and there was a chance to do this in National Service. Just before I left Giggleswick I went down to Hornchurch, by train, to be graded as suitable, or not, for National Service aircrew. I did a whole series of aptitude tests in those two days, and though I wanted to be a pilot, they were doubtful about this, and wanted to put me down as a navigator ...

"They didn't think my aptitude was right, but they decided to allow me to try as a pilot. As I wanted to go to university in two years I decided to try for an early call-up, and I was in, on a flying course, on the day that I was 18."

Mike Costin, too, had the sort of childhood where engines, machines, and all mechanical things, never seemed to be very far away. Mike, like Keith, was never overawed by personalities, or reputations. He recalls how his father's business – an artistic form of interior decoration – rapidly built up in the London of the 1920s and 1930s:

"Father used to say 'I paint houses. The only difference between the other painters and me is that I carry my brushes in my top pocket.'

"All the top people in London had to come to him to get their jobs done. Lord so-and-so, or Lady so-and-so, had seen a room done somewhere, wanted their room done like that, an oak-panelled room, a pine-panelled room, marble or whatever. He was actually a terror in the 'Establishment' because they couldn't do without him. There wasn't always a lot of money, though. I remember that he did a deal with the professions in North Harrow in exchange for a bit of decorating, we would get some free medical or dental treatment ..."

All three Costin boys went to the Salvatorian college in Harrow Weald, which was run by the Catholic Salvatorian order. Mike was ten when war broke out, and 16 when peace returned in 1945.

"I was influenced by Frank's activities," Mike now remembers. "From a very early age he had been totally involved in aeroplanes – there used to be copies of Flight and Aeroplane all around the house. I left school at 15l/2, and I decided to apply for an apprenticeship at de Havilland. It wasn't local, of course – it was quite a way from Harrow to Hatfield – and it wasn't Frank's influence, for he was already away from home, with Percival Aircraft, where he was Project Design Engineer. He didn't actually move to de Havilland, as Aerodynamic Flight Test Engineer, until 1951.

"I thought de Havilland would be an excellent place to be – they had no fewer than 1200 people in the technical school. I wrote to them, got an interview, and was accepted as a trade apprentice, as a fitter, and that was a 4l/2-year apprenticeship.

"I left school in July, but the de Havilland entry in those days started in early January, so I had time to spare. In the meantime a school friend of mine had a father who owned a string of bicycle shops – I worked at one of them, repairing and rebuilding cycles, wheels, three-speed gears, and everything.

"When the time came to start work, I went into digs in Hatfield. I was earning 26s (£1.30) a week, but my

digs cost 35s (£1.75) a week, so I needed help from my parents. They weren't very well off, but somehow they survived, and they helped me.

"De Havilland gave me fantastic training. I had nine months of basic training, for instance, at Salisbury Hall, near London Colney. The academic side of training was all at Hatfield, just inside the gates where there was a collection of wartime huts.

"At that time I didn't have a thought about cars, or anything else. I was totally bound up with aircraft, that was my horizon. I didn't have any great ideas. I didn't see that I could have any great qualifications to do any more, but I was always in there, trying ... After two years, though, I must have been doing fairly well, at the academic level, because I was upgraded into an engineering apprenticeship, which put me on a different level. When you start out as a fitter you have basic training, then you go through the fitting shops and you are trained as a fitter – but as an engineering apprentice the training was wider – into foundries, press shops, laboratories: I went to 14 different departments, and it was an ideal grounding."

When he was 16 years old, Mike had got his first

COSWORTH – THE SEARCH FOR POWER

Before Mike Costin became a director of Cosworth he had begun his career as an apprentice at de Havilland aircraft, working on such jet airliners as the Comet.

mechanised transport, a 250cc unit-construction New Imperial motorcycle. Like the BSA which Keith had bought:

"It wasn't serviceable at the time, it had a gearbox layshaft which was worn out. I saved up, and bought a new layshaft from Colliers of Birmingham. They screwed me, I know that now – and these days I would have the buggers for breakfast – because the shaft hadn't been hardened, and in about five minutes it ruined itself. At that point I sold the bike, because I couldn't afford to keep running it, so I went back to a pushbike for a time.

"I then had another motorbike, an old BSA 250cc, then ended up with a 1934 BSA Blue Star 500cc single. I had gone back to live at home for the last year of my apprenticeship, and as I was at Panshanger, qualifying for my maintenance licence, I used the plonking old BSA for transport.

"I used to ride 26 miles each way, starting at Panshanger at 7.30am every morning. In that year, too, I was doing four evenings a week at night school. We used to have one full day off work to go to college, and four nights at night school. That was a fair old flog …" At the conclusion of his apprenticeship, and having won two deferments to successfully sit his ARB examinations, Mike then went into the RAF for two years of National Service. Back from a routine stay in the forces, he returned to de Havilland, moving straight into an office designing test rigs on systems, mainly for the jet-propelled Comet, but also including Vampire work and "whatever was going – it was very

interesting …" There was also another side to the work, that of accident investigation of components and systems on military aircraft.

"The first car I used wasn't actually my own. Peter Ross had started his apprenticeship when I did. He had a nice, pristine, 1928 Austin Seven Chummy, but it didn't stay that way, it got modified. Through Peter I met Derek Wootton, the famous bloke who Colin Chapman got to follow back to his workshop after a 750 Club race meeting. Colin was in his Mark III race car, Wooty in his clapped-out old Austin Chummy with the Ford 10 engine. Chapman was having great difficulty in keeping up with him, but when they got to the end of the trip he saw that Wooty was wearing dark glasses. Chapman then said, "What the bloody hell are you doing with them on, at this time of night?" to which Wooty replied, "Well, if I don't wear them, my eyes water …"

"Now, Wooty was a mad-man, a great enthusiast, and he had a barn full of Austin Seven and Ford 10 pieces. I started to use a car which belonged to Derek Wootton – he had two cars and I used to borrow one.

"There was one amazing occasion, when I was driving along with my wife-to-be in one of them, a 1937 Austin Seven Ruby, when suddenly, whoosh, a wheel came off the car. I rescued the wheel, and had a look round the car, and found that all the wheel nuts were loose.

"Wooty had come round to the garage during the day, and because he'd wanted the wheels and tyres from one car, put on the other car, he'd swapped them over. He'd just put the other wheels back on 'my' car, but he hadn't bothered to tighten up the wheel nuts, and he hadn't told me! I haven't been able to live it down, with my wife, ever since."

At this point, we might reflect that one of the most important early influences on the founders of Cosworth was aircraft engineering, and the aircraft themselves. If Keith had not gone on to fail his pilot's training course, and if Mike had not met Colin Chapman by a series of coincidences, the first meeting, the formation of a friendship, and the foundation of Cosworth might never have occurred.

In the meantime, Keith was also enjoying himself, and eventually moved up to running his first car. His National Service experiences, as you might guess, were both flamboyant, and eventful. After 12 weeks of square-bashing at Kirton-in-Lindsey, and initial Tiger Moth flying experience at Digby (not far from Sleaford):

"My flying of Tiger Moths suitably impressed the RAF, so I was re-graded as a pilot. I went on to do 60 hours in Chipmunks at Booker [the airfield near High Wycombe], then went on to Holme-on-Spalding-Moor [near Market Weighton] and did about 70 hours on twin-engined Oxfords."

At that stage disaster struck for the prospective pilot for: "I was then flung out for 'dangerous and incompetent night flying' – I actually went to sleep in the circuit. I'd had some medical troubles – I had been chasing model airplanes round in a field, tripped over and sprained my ankle, they'd taped me up, and I now know I'm allergic to Elastoplast ... I was trying to catch up on the course, having been off for a time. Anyway, I was within ten hours of getting my wings, but I never got them.

"When I was thrown out as a pilot, I was immediately sent to do navigation, and I went down to RAF Thorney Island, near Portsmouth. I studied navigation, found that I could do this without any trouble, and I also proved that I had a strong stomach. We went on many bumpy flights in Ansons, four or five of us, and occasionally I was the only one to put in a chart for an exercise because everyone else had been green, and sick.

"Now I don't compromise easily – a lot of people will tell you that [They did – AAGR] – and my lecturer in astro-navigation was a blithering idiot: we used to have big arguments about his theories about star shots. I simply won't accept anything that is wrong;

Throughout his adult life, Mike Costin was fascinated by aerospace, and with flying, and for many years flew gliders for enjoyment.

theories that are wrong. I can spot the bullshit factor at a 100 yards range! If anyone makes a statement about a physical or mechanical phenomenon, which is actually suspect, I have a little automatic mental mechanism which says 'Hang on, is that right?' then it starts another mechanism to work out what is right.

"Because I'd started the course late, I was very tight for time. Then I had cartilage trouble in my knee – a rugger injury – was carted off to Halton hospital for it to be removed, and got water on my knee. Then I spent time at the rehabilitation centre at Headley Court. In the end I couldn't complete my navigation training before I left after two years, though I was still top of the course. Actually I was allowed out early, still as an Acting Pilot Officer/trainee Navigator, and went straight to Imperial College, London, in 1952."

Even before he joined the RAF, Keith developed a passion for Scott motorcycles:

"The Flying Squirrel, which had a water-cooled, parallel-twin, two-stroke engine with deflector pistons, well angled forward in the frame, made a very interesting noise when it was actually firing on both cylinders [here the famous Duckworth cynicism for other designers' work, well-developed in later years, was being honed]. I was still playing with Squirrels, whenever I had the time, when I got to university.

"In the RAF, three of us, who all came from the Leeds and Blackburn areas, clubbed together to buy a car, an old Singer 12 saloon, the one with the overhead cam engine. It did a few trips from Kirton-in-Lindsey, and from Digby, but it was a real heap, and eventually I think we just abandoned it."

Keith, as you might expect, had trenchant views about the right, and wrong, universities to learn all about engineering:

"Most people told me 'If you really want to be an engineer, don't go to Oxford or Cambridge, but go to where engineering is actually taught as an intended subject,' and that Imperial College was the place.

"So that is where I went, to take a mechanical engineering course. I knew that if I wanted to get anywhere in life, I needed a degree. But there was never a Duckworth 'Master Plan' – there never has been one. I think that people who plan like that have a mental deficiency, and a very high opinion of themselves. Later on, at Cosworth, nothing upset me more than interviewing graduates who wanted to see how their life could be planned for the next few years – if they had wanted planning, they should have joined the Forces, or the Civil Service! People

like that have no sense – they should realise that their progress in life is dependent on the competence that they demonstrate – it's nothing to do with the passage of years, or of seniority. One of my principles is that young fools go on to become old fools …

[Interviewing Keith while preparing this book usually resulted in at least one major philosophical 'lecture' like this, every hour, if not more frequently. His colleagues assure me that business life used to be like that too …]

It was in his first year at Imperial College that Keith began to get interested in motorsport. Some of his new-found friends were interested in motor racing, and visits to the circuits – mainly Goodwood, Brands Hatch, and Silverstone in the early 1950s – soon followed. At first he was still running a Scott motorcycle, but eventually graduated to an Austin Seven Ruby saloon.

The Ruby, like all such ageing Austin Sevens, had very erratic brakes, and on one notable occasion Keith was driving down Regent Street with his future wife, Ursula, by his side, when hard braking ahead of red traffic lights resulted in the car swapping ends and going through the (still red) traffic lights backwards! No-one was hurt, but Ursula was not best pleased.

"I also rose to the delights of riding a Triumph Speed Twin motorbike, which had a sidecar on it, so I did my share of sidecar driving. That included the novice's obligatory visit over a kerb! The owner, Noel Davis, who became Chief Executive of VSEL (which is a large shipbuilding and engineering concern), was very nice about that …"

At the end of that academic year he took a vacation job, one as far removed from high-tech as could be imagined, even by the standards of the day:

"I went to the National Oil and Gas Engine Co in Ashton-under-Lyne, one of the groups making middle-size (not full ships' size) stationary engines.

"I can well remember helping someone tap out a 2½in Whitworth head bolt in the bottom of a cylinder liner – and those engines could have 12in bores.

"When I arrived they'd just had a very jolly explosion, where a turbocharged gas engine had mixed gas into its crankcase, which had gone up, blown the inspection doors right off and gone out through the rear corrugated iron wall of the building."

In that same summer, though, Keith convinced his mother that he should be allowed to buy a Lotus Six in kit form and that some of the money his father had left him should be invested in the kit. Keith admits that his mother didn't even know what a Lotus Six was, or looked like. Right from the start, he decided that his Six had to be properly built, with the best components. It was not about to be a scrap-yard special:

"So off I went, up to Lotus, which was in the pub yard in Hornsey, got hold of the specifications, the price list, and I looked at all the options that I could have, and paid my deposit. I made the bold decision to use a Coventry-Climax engine, and an MG gearbox – that was very bold, because the Climax was the most expensive of the engine options, about £250 at the time, I seem to remember. 'I saw that I needed Ford axles, which needed to be sent off to be modified. They were E93A parts, available from my local Ford dealer, so as there didn't seem to be much price difference between new and secondhand prices, I managed to buy a new rear axle, and other new Ford bits. "At the beginning of the summer holidays, I borrowed a trailer, went down to Hornsey, and collected the kit." Perhaps Keith met Mike Costin for the first time during those visits, but neither now recalls an occasion. Even though he was then struck down with glandular fever during his second year ("I was too ill to take second year exams, I had to take a second second year, so my three year course actually took four years"), Keith installed the Lotus kit in the workshop in Wilpshire, and got on with building it. At the time he rather fancied himself as a budding racing driver, and thought the Six was the ideal way to prove his point. The problem, however, was that his ambition was way ahead of his abilities:

"I did, in fact, race three times. I finally decided to give up because I shunted the chicane at Goodwood, when the VG95 linings picked up in the drums, and the wheels didn't unlock when I took my foot off the brakes. I went straight into the chicane, which was a solid bank with a row of geranium pots on the top. I ended up against the bank with a geranium in my lap.

"Earlier on that day, I'd actually gone through Fordwater, that's the very fast kink, where there's a change of surface, and the car had leapt up and gone sideways for a way, before I straightened it up.

"I remember thinking, 'Jesus, you're not with that, not even vaguely with that, are you?' There was a great deal of luck that it covered the next piece of road without going off. I'm hopeless, my hand/eye co-ordination is poor. It upsets me. Full stop. It upsets me that I could never be competent in the Uhlenhaut mode, that I'm not blessed by being able to drive properly.

"Now Mike, on the other hand, I've never seen him over-correct a car. When the back end goes he just puts on the right amount of opposite lock at the right time, the car carries on sliding, and mysteriously as the kerb approaches it stops sliding and carries on in the right direction. That is totally beyond my imagination.

"Later I decided that there seemed to be two categories of racing driver – those who could drive by natural ability, and those who actually gained competence by experience. I thought that those who had the natural ability were most likely to win the races, and that I was firmly in the other category. I decided that I never did the right thing, the right amount, at the right time. I soon learned what proper driving was about, when I went out with Mike."

Mike Costin, in the meantime, who had rejoined de Havilland after National Service in November 1951, had also started to work at Lotus while keeping his job with the aircraft company. The Lotus connection all started with Peter Ross, and his cousin Adam Currie, who had bought Colin Chapman's Lotus Mk 3B. At the time Colin Chapman's business partners were the Allen brothers, Michael and Nigel, who finally walked out on an unsatisfactory working arrangement, leaving Chapman on his own.

"Towards the end of 1952," Mike recalled, "Peter told me about Colin Chapman – I hadn't met him then – about his cars and his big ideas, and that he wanted help. Through Peter, I met Colin, and eventually we struck up a deal. I would work there part-time (in the evenings) but I would keep my job at de Havilland, which I did for the next two years or so.

"The object was to build Mk 6s at a profit, to subsidise Colin in racing. I actually built Colin's racing engine, but I also did the production engineering for the Six, I did all the thinking behind that. Colin didn't actually pay me any money – oh no, not Colin! – but I got gallons and gallons of petrol instead.

"It was a busy life. I used to finish work (we were living in Hatfield) and I used to get away from work at about 6.00pm, start again in Hornsey at 7.15pm, and work through until one or two in the morning. Then it was back home, and back to work the following morning. I was already married and my wife didn't see much of me at the time. She was very understanding.

"I used to get back into Hatfield every morning, with packets of fags to use as bribes, drawings, pieces to be treated and welded, bits of material to be scrounged – it was a bit naughty, the 'foreigner' syndrome, but as Colin and Lotus were already winning, and we were getting famous, I managed to enthuse a few people.

"That year we did a deal, that I would do the 1172cc

Like Keith Duckworth, Mike Costin was always a 'hands-on' automotive engineer. Here, in 1969 (the high-mounted struts for the aerofoil on this F1 car give us a fairly clear idea of the date), he makes adjustments to a DFV during practice sessions for an F1 race.

races, and Colin would do the 1100cc races. I hadn't done any racing before that time; in fact, I'd hardly been to any events as a spectator. In 1953 there was Colin and myself at Hornsey, nobody else at all; then one or two other people joined us in 1954.

"That was the year when Chapman designed our first so-called aerodynamic car, but I wasn't very impressed at first. Fortunately, my brother, Frank, had joined de Havilland by this time – he was in charge of flight test aerodynamics at Chester – so I shipped the balsa model which Dave Kelsey of Progress Chassis had made for us, up to Frank, by the inter-factory airlift, and asked him what he thought, and could he improve it? He could – he totally changed it, into the familiar shape of the Mk 8.

"Up to that stage Frank had been totally uninterested in cars – he only thought of aeroplanes. But I kept on at him, and said 'It's great sport, and you could do some interesting aerodynamics.' He made a good job of the Lotus Mk 8, and that's how he got drawn into automobile engineering."

By the late 1950s, therefore, Mike Costin was Colin Chapman's right-hand-man in every way, and had taken on the grand title of 'Technical Director.' Throughout the period when Chapman's methods – and Lotus – was all about advanced design, exhortation, and close-to-the-wind wheels and deals, Mike was his sheet anchor, the best car and engine builder at Hornsey, and the most practical personality on the ground.

Keith Duckworth, on the other hand, was enjoying himself at Imperial College – rather too much to get a lot of work done. Returning to start his second academic year, he moved into digs in Lavender Hill Gardens, Clapham, to find a young man called Bill Brown installed on the other bed in his room.

Keith's friend Brian Bannister, who had provided the lift down from Blackburn to London in a Triumph Roadster, expressed the opinion that Bill Brown was going to be a very boring room-mate. But after an evening spent together at the local pub, Keith was staggered to find himself: "drunk under the table by this nineteen-year-old who had already spent a year on the buses. I thought this was a very reasonable start!"

From that moment, the two undergraduates became firm friends. Bill hailed from Hartlepool in County Durham, and eventually bought Keith's Austin Seven Ruby, at one time suffering from police attention over its roadworthiness failings, and eventually turning it into a special.

Keith now admits that the two worked very hard

on their social life in London, but that neither of them actually worked very hard at their studies. The tutors eventually suggested that Bill Brown should leave when he failed a set of examinations, and though he later returned to try again, he never achieved those coveted initials 'BSc'. By the time Keith set up in business, Bill Brown had joined the RAF, to complete his National Service. Keith, on the other hand, had scraped through. Many people, including the author, are surprised to learn that he did not get a toweringly successful First Class degree:

"I passed, just passed. No way was I going to get honours. In those days the people who got honours were the ones who talked to walls. I just scraped through with a pass, and I think I was quite lucky to qualify. I made quite a few mistakes. One was that we had to write reports of the work we had done on the various gas engines and oil engines. Most people just copied the previous year's reports, but not me. I actually wrote a critical analysis of whether we had learned anything, and in most cases I came to the conclusion that the measuring equipment, and the way that the experiments were done, didn't prove anything. I wrote this down at great length, and my conclusions were that it was not a worthwhile exercise.

"As this was totally new to the examiners, I got very poor marks for my course work. But I reckon that that is the foundation of why I am a good development engineer.

"I was always in trouble in passing exams, because I didn't like learning everything as a parrot. While I have a good memory, I wouldn't spend the effort to programme it. I really only learned the things I could understand. In exams, where I hadn't learned the equations, I just had to sit down and work everything out from first principles, so I never did sufficient in the time available, I didn't answer enough questions.

"But there was no way that I was going to adjust my principles for the sake of passing exams. It is a fundamental that I have to understand what I am doing, and that is what turns me on."

Before examination time, however, Keith had visited Lotus several times, always in search of bits and pieces for his Six, and spent the whole of one summer vacation at Hornsey:

"I decided that working on sports cars was a more congenial way of vacation training than tapping vast threads for gas engines. I wasn't paid much, but I did at least get a nominal sum. During that time I worked in all the shops, and this would be the time that I met

Mike. I was given astonishing responsibilities really. I was working for Graham Hill in the gearbox shop – he wasn't a full-time racing driver at that stage – and he liked to give the impression that he was the only bloke who could assemble racing Austin A30 gearboxes. One time, when he was away somewhere, racing, I was asked if I could assemble boxes. I could, and I did. It wasn't as difficult as Graham had tried to make out. After all, I had a collection of bits, there were instructions for building standard boxes, and a picture, so I thought that was enough.

"There were a few bits to shim, here and there, but since they all had to go together in some sort of logical order I soon worked things out."

Then, in 1957, Keith's final examinations were upon him, and it was time for him to start looking for a job: "I went on the usual university 'milk-round,' looking for a post-graduate apprenticeship. I certainly hadn't decided to start my own business, and I hadn't considered working for Lotus full-time. I went for interviews to Rolls-Royce Aero Engines, and to Napier. I was offered graduate apprenticeships by both firms,

LOTUS – THE 'MIDWIFE' FOR COSWORTH

WITHOUT Lotus, and Colin Chapman, Cosworth Engineering might never have been born. Although Keith Duckworth and Mike Costin both lived in London in the 1950s, and both were interested in motor racing, they might never have got together if it had not been for Colin Chapman, his exciting sports cars, and the cramped Hornsey premises of the Lotus Engineering Co Ltd.

Keith Duckworth's first Lotus connection was the purchase of a Six, in kit form, which was followed by visits to Hornsey to buy bits and pieces. From there, it was only a short step to 'lending a hand' at Lotus, in the evenings.

Mike Costin first learned about Lotus cars from his friend Peter Ross, and a friend of Peter who had bought the Lotus Mk 3B, and it was not long before he was attracted to Hornsey as well, first of all to work on the cars in the evenings. By 1956 Mike was working full-time at Lotus, Keith met him on one of his irregular visits and the rest, as they say, is history ...

In many ways, Colin Chapman was the mentor who guided Mike Costin and Keith Duckworth to their own greatness. Both worked for him at Lotus in the 1950s, both appreciated his instinctive genius for advanced engineering – but both became frustrated with his unorthodox business methods.

but I was very attracted by Napier. They were still making Deltic engines, and Nomads – both great, crazy, engines, it would have been interesting work.

"I was very tempted by Napier, because they seemed to be doing even more daft things than Rolls-Royce. I must say, there was the prospect of working with Nomads – an H24 two-stroke diesel compounded with an exhaust driven turbine through an infinitely variable drive. In fact I'd already accepted Napier's offer, but then I sat back and considered that all such apprenticeships would probably have to start by filing blocks of metal for weeks, and I didn't really think I needed that.

"Now what was really fascinating was the insight offered by the report, which I got from Rolls-Royce after my application, that: 'They would take me on for a graduate apprenticeship, but that they had severe doubts as to whether I was suitable to be a member of a team …' They'd actually picked up my personality, even though I was quite shy at that time, and I would have thought that I was introverted, so I think that was quite the brightest thing that an interviewer ever worked out about me. His conclusion was exactly right, and I was still only 24.

There was also another opportunity:

"I was also asked if I would stay on at Imperial College, and do research into the tribology, the science of lubrication, which was still relatively new. That didn't interest me though …"

Then came the breakthrough, the event which was to start Keith along the path to fame and fortune in the motor racing industry:

"Graham Hill was about to leave Lotus, to become a full-time racing driver. I went along to Lotus, to see Colin Chapman, and he offered me a job, straight out of college, as a gearbox development engineer. Rather unkindly, therefore, having already accepted Napier's offer, I turned them down, and went to work for Lotus, at a salary of £600 a year."

Keith admits that there was some concern at home, in that he wasn't joining a large company. However, since his father had always been something of a rebel – "They said he'd never become a member of the Cotton Exchange unless he was a Mason, but he just retorted 'Well, we'll see about that …'" – there was no real resistance. For Keith, it was a great opportunity.

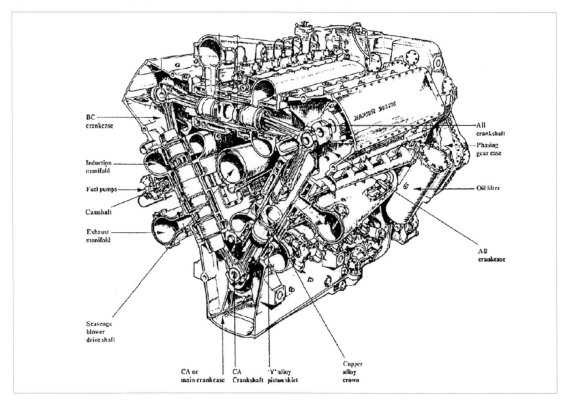

When Keith Duckworth graduated from London's Imperial College in 1957, he dabbled with a job offer that came to him from Napier. He would have been working on 'daft' engines like this famous Deltic power unit which, among other things, powered by BR Class 55 express railway locomotives, and many different military boats.

2: EARLY DAYS IN NORTH LONDON

When Keith Duckworth joined Lotus in the autumn of 1957, he was embarking on 'Mission Impossible.' His job, quite simply spelled out by Colin Chapman, was to turn the troublesome new five-speed gearbox – already nicknamed the 'Queerbox' – into a reliable proposition. It didn't help that he was the first graduate to start working at Hornsey, and was greeted with a notice on his locker stating: "Who needs experience, I'm a college graduate." "When I arrived," Keith says, "the 'Queerbox' had never managed more than 50 miles before the crown-wheel-and-pinion failed. The previous incumbent in the job was Graham Hill, but he was doing more and more racing driving.

"At the time Lotus had sent a 'box down to a big company on the North Circular Road, who were doing tests on a 4-square rig, putting torque on the box and measuring deflections – quite a lot of intense effort was going on.

"The 'Queerbox' had its selector mechanism running through the middle of the gears themselves, with a quadrant gearchange. It was an all-indirect gearbox. Drive came in through the cluster of gears, the input shaft was the bottom one, while the crown wheel and pinion, which had a ZF limited-slip differential, was at the back. It was a very short gear cluster indeed."

This was the gearbox which had been designed for Chapman by Richard Ansdale. Later, Ansdale, a very experienced designer, was to be involved with the marketing of Wankel engines in the UK, and with the birth and concept of the Lotus-Ford twin-cam engine.

The box was first shown, in public, in June 1957, as an integral part of the design of Lotus's first single-seater racing car, the 12. A year later, while Keith was still working on the development of the design, it also made an appearance in the Lotus 15 sports racing car.

Anyone with half an hour to spare, and the sort of engineering insight which is not overloaded by talk of tolerances, mechanisms, lubrication levels, and assembly methods, should encourage Keith to talk about his struggle to make the 'Queerbox' work, and work well. It is a riveting story of enterprise and first principles (on Keith's side), fighting against expediency and a reluctance to invest in change (by Colin Chapman). Mike Costin, wisely, kept well away from it all.

"The two main problems with the 'box," says Keith, "were that the gears had very short internal splines to locate the selector linkage, and that the crown wheel and pinion was not getting enough lubrication. I looked at all this, and the failed crown wheel and pinion gears, and reckoned that the oil wasn't getting where it should. I made up some shields and tinware inside the housing, then some jets, convinced myself that oil would now get up to the gears, and that if we assembled it properly, with the right offset, that there was a fair chance that it would work."

Placidly, and somewhat complacently, he then summarised:

"The first crown wheel and pinion that I assembled, with all these bits and pieces, went on for ever. That ceased to be a problem."

Keith Duckworth's task at Lotus was to turn the 'Queerbox' transmission into a viable unit. He found a solution, but Colin Chapman would not authorise the capital expenditure to put it into effect. (Courtesy: Karl Ludvigsen)

Far right: This was the Duckworth 'queerbox' installed in a Lotus race car. Frustrated by Colin Chapman's attitude to his suggestions for improvement, Keith eventually left Lotus to start his own business. (Courtesy: Karl Ludvigsen)

Meantime, ZF was building a new batch of gearboxes. Keith then had to travel to West Germany ("It was the first time, the very first time, that I'd ever been out of the country!"), to show them how to add all those shields and jets.

"There was an oil force-feed to the gears, but I had to reposition the jet. Even so, although we could make the crown wheel and pinion work, the gear change was hopeless. It seemed easy to arrange the change through the centre of the gears, but there was so little space.

"Certain people didn't seem to understand anything. It was no good doing all the sums, and the drawings, if there was no understanding. There's a lot of difference between regurgitating knowledge, and actually being able to understand how things work."

[Time, now, for another commercial for the Cosworth philosophy ...]

"There is a fundamental thing about Mike and me which is different. We are understanders, we think out how things actually work. It really is me who has taught Mike to do this. What is quite remarkable about Mike, and Ben [Rood], is that I found them early on, and they are still the only two who really understand what I'm about, and what everything is about. They are the only two who have been good disciples.

"By the way, I think that Colin Chapman was the brightest and quickest bloke I have ever met. Technically he was the brightest I ever met in conceptual thinking – the amount he could do in a short time was prodigious. He'd go away one day, having decided on something, and come back the following morning with a complete drawing, having done it overnight. But he wasn't that good at detail design because he didn't have enough grasp of limits, fits and running clearances."

Even so, Keith could not persuade Chapman that the 'Queerbox' was a hopeless case:

"All kinds of people tried to design a positive stop system: Len Terry was at Lotus by then, he actually drew up the parts. I used to say that this wouldn't work, and that wouldn't work. Eventually Colin said I should design the stops myself.

"It was incredibly difficult, requiring incredibly precise positioning, but I actually managed to make a positive stop change that worked. The problem was that we really needed to lengthen all the gears, only by about $\frac{1}{10}$th of an inch, so that wear and radiusing on the gears and the shaft wouldn't be critical. That, though, would have meant a new casing, but Colin said he couldn't afford that, it would have meant machining new gears and a new casing: 'You've got to make do with what you've got.'

"I was very weak, very feeble, I shouldn't have allowed this to go on for so long. Richard Ansdale was continually proposing modifications, such as a synchromesh proposal – but although that would have helped in down changes, it would have hindered as you went up through the 'box. There was also his proposal to use the first-gear pair of gears as an oil pump, but I did a few quick sums and worked out that this was going to pass 3000 gallons every hour, so the mechanical losses were out of this world ...

"In the end, I said, 'Well, Colin, if that's the case, I'm not prepared to waste my life developing something that will never work.' I was working morning, noon and night anyway, for my £600 a year. By that time I knew it was never going to work as it was designed. I could see that it was still unsound ..."

After ten months of frustration with the awful 'Queerbox,' Keith was ready to leave Lotus. (Once he had left, Chapman handed over 'Queerbox' development work to Steve Sanville – but Steve was no more successful than Keith had been). Before this, however, Keith had struck up a friendly working relationship with Mike Costin. As Mike recalled:

"I used to build all the racing cars in those days, and Nobby Clarke was production manager. I was really in charge of building all the prototypes. Jack Field was in charge of the stores, upstairs in the loft.

"Straight away I could see that Keith was a bright bugger, even in that vacation job. I got to know him better when he came to Lotus, straight from college. My regard for his ability was enhanced as soon as he started working – the sort of jobs he was doing, his approach, his handling of mechanisms, of understanding how they worked, and his judgement of what would work and what would not.

"He could take anything from start to finish, from concept, to layout, to the design details, to making the prototype bits, to assembling it himself, to showing how it would work and understanding the principles involved – I was totally sold. He was the brightest thing I had ever come across.

"I always had a very high regard too for his academic knowledge, it was far higher than mine. The bloke who can really understand the law of physics – the world goes round on the laws of physics – had an advantage. The whole thing is common sense, and Keith had a lot of that.

"Colin couldn't stand that this bloke was so bright.

He was very forthright, and he wanted an explanation of everything, he wanted to discuss everything. Colin didn't want to know: he wanted to do it that way, even if proved to be wrong – and, by the way, he wanted it done yesterday."

The idea of setting up in business took time to germinate, but both Keith and Mike can really thank Colin Chapman for forcing them to think about it. "While I was at Lotus," Keith told me, "we discussed setting up in business, because Mike had decided he didn't like Colin Chapman's business ethics.

"Colin was a stranger to the truth in many ways – he used to lie for no reason! I think he did that to make life complicated, to keep his mind agile. He always needed a lot of things to consider. If he told different things to different people, he was going to have some explaining to do, so he kept his mind sharp in digging himself out of the holes that he had himself created …

"While I worked there I lost engineering arguments that I should have won, because he marshalled his thoughts and his facts so much quicker than I could, so I would find myself agreeing with something that was wrong. He would get his way by throwing in red herrings. I am so undisciplined, and such a persistent thinker, that I would chase the red herring and lose the drift of the argument.

"Eventually I could counter this by saying: 'Yes, Colin, I've heard everything you have said, I've still got the odd doubt in my mind, I'll let you know in the morning,' then I would manage to avoid agreeing to things that I thought were daft." Keith, in any case, was completely convinced that he wanted to enter a partnership with Mike Costin:

"I thought Mike was supremely capable. We actually are a brilliant pair – he is still a racing mechanic by nature, whereas I tend to think too long. If you are a racing mechanic you do the things you can in the time available. I'm a bit too slow, I try to do the right thing. Mine is the right way to go if you want to go away and win a lot of races."

Mike's reasons were more basic. He was chief mechanic in charge of the racing team, did some of the test driving, and had his share of the 'all-nighters' that seem inevitable in such organisation. He didn't seem to be getting anywhere in life, he wasn't seeing enough of his family, and he was wearing himself out:

"I used to have my seasonable ups and downs," Mike recalls. "At the beginning of a year I'd be reasonably rested, but at the end of the season, by October time, I was finished. I was very unhappy [the

words, and adjectives, were much stronger in the original interview!], because we would still be in all sorts of panics and disasters. Life was bloody difficult. Regularly I used to talk about leaving – I was sure that life shouldn't be like that.

"Colin was really an impossible person to deal with, but he and I had a relationship which was extremely good. We only had two or maybe three major rows. He knew he could push me a hell of a long way – he was a very fine judge of that limit."

The fact was that by the summer of 1958, Mike had taken to Keith, and Keith to Mike. Both thought the other was a 'useful bloke' [that's another standard form of professional recognition at Cosworth, even in the late 1980s], and that they should go into business together.

Choosing a name for the projected new company – Cosworth – was easy enough, for it meant using parts of each other's name. COStin and DuckWORTH worked quite well; would anyone have been as impressed by a company called 'Ductin' instead?

Aims and ambitions? This was simple enough. Keith says:

"We thought it must be possible to make an interesting living, messing about with racing cars and engines. That was the total objective behind the formation of Cosworth Engineering – the total objective." Mike's view was similar:

"We thought we would set up a company in motor racing, and get work. It was as general as that. Lots of people wanted work doing – they wanted things designed, developed, engineered, manufactured, modified, raced, maintained – and there was plenty of work around."

When the decision was made, Keith buttonholed Colin Chapman, spent two-and-a-half hours telling him what he had come to think of his organisation, his gearbox, his unwillingness to invest in change, and of his methods.

He then told him of his proposal that Mike and he would be starting their own business. The crafty Colin Chapman, however, might have picked up advance vibrations about all this, and had just persuaded Mike Costin to sign a new three-year service agreement to stay at Lotus. Immediately, therefore, he insisted that Costin could not leave, and that furthermore extra-mural activities were forbidden. He would not allow him even to contribute to Cosworth's activities until that agreement expired.

This was a serious blow to a project which was

still unborn, but the miracle of it all was that Keith decided to go ahead in any case, Mike decided to stay on at Lotus, and a relationship between Cosworth and Lotus was forged, and expanded, in the years which followed.

"I had no choice," Mike recalls, "for I was totally impecunious, with a wife and three kids to support. I'd been earning £12 a week at Hatfield, which rose to £15 a week when I joined Lotus in 1956, and now I was on about £1000 a year. It could have been worse, but I didn't even own my own house – I didn't own a house of my own until I moved to Northamptonshire."

Keith, on the other hand, could afford to take a bit more risk, for he had a little family money behind him: "I had enough money to buy a dynamometer. As far as I could see, none of the other tuning firms were even using a dyno, which I thought was incredible. At least if we used a dyno, we could prove that we were getting somewhere.

"I had £1000 of my own earmarked for a dyno, but it only cost £600. The wonderful situation is that the supplier was worried about my creditworthiness; I'd put in the order from Cosworth Engineering on something very similar to bog paper. They put some

credit inspectors on to the job to find out if I was creditworthy – and then they went and asked Mike, and Mike kindly said that I was!

"I could still afford to get started on my own. Mike and I decided that there was a reasonable chance that the other people who were fooling around with racing cars and engines weren't all that bright."

At this point, please note, Keith had never tuned or modified a single engine, but thought he was "sufficiently numerate, and practical" to be able to tackle that sort of thing.

And so it was that a new company, Cosworth Engineering Ltd, was set up, and incorporated on 30 September 1958. The company's authorised capital was £100, of which precisely £2 – one £1 share each for Keith and Mike – was actually issued at the time. It was not until June 1963 that the remaining £98 was issued, all of which was taken up by Keith himself. Then, as at all stages until the sale to UEI in 1980, Keith was by far the largest shareholder in the company. The share capital was not to be increased until 1966. But where was Cosworth to operate?

"Even before Cosworth was set up, in 1958," Keith relates, "I was living at John Campbell-Jones' house in

Dan Margulies posing in front of various cars at the Shaftesbury Mews garage, Cosworth's very first home at the end of the 1950s. At the time Keith shared facilities with John Campbell-Jones and Margulies. Cosworth has changed considerably since then. (Courtesy: Dan Margulies)

COSWORTH – THE SEARCH FOR POWER

North Kensington – a very posh house, because his father was a very great architect. I had met John on one of his visits to Lotus.

"My own first premises – working on my own – were in John Campbell-Jones' garage in Shaftesbury Mews, London W8 – not far from Kensington High Street – which also had Dan Margulies in it."

This historic site (for Cosworth fans) no longer exists as a garage, for it has been converted into stylish neo-Georgian houses.

"The very first work we did was to build a jig for the Vanwall F1 cockpit bubble canopy; then I started work preparing Dennis Taylor's F2 car."

This, of course, was only the beginning, for Keith needed a more permanent home: somewhere to install his dynamometer, and get on with the developing, tuning and building of engines. At around the same time Keith also married Ursula, whom he had met at a dance, finding out that she was studying French and German at the Institut Français. "All the time I was looking for premises. Eventually, I answered an advert for buildings occupied by Hubbard and Wink, who

were firewood merchants, and took over from them. They were using some old coaching stables adjacent to the Railway Tavern, at 43 Friern Barnet Road, Friern Barnet, in North London. They used to bring in trees, and chop them up for firewood!"

This site, about eight miles north of London's West End, was by no means 'des res.' Early employee Bill Pratt's memories include the fact these stables were in a total state of disrepair, still had the hay baskets on the walls, and had an upstairs section which was completely unsafe. Regular hunts had to be mounted to keep down the rat population:

"Keith used to use the bit under the stairs as an office. His wife, Ursula, used to come in at 6.00pm, make him a meal, and catch up with the paperwork. She was also the cashier, and used to take the money across the road to the bank. There were no toilets on the premises, so we had to walk up to the local railway station if we wanted to go." The Railway Hotel, by the way, was later refurbished, and renamed as the Turrets Hotel.

It wasn't a palace, but it was available, so while

Cosworth's very first task was to build a jig to support the formation of a prototype cockpit canopy for the Vanwall F1 car. The introduction to Vanwall came via Frank Costin (Mike Costin's brother), the de Havilland-based aerodynamicist who had shaped the very successful Vanwall race car.

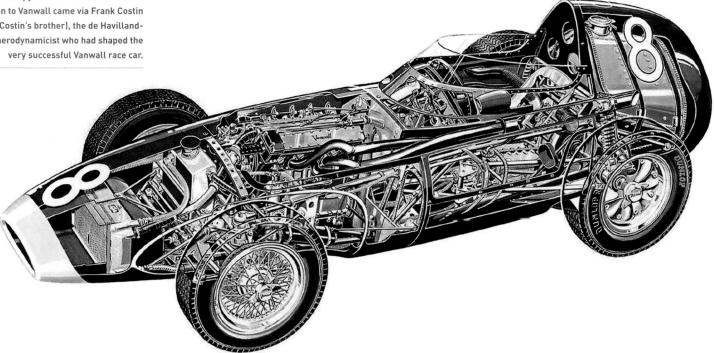

Keith installed his precious dynamometer in the bottom booth ("I didn't apply for planning permission, nothing formal like that, we just got on and did it. The exhaust pipe went straight up through the roof."), Ursula went house hunting. Before long Keith had moved in to Northwood Gardens, also in Friern Barnet, close to the disreputable Cosworth premises.

In the beginning, Keith worked at Friern Barnet by himself, for Mike Costin was securely tied to Lotus, becoming more and more of an executive, less and less of a designer, as Lotus entered Formula 1 racing, and as the Elite road car staggered into production. Apart from the important Costin-Duckworth link, however, there was one further link which would eventually become important to Cosworth – that Lotus built the first few Elites at a scruffy old building in Kenninghall Road, Edmonton. This building would eventually become Cosworth's second home.

Keith has very clear memories of Cosworth's first trading year, and the work he was doing to establish the business:

"I was working there on my own, looking after Coventry-Climax engines for Lotus Elites, for Graham Warner of the Chequered Flag, and for Ian Walker, and I was still looking after Dennis Taylor's F2 car. I then started doing engines for John Brown's Elvas, plus making new wishbones, and a different front suspension.

"The first bloke I ever employed was Les Spilsbury, an Australian who was over here as a dirt track rider. For the best part of a year he helped me to rebuild Climax engines. I spent most of the day chasing spares, and rebuilding engines at night. The next to arrive was Bill Pratt – he came from JAP engines, who were just around the corner – who finally retired from Cosworth in 1989, and then we got George Duckett, who was still building F1 engines at the end of the 1980s. Bill Brown, too, although he was still in the RAF, he'd got himself a posting somewhere up the Great North Road, and he used to come down at weekends to help out.

"Ursula was keeping my books for me during the evenings. It has been observed that I always employed the 'Jewish Accountancy System.' You extract your money promptly from customers, ensure that you pay up promptly, so that at any time the money in the bank represents your position, and you don't have to do much paperwork.

"I used to like the 'three nail' system on the office wall – paid, unpaid, and pending – and I always made sure I was paid promptly. Fortunately, I always seemed

to have enough sense to realise that unless my regular income exceeded my outgoings, then bankruptcy was certain."

Then, as later, Keith, a paid-up member of the hard-headed North Country fraternity who sees great merit in making money, was determined to stay afloat. In the meantime, he had met a resourceful machine shop owner from Walthamstow, Ben Rood, who seemed to be able to make anything, from any metal, to any specification.

Furthermore, he was remarkably quick, accurate, and possessed of the same mind as Keith himself. Ben Rood originally met Keith at a Brands Hatch race meeting, when he was still working for Lotus. Once Cosworth was formed, and various parts had to be machined, Ben's business, Rood's Engineering, got the work, as Ben recalls:

"I only had three or four people working for me at the time. I went to see Keith to see what he needed, and started making pieces for Cosworth, more or less on a daily business. The important thing, the unbelievable thing, is that he used to pay me – without being asked. Everyone else was hanging fire, and taking as long to pay as possible, but Keith would actually corner me

BEN ROOD

BEN Rood, technically speaking, was a Cockney, for he was born in Bethnal Green, within the sound of Bow Bells, in 1926. He was born above a shop where his father was running a confectionery business, and also made ice cream. Shortly afterwards, the family Rood moved out to Essex, to the Bucks Hill and Loughton areas.

Soon after leaving school, for the war had broken out, Ben began to work in a local engineering factory. Not only did he make models, but he soon had a lathe of his own, and bought his first motorcycle. After serving in the Army, in REME, he joined Browns Engineering in Loughton, and soon committed himself to a life in engineering:

"I never really thought about doing anything else. I always thought about engineering, and engineering problems. I used to go and lie in the bath reading *Machinery Handbook*.

"Later on, after the Army, I got involved in motorcycle racing. I went off and built myself a grass-track racer, and began to win about one in four of the races I entered. Then I got interested in road racing. I bought an Excelsior Manxman which had a split cylinder head. This didn't respond to any form of repair so I thought 'I know, I'll make a head and a cylinder barrel' – which I machined up from solid, believe it or not."

Later Ben moved up to a Mark VIII Velocette, a genuine 250cc racer, which he drastically lightened, raced for the Velocette 'works' team in the Isle of Man, and for which he eventually designed a twin overhead camshaft engine:

"One day I decided to do a twin-cam head. It didn't look too difficult, so I kept the original shaft drive, operated the valves through a train of gears, and built it all myself." This, mind you, with no formal engineering training, and very simple machinery! Later an enthusiast called Gerald Smith, who raced a 500cc F3 car, asked Ben to produce a twin-cam head for his 500cc Norton – which he did by using the same basic casting, but many different machining details. In the same period Ben also started making complete engines – the Hogan-Rood engines – for hydroplane racing. These were very successful, for instance, in the hands of the Stacey brothers (who were brothers of Lotus F1 driver Alan Stacey).

One thing led to another: Ben started maintaining Gerald Smith's car at race meetings, and before long he came across Keith Duckworth, also visiting to see how his Lotus 'Queerbox' parts were performing.

Rood's Engineering, a small machine shop concern, was founded in 1954/55, and it was while searching for business that Ben started to make engine pieces for Cosworth. Once the Formula Junior business took off, that rapidly grew to the point where Ben was working almost entirely for Cosworth – and the rest of the story belongs to the main text of this book.

Ben died in 2011.

Early in the life of Cosworth, Ben Rood became an indispensible part of the fledgling team's organisation, with his love of all things mechanical, and the way in which he could organise accurate machining methods using the very minimum of capital.

and say 'We owe you some money,' and write out a cheque."

By mid-1959, however, the Formula Junior phenomenon was beginning to spread across Europe. It was inspired, in the first place, by the Italian Count 'Johnny' Lurani, as a nursery for budding drivers, with the intention of using modified mass-production engines. The engine size limit was to be 1000cc at a particular weight limit, or 1100cc if the cars weighed somewhat more. At first the Fiat 1100's long-stroke

Millecento engine looked like being the most tuneable unit, so Keith began a development programme on this design. Fortunately, however, one of Keith's college friends, Howard Panton, had asked Keith to make him a Junior car, which was already part built, and to be powered by a Fiat engine. Howard, who had gone on to work for Ford, then told him about the imminent arrival of the ultra short-stroke 105E design. Ford's Walter Hayes, who later did so much to bring Cosworth into Grand Prix racing, described FJ as: "eventually a Ford formula, because we had a modern engine with an un-burstable bottom end." In Keith's own words:

"To me the 105E sounded like a reasonable proposition because of its design, so as soon as possible I got hold of a couple of engines and started work on them." Not only that, but through his continuing relationship with Mike Costin, Keith landed the order for providing engines for the first mid-engined, Lotus 18, Formula Junior cars. But there was an alternative, as Mike Costin pointed out:

"When Lotus came to build the FJ Type 18 in 1959/1960, there was somebody around called Graham Hill, who was a director of Speedwell. The natural engine to choose was the Speedwell A35 BMC unit instead of the Ford. There were great battles, and in the end we built up two prototypes, put one engine in each, and ran one against the other. Fortunately Lotus decided – with no bias of course – to go the Cosworth way."

But this is no fairy story, and Keith makes no secret of his problems in that fraught period late in 1959. Keith's target was to have two engines ready for use at Boxing Day Brands Hatch – one for Lotus, and one for Graham Warner's Chequered Flag Gemini – and with a delivery deadline looming up, he couldn't get the 105E engine to work. The memory lingers on:

"There were two snags, which went in parallel. One was that we couldn't get camshafts which would run through surge periods at about 6000rpm, and at 7400rpm. The other was that we got inconsistency of performance from day to day. The same engine performed differently on a Monday, from the previous Friday. We would get 75bhp on one day, and more than 80bhp on the next.

"In the end I concluded that it was all due to humidity. We were using so much combustion chamber squish that I decided that the only possibility was that, under certain conditions, the squish was actually trying to blow the combustion flame out: somehow or other it was quenching the fire. We cured that by removing the squish, by carving great lumps out of the cylinder head, then milling some more off the head to restore the compression ratio. That worked well, and we left things the same way for the whole of the life of the 105E-based engines.

"But there was still the problem of the Ford valve gear. At that time I hadn't designed many cams – I'd designed a special profile for the 1100 Climax which didn't seem to be much different from the standard one. My problem was that I had read the books on cam design and I had believed them. That was fatal. Even so, those people seemed to be fairly knowledgeable about the various types of profile, and acceleration diagrams."

[Another pause, here, to eliminate the long Duckworth lecture on camshaft design, valve springs, surging, and accelerations, which followed ...]

" ... At first we used a cam profile that was very mild by comparison with my later efforts, and especially compared with BMC racing cams of the day. But this caused quite catastrophic spring surge at just below 6000rpm, and the engine wouldn't go through it at full load. We were wearing out cams and tappets as well. If we offloaded the test bed, then took a run at it, we'd get there, and it would work reasonably well at up to 7500 or even 8000rpm.

"We looked at everything in the valve gear, we had different frequency springs, stiff pushrods, stiffened rocker assemblies, steel camshafts, but we could never get through that period. Much later I finally concluded that the problem was in the support of the rocker pillar on top of the cylinder head. At this stage we were about to go broke, because we couldn't deliver engines, and get paid for them. If we couldn't get a commercially viable racing camshaft, we would go broke. I had just been refused a £30 bank overdraft – I thought the bank manager was a dreadful judge of character! It was the one and only time that we nearly went under. There's no doubt – we were in a bit of bother ..."

Did he ever consider abandoning the project, I wondered?

"No, I don't think so. I've got a fierce determination. The more I can't understand something, the more I worry it out – I believe that in engineering there is always an answer, it's just that we are often too dim to see it. Even if the solution was quite expensive, it was better than going broke. A solution was suddenly going to be worth quite a lot of money – and I didn't think any other tuner had solved the problem at that time.

"I do think the prospect of bankruptcy at Christmas 1959 sharpened up my thinking process. I just wasn't prepared to have to go out and get a job, with my tail between my legs, having failed to manage on my own."

Keith couldn't consult Mike about this problem ("Once he gets on to something as mathematical as that, Mike is in a great deal of trouble ..."), but fortunately he could consult Ben Rood, who had already progressed to making camshafts for his own racing motorcycles:

"Ben almost has Newton's Laws programmed into him, I think they've been there from birth, but he'd had no mathematical training, or theoretical training at all. He could work from incremental tables, and use lift figures to give a smooth acceleration diagram, even though he didn't know the theory behind it.

"We'd tried everything by then, and decided we'd have to change the cam. I think I probably spent most of my time, for a week, trying to think as to what mattered, on cams.

"I'm fairly difficult to live with when I'm in that sort of situation. By the time you've got a great picture going, to get a multi-parameter problem assembled in your mind, it's a bit difficult to keep it there. If the phone rings, or somebody asks me something, I can be put back about three hours of mental model construction – in such cases I'm not very keen to be disturbed."

The result was that Keith and Ben completely revised their views on camshaft design, went for constant acceleration curves ("I reasoned that I didn't know what 'jerk' was all about, and so I was fairly sure that the valve gear didn't know it either. I thought that all the arguments about 'jerk' were grossly over-rated"), and produced a completely new profile:

"We ran it, the surge had miraculously disappeared, it went straight through 5800rpm, and we were clear, right up to 9000rpm and beyond. We had an engine that could race, that would produce 75 to 80bhp.

"That was when I decided to stop reading books, which only tended to mislead me. I decided that it was always better to work things out from first principles. One of my most important sayings, as a result, is that; "It is better to be un-informed, than ill-informed". After all, if you are un-informed your only option is to sit down and think about a solution. If you think hard enough, it is even conceivable that you might get to the right answer.

"Unfortunately, for Boxing Day Brands we only

Cosworth's early reputation was founded on the remarkable way in which it learned to race-tune Ford's overhead-valve 105E engine. This was the base engine on which all the miracles were wrought.

COSWORTH – THE SEARCH FOR POWER

1958-1961: THE STRUGGLE TO MAKE MONEY

BUILDING a reputation in the motor racing business is often easier than building a bank balance. Even though Keith Duckworth's early business philosophy ("It must be possible to make an interesting living") was justified, it was hard work. At least, as he so gleefully pointed out in later years, no-one could accuse him of profiteering! Here is Cosworth's basic financial record for the first three ('Friern Barnet') years:

Financial year after tax	Turnover	Profit (loss)
Year ending 30 September 1959	£3666	(£744) loss
Year ending 30 September 1960	£21,591	£2215
Year ending 30 September 1961	£68,507	£2525

IN the first year, the loss was caused by 'start-up' costs, not least the purchase of the dynamometer, and, at that stage, Keith Duckworth was Cosworth, preparing, rather than manufacturing, engines. The second year included the crisis period when Keith was even refused a £30 bank overdraft to pay his telephone bill, but it was also the period which saw mass deliveries of Formula Junior engines get under way. In the third year Friern Barnet was already bursting at the seams, for Cosworth had become the prime supplier in the Formula Junior engine business.

had a single cam and one engine together, complete with Ben's tappets and a steel camshaft. That was for Gemini. We built it on Christmas Eve, we did a test bed run, it went straight to Gemini, and they took it to Brands.

"Except for the twin carbs and a special exhaust manifold, Lotus, for that race, had to turn up with a standard engine! Their car was brand new, not even tested, so the suspension was set too soft."

What followed, in retrospect, was hilarious, but at the time it was another major set-back, as Keith remembered:

"Gemini obviously didn't tighten up their flywheel bolts, so in practice the damned thing fell off, going out through the bell housing, and knackering the crankshaft. That put Gemini out of the race.

"Well, Mike and I then took Lotus's standard engine, and the broken Gemini engine, rebuilt the Lotus engine using the standard crank and most of the racing bits from the Gemini, and cobbled up half a racing engine for the Lotus. He finished, he didn't win, but at least it was a good start."

This is where the fairy story clicks back into gear. The next appearance for the Lotus 18, complete with Cosworth Ford 105E engine and A2 camshaft, was at Easter Goodwood:

"Lotus wouldn't run a dry sump at the time, they kept to a wet sump, which surged very badly, so when Jim Clark set the tail out, and held it out, the bearings ran. We had to get a new set of crank bearings, from the Ford dealer in Chichester – they sent them up the road by bus! – and there are pictures in Lotus books of Mike and I working on the car, tipped on its side, so that we could change the bearings in situ, and modify the baffling to the sump.

"It raced like that, with Jim Clark going out, and winning" – it was the very first outright victory by a Cosworth-tuned Formula Junior engine. Suddenly, the fledgling Cosworth company was submerged in orders. Mike Costin recalls that in February 1960 Lotus had only three orders for its first 25 FJ cars, but that:

"... by October, we had made 125 cars, which means that Cosworth had supplied that many engines to Lotus alone, never mind Gemini, Elva and others.

"We would buy engines in batches of ten, send them down to Friern Barnet, where Cosworth would strip down, machine everything, modify everything, build it up, test it and send it back. The cost was £145, and Cosworth would keep the standard pieces. That was the deal.

Very soon the place was cluttered up with unwanted standard parts, but no-one had the heart to throw them away. Not only that, but Cosworth had also started to supply special 105E parts, particularly camshafts, to other tuners and engine builders. Keith was quite happy to do this:

"Everyone was trying to tune 105Es at the time, but our A2 was the first cam that actually worked, and it remained the only one that would work for years afterwards. We used to sell it to our rivals for the outrageous sum of £17.10s (£17.50), to allow them to keep going.

"We made our own master profiles, but Leonard Reece used to make the cams for us. Later we made a simple modification – we added $\frac{1}{32}$in of lift and extended the opening period. That was the A3."

In the meantime, the de Havilland/Mike Costin connection struck again. When Mike had been training at Hatfield, one of his colleagues was a young man called Brian Hart. Brian stayed behind to do a further two years, in Flight Test and experimental work, doing airframe and engine design. Then, one day:

"I'd started racing. I went along to Friern Barnet to buy a camshaft to go in my Formula Junior car, then one thing led to another. Before long I started working there in the evenings, then I finished up working there full time. It was the "thin edge of the wedge" business – I caught the feeling, and the exciting atmosphere in the place."

AUTOSPORT: 25 MARCH 1960

"THE 1960 European racing season got under way with the 39th BARC meeting at Goodwood ...

"A 10-lap Formula Junior race followed and proved to be the race of the day. Among other reasons for this distinction it marked the car racing debut of world motor-cycling champion John Surtees ...

"Surtees, driving Ken Tyrrell's Cooper Junior, and Jim Clark in a works-entered Lotus, accelerated neck-and-neck from the flag and went into Madgwick very close together. The rest of the field were in a close-packed bunch some way behind the two leaders, with Trevor Taylor's Lotus leading. D Mason (Elva) spun off at St Mary's and retired, and at the end of the first lap Surtees was in the lead, mere inches ahead of Clark's Lotus, Clark paying him the compliment of slipstreaming him on his first outing. On the second lap Clark and Surtees went into Woodcote side by side and the popular Scot came through in the lead; Trevor Taylor had outstripped the rest of the field and was moving up to challenge the leaders, while Chris Lawrence's Deep Sanderson was far behind and sounding very sick. From the third lap the first three cars were out on their own; Surtees momentarily passed Clark on Woodcote on the fifth but was soon retaken. On the sixth lap Taylor slipped past Surtees coming out of Madgwick and from then until the last lap the order remained unchanged. All three were driving on the limit and were only a few yards apart until, on the last lap, Surtees took Taylor on acceleration out of Woodcote to finish three seconds behind Jim Clark and 1.4 seconds in front of Taylor ...

"The fastest lap, achieved by Clark at 1min 35.6sec, constitutes the first lap record for Formula Junior cars at Goodwood ..."

This, then, was a famous occasion – for the two Lotus cars were using Cosworth-prepared Ford engines; it was the first race ever to be won by such an engine, and one which established the Lotus 18 as a dominant Formula Junior car.

Cosworth's very first racing success came at Goodwood at Eastertide in 1960, when Jim Clark drove this Ford 105E-engined Lotus 18 to a narrow victory ahead of John Surtees in the Formula Junior event. After which the floodgates opened ...

"Eventually I was building engines, doing detail drawings, and some development work. I was racing a lot at weekends, too – it was a busy old life."

Business was booming, Keith was having to spend too much of his time managing the business, and could not get back to his favourite occupation, which was designing new parts, and tuning engines. Except for Mike Costin who was still not free to join Cosworth as a working director – that move did not take place until August 1962 – the other important partners all arrived at around the same time. Ben Rood recalled

Cosworth's original reputation was founded on the remarkable way that the company could power tune Ford's rugged early-1960s type of four-cylinder engine. This cutaway drawing shows the five-bearing 1.5-litre version of the power unit, on which the later Formula Junior engines, and on the Cosworth-refined Lotus-Ford twin-cam power unit were both based.

COSWORTH – THE SEARCH FOR POWER

Cortinas powered by the Cosworth-developed 'GT' version of the short-stroke engine had great success in rallying. This was Roger Clark on his way to third place in the Circuit of Ireland rally of 1965.

that his machine shop business was working so much for Cosworth that he was in and out of the business constantly:

"One day I said to Keith, 'What about me working with you all the time?' and, almost simultaneously, Keith said, 'What about joining me at Cosworth?' So, we did that. I was more or less the 'Self-Employed Director' for a time, since I kept Rood's Engineering going, more or less independently, for the next few years.

"I now see myself as a sort of uneducated Keith. Like him, I have an interest in mechanisms, but he's had the advantage of a university education. We've always got on very well, in business and out of it. We used to drink a lot of beer together. In the early days we used to finish up in the pub two or three nights a week, not to booze, but to talk. We'd spend our evenings talking until 1.00am, in the car, in the car park, outside. I was a great 'shop-talker,' and I always wondered if Keith got fed up with me always talking shop. Little did I know at that time that he could never get fed up with that ..."

Bill Brown, too, had been persuaded to join Cosworth at the end of 1960 after completing his stint in the RAF, to become the general business and sales manager. The workload at Friern Barnet was so frantic, too, that Bill also produced some of the early detail drawings. Keith, at last, could get on with his designing and testing, leaving much of the administration to someone else, and Ursula could go back to becoming more of a housewife than a part-time book-keeper.

By 1961, and even though Cosworth (in Ben Rood's words) was "producing Formula Junior engines like shelling peas," the dreadful old Friern Barnet premises were overcrowded, and quite unsuitable for further expansion. Up to 14 people were now jostling for space in the old stables, so Keith had to contract out quite a lot of the work:

"We had our manifolds, for the Weber carburettors, and our sumps, fabricated outside. We didn't provide exhaust systems at all, that was the responsibility of the car builder – we just supplied recommendations about lengths and pipe diameters."

Even at this stage, too, there was the first 'works'

While Cosworth's race engine reputation was still being established, the changes it could make to Ford 'works' rally engines were also coming through – this was Peter Hughes' Cortina GT, which won the East African Safari of 1964.

Cosworth's first contract with the road-car side of Ford-UK was to design and develop the inlet manifold for a twin-choke Weber carburettor, to power the four-cylinder engines.

The Lotus-Ford twin-cam engine, 'improved' and coded TA by Cosworth, was used in a wide variety of cars produced between 1962 and 1975. This is the neat and very agile two-seater Lotus Elan for which the engine had originally been designed.

The TA-type Lotus-Ford twin-cam engine was fitted to the Escort Twin-Cam. Immediately after its launch, Roger Clark proved how effective it was, in a TV rallycross event at Croft.

This was a display unit, of the Lotus-Ford (TA in Cosworth language) twin-cam engine, and its related Ford transmission, complete with two twin-choke Weber carburettors.

contract from Ford. In 1963, not many new Capri GT and Cortina GT customers realised that they were driving round behind pieces of Cosworth engineering. Keith recalls that:

"Ford obviously took notice of our winnings with the 105E engine. Quite early on, we were sent a Capri engine (the awful Classic Capri of the early 1960s, that is) in 1.3-litre form, to try to do something with it. We produced the camshaft for that, and an inlet manifold – the two-ring type of manifold which had a Weber carburettor sitting on top of it. This is why we were always so popular with Weber, because we introduced Ford to Weber carbs for the Classic Capri, and for the Cortina GTs. I can remember rushing around for a time in a car with that engine fitted.

"By the way, the surge problem was still there with the Cortina GT camshaft. I was very surprised that Ford cleared our cam to run up to 6000rpm, for I could hear it surging, quite clearly, at about 5800rpm. In the end I sold the design of the GT cam to Ford for £750, but I had to have a great argument with one of the buyers about that.

Fortunately, in 1961 Lotus had just vacated its old development workshops in Edmonton, where the prototype Elite road cars had been produced. Mike let Keith know of this move, and it was not long before Cosworth Engineering took over the lease, and found its larger (though still temporary) home.

COSWORTH – THE SEARCH FOR POWER

3: BIG MOVES – TO NORTHAMPTON, AND INTO F2

"Nobody else has been outstandingly successful, and made money, and managed to stay in business, by making racing engines ..."

"We'll draw a line about 15 miles each side of the M1 motorway, and look anywhere in that band ..."

Cosworth Engineering was still only three years old when it moved in to the ex-Lotus premises at 2 Kenninghall Road, in North East London and there was still no place for glamour, and glitz. The premises, to be frank, were only slightly less seedy than those vacated at Friern Barnet, for the factory roof was of corrugated iron, as were the big slide-away doors, and the yard was usually littered with oil drums, wood, and odd bits of building material.

In the meantime, Cosworth also installed some machinery in Ben Rood's workshops in Walthamstow, and before long Rood's Engineering was working full-time for Cosworth. As soon as Cosworth established a stores department, a young man called Jack Field moved in to run the operation:

"In the very early 1950s I got to know Lotus, when Colin Chapman had the sheds behind the pub in Hornsey, and it was there that I met Keith and Mike. I was actually working the sales counter in a Vauxhall/Bedford dealership across the road.

"Before he was even working full-time on his cars, Colin used to call in on his way to work with British Aluminium, leave me a list of bits and pieces, nuts, bolts, valve guides and what have you, then call back in the evening and collect them, take them away and use them to build his cars.

"Then, when Lotus put up a stores, in the roof, he asked me to join him. It was the usual Chapman story: 'We can't pay you a lot of money, but we're going to become one of the largest manufacturers in the UK, so you'll finish up as a rich man.' I didn't believe him, but as I was a bit of an enthusiast, I joined him, and stayed for about three years. I left Lotus at about the time Keith left to set up Cosworth.

"I left because I couldn't afford to get married on the salary Colin was paying me. I went back to the dealership for a time, but because I was selling parts off the back of the garage's van, I used to call in at Friern Barnet, and kept showing an interest.

"Eventually, I went to work for Cosworth, running

By 1961 the original Friern Barnet premises had become extremely cramped for the ever-expanding Cosworth business, so a move to an ex-Lotus building in Edmonton was a real step-up for the company. That site had originally been where the very first Lotus Elite took shape. Cosworth would soon outgrow this building, and move on to the purpose-built Northampton factory in 1964.

the stores, acting as van driver, and if there was an engine to pack I'd make the packing case first! I was also doing the buying, and some of the selling, but eventually I released the buying, released the stores job, and I've been selling – or marketing – ever since.

"At Cosworth, though, everyone seemed to have a hand in sales. Bill Brown and Keith used to go to the races, Bill used to do all the deals with Lotus, everyone just got stuck in. I worked very long hours – we started late, but we finished late, and we also used to work at weekends. Fortunately I stayed married – it helped that my wife had been the switchboard girl at Lotus, so she really knew what she was letting herself in for."

At this time Cosworth was selling a great variety of modified Ford 105E engines for Formula Junior cars, sports cars, and even as options for the Lotus Seven road car.

"We gradually changed over from 1-litre to 1100cc," Keith said, "by which time we were having special cranks made, mainly by Laystall, we had special pistons, in fact by the end of the programme we made so many special bits that there were really only the block and head castings that were not special – and that was because the rules didn't allow us to do those."

At the same time, the company was financially sound – something which could not be said of many of its rivals. Keith Duckworth:

"We always used to pay our bills promptly, and tried to get paid promptly. The one thing that assures attention from suppliers is to be the one who pays his bills on time! I even managed to survive by not being paid regularly by Lotus. There was once a terrible drama, when there was £3000 outstanding from them at the end of the first year. I don't know how we survived then.

"I can remember going to see Fred Bushell at Lotus, who said he'd have a cheque in the post. I remember looking at him doubtfully, and I can also remember that I got a significant lecture for looking at him quizzically as if I didn't believe him. He actually tore me off a strip for not believing him – but a couple of weeks later the cheque still hadn't arrived, though it did arrive in the end.

"We never had an overdraft during the years that I owned Cosworth – or if we did it was purely for technical purposes, just for a week or so. I managed to buy all our equipment on a totally self-financing basis. We were a fairly high cash-generating business, right from the word 'Go.' Because I owned the company, I

had a very personal view of what to do with profits. When we had enough money, I used to go out and buy some machinery. I wouldn't buy anything until we had the money to pay for it – that's a good North Country habit."

[Time, now, for another short Duckworth lecture ...]

"I think that borrowing is one of the biggest immoralities there is. The more I think about life, and the credit society, the more irresponsible I think it is. I don't think that the moral fibre of most people makes it possible for them to be offered lots of credit."

[Back to the growth of Cosworth ...]

"I never had that feeling that I wanted to be a millionaire, not just for the self-esteem. Colin Chapman, though, he was definitely like that, but I could never understand him. Because of the tax regime of the day, we tried to invest almost all of our profits, and that's how we came to have so much capital equipment. In practice, that's why we were really forced into an expansion that neither Mike nor I really wanted, because we had a lot of capital machinery hanging round. But it was better to buy them, than to take the profits as salary, and pay 98 per cent income tax. It wasn't until years later that I realised how rare Cosworth actually was in this respect. There were lots of tuning firms, but nobody else has been outstandingly successful, and made money, and managed to stay in business, purely by making racing engines.

"When I totally owned the business, I always tried to hold enough money to see us through a bad period. When I was in total control of company finances, I never paid out any more than I wanted to do. I didn't pay myself much either, because I lived fairly simply. I seemed to work nearly all the time, so I didn't need much money to live on."

Cometh the hour, cometh the man. Keith also acknowledged that Cosworth was founded, and grew up, at exactly the right time.

"Formula Junior happened at the right time for us, because it allowed me to design bits of engines progressively. The other factor was that we were always encouraged to think about engine design, and development. It was mainly our deep thinking, and our approach to life, which made us different."

In 1962, with Cosworth's FJ engines used by as many teams as could reserve places in the queue, Keith had a chance to widen his reputation. He had already heard about the secret new Elan, and the Lotus-Ford twin-cam engine project, which were under development, but until July 1962 (only three months before launch)

In every way Walter Hayes, Ford's accomplished Public Affairs Director in the 1960s, was 'the Godfather' behind Cosworth's move up to designing the FVA and DFV race engines. He later guided Cosworth to even greater things in the 1970s and 1980s, before joining Aston Martin as chairman.

he had not been invited to work on it. By this time, to quote a distinguished Twin-Cam restorer, Miles Wilkins, "the whole project was in a bugger's muddle."

"The head had been designed by Harry Mundy," Keith related, "then drawn up by Richard Ansdale. Colin approached us, not only to make a racing version of the engine, but to sort it out to go into a production car. It wasn't all bad, but at the time the head joint wasn't sound, the head structure wasn't any good, and its ports didn't look like ports ought to look. By that time we thought we knew a lot about ports – we tended to bore them as far as possible, to keep them straight, to make sure there were no valve guide bosses to get in the way, because we were trying to take air round the bend and through the valve with as little disturbance as possible.

"We had, after all, got more than 100bhp/litre from the pushrod 105E engine, which was GP power of only five years previously, and were managing to run that pushrod engine up to 10,000rpm, nearly 10,500rpm. I didn't think the ports were as free-flowing, or as straight, as they should be. We did think we had a fair idea of how you should get air, at high velocity, through ports, and to work properly. So we straightened up the ports – we just arbitrarily redesigned them – then we added a bit of structure into the head too.

As Miles Wilkins noted, in his book *Lotus – the Twin-Cam Engine*: "Therefore, the final shape of the head, including the oil breather arrangement, was produced by Keith Duckworth."

Once Cosworth had sorted out the final specification of the Twin-Cam cylinder head, race-engine development went ahead smoothly, many engines were supplied to Lotus for fitment to Lotus-Cortinas used in saloon car racing, along with units sent to Ford for use in rally cars. Not only was it Keith's airflow development which made a difference, but the design of several new camshaft profiles.

Although Duckworth always insists that there was no 'master plan,' and that he never actively wanted Cosworth to expand, the company did not run itself. Each new motor racing season brought new regulations, new challenges, and a new queue of customers who wanted engines to suit. Forward planning, according to Keith, only took place once a year:

"We used to spend the first week of our annual holiday shut-down having a running board meeting to work out what the strategy should be for the next year. We'd already had to change our views about "making

an interesting living, messing about ..." Every year we'd have to sit down and think "What on earth are we going to do next?" We'd all been so busy running our various departments throughout the year, that the only time there was any peace and quiet was when everyone else went on holiday for two weeks.

"The four of us – Mike, Ben, Bill Brown and I – would meet, and try to discuss strategy. Originally we met for whole days, but then it became a question of mornings only. Three of us didn't mind thinking, and talking, until the late hours – but not Bill.

"There was one epic meeting where we asked Bill how many of such an engine he thought he could make. He said he didn't know, so I encouraged him to go away and have a think. At that moment Bill stood up, glared at all of us, and blurted out 'It's all right for you, you don't mind thinking all the time. Me, I find it bloody hard work!'"

Even so, Mike Costin insists that the relationships were usually harmonious:

"The secret was that we always accepted Keith was ultimately the guv'nor. It was largely a case of personalities – he did, after all, own the bat, the ball and the pitch, but we all had, and still have, a high regard for his abilities. Some people say that he got bees in his bonnet. I don't agree. Let's just say that

Ford's original Lotus-Cortina, built by Lotus from 1963 to 1966, used the 8-valve Lotus-Ford twin-cam engine which Cosworth had turned into a powerful and viable road-car power unit.

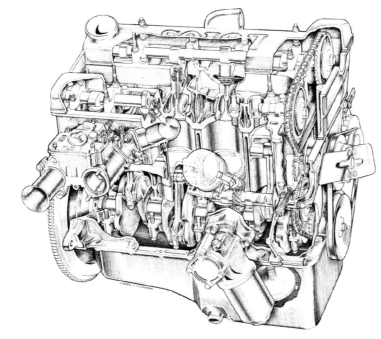

Although the neat 8-valve twin-cam Lotus-Ford engine was not a Cosworth design, under project code TA it needed the company's expertise to turn it into a reliable power unit which could be race-tuned to a remarkable degree. Much of Cosworth's expertise went into improving the structure of the new aluminium head, and into improving the breathing.

teacher. My engineering education has been brought about by Keith, not by Colin Chapman, by always being totally involved with Keith. If there was ever anything I didn't understand, Keith has taken me back to square one, to discuss it. Keith doesn't have any books full of formulae – he develops every theory from scratch.

"It's simple really. I've never been overwhelmed, or threatened by this mountain of intelligence. I've never worried about an earthquake. I just accept that Everest is there."

Keith saw it a little differently:

"Obviously, by thinking deeply, and by holding my own views, whenever anyone says something with which I disagree, I will try to say 'How do you come to that conclusion?' Because of questioning everything, I am more or less socially unacceptable.

"On the clock which I gave to Mike to commemorate his 25 years with Cosworth, the caption I had put on the side was: 'From the idealist to the realist. Together, in Cosworth, we beat the world.'"

The fact was that, in spite of Keith's modest intentions, his fledgling company had taken on a momentum of its own, and it was expanding all the time. Not only that, but after four sometimes frustrating years, Mike Costin finally came to the end of his service contract with Lotus, and moved to Cosworth, to take up his directorship. Mike sums up the new relationship like this:

"Keith was the dictator, and the engineer. Bill was not a great engineer, but he was a good administrator. Me, well, I don't call myself anything, really. Apart from three years at de Havilland where I was on a drawing board most of the time, I wouldn't say that I was a draughtsman. I wouldn't say that I was proud of my drawing.

"My designing was always done as sketches, but the sketches had every radius, every limit, every finish, every heat treatment. I used to keep notebooks, stacks of the things. I used to spend quite a lot of time in the drawing office, commenting on things.

"I had, and still have, an input to design, through discussing for hours and hours with Keith how things have to be designed, but I'm not the designer. When it came to all the big engineering decisions, the big jobs, all three of us – Keith, Ben and me – could get together, and we could all talk about, say, how we were going to tool something, how we were going to design something. We could all talk about every aspect of the job, we were all relatively interchangeable, though we each had our own areas of responsibility."

sometimes he had particular topics of the day! If he had to go on and on about something, it usually meant that other people hadn't understood, that they hadn't got far enough down the road.

"Keith, I've always said, should have been a

For the first time, since 1958, Keith could concentrate on design work, while Mike could get on with the development, the production engineering, and dealing with the customers. Within two years of moving, the workforce had doubled, and Keith began to mull over a new design project:

"I didn't mind that it was going to take a lot of thinking. For years I've been perfectly happy to sit down and think out a problem, I don't even find it hard work."

By the beginning of 1963, the motor racing authorities had decided to bring Formula Junior to an end, not least because it had become dominated by Ford engines, almost all of them built by Cosworth! For 1964, and in place of Junior, it was decided, there would be two new International formulae, a new 1-litre Formula 3, and a new Formula 2.

Formula 3 was really to be 'son of Formula Junior,' and would still require homologated road car engines to be used, although a new limitation was the use of just one, single-choke, carburettor. For Cosworth, this meant reworking the existing FJ design, and producing the new MAE ('Modified Anglia Engine') unit, a real screamer which could rev to 10,000rpm and beyond, while producing 100bhp/litre through a single carburettor choke.

The new Formula 2 sounded much more challenging – and much more interesting for Cosworth. Quite simply, the regulations allowed: "... racing vehicles of a capacity limitation of 1000cc. Maximum number of cylinders, 4. Minimum weight of car, 420kg."

Keith and Mike began planning a new engine immediately, and within weeks *The Autocar*'s sport column rumoured that: "Cosworth Engineering is developing a twin overhead cam head to suit the 1000cc 4-cyl, 5-bearing, Ford engine."

That rumour, as it happened, was well wide of the mark, though it showed how far Cosworth had advanced in a few years. The motor racing 'establishment' (and there was nothing more 'establishment' than *The Autocar*'s Peter Garnier and Harry Mundy) clearly believed, now, that Keith was capable of designing anything.

During 1963, Keith evolved his new engine, the first Cosworth unit to have its own purpose-built cylinder head. Called SCA ('Single Camshaft, Series A'), it was still based on the same 'bottom end' as ever – the successful 5-bearing Ford cylinder block, but this time it was topped by a new aluminium cylinder head, with the camshaft mounted above the valves.

"In a way, this was a logical step from the old Formula Junior engines of the past, for the head still featured a line of vertical valves, two per cylinder ('It was really an overhead cam version of the last of the Formula Juniors'). This time, though, the camshaft was

From 1968 to 1970, Ford's 'works' rally team used Lotus-Ford (Cosworth TA) engines in its Escorts in the world's toughest rallies. This was Hannu Mikkola in the 1969 Monte Carlo rally.

KPU 392C was the magnificently prepared Lotus-Cortina which Sir John Whitmore used to win the 1965 European Touring Car Championship.

The Lotus-Ford twin-cam engine – Coded TA by Cosworth when work was carried out on it – was a neat fit into the engine bay of a Ford Lotus-Cortina.

Long after Cosworth had moved up to designing and developing the FVA and DFV race engines, its preparation work continued on pushrod-engined Ford power units. This was Lucien Bianchi driving a 'works' Cortina GT on the gruelling East African Safari of 1967.

upstairs, and there were no pushrods or rockers to add to the weight, the inertia, and the flexibility of the assembly.

Because the new SCA engine appeared soon after Rover had launched the 2000 model, some know-alls suggested that Keith had copied the layout of the Heron-headed Rover. The fact was that Keith's engine had already been designed months before the Rover made its public bow and, in any case, as Keith retorted:

"I never copy anything. My simple argument was that at the compression ratios we could use, and the valve sizes needed to ensure good breathing, then a bath-tub type of chamber ended up masking the valves. It was an awfully long way round their periphery. I argued, with myself, that if I put the combustion chamber in the piston, then for most of the time the valves would be out of the way, and that they wouldn't impede the flow. In fact, I'm not even sure I knew about Sam Heron, and his theories, when I started to design the SCA."

The steeply aligned inlet port of the SCA owed much to the Mk XVII pushrod engine of the previous year, which was heavily modified by having tubular downdraught inlet ports brazed into the casting. It wasn't cheap, or easy, to make, but at least it proved that there was an improvement in gas flow. The SCA, in some ways, mirrored that approach.

"The SCA was the first cylinder head that I ever designed, and now I think there was quite a lot wrong with it. We had all sorts of trouble with the combustion – we couldn't make it burn – but it was still good enough to win a lot of F2 races. In the end, there was so much spark advance, that it wasn't reasonable. We ended up with 49 degrees. The SCA chamber suffered from a lack of circumferential swirl.

"It might not have been right, but we had to make it work. It won the Formula 2 Championships of 1964 and 1965, until the second Honda engine of 1966, with four valves and twin overhead camshafts, tungsten carbide rockers, and torsion bar valve springs, appeared in Jack Brabham's cars. We'd run out of breathing at about 11,000rpm so we obviously needed more valve area. That's what really started me thinking about 4-valve heads.

"Mike and I exercised great ingenuity – we had ports that curved round, we had the piston of the week, with every kind of shape, dint, and odd hole – but the combustion was not good, the mixture never burned properly. At that stage of development with the company so small, we had to make things work: we couldn't afford to spend a lot of time developing it."

[Now comes the most famous Duckworth aphorism of all time …]

"Development, of course, is only really necessary to rectify the ignorance of the designers."

Cosworth's, and Keith's standards, of course, have always been incredibly high. The fact that the original carburetted 1-litre SCA of 1964 produced 115bhp, while the final Lucas fuel-injected type produced 143bhp, is brushed aside:

"Frankly, with the SCA, I was sorry the moment after I'd done it! I think that it was the 'Heron' type of head that did it. I can later remember arguing like hell with Harry Mundy about this. I was staggered when he used a Heron head on the Jaguar V12. Harry was very stubborn about things, but then so was I. I had some trouble in relating to him, but never to his boss at Jaguar, Walter Hassan."

By 1963-1964, however, Cosworth had already begun to outgrow its premises. Even in two years, the place was bursting at the seams. Keith could not face the idea of expanding an old and unsuitable building that was not his, so he began to cast around for a new location:

"We were still leasing, so now that we'd made a bit of money, we could afford to buy a place. I suppose I wanted to move a bit further north, to be a bit nearer home – I'm not that keen on London at the best of times – but we had to be within reasonable reach of airports, and people who were in racing, most of whom were in the south.

"Therefore we said 'The M1 motorway has just been built, so we'll draw a line about 15 miles each side of the M1 motorway, and look anywhere in that band.'

"None of us had actually been to Northampton when it was first mentioned, but we knew an architect who knew about the place. I think it was Bill Brown who first suggested that we should go and look up there."

Ben Rood remembers this rather differently:

"I never actually got round to looking at sites, but it just so happened that a friend of mine, for whom I was doing a hydroplane engine, had connections in Northampton. He told me about land being newly developed, and suggested we went to have a look. So, if I hadn't still been interested in hydroplane racing, we might have moved somewhere else."

Keith now takes over the story:

"We thought about a site with development grants, and I think we were tempted by Wellingborough or Kettering, both of which were assisted areas, but we decided they were too far away from our customers. Northampton, simply, was the best bet. Anyway, we all went to look at Northampton, where we found a piece of land in what was to be St James Mill Road – it was still a field, actually – and I believe we paid about £8000 for the site.

"There wasn't even a proper road there when we started building. We put up the first building on the estate; we occupied it before the road was complete."

'Jimmy's End' was south-west of the town centre, close to the River Nene and the Grand Union Canal, and almost overlooked by the main line railway, as it swept into Northampton's main station. It was a far cry from the hustle, bustle, noise and dirt of industrial north-east London, but this was where Cosworth was to make its permanent home.

Keith, prudent in all things commercial, took the trouble to buy more land than he originally needed, but the first Cosworth factory building at Northampton (later to be known as 'Factory 1,' and still the core of the HQ/management building to this day), occupied precisely 6800ft^2, plus 720ft^2 for dynamometer cells.

By comparison with what had gone before, it looked, and felt, palatial – yet another 3000ft^2 was needed within two years, and another 12,000ft^2 had to be added 18 months after that. At the beginning of 1971, another 22,000ft^2 was built on land across the other side of St James Mill Road.

Brian Hart, still combining a Cosworth job with a growing reputation as a racing driver, was one of the

The first of the Cosworth-evolved engines for the Cortina GT appeared in 1963. Only the badge on the rear wings – and the road-car performance – gave the game away!

Ford's 'works' rally team used Cortina GTs, then Lotus-Cortinas, with great success in rallies all round the world – this being David Seigle-Morris in a GT in the French Alpine of 1964.

The Duckworth-developed pushrod engine for GT models, designed in 1961, was such a success for Ford-UK that tens of thousands were manufactured, and the design stayed on the market well into the 1970s.

The SCA of 1964 was the very first Cosworth-developed engine to have its own cylinder head, and single-overhead-camshaft valve gear. Here, Keith Duckworth is seen tinkering with the SCA in Jim Clark's Lotus F2 car at Pau in 1964.

COSWORTH – THE SEARCH FOR POWER

The SCA of 1964 was the very first Cosworth-developed engine to have a specially-designed cylinder head, which featured downdraught inlet ports. Here is an early type seen on test at Edmonton.

first employees to go up to Northampton, where he stayed until 1969:

"A few of us – Jack Field, Bill Pratt, George Duckett, and I – went up to Northampton at an early stage, and actually helped to build the place. I was responsible for building some of the test cells, sometimes as bricklayer, then with pipework, in fact anything to get us going. Cosworth would always prefer to do something on its own, properly, than to pay for someone else to do the job."

Bill Pratt once boasted that the move really didn't cause any 'down time:'

"We never stopped building or testing engines. We finished testing in London, then brought the next engine up to Northampton for testing. It was a very smooth change."

Keith remembers the snags of sharing a newly-developed estate with other concerns:

"At first there was a factory across the road which boiled up rotten animal carcases to extract glue – that stank awfully on the days when the wind was in the wrong direction.

"This was the time when we regularised everything with Ben, for we'd originally bought half of the machinery that was in his Walthamstow place. It was at this time

that he closed down Rood's Engineering, and became a full-time Cosworth director.

Cosworth was employing no more than 30 people at this stage, but by no means all were attracted to the idea of living in Northamptonshire. One of the first tasks facing the four directors was to recruit more labour. The final moves took place towards the end of 1964, as *Autocar* noted:

"Mike Costin phoned last week to say that we shall shortly have to contact him at Northampton, instead of Edmonton. Instead of Edmonton 7694, it will be Northampton 51802/51803 after Christmas time ..." [But don't try to ring those numbers today, they changed many years ago!] The company, newly-established in Northampton, was now set to get bigger and more important in the years which followed. Brian Hart recalls that the workforce rocketed to around 50 within three years, after which it continued to grow, inexorably.

Neither Keith Duckworth nor Mike Costin wanted to run a large business ("The one thing we both agreed on," Mike Costin says, "was that we didn't want to expand"), but, on the other hand, they were not about to turn away business when it came knocking on the door. This, however, was only the start. The 4-valve revolution was just around the corner.

MAKING MONEY AT LAST

ALMOST as soon as Cosworth was established, turnover and profits began to surge ahead. Never again would the company have to rely on its bankers for support, with the business expanding as a result of Lotus-Ford Twin-Cam, Formula 3 and SCA Formula 2 engine work.

The financial 'Year End' was soon moved from 30 September to 30 April, which explains the 19-month accounting figure for 1963. The move to Northampton took place at the end of 1964.

Financial year	Turnover	Profit (loss) (after tax)
19 months ending 30 April 1963	£156.696*	£5885
Year ending 30 April 1964	£157,340	£11,973
Year ending 30 April 1965	£183,191	£23,775

* This equates to £98,966 for a 12-month period.

THE period ending 30 April 1963 was still bound up entirely with the manufacture of pushrod Ford-based engines, and the race-tuning of Lotus-Ford twin-cam engines.

In the next year, the first single-overhead-cam SCA F2 engines were built, along with single-carburettor Ford-based F3 engines.

The year ending 30 April 1965 saw Cosworth concentrate on F3 and SCA engine manufacture.

You've heard of a 'green-field' site? The Cosworth factory at Northampton was built in just such a location. It was in this modest building that the first of the company's 16-valve engines was built.

4: FAME IN F1 – THE DFV PROJECT

"I am responsible, by a completely original piece of thinking, for the modern narrow-angle 4-valve head."

"I have a vast natural curiosity, so I'm always inventing things ..."

Although the credit for the design of Cosworth's famous mid-1960s racing engines belongs to Keith Duckworth, their success was only guaranteed by the vision of two other men, Colin Chapman of Lotus, and Walter Hayes of Ford. Between the three of them, there was enough energy and vision to run any large project.

The inspiration, the driving force behind it all, was that Chapman, and Lotus, needed a new Grand Prix engine; Ford was persuaded to finance it, and both agreed that Keith Duckworth was the man to do the job for them. Even so, this was not a project which came together in a hurry. The basic timetable looked like this:

1961-65: Grand Prix (F1) racing run to a 1½-litre engine formula. Like most British car constructors, Lotus relied on Coventry Climax engines.

Nov 1963: FIA announced new GP formulas, to take effect from 1 January 1966. F1 engines to be normally-aspirated 3-litre, or 1.5-litre with 'supercharging.' F2 engines to be 1.6-litre normally-aspirated units, based on a road-car cylinder block.

Feb 1965: Coventry-Climax announced that it would withdraw from F1 engine building at the close of 1965.

Spring/ Summer 1965: Colin Chapman persuaded Ford to back the design of a new 3-litre F1 engine.

Oct 1965: Ford revealed F1 and F2 engine plans, with Keith Duckworth contracted to do the job.

Sept 1966: First (prototype) appearance of 4 cyl F2 engine, the FVA.

Mar 1967: First F2 race held at Snetterton – Cosworth FVA-engined cars took all awards.

Apr 1967: Cosworth's first F1 engine, the DFV revealed.

June 1967: DFV-engined Lotus 49 won Dutch GP in its first appearance.

Although Keith Duckworth already thought that he was capable of designing a complete racing engine, he was still too canny, still too much of the careful-with-his-money Northerner, to go ahead on his own, without the backing of a major client. In 1964-65, with the SCA on the way to proving itself in the current F2 championships, Keith was already involved in the design of a 4-valve 1600cc engine (FVA) for the new F2 formula and although he already felt capable of designing a complete racing engine he was not harbouring any firm F1 ambitions.

Ford's ebullient director of public affairs, Walter Hayes, on the other hand, had already added Keith's talents, and those of Cosworth, to his personal memory bank. He also had close links with Colin Chapman.

"I joined Ford in 1962, from Fleet Street," Hayes told the author just before he retired, "at a time when Patrick Hennessy was beginning to build the company in a new fashion. The Cortina was already in the melting pot and it was going to open up the market in ways that had never been done before.

"Within a very few weeks of joining Ford, I decided that we would go into motorsport with it. Since I had a very broad brief, I could suggest anything that I liked to do. Even before this, though, when I was editing the *Sunday Dispatch*, I had hired Colin Chapman to write a new type of motoring column.

"By that time, too, I already knew about Keith Duckworth. He didn't strike me as the type of person who could ever work for another boss for very long. It wasn't that he was aggressive, or silly about the superiority of his ideas – it was just that he always liked to be in a position to follow his own ideas right through.

"Keith had a lot to do with the engines in the first racing Lotus-Cortinas. I recall that those cars were so good that I once had to say to Graham Hill: 'Don't go too far ahead of the Jaguars, because the TV people can't see that you're beating them if they're back out of sight ...'"

When Coventry-Climax announced an imminent end to its Grand Prix engine building activities, it shocked everyone, not least Colin Chapman, who had built up something of a special relationship with Walter Hassan, Peter Windsor-Smith and the Coventry-Climax workforce in Coventry. Everyone had assumed that Coventry-Climax would continue into the new era, but as Walter Hassan later wrote, in his autobiography *Climax in Coventry*: "... we planned a clean break. Peter Windsor-Smith and I never even got round to sketching out 3-litre layouts, although we had a clear idea of the sort of engine we *would* have designed."

The problem which faced Lotus had obviously been relayed to Coventry, well in advance, as Hassan later wrote:

"The design of a completely new power unit of twice the size [as the 1½-litre V8], with all the development costs, was more than we could swallow, especially as we had been led to believe from the customers that they would not pay up."

Lotus, like Cooper, Brabham, and other constructors, did not have the financial backing to fund a major new programme. During 1965, however, Colin Chapman approached Keith Duckworth, asked him if he could produce a new Grand Prix engine, and offered to find the money to finance it. Keith replied that he had already decided to design a 4-valve F2 engine anyway, and that if that worked, then he really didn't see why he shouldn't combine two of them, and make a V8. He then said:

"Well, let's suppose we have to make five engines, do the design, and a bit of development, on the back of an envelope basis, about £100,000 will be needed to do the job properly."

There was no detailed analysis, it was purely a 'think of a number' exercise.

Chapman's first approach was to the Society of Motor Manufacturers and Traders (SMM&T), but although he was as persuasive as only a Chapman looking for backing could be, he got nothing but sympathy – and the ear of the SMM&T's President. Next, it was time to look for a Fairy Godfather from industry. As Chapman told motor racing authority Doug Nye, some years ago:

"On first contact with Ford, they didn't want to know, so we then had meetings with David Brown of Aston Martin in London. He was very interested, but he wanted far more control of the project than Keith was prepared to give him: he virtually wanted to buy Cosworth. Then we tried [Sir Daniel McLean] Macdonald of the British Sound Recording company,

Walter Hayes of Ford (to the left of this study) was the midwife of the DFV, easing the passage of the engine through Ford's complex systems, which left Keith Duckworth (right) to get on with the job of designing it.

and there were several other interested parties, but we didn't really seem to be making much progress."

Keith had approached Geoff Murdoch of Esso (Lotus was contracted to Esso), but also drew a blank. In the meantime, Chapman had already discussed the project with Walter Hayes, as the Ford man later recalled:

"I had got to know Colin well by this time, and I sometimes used to go round to Colin's house in Hadley Wood, for dinner, and a chat. On one occasion he said to me 'This is getting serious, I don't suppose you would do an engine, would you?' Now, every time I saw Colin, he would have nine or ten ideas to discuss, he wanted to work on all of them at once. So, at that point I only needed to say: 'Well, it's funny you should be saying that, because I rather think that I would like to do an engine now. I think we've earned our spurs at the lower level of the sport. I've been thinking about ways that we might go further, but I've been uncertain as to which way to go.'

In 1974, how could it be that Keith Duckworth and Colin Chapman of Lotus were still looking so pensive about the DFV engine, when it was already the most successful F1 engine in the history of the sport?

Harley Copp was Ford-UK's technical director in 1965 when Walter Hayes needed support at board level to get the DFV project approved. He was always an enthusiastic supporter, and (with Hayes) attended the DFV's triumphant debut race in Holland in June 1967.

"In those days I was even considering trying to do a GP engine 'in house,' but that would have been vastly expensive, and anyway at that time I didn't know that you needed a special kind of expertise to do a racing engine. Colin then said to me that he thought Keith could do it. I knew enough about Keith by then – the only ability I've ever really had was to be able to pick people. I've always been able to smell them out from quite a distance.

"What was interesting to me was that Colin really didn't know anything about engines, I sometimes think he knew less than me. Whenever he sketched a car, he would draw it very exactly, but at the back he would just draw an oblong box, and write "Engine" on it. But he'd already worked out how to make a very light car on the drawing board he always kept at home. He sketched out the car with the engine actually bolted on, as part of the structure."

Before long, Walter Hayes was sold on the idea, but before trying to sell the idea to Ford, he first of all had to prepare the ground. His chairman, Sir Patrick Hennessy, was also President of the SMM&T, and Chapman's request to that body had to be progressed before he could go further. In the meantime, Harley Copp arrived from Detroit, to take over as Vice President of Engineering at Ford of Britain. Walter Hayes soon discovered his new colleague's love for motorsport, and began to discuss his projects, and his dreams, with him:

"I talked to Harley, I talked some more to Keith, then to Colin. We had lunches, and dinners, and things, to see what could be done."

In the end, it was Chapman who burst the logjam of understanding. As Nye's narrative makes clear, when he was invited to dine with Harley Copp, Hayes burst out with: "Look, you're missing out on the best investment you have ever made … for £100,000 you can't go wrong."

Copp was convinced, and Hayes then thought it was time to talk things through in detail before formally asking for backing from his fellow directors:

"Keith then did what Keith has always done. I don't think that diffidence is the word, but what he does is to put up such a level of deterrence, to make sure that other people are really as enthusiastic as he is. Then he agrees, but he never actually tries to sell anything.

"Then we got down to the question of what kind of engine it should be. I then had a very good idea, and put it to Keith: 'Why don't we start with a four-cylinder engine for F2, then double it up, and make it into a V8? That way, half of it will be good for the Lotus Cortina too, and all of it will be a Grand Prix engine?'

"Nowadays, when anyone talks about the DFV [Double Four Valve], everyone forgets the FVA [Four Valves, Series A], but this was always an essential part of the programme for me. Big brother was fine, but little brother was equally important. It was always an important part of our agreement, that I wanted to see the little one built first, because frankly I thought that if the little one worked, then the big one was sure to work."

Keith took the pragmatic attitude that if the four-cylinder F2 engine worked well, and produced around the 200bhp which he thought was needed to make it competitive, then it would be worth going on to design a new F1 engine of about double the size.

And so, between the three men, it was settled. Assuming that Ford's various policy committees would 'buy' the project, Keith Duckworth would design a new F1 engine, Ford would pay for it, and Lotus would have first use of it. The difficulty for all concerned, however, was to get accurate cost estimates. Walter Hayes had a horror of going into such a programme without enough money to back it:

"The worst thing you can do, at Ford, is to cost

a programme, then have to go back to ask for over runs – for more. In any case, when we were going into business with an outside supplier, we always wanted to be sure they were happy too. But Keith thought he could do it for £100,000, and that's what we agreed upon."

While all this was going on, Cosworth was settling into its new factory at Northampton, grappling with the development difficulties with the SCA engine (but still winning a lot of Formula 2 races), selling lots of pieces for race and rally-tuned Lotus-Cortina Twin-cam engines, and turning out masses of single carburettor MAE engines for use in Formula 3. While Keith began to apply his enormous intellect to the double challenge which he was about to face, Mike Costin, Bill Brown and Ben Rood stayed behind to 'mind the shop.'

In the meantime, at Ford, there were two financial hurdles to be crossed. Walter Hayes and Harley Copp had to face a Ford of Britain Policy Committee meeting where, under 'Any Other Business,' Walter Hayes casually said:

"Yes, Harley and I would like to do a Grand Prix engine."

To you and I, the sum requested (£100,000) was a lot of money at that time, but as it was only one tenth of the amount previously budgeted for adding synchromesh to the bottom gear of Ford's small passenger car gearbox, to make it suitable for use in the Cortina, no one really flinched.

"After that," says Walter Hayes, "I had to go over to Detroit, to sell it at an annual review of world motorsport policy. It was rather a terrifying occasion. I said that I wanted to go ahead with a Grand Prix engine programme, and Mr Ford [Henry Ford II] who was sitting at the head of the table, said: 'Well, what is this engine going to do for us?'

"To which I replied: 'Well, in my opinion, it will win some Grands Prix, and I also think that it will win a World Championship.'

"'And how much is this programme going to cost?' said Mr Ford. Now I can't remember how the figure had altered slightly, but I remember that I said 'Oh, $323,000.'

"Fortunately for me, the budget for the Ford USA motorsport programme had been presented immediately before I walked in, so $323,000, by comparison, did not seem quite as enormous to them as it did to me."

The project was sold, and all that was necessary was for contracts to be drawn up, responsibilities to be agreed and for Keith to start work in earnest. Cosworth was to get £25,000 on 1 March 1966, when the contract was drawn up, a further £50,000 on 1 January 1967, and the final £25,000 on 1 January 1968. It was agreed by all concerned that the first £25,000 was to cover the design of the four-cylinder F2 engine, which was to use Ford's five-bearing 120E cylinder block.

In those days everything was much more casual than it later became. Rumours of a joint Cosworth/Ford programme were spreading by September 1965, and Ford made an official announcement in October 1965. Keith then worked hard for the rest of 1965, and the early months of 1966, but there was still no official contract to cover all the work!

"Then came the question of getting Keith to sign the contract," Walter Hayes remembers. "I don't think Keith had ever signed a contract before, and I don't think he had any lawyers. He wouldn't have wanted lawyers anyway, because that profession was already on his list of 'Bad Things.'

"So I wrote him a letter, then our lawyers said he had to have a contract, but when he saw one of our contracts he actually called me and said it was all too complicated: 'Do you want me to read the contract, or shall I design an engine instead – I haven't time to do both?'"

In the end Keith signed the vital piece of paper on 23 June 1966, by which time the first FVA F2 engine had started test bed running! Not that the signing of a contract was ever likely to kill the project, as Walter Hayes still insists:

"The main thing was that we all had the same objective. After all, if you have some beautiful girl who wants to marry you, the last thing you worry about is a contract. If you want to marry her as much as she wants to marry you, the rest is easy."

By 1965, in any case, Keith had already decided to tackle the design of his first 4-valve twin-cam cylinder head. His aim was to get better combustion and increased gas flow. Technically, and personally, he was sure he could do a good job, but the support of Ford made this financially feasible as well.

Although Keith insists that he doesn't read books ("I'd stopped consulting experts very early on, even before I did the SCA"), and that he never copied what other people have done, he was clearly well informed about design trends in racing engines. He had, for instance, seen how many noted companies had stayed loyal to part spherical combustions, through thick and thin, but he was not convinced that they were still relevant:

"The hemispherical head was correct many years ago, when engine strokes were very long, and the compression ratio you could get on available fuels was fairly low. Therefore, with a flat-topped piston, and two large valves fitting nicely into the chamber, and a sparkplug fairly near the centre, you got rather a nice chamber. Flame travel near the plug was good, and the whole chamber was a nice shape.

"Once bores started getting bigger, and the usable or sensible compression ratio went up, then people started adding lumps to the top of pistons, and if there was a 90-degree included valve angle what remained was really a pent-roof chamber anyway. The chambers became orange peel shaped, with valve pockets in the side of the pistons.

"Even the first 4-valve engines of the 1960s, which were motorcycles (and Honda did an F2 engine to compete with our SCA), still had 80 or 90 degree included angles.

"When I came to design my first 4-valve head, I looked around, said, 'Well, hemispherical heads, they should have been turfed out yonks ago, they're wrong, and those angles are all wrong.' My criteria were that I didn't want any surplus combustion chamber area, I wanted to use a pent-roof combustion chamber with the valve angles adjusted to make a flat top piston reasonable, with a compression ratio of about 10.0:1.

"It means that I am responsible, by a completely original piece of thinking, for the modern narrow-angle 4-valve head. In terms of airflow, and flow management, today's F1 engine uses exactly the same principles that I established 25 years earlier."

No one else, it seemed, had thought this through in recent years, and there was only one learned journal that Keith trusted: Ricardo's *The High Speed Internal Combustion Engine*:

"I really did think he was pretty good. However, quite often he put in the Latin phrase 'ceteris paribus' (other things being equal) the problem being that, in real life, you usually cannot make the ceteris paribus! If you could change just one thing at once, in a combustion chamber, and measure the effect, you might learn something, but that's impossible. However, I have a vast natural curiosity, so I'm always inventing things. I've always liked to make advances."

Even by this point in his career, Keith had decided that gas-flow rigs had little or nothing to tell him. More than once he told me that gas-flow rigs can show that certain changes to a head will improve the flow, but that the engine, on test, will actually be worse. In later years one of his most famous habits was to say that he could look at an engine, feel around in the ports with his fingers, and know if it was 'going to flow, or not':

"We always knew that the basic velocity in the ports was important, and the conditions around the valves and seats was equally important. Anyone who applies air flowing techniques arrives at bigger holes than I consider to be sound."

There are some aspects of gas flow management that Keith, and his colleagues, clearly thought they knew more about, than their rivals, for further discussion on the subject was always diverted. Keith would rumble, huff and puff, then abruptly clam up. On two occasions, his experienced knowledge of cylinder head design, have entered folklore. An early visit to Ford USA, in Detroit, led to him being asked to inspect one of the race car cylinder heads of Ford's huge-capacity V8 engines. He was apparently amazed by the sheer size of the inlet ports, and was heard to suggest that arrows should be cast on the port walls, to tell the air which way to go. Then there was the time in the early 1970s that Chrysler-UK's motorsport department couldn't make the 16-valve Avenger-BRM engine work, and took a head along to Cosworth to ask for advice. Keith helpfully looked at the head, squinting at the chamber and ports from every angle, grinned, then roared with laughter, and suggested that the engine should be junked. Chrysler UK didn't like what they were told, but the fact of the matter is that the engine never worked properly, and it was eventually junked.

Keith himself, however, was not infallible. In 1965, at the start of the Ford F2/F1 programme, he carried out a lengthy, and carefully considered, non-starter of his own:

"When I did the first-ever schemes for the 4-valve head I produced a diagonally opposed layout, with one inlet and one exhaust valve on each side of a pent-roof chamber. There was a compelling reason for this – I was looking for the circumferential swirl that the SCA had never had.

"In fact I had schemed everything, and drawn all the pieces, before it dawned on me that, relative to a central sparking plug, a circumferential swirl was in fact stationary – with the SCA, and a plug to one side, the swirl was effective. On the SCA layout we got some swirl, whereas with a central plug there would be no significant movement relative to the plug, and propagation of the combustion flame would not have

VALVE ANGLES – AND HEAD LAYOUTS

IN racing car engine design, is there anything new still to be invented? In detail, yes, but in concept, probably not.

Keith Duckworth, not a modest fellow where his own achievements are concerned, made one emphatic claim – that he, and he alone, developed the 4-valve, twin-cam, narrow valve angle cylinder head for use in racing engines. As a package, that's true enough – what is interesting is that each of those features was developed individually, many years earlier.

When I was originally writing this book, Keith lent me his own personal copy of Griffith Borgeson's book *The Classic Twin-cam Engine*, stating kindly that "It might teach you something." He was right, it did. Keith might have been impressed by the author's knowledge of old engines, but not by his ignorance of new ones. Near the back of the book there is a posed picture of personalities around the DFV engine. The caption reads: "Colin Chapman, Jim Clark, Graham Hill and friend at the dawn of the Ford-Cosworth era." The 'friend' is DKD himself!

No-one, for sure, had produced and raced a head like that of the FVA/DFV before it was evolved by Keith Duckworth. However, the origins of each feature seem to stack up like this:

TWIN OVERHEAD CAMSHAFT CYLINDER HEADS

THERE'S no doubt that the first twin-cam head to appear in public, to race, and to win, was that used by the 7.6-litre Peugeot Grand Prix car of 1912. That self-titled doyen of technical motoring journalism, Laurence Pomeroy Junior, later wrote that these cars had "startling technical novelty."

Who actually inspired the engine? There has always been fierce debate about this, especially as three of the team's drivers (dubbed 'The Charlatans!') were said to have great influence over designer Ernest Henry. That distinguished race engine designer Harry Mundy once insisted that one of those drivers, Georges Boillot, was the real inventor. Most historians, though, now credit Henry for the drafting, if not for the original inspiration itself.

The Peugeot engine, however, was not just a twin-cam, but it also had four valves per cylinder, opposed at an included angle which Pomeroy quotes as 45 degrees, looks more like 90 degrees in drawings, and according to Borgeson "may have been 60 degrees." No-one now knows, and no engines survive. The specific power output, very competitive for those days, was variously stated as 148bhp, 175bhp and (by Pomeroy) 130bhp. A Cosworth race engine of the early 2000s was up to 15 times more efficient.

Even though Mercedes-Benz then won the 1914 Grand Prix with a single-cam/4-valve engine, the twin-cam lesson had already been absorbed by many other designers. Except, that is, for Bugatti, who stuck stubbornly to his own ideas throughout the 1920s.

FOUR VALVES PER CYLINDER

HERE was a feature which came and went. There were four-valve engines of a sort, even before the arrival of the Peugeot and 4-valve engines as a result of the desire to copy the Peugeot, yet many Grand Prix engine designs then reverted to two valves per cylinder until the 1960s.

Famous '4-valve' engines of the prewar period included W O Bentley's single-cam designs, the M25/M125 series of Mercedes-Benz Grand Prix engines of the 1930s, the 8CL Maserati units, and, of course, the legendary Rolls-Royce Merlin aircraft engines. The type was rarely seen at all in the 1940s and 1950s. On the other hand, successful engines like the straight-eight and V12 Delages of the 1920s, the straight-eight Alfa Romeo twin-cams of the 1930s, the V12 Ferraris of the 1940s and 1950s, the Mercedes-Benz M196 F1 engines of 1954/1955, and almost all the successful Coventry-Climax F1 engines, relied on part-spherical combustion chambers and two valves per cylinder. Four-valve redesign was later carried out on the Offy, and on the Coventry-Climax FWMV.

The first successful 4-valve race engine of the postwar era was the Borgward F2 engine of the late 1950s, followed by the last of the Coventry-Climax V8s, in 1965, this pre-dating the Cosworth FVA by one season. As Coventry-Climax design chief Walter Hassan wrote in his memoirs (Climax in Coventry): "Technically this was the right thing to do, although very few racing engines with such a layout had been used since the war."

It took a long time for Coventry-Climax to develop an engine which produced more power than its two-valve predecessor, but in the end Jim Clark won five F1 races with the same engine in 1965, thus securing the World Championship for himself, and for Lotus, in 1965.

Although the motor racing world was then on the brink of going 4-valve in a big way (Coventry-Climax with the unraced 1½-litre flat-16, BRM with the unraced version of the H16, and Ferrari with a V12), it was Cosworth, first with the FVA, then with the DFV, which got there first. After that, everyone else rushed to catch up.

VALVE ANGLES

LET'S get one definition out of the way, right away. 'Valve angle' is actually short for 'valve included angle', which Harry Mundy always insisted should be stated as 'valve opposed angle' – and is the measure of the angle between the inlet and exhaust valve stems in a cylinder. In most cases the valves are symmetrically disposed around the centre line of the cylinder itself.

Once the layout of twin-cam racing engines had settled down in the 1920s, many designers settled on part-spherical combustion chambers, with widely spaced valves. A typical opposed angle was 90 or even 100 degrees – this allowing the use of two large-diameter valves whose heads would not push too far down into the bore when fully opened.

Bentley, which used a fixed cylinder head, and which had used the prewar Humber engine as its inspiration, settled on a 30 degree included angle which, if the designers had only realised it, was almost the benchmark set by Cosworth with the FVA five decades later!

The famous Alfa Romeo P2 and P3 engines all had 90 or 104 degree layouts, while the Miller-inspired Bugatti twin-cams of the 1930s used a 90 degree angle. In the 1930s Mercedes-Benz settled on 60 degrees for its M25 units, then 70 degrees for the M125, and 56 degrees for the M165 1½-litre V8s of 1939.

The trendsetting F1 engines of the postwar period were the Alfa Romeo Alfetta (100 degrees), the Ferrari V12 4½-litre (60 degrees), the Mercedes-Benz M196 2½-litre (88 degrees), Vanwall (60 degrees), the Coventry-Climax FPF (66 degrees), the 1½-litre BRM V8 (80 degrees), and the Coventry-Climax FWMV V8 (60 degrees). The unraced flat-16 Coventry-Climax unit of 1965, which promised to be the most powerful 1½-litre F1 engine of all, used a 48 degree angle.

It was that gradual trend which Keith Duckworth nudged one entire stage further – the four-cylinder FVA of 1966 had a valve angle of 40 degrees, and the V8 cylinder DFV of 1967 used a 32 degree angle. A new benchmark had been set.]

No, this is not a Cosworth engine, but the mighty Rolls-Royce Merlin aero engine. Keith Duckworth studied this engine, and many others, when formulating his own ideas about 4-valves-per-cylinder layouts.

been assisted. To make it work, I would have needed three sparking plugs, and I thought that was silly.

"So we scrapped the whole scheme. I'd done a complete set of drawings by that time. It was going to be difficult to plumb anyway – there would have been a set of inlets and a set of exhausts on each side."

Keith, however, had always been ruthless, perhaps too ruthless, in cancelling projects which do not seem to be going well:

"Undoubtedly I have been wrong, sometimes, to stop projects being continued through further stages of development. Originally that was because we couldn't afford to produce triumphs of development over design. If, at that stage, we looked at a drawing, or a prototype, and it all looked fairly hopeless to me, if it was going to cost a fortune to proceed with, then I would stop it at that time.

"My first impressions are usually the right ones, I obviously have a lot of intuition. I sometimes look at things and think: 'Crikey, there's something wrong there.' If my intuition fails me, and it gets past me, then Mike can usually sort it out. Mike has a fantastic mind, almost his own computer. He's wonderful value to all of us, because he can turn over an idea in his mind, look at a drawing, or at a component, and come out with the answer 'Yes I like it,' or 'No, it doesn't

sound very good.' He has about a 95 per cent chance of being right. He's a wonderful counter to me, because I tend to be inventive and throw ideas out, when Mike will then say: 'Oo-err, I don't like that.' He can never explain why, but he always seems to know whether things are going to work or not."

Keith thinks that many engineers are too proud to admit to their mistakes, and throw good money after bad to try to dig themselves out of a crisis. In the late 1960s he was amused to find BMW trying to produce a competitive F2 engine, first with the radial valve, two-stage valve gear 'Apfelbeck' engine (Jack Brabham once christened it the 'high and heavy' engine, and that name stuck), then with a diagonal valve head of the type which Keith had already abandoned, and finally with a conventional 4-valve twin-cam arrangement. In the end, as Duckworth gleefully confirmed, BMW bought an FVA, tested it, and stripped it out, to get the measure of what they had to beat.

The moral of this story is that the Apfelbeck appeared in 1966, the 'Diametral' in 1968, and the FVA clone in 1970. It took BMW four years, and tens of thousands of hours, to produce a competitive engine. Keith Duckworth, by thinking hard about every aspect of the design, produced a race-winning engine in about a year.

The story of the design, straightforward development, and sensationally successful race-winning career of the FVA (Four Valves, Series A) is well known. Keith started work in July 1965, the first engine ran on the test bed in February of 1966, Mike Costin first tested it in a Brabham single seater chassis later in the summer of 1966, deliveries began early in 1967, and it was immediately dominant when the new Formula 2 series began in March 1967.

It went on to dominate F2 from 1967 to 1971, there being no other engine – Ferrari, BMW, or whatever – that could match it. It was only the fact that it could not easily be stretched to a full 2.0-litre size in the early 1970s – it was, after all, based on Ford's 1.5-litre cylinder block – that allowed BMW to catch up. By this time, in any case, Cosworth had turned its attention to other projects.

"But we still didn't have a clue about costings," Keith recalled. "The FVA, in the 1960s, was sold for £3000. I can well remember wondering, not what it cost to build, but what the market would stand.

"I discussed this with the others: 'If we're going to sell 20 of them, maybe 40 of them, for a couple of years, how much can we sell them for?' I asked Bill and

Powered by an FVA engine, the Alan Mann Racing Escort dominated the British Touring Car Championship in 1968, with Frank Gardner the accomplished driver.

RAPID EXPANSION WITH 4-VALVE ENGINES

IF Keith and Mike had not wanted Cosworth to expand (as they still insist about their business philosophy), they should not have designed such successful engines. Once the phenomenal FVA and DFV engines were launched, there was a growing queue of customers. In two years – 1965 to 1967 – Cosworth doubled in size, and the business became a high-tech operation.

Financial year	Turnover	Profit after tax
Year ending 30 April 1966	£225,012	£30,796
Year ending 30 April 1967	£347,407	£36,145

THE first 16-valve twin-cam FVA F2 engines were delivered in the year ending 30 April 1966, but many more were delivered in the following 12 months. The first £25,000 for the FVA/DFV contract was received during this period. In the year ending 30 April 1967, Cosworth received another £50,000 towards the DFV work, with first deliveries of the engine (to Lotus) taking place just before the end of April.

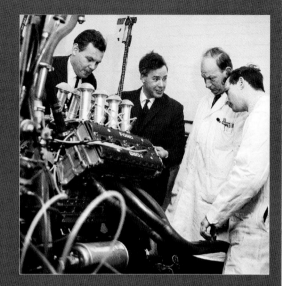

The 'Famous Four' in 1967 when the DFV engine was still very new. Left to right: Bill Brown, Keith Duckworth, Mike Costin, Ben Rood.

The FVA was the very first of a long-line of Cosworth engines to use twin overhead camshafts and four valves per cylinder. Built as a 1.6-litre Formula Two unit, it was a neat and extremely effective power unit in the 1960s. This was the very first to be installed in a race car – an F2 Brabham – for testing in the autumn of 1966.

Mike if we could make them for that, and we hadn't a close idea. Ben hadn't an idea either. It was then that I made a typical chairman's decision. I drew myself up, glared around, and said very loudly: 'We'll charge £3000. If we can't make that f***ing thing for £3000 a throw, we should f***ing well give up!' That was how we arrived at the price."

The FVA, therefore, was the first high-tech, low-volume, engine to be produced by Cosworth from its new factory in Northampton. Based on the sturdy cast iron Ford block, it had a light alloy cylinder head casting (like most such castings for many years, it was made for Cosworth by Aeroplane & Motor Aluminium Castings in the Midlands), with twin overhead camshafts driven from the nose of the crank by a series of gears. There were 16 valves, fuel-injection by Lucas, and the name of 'Ford' was proudly cast on the camshaft cover. Target power, when the engine was designed, had been 200bhp, but this was handsomely beaten on a very early test run. Most engines delivered in 1967 produced 220bhp, and this figure was increased considerably in the years which followed.

"But I still got it wrong in one way," Keith said. "I had set the valve angle at 40 degrees, but that left me with a chamber which was too big. We found we could run with even higher compression ratios, and ended up with a piston growing up into the head. That's one reason the DFV angle came down even further, to 32 degrees." By the spring of 1966, therefore, Keith had proved, to his own and to Ford's satisfaction, that his ideas on gas-flow, cylinder head layouts, and structural design, were all sound, and he sat down to design the Grand Prix engine.

At an early stage Keith had to give it a project code. Like his opposite number in the motor racing business, Mike Hewland, Keith had a healthy disregard for flowery names. Christening the new engine was easy – it was really double the FVA, in some respects, so it became the DFV, or Double Four Valve, engine.

[Mike Hewland, for instance, was known to christen his transmissions by names like 'LG' – for Large Gearbox, or 'DG' for Different Gearbox ... he and Keith had a lot of practical sense in common.]

Keith Duckworth's regime, established to design the DFV, has been chronicled before. Using his drawing board at home, a few miles away from the factory, he settled down, in peace and quiet, to think things out. Mike Costin remembers that the initial thinking process

Much of the original test and development driving connected with the FVA engine was carried out by co-founder Mike Costin (who was a skilled race driver as well as a peerless development engineer), here seen talking to John Dickens, his race mechanic at the time, but later to become a director of Cosworth in the late 1980s.

Perhaps testing of the original FVA-engined Brabham usually went smoothly, but in this study of Mike Costin in mid-session at Brands Hatch in 1966, he looks less than completely happy about something!

went on for weeks, and that the biggest agonies seemed to centre around one vital 'benchmark,' the position of the holding down bolts for cylinder heads:

"In the end," Mike told me, "I really had to read the riot act, and point out to him that unless he made up his mind about these, we'd never get the DFV built at all."

Keith agreed, but justified the delay, not as indecision, but as careful analysis:

"I tend to 'think' with a pencil. The problem is that you start off with what you were originally thinking about, but by the end of the first page you've already decided that what you started with was a lot of nonsense. So now perhaps we'd better start again, from there.

"Mike reckons that it was always worth my while going away and spending a lot of time designing something to be small and simple. The longer I spend at it, the greater chance there is of it working. He doesn't think many designers do this. They sit down with a problem, think of a solution to it, then they draw it. They are so relieved to have found a solution at all, they don't think of any alternatives. When I design anything, I think of about six ways of doing the job."

Sometimes working up to 16 hours a day, and straining his eyes so badly that doctors feared for his well-being towards the end, he spent nine months and, incidentally, lost 40lb in weight: "As I was at home for all my meals, I deliberately went on a diet, which seemed to consist largely of steak and cabbage, and as a result I lost 40lb."

It is quite untypical of Keith that he later minimised the sheer effort involved: "In those days, when I started with the DFV, it was without management systems, with a fairly simple mechanical fuel-injection system. It was possible for one bloke (me) to be sufficiently knowledgeable about all the aspects of the engine, to do a design as a one-man job. Later, when we got on to the days of turbocharged engines, and electronic management systems, that was more unlikely."

At about the time Keith conceived the DFV, he hired Mike Hall, from BRM, as his de facto chief designer. Mike had been closely involved with the successful BRM V8 engines of the early 1960s, but had become alarmed at the problems thrown up by the massive 3-litre H16 which BRM was developing for the new Formula:

"Geoff Johnson drew that up for Tony Rudd on a clean sheet of paper – a *very large* sheet of paper. It was a masterpiece of draughtsmanship, but I think that's all I could say for it. In fairness, it wasn't his concept.

"We knew a lot about V8s, so my feeling (shared by one or two others) is that we should have gone for a compact V8. As it turns out, that is precisely what Keith was thinking, but at BRM we didn't know that at the time. Strangely enough, BRM had already been involved with 4-valve heads for the V8, for they had bought a stake in Weslake, where Peter Berthon and Aubrey Woods had designed one, still with the same valve angles as the existing V8.

"When I arrived at Cosworth, the drawing office at Northampton consisted of Roy Jones, Pete Stemp, me, and the odd youngster. There would only be 40 or 50 people in total, at Cosworth, then. Keith didn't design in the office – he worked from home. I used to have to go up to Keith's house once a week, where we used to talk about everything. In the main, I designed most of the accessories on the DFV, I did the inlet manifolds, the water pumps, the accessories down the side.

"Keith would provide schemes for what he wanted, fairly vague in the case of accessories. However, he knew enough to say that he wanted the pumps to be a certain diameter, and where the volute should go.

MIKE HALL

WHEN he joined Cosworth in 1966, Mike Hall was already 36 years old, and had a depth of engineering experience covering activities as diverse as Rolls-Royce diesel engines, Raleigh moped engines, and the BRM organisation.

Born and bred a Midlander, where his father was an engineer with his own business ("We had a lathe in the garage, at the bottom of the garden"), he joined Rolls-Royce in 1947, served a five-year engineering apprenticeship at Derby and Belper, completed his National Service with REME in West Germany, then returned to Rolls-Royce:

"I became a research and development engineer in the diesel engines division, went from there to the detail drawing office, then graduated fairly quickly from there into the design office. My project engineer at Rolls-Royce, Geoff Topliss, then left to go to Raleigh Industries in Nottingham, to set up a motorised division. He asked me to join him there, where I stayed for six years, actually working in the Sturmey Archer division, designing small two-stroke engines for mopeds and scooters."

In the meantime, Mike had also taken up motorcycle racing, and competed in the Isle of Man TT races, tuning his own engines, and getting parts made by the firms he was working for. For a year he was tempted to move away from Raleigh, to work with Joe Ehrlich at the Bristol Siddeley 'small engines' division, at Leavesden, near Watford:

"Then, I went to work for BRM. The original connection was that I bought my first racing motorbike, an AJS 7R, from Raymond Mays, but that was in 1948, and this was 1962. I wrote to Raymond Mays, he passed the letter on to Tony Rudd, who eventually offered me a job as a development engineer ..."

Mike's original work was with BRM's 'contract jobs' (Lotus-Cortina engines for racing, 'King Kong' engines and gearboxes for Chrysler USA), but then came a chance to work on BRM's successful 1960s racing units:

"I got the job of developing the 'Tasman' version of the 1½-litre V8. I did nearly all the work on that – it started as an 1800, then a 1900, and I think I got it out to about 1950cc.

"In tandem with that, BRM designed a 1.0-litre F2 engine [which competed with Cosworth's SCA], and I had the job of developing it. To make it an economical proposition, we had to make do with a cylinder head from the V8, which was always a limitation, as this was really a 750cc head and porting, which never gave the cam lift or the valve sizes that we needed. Geoff Johnson designed it, and he came to work for me at Cosworth in the 1980s."

It was while he was at BRM that Mike met Keith Duckworth: "I used to go to all the races, particularly F2 events, and so did he. We got to know each other, and eventually I decided that Cosworth would be a good place to work. We talked to each other at various events, had a drink in the hospitality tents, and by this time I wasn't enjoying the way things were going at BRM with the H16 F1 project.

"I virtually said to Keith, 'I'd like to come to work for you,' but this went on for six months before I eventually moved to Northampton. I suggested to Keith that I should be a development engineer, because that was what I was doing at BRM. Keith didn't think he wanted one of those, so I moved to Cosworth as a designer."

By this time the motor industry already knew that Cosworth was preparing to build Formula 1 engines. It was no surprise to Mike, therefore, to realise that his first job was to work on the design of the DFV.

What a baptism!

Even so, I had to do a lot of detail design development on my own."

Ford offered help and support, at all times, but Walter Hayes was careful not to smother Cosworth with sponsorship:

"I was very careful to offer Keith help, but not to sit on his shoulders during this period of time. It was obvious that we had much greater engineering resources than he had, particularly where metallurgy was concerned.

"Occasionally he would come down to Dunton, to see Harley Copp, and he used to wander around talking to engineers, but it was always obvious that he would do his programme, his way.

"It was at about this time that I discovered something quite remarkable about him – that he designs everything, completely, in his mind before he starts drawing. For the original DFV, he did all the thinking, and he did all the scheming and designing – it really was the nearest thing to a one-man engine that there ever has been.

"Well, in later years, people would sneer that it

The DFV first ran in the original Lotus 49 F1 car in April 1967 – this is mechanic Dick Scammell driving the car from its transporter to the race track at Snetterton on that important day.

Although it was built around a 90-degree vee angle, the DFV was surprisingly well-packaged.

This was how the Cosworth DFV engine became instantly famous in 1967 – by powering Lotus's new Type 49 F1 car, with Jim Clark at the wheel.

wasn't a Ford engine, but it absolutely was a Ford engine, because he did it all for us."

Ford, and Walter Hayes, in the meantime, were keeping the general layout of the new engine completely under wraps:

"I actually leaked the existence of an F1 plan to Denis Holmes of the *Daily Mail* at a foreign motor show, and it was only then that I discovered how romantic people were getting about engine layouts. They were talking about V12s, H16s, and here was I wanting a V8. I didn't see why a V8 should not work, for I've discovered that in racing what you really need to win is dedication to the utmost simplicity.

"Even so, I had to swear the only people who knew, into secrecy. I said that if anyone stood up and revealed that it was going to be a V8, it would be laughed out of court because everyone else seemed to be going for more complex engines.

"I was right. When we unveiled the engine in our Regent Street offices, in London, there was a bit of stunned silence at first."

There was, in fact, an enormous amount to be done if the engine was to be race-ready early in 1967 and Keith was quite determined to control every aspect of the design. At one time he came dangerously close to damaging his health, and it was only a serious, though temporary, problem with his eyesight which caused him to back off a little. Perhaps Walter Hayes' memory took on a touch of hyperbole over the years, but he insists that:

"I think that obsessive is a dangerous word to use, because I think the last word I would apply to Keith is 'obsessive,' but the fact is that at one time the pressure on him caused him not to leave his drawing board for nearly ten days and nights. But I could see why he did this – it was his engine, and it was a masterpiece. It was really a piece of unique sculpture."

According to Mike Hall, whose contribution to the birth of the DFV should never be ignored, Keith never had any doubt that the new Formula One engine would work, first time, and give the predicted power.

"In our wildest dreams, we even hoped that it was going to win straight away, but I don't think anyone really expected it to win, in Holland, on its first race."

The torsional vibration problems which led to timing gear failures soon became known, as did problems with the lubrication system, as Mike recalled:

"Let's face it, the original system was a cock up. The oil drains and vents weren't sufficient, the 'blow by' was trying to get up, the oil was trying to get down, they met in the middle, and it wouldn't drain. That's why we had those temporary external pipes on the early engines."

The fact is, however, that Keith had expected the DFV to produce at least 400bhp when it first ran up to power, and that target was slightly exceeded at once. In the spring of 1967, therefore, Cosworth's immediate problem was not to meet its performance targets for the engine that was to underpin its future, but to build the five engines demanded by the Ford contract.

While all this was going on, Colin Chapman was designing a new F1 car, the Type 49, and Walter Hayes had influenced a major change in the Lotus driving team:

"I had a bit of conflict with Colin Chapman when I insisted that he took on Graham Hill. With other teams, I had already observed that they had No 1 drivers and No 4 drivers, with nothing in between. I felt that

Five of the most important characters in the early 'marriage' between Cosworth, Ford and Lotus – spotted at an F1 GP in 1967. Left to right: Jim Clark, 'Jabby' Crombac, Keith Duckworth, Colin Chapman, and Dick Scammell.

this really meant that they produced one absolutely gorgeous car, and another that really was a lot less than gorgeous. I thought that if I could insist on two

demanding drivers, my engine could be in two first class cars.

"Jim Clark and Graham Hill were two great names, but I also wanted to make sure that there were two No 1 cars to be driven. Well, of course, there was conflict as to who actually was the No 1 driver, but everyone really knew that Jim was always tops in Colin's eyes, and Graham Hill was sensible enough to never argue with that. There were huge personal differences, too – Jim was a ballet dancer in a car, while Graham was a real powerhouse: their driving techniques were completely different."

The new Lotus 49's design relied on the DFV for much of its structural integrity, so it could not be completed much before the first unit was handed over on 25 April 1967. It was too late for the car to tackle the Monaco GP, so the first appearance was re-scheduled for the Dutch GP, at Zandvoort, on 4 June. Lotus, however, had a further problem with drivers. Jim Clark's earnings had risen so much that his advisers had told him to take a 'tax break' (to live out of the UK) for a year. Accordingly, he not only shared a flat

AUTOCAR: 8 JUNE 1967

PART of Peter Garnier and Innes Ireland's joint report on the Dutch Grand Prix read:

"JIM Clark, driving the brand-new Lotus Cosworth-Ford 3-litre V8 Formula 1 car in its first race, scored a convincing win in last Sunday's Dutch Grand Prix at Zandvoort – leading the race unchallenged from the 16th of its 90 laps. Graham Hill had put up an equally impressive performance in the second of the Lotus-Fords during practice, securing pole position on the grid ...

"Colin Chapman produced yet another masterpiece in racing car design. It is what one might truly call 'a new car' ... The new Cosworth engine is obviously giving well over 400hp, and is a beautiful example of brilliant thinking and engineering ..."

AUTOCAR: 15 JUNE 1967

IN Eoin Young's 'Straight from the Grid' column:

"I gather there is no truth in the rumour after the Dutch Grand Prix at Zandvoort that Formula 1 will now be called Formula Ford. But judging by the looks on people like Jack Brabham, Ron Tauranac, Raymond Mays and Bruce McLaren as they surveyed the new Lotus, the rumour did have a spark of feasibility."

AT the end of that 2hr 15min race, Jim Clark's Lotus 49 had not only won by 27 seconds, but it set new Formula One performance standards into the bargain. The DFV era had begun.

After the launch of the DFV, Keith Duckworth decided that as a successful businessman he deserved a few toys, so bought this Brantly helicopter, just for fun. Even though the trenchant Duckworth always described the helicopter principle as 'fundamentally unsound' he came to love such machines.

This was the BRM V12 F1 engine of the early 1970s which threatened to defeat the DFV, but suffered a lack of development.

Competitive throughout the 1970s, the flat-12 Ferrari engine was the unit which gave the DFV the most trouble.

Even after 14 years of development, the DFV was still competitive, and was still neatly packaged. This was a 1981 unit, ready for delivery to a customer.

in Paris with journalist Gérard ('Jabby') Crombac, but he also had a place in Bermuda. The honour of making the very first test drive in the 49 went to Mike Costin, and Lotus mechanic Dick Scammell (who later became a much-respected director, and then managing director, at Cosworth) also built up some mileage, but all the serious testing of the 49, thereafter, had to be carried out by the team's 'new boy,' Graham Hill. Jim Clark's first introduction to the Lotus 49/Cosworth DFV combination was actually in Holland, before practice began, in a car which had not then turned a wheel!

As everyone now knows, the Lotus 49, and the Cosworth DFV engine, made an explosive impact on Grand Prix racing. Graham Hill's car took pole position at Zandvoort, and no other type of car was to take pole position until a year later. In the Dutch GP, Graham Hill led from the start, but retired after 11 laps, the timing gears in his DFV broken. Clark, who had started eighth on the grid, soon took over the lead, and held it to the very end. Ford, and Walter Hayes, might have hoped for a debut victory, but were not about to make a song and dance about the new engine at that stage – just in case there was a fiasco, or the engine (perish the thought) was not competitive. Walter Hayes played it all very quietly:

"I told Harley Copp that we should go quietly to Zandvoort to have a look. We hired a very light, single-engine aircraft in Southend, and flew to Holland, where we were met by a car. That evening we dined with Ted Edwards, managing director of Ford Holland.

"We went to the track, we saw the victory, we shook hands, and then we slipped away. On the way back to Schipol airport we stopped the car outside a shop, bought two bottles of beer – no champagne, certainly not, we hadn't made any such plans – which we then drank in the car, on the way to the plane."

Neither Hayes nor Cosworth did too much shouting about that first result, as they all knew how fickle the fortunes of motor racing could be. The DFV, indeed, had already shown its frailties – the lubrication problem would soon be sorted, but the timing gear problems would not be eliminated for two or three years. Right away, though, it was clear that the Lotus 49/Cosworth DFV combination had changed the shape of GP racing for ever. For the rest of 1967, a Lotus 49 led every race that it started, and by the end of the year there was still no challenge in sight.

Keith and Mike, whether or not they were prepared to admit it, were delighted that they had made such a startling entry into motor racing's top level, but Walter Hayes was not so sure:

"Almost at once I began to think that we might destroy the sport. I realised that we had to widen the market for the DFV engine, so that other teams could have access to it for 1968. In the next-to-last race of the year, we went to Watkins Glen. It was the first time we had raced in the States, and since we had got our investment money from there, I was particularly anxious that we should shine.

"Jimmy and Graham were particularly foolish in practice, blowing one another off from pole position.

It was at that point that I said to Chapman: 'Will you please tell your drivers to report to me, in my room.' I was playing the headmaster, but on that occasion I had to.

"They came to my room, and I said, 'Right, we are now going to decide who is going to come first, and who is going to finish second.' There was no argument about this, and don't forget that I was talking to two of the best drivers in the world. Even so, Keith says that he had never heard anybody in his life say such a thing.

"I tossed a coin, Graham called, and Graham won. At the moment I said: 'Fine, Graham, you can come first, and Jimmy, you come second.'"

Except that Murphy's Law then intervened, for Graham's ZF transmission began to give trouble during the race, Clark led until it was too late for 'team orders' to be applied, and even then his car almost let him down when a rear suspension link failed. Lotus and Ford got their expected one-two, but not in the order agreed in the Glen Motor Court the previous day!

On his way back from Watkins Glen, with the race trophy cradled on his lap, Walter Hayes recalled his original forecast for the Cosworth DFV to the Policy Board: "In my opinion it will win some GPs, and I also think that it will win a World Championship." One half of this prediction had already been realised. The second would follow in 1968.

A happy man at his work – Jim Clark in a Lotus 49, newly branded with Players Gold Leaf, at the beginning of 1968.

5: BELT-DRIVE — BDA AND ITS SUCCESSORS

"He had to be a great character, the whole Cosworth thing wouldn't otherwise have worked ..."

"You can't believe how quickly I arranged for an engine to be slotted into an Escort. You should have seen Stuart's face when I showed it off, and as for Walter Hayes ..."

"By the mid-1970s BD work probably accounted for about half of our turnover."

"Alf Vickers put sufficient organisation into us. I really do not think we could have built 100 GA V6s without his advice."

Once the DFV had proved itself in Formula 1, Cosworth suddenly found that it was famous. Companies which had previously ignored the company suddenly began to offer work, and several ambitious young men started asking for jobs.

When Ford decided to make the DFV engine available to other teams, it put the business under strain. In no time at all, the original buildings were full, and an extension had to be erected. Before long, too, that was full, and yet more buildings were put up in Northampton. This put Keith and Mike in a real dilemma. They had never planned a massive business expansion, but they were certainly not willing to turn away good business at this time.

It would have been ludicrous for motor racing's most fashionable business to carry on operating as a £100 limited company, but Keith, in any case, had already taken steps to change Cosworth's financial structure. Even while the FVA/DFV design and development programme was going on, in 1966, for the first time since Cosworth Engineering was set up in 1958, the issued capital was increased – from £100 to £1000.

Mike Costin, Ben Rood and Bill Brown's families all received shares in this expansion, and the company's structure was therefore stabilised for the next decade. Keith, however, saw no need to look around for other sources of money – as ever, he was much the largest shareholder in the business. Even so, Cosworth was still a small company. In the financial year ending 30 April 1967, Cosworth Engineering's annual turnover was £380,470, and its after-tax profits were £44,238 – though that profit was nearly 50 per cent higher than it had been a year earlier.

Keith's 'Jewish accountancy' methods had clearly worked well in the early 1960s, for the company's reserves were no less than £112,188. (For comparison, by 1967 Lotus was a much larger company, and was making at least five times as much money as Cosworth – in 1967 its pre-tax profits were £324,000.)

The huge success of the DFV, especially by 1969, when it began to be supplied to teams like McLaren, Tyrrell, Alan Mann, Frank Williams and Brabham, and the continuing success of the FVA and all the pushrod engines, helped to expand the business. The 1967 financial figures were soon left behind. In the year ending 30 April 1968, after-tax profits surged ahead to £71,035, and a year later that figure increased, yet again, to £111,396.

Cosworth was, as Keith has always been proud to repeat, a remarkable and efficient little company – not only successfully in business to make racing engines, but always expanding, and always making a profit. It was also an essentially practical, and down-to-earth business, and the directors knew that new work would always be needed to keep the designers, and the workforce, occupied. By mid-1967, with the DFV not even blooded on the race tracks, another major design project – the BDA – was under way. Mike Hall, who shouldered the entire design job, remembered it like this:

"It all started in May 1967, very much as a

The BD series was designed at Cosworth by Mike Hall, and was the first Cosworth engine to use belt-drive to its camshafts. It had a phenomenal life, and reputation, being built in many different versions for two decades. This was the Ford Escort installation of the mid-1970s, complete with a light-alloy cylinder block.

'handshake job.' Harley Copp, who was Ford's director of engineering, Walter Hayes, and Henry Taylor, who was competitions manager, were in on it. For a time, very few people at Ford knew about it. I only dealt with Henry Taylor. It was all rather informal. I don't think there was a written contract but Ford gave us some money [Keith remembers it as £40,000, and a £1 royalty on every engine subsequently made] and asked us to build about ten complete engines.

"There was no specific performance target, though naturally it had to be better than the Lotus-Ford Twin-Cam. We aimed for 120bhp for the road car's engine, which it achieved quite comfortably. At the time we even found that it would run on 2-star petrol.

"There was never any intention, though, that Cosworth would build the engines in quantity. Ford was going to look after that – we were just the design and development contractors. We started in May 1967. I designed the whole thing, with the help of three or four detailers, and the first engine must have run in June 1968. That, by the way, included developing all the patterns, and as we didn't have a foundry in those days we had to get heads cast by Aeroplane & Motor, in Birmingham."

This was the genesis of the famous BDA engine, the Ford-based 16-valve twin-cam unit, which was to mean as much to Cosworth, and to Ford, in the next three decades, as did the DFV. Lovers of 'Cosworth-speak,' by the way, will already know that BDA means 'Belt-Drive, Series A' – a description which refers to the way the camshafts were to be driven. Mike Hall told me:

"Basically, it was a requirement for a 4-valve, four-cylinder engine, the productionised version of the FVA Formula 2 engine, for use in a road car. It was to replace the Lotus-Ford Twin-Cam, and it had to be suitable for racing, for rallying, and for use in a road car. All the work we did here, initially, was for the engine to go into a Lotus-Cortina. In fact the first road work we carried out was in two Lotus-Cortinas – I ran one of them for around 40,000 miles."

This was the first of several Cosworth engines to be completely designed by Mike Hall, who recalled that, in 1967:

"The BDA was my first total job, here. Keith was totally pre-occupied with the development of the DFV, which had timing gear problems, and the like. He was away from Northampton a lot, at the races, and he liked to be able to concentrate on everything that was happening with the DFV."

Keith Duckworth confirmed this:

Above all, the BD was always a very neatly packaged engine, with the Weber carburettors close to the head casting, and a plastic cover surrounding the belt-drive to the twin-camshafts.

"I made suggestions as to how it should all be done, and what should be changed from the FVA, but Mike Hall did all the actual designs."

It might be romantic to suggest that the BDA was a 'productionised FVA,' but the truth is much more mundane. Except that both engines used Ford 'Kent' family cylinder blocks, twin overhead camshafts, four valves per cylinder and valves opposed at 40 degrees, they were almost completely different in detail.

The Formula 2 FVA, after all, had been designed around the 'pre-crossflow' 1500cc cylinder block of the current Cortina GT, and had extremely oversquare, non-standard, bore/stroke dimensions, whereas the BDA was to be designed around the taller 1600 crossflow (or 'Kent') block, retaining the same bore and stroke as other engines used in Cortinas and Capris.

"The head, basically, was very similar to the FVA," Mike Hall told me. "It had the same valve angles, though the valves were different sizes, the ports were different sizes, and they had to be aligned so that they would easily fit a road car."

When the engine was unveiled in 1969, the real surprise, for the pundits, was to see that cogged belts were used to drive the camshafts – for this was the first such use by a British concern. Glas had been the first company to fit cogged belts to its production engines, but the seal of approval had come from Fiat, in 1966, when a belt was adopted for the new twin-cam engine fitted to the 124 Sport Spider. At Cosworth Mike Hall, rightly, claimed the Cosworth innovation for himself:

"Belt-drive was fairly new in those days. It was my idea to use it. It was fairly obvious that we couldn't use the gear drive from the FVA engine, because apart from the expense it was also very noisy. This engine, don't forget, had to be used in road cars as well as in motorsport."

[Keith emphasised the noise problem by quipping that: "at odd periods you get gear crash occurring and it makes a noise enough to wake the dead ..."]

"There was a choice between a chain, and a belt, but the belt proved to be very light, efficient, and quiet. Obviously we talked a lot to Uniroyal, right from the start, but what worried us all was not the efficiency, but whether the belts were going to survive.

"Completely unbeknown to me, it turned out that the belt I needed from Uniroyal, to fit my design, happened to be exactly the same length as that which Fiat was using in the 124 Sport engine. How convenient – it saved us a lot of development time and money.

This Ford cutaway display engine, shows the intricate and demonstrably well thought-out layout of the BD power unit, with many of the details which would find favour on other engines designed by Cosworth in later years.

One of Ford Motorsport's most intriguing 'might-have-beens' was the mid-engined GT70, which was intended to be a 1970s rally car. One of several proposed engined options was the Cosworth BDA. This car was cancelled after several prototypes had been built.

"Once we had increased the width of the belt, and added an extra idler to give sufficient belt 'wrap,' there was never any belt problem with the BDA. Even in the 1980s, though, I noticed that certain people continue to have trouble with their belt-drives ..."

He was much too much of a gentleman to spell out which engines he was referring to.

Then, as later, Cosworth was never willing to do a rush job, a bodged job, or merely 'make do' by modifying an existing design. To modify the FVA was never even considered, as the list of changes summarised by Mike Hall makes clear – the head casting was new, the exhaust ports curled over, the water flow was utterly different, the cam carrier design was simplified, the valve actuation was changed, the oil flow along the head was different, there were carburettors instead of fuel-injection ...

It was, in effect, a new engine using race-proven principles. Not only that, but it would soon become a very effective competition engine. Keith and Mike both thought that the bore/stroke ratio was unfavourable, and would hinder its potential, but they were amazed to discover that it would rev very fast indeed.

When what Keith describes as an 'FVA/BDA' was built (FVA bottom end, and much over-square layout, mated to a fuel-injected BDA top end), it produced 238bhp in its first power test, at least as much as any 1.6-litre FVA had ever produced. Which was better? The ever-diplomatic Mike Hall put it this way:

"I think there was very little between them. If anything the BDA could have been slightly better, and I think that was only due to the efficiency of the cambelt system – a belt instead of a lot of gears all churning around."

Like several other engines, or derivatives of its own engines, that Cosworth was to design in the 1970s and 1980s, there was never any question of the BDA being built in quantity at Northampton. The factory, quite simply, was not intended for series-production use and could not cope.

At first it looked as if Ford hadn't decided how to use the new engine. Cosworth's original commission had been for an engine to replace the Lotus-Ford unit, which at the time was only used in the Lotus-Cortina. Nothing came of that. Then, in time for the launch of the Capri coupé in January 1969, Ford built a handful of BDA-engined Capris. One hundred such cars, it was suggested, might eventually be built. Cosworth built 32 engines but nothing came of it.

It was not until Ford's new competition manager, Stuart Turner, met Keith Duckworth over dinner at the author's home in the Midlands, that the definitive solution was hatched – the BDA would find a home in the Escort in 1970. You could say that Keith and Stuart took to each other in a big way, that evening, for they

Stuart Turner became Ford-UK's competitions manager in 1969, and soon persuaded his bosses that they should fit Cosworth's new BDA into the Escort bodyshell. The result was the Escort RS1600, and the rest, as they say, is history ...

talked for hours about every aspect of motorsport. As Stuart later commented:

"I've always been lucky to work with great characters, because otherwise business can be too grey and dull. Keith was a great character, no doubt about that. The very first time I ever saw him in a Ford environment, he was arriving at Dunton [the Ford design centre in Essex] in his helicopter, and there were firemen everywhere in their gleaming brass helmets, with a beaming Duckworth grinning at the hilarity of it all – it was almost like a Royal visit, and he loved that ...

"Once I got to know him well, I tried to get an agreement with him – every time the DFV engine won a race we would call it a Ford, but every time it failed we would call it a Cosworth! I really can't see why he wouldn't have that. He had to be a great character, the whole Cosworth thing wouldn't have worked otherwise. If you're going to motivate a roomful of engineers to create something in your image, you've got to be self-confident.

"Keith was always confident in his own abilities, but I never found him arrogant, though I gather other people did. He was humorous, entertaining – but he could also be boring: can't we all? The problem, though, was that he used to get bees in his bonnet. If I wanted information from Cosworth, and I was in a hurry, I tended to call Dick Scammell for a mere 20 minute chat, because I didn't have time for a short 'talk' with Keith."

As far as Cosworth was concerned, however, the BDA then took on a life of its own. In the initial stages Mike Hall wrote out all the specifications, consulted with Ford on the question of making all the pieces, but was not originally involved in building engines or supplying parts:

"In those days we were still very small. We couldn't have made the parts anyway. We were up to our ears trying to make DFV parts at the time. I know it doesn't sound very romantic, but here was a job, we did it well, then we handed it over to Ford, and thought: 'Right, that's that, let somebody else have the job of producing the engines.' Harpers of Stevenage – they had once built Vincent-HRD motorcycles – were the first to assemble BDA engines for RS 1600s, but several other companies later got involved.

"But yes, of course, it was, and it still is, an engine to be proud of. I certainly didn't lay it out to have an incredibly long life, or for an incredible number of derivatives to be made. Somehow, it just snowballed into the 'Meccano set' that we now have. We still make a lot of versions, one way or another. By the mid-1970s, indeed, BD work probably accounted for about half of our turnover!"

Ford, in fact, was very relaxed about the modification of the BDA engine, not only by Cosworth, but also by several other companies. Some of the most successful derivatives of the original BDA – the aluminium cylinder block, and the turbocharged versions, for instance – had little or no connection with Cosworth. Even at the end of the 1980s, 20 years after the BD series was designed, Cosworth was still building kits in their hundreds, and parts in their thousands. More than any other race engine supplier, Cosworth diligently serviced its old engines, as Jack Field told me in 1989:

"People have got to the stage where they expect Cosworth to be able to supply the bits they need, even if they're not exactly sure what type of engine they've got. We have our pride – not only do we like to supply parts (it's very profitable, you know), but we always like to be able to supply the correct bits, too.

"I could still supply pistons, gasket sets and valves for MAEs and single-cam SCAs; even a few bits for Lotus-

By the late 1970s, the Escort RS1800, renamed Escort RS, was one of the world's most successful rally cars. This is 'works' driver Björn Waldegård on his way to second place in the 1978 RAC rally.

Ford twin-cams. But we're still building complete new BDs, or should I say complete kits of parts to build BDs: if you look across the road, in Ben's machine shops, you'll see new cylinder head castings being machined.

"At the moment [1989] our turnover on BDs is still going up. We've done quite a lot for Caterham, for the Super Seven, then we supply BDPs to the States, to run on methanol. There are probably 1250 complete BDPs out there in the States, running and winning races."

Once the BDA engine was up and running in the early 1970s, Cosworth, and several other concerns, started the never-ending business of race and rally-tuning it. One way to gain power, of course, was to enlarge the engine, which Cosworth speedily began to do.

In rallying, if it had not been for Stuart Turner's devious and inventive mind, there might have been no incentive to make the engine bigger, as the original BDA engine was a 1.6-litre unit, right up against the class capacity limit. Stuart knew that Twin-Cam success had always been frustrated by this class limit, and he was determined that it should not happen again. Keith Duckworth now takes up the story:

"By a strange and very lucky coincidence we found that top tolerance engines with the longest strokes and the biggest bores slipped over the class limit to 1601cc. Well, of course, it would have been quite unfair to allow the engine to be homologated in a smaller class, so we had it approved at 1601cc instead!"

The tolerances in question were minimal, and in fact the BDA used the same engine bottom end as the 1598cc Cortina GT/Capri GT pushrod unit, but no-one seemed to mind. Publicity material, and the homologation forms, quoted a marginally longer stroke, and the job was done. For the next few years, however, there was a struggle to gain more capacity, as there was a definite limit to the enlargement of cylinder bores which could be carried out without ruining the integrity of Ford's cast iron block. Cosworth, on the other hand, was adamant that an increased stroke dimension was not the way to go.

Ford's engine specialist at Boreham, Peter Ashcroft, nagged away at the foundry to make changes to the cores, eventually getting his way, which explains why a special casting known as the 'Ashcroft block' eventually came along. But there was more to come, from an outside source. Brian Hart, once one of the stalwarts who had helped to build the Northampton factory test cells, had eventually pulled out of racing, and set up his own engine-building concern in Essex:

"I stopped racing for Team Lotus when I realised how slow I was, compared with Jim Clark, then I moved down to Harlow, set up Brian Hart Ltd, and started by servicing the highly-successful FVA Formula 2 engine.

"Then we started working on BDAs – there were plenty of parts available from Cosworth, it was really the kit engine of the 1970s – but I soon saw that it needed to be larger, and that the cast iron block was the limiting factor.

"We could recognise a need for a new 2-litre sports car and Formula 2 engine, and because of this I started looking at the BDA engine. I may have been overconfident at the time, but it worked – as I was drawing-board trained, and I had already done quite a lot of design work at Cosworth, I decided that I knew enough to design a light-alloy version of the cylinder block, with siamesed bores and other changes. I also did away with liners – we ran the pistons direct in the bores, which were suitably plated. That gave me 2-litres, right away, and it was a lot lighter too."

It was a complete 'private-enterprise' project, first raced privately in 1971, but no sooner had the first block been cast by Sterling Metals, and machined at Harlow, than fate intervened. Early in 1972, when Peter Ashcroft was on one of his regular visits from Boreham (on this occasion, actually to talk about engines for the 'works' Escorts entered for the East African Safari), he actually fell over the evidence, in the workshop. Brian remembers that Peter actually tripped over the casting, and exclaimed: "What the devil's that?"

Peter looked at the block, and was immediately impressed. "You can't believe how quickly I arranged for an engine to be slotted into an Escort. You should have seen Stuart's face when I showed it off, and as for Walter Hayes …"

Within months that block had been adopted by Ford, put into production for late-model RS 1600s (and, to follow up, in the RS 1800s), and eventually became a very major alternative to the cast iron block used in many of Cosworth's own kits. Keith, being Keith, did not rush in to give this new block his immediate acceptance, for he had a serious objection to siamesed cylinder bores, and their effect on the integrity of cylinder blocks – in fact it is a feature he would never willingly design into a new engine. Brian thought that it took years for Keith to come to terms with the merits of this block, but knows that eventually he was won round. Mike Hall confirmed that Keith originally didn't approve of the aluminium block:

"I think it's fair to say that the whole BD engine

The BD was an amazingly versatile power unit, which was still winning at world level more than ten years after it had been unveiled. This was the charismatic young Finn, Ari Vatanen, who drove Ford Escort RS types to win the 1981 World Rally Championship.

The Caterham Super Seven was launched in the 1970s, and would sell strongly for the next 50 years. In 1983 the BDR derivative of the versatile BDA engine proved to be a comfortable fit for the latest Caterham chassis.

project suffered a bit from Keith's NIH ('Not Invented Here') attitude at this time. It was invented at Cosworth, but really not by Keith. He was never very interested in it. Keith's standards were very demanding. He admits that sometimes he finds it difficult to give credit to anyone for doing a good job. But then I did the next job, and the next job, and I'm still here, so I guess he respects what I do."

GA – Cosworth's first V6 project

In the early 1970s Walter Hayes decided to move the Ford-of-West-Germany motorsport operation into motor racing, with the department successfully developing the Capri RS 2600 as a Group 2 touring car. But it wasn't easy, as Walter Hayes recalls:

"I tried to find a German Ralph Broad, or an Alan Mann, but there wasn't that sort of cottage industry in West Germany. I had to come back to the UK for that."

The original Capris used German V6 engines, which were race-tuned and developed by Harry Weslake's

When Ford needed a more powerful Capri for Touring Car racing, it introduced the RS3100, while Cosworth produced the four-cam GA version of the engine. Jackie Stewart, recently retired from F1 competition, posed with the RS3100.

concern in Sussex, but by 1972 it was clear that the engine was running out of stretch, and potential; it was stuck at about 320bhp. A bigger and more powerful engine was needed. Fortunately, a change of regulations allowed manufacturers to use alternative cylinder heads in touring car racing, but at least 100 sets of parts had to be built to allow Group 2 homologation to go ahead.

"I first met Keith when we were running BDA-engined Escorts in European Championship races," Mike Kranefuss recalled. "My English wasn't good enough, then, to realise the stories he was telling – but people around me would suddenly start grinning and laughing, or even looking upset – I improved, later.

"By this time he had produced the DFV, which was winning everything, and everyone I knew was in awe of him. So, when I first visited him in Northampton, I was expecting him to be in a welcoming and wonderful office – but I found that it was crummy and small instead.

"He never struck me as a man who was completely sure of anything. He seemed to have an unbelievable talent for swallowing all the influences, all the elements which would eventually let him decide what he thought the best engine solution was, and we could never really get a straight answer out of him, certainly not immediately.

"If I asked him a question – if anyone asked him a question – there wasn't one answer. There were several different answers."

Even so, Kranefuss was impressed. In 1972, Ford decided to abandon the Ford-Cologne V6, and to use the entirely different Ford-UK 'Essex' V6 engine instead. Cosworth was therefore commissioned to 'do a BDA,' to design a four cam engine conversion for the 'Essex' engine, with a target of more than 400bhp! This was the Cosworth GA project, an engine designed completely by Mike Hall.

It is now well-known that Ford and Cosworth had a great deal of trouble with this project. There were two interlinked problems – one was that Ford wanted to push the capacity of the racing engine out from 3.0-litres to 3.4-litres, the other was that the production cylinder blocks had castings of very variable quality and construction. The standard engine, of 2994cc, used a cylinder bore of 93.66mm, but Ford wanted that to be increased to 100mm for the GA racing application. Although theoretically there was a great deal of cast iron 'meat' in the metal surrounding the bores, this was a near-impossible task, as Mike Kranefuss confirmed:

"Out of 200 blocks we took from the foundry, we ended up with only one or two which survived the machining process. There were moments when Keith was absolutely disgusted with the whole business. He couldn't relate to this sort of awful quality, the unions didn't like us going into the factory to try to sort it out, and Keith simply couldn't stand stupid people."

Keith repeatedly made the valid point that, in any case, production engine castings are rarely strong enough to cope with the stresses of racing engine horsepower. After all, he said, if a casting could put up with two or even three times the power, without breaking up, then it must have been badly overdesigned in the first place.

[When I then suggested that BMW must have been proud of its four-cylinder block, which was used as the basis of the turbocharged F1 engine, Keith flatly refused to believe that the block used was standard, or even nearly standard.]

Mike Hall told me that Cosworth had to "fiddle around," within the regulations, to make the block survive, that four-bolt bearing caps had to be used, but that blocks still failed. Nevertheless, Mike did a great design job:

"This was my favourite engine; I was proud of what I did. I designed a cylinder head which could be used on both banks – there was just one cam carrier casting, and one cam cover casting too. The cams were belt-driven, in fact the engine looked to be festooned with belts."

Much of the 'bottom end' detailing, crank balancing, and related work, was done for Mike by Graham Dale-Jones. Except that the machined faces were not parallel with the cylinder head face, the general layout of the GA's top end was like that of the famous BD, for it had four valves per cylinder, a central sparking plug position, and a valve-opposed-angle of 40 degrees. The camshaft profile used was the same as that also employed on the Chevrolet EA, and the racing BDG engine.

In fact there was provision for up to three plugs/cylinder in the design, but tests showed that this arrangement provided no more power and torque than the classic single plug layout, so was speedily abandoned.

The engine began test bed running in the winter of 1973/74, and the Capri RS 3100 for which it was intended was unveiled in November 1973, but as this was the period in which the Energy Crisis was gripping the world's motor industry, it was a project which ran into trouble from the beginning. By the time it was made public in the spring of 1974, Ford's own motorsport plans for its use were on the wane. Even so, Cosworth fulfilled its own side of the bargain. Rated at 420bhp at first, it was eventually improved to 455bhp, and achieved reliability and success.

Keith insists that the necessary quantity could never have been made if Alf Vickers had not recently agreed to become a production consultant at this time, and had sorted out machines, planning, and the whole process.

Ben Rood's machine shops managed to produce the 100 sets of parts which Ford needed for homologation purposes, with about 30 of them being built up as complete racing engines for Ford-Germany, supplying the balance (as boxed kits) to the Boreham motorsport centre. Ford then quoted £4000 for a kit of parts, and a further £750 to build up an engine.

To machine the 200 GA cylinder heads which were needed, Ben Rood devised the simple 'machining between centres' method, which is still used to make Cosworth engines in modern times, even the volume production castings, and Mike Hall remembered it as the first complete engine that Cosworth actually built in numbers.

In 1974 and 1975 the 'works' Capri RS 3100s won major races at the Nürburgring, Zandvoort, Hockenheim, and Jarama, beating the bewinged BMW 3.0 CSLs in every case, but the project was then terminated.

The engines, however, found a new home in F5000 single seaters, where drivers like Alan Jones found the 3.4-litre quad-cam units to be more than a match for the 5.0-litre pushrod Chevrolets favoured by other teams. Even so, many of the Cosworth-built kits hung around at Boreham for some time.

In later years the engine saw something of a renaissance for use in non-homologated cars, particularly as Swindon Racing Engines (which had the original service/rebuilding contract) began manufacturing light-alloy versions of the cylinder blocks, which pared a great deal of weight from what was always a bulky engine.

Cosworth in the early 1970s

This was the period when Cosworth was eased into a massive expansion of its machine facilities, when a new building (later dubbed 'Factory 3') took shape

The RS200 of 1985/1986 was a ferocious Group B beast, complete with rear/mid-mounted BDT engine, and four-wheel-drive. This particular car was retained by its original designer, John Wheeler, and later used in Historic events all over Europe.

TURBOCHARGED BDS

TWO decades after it was born, as a 120bhp road-car engine, the BDA had evolved into a fire-breathing, 650bhp, rallycross engine of awesome character and performance. Yet Cosworth had little or nothing to do with the turbocharging of one of its most famous designs. The turbo story really began in West Germany, with Zakspeed, where turbocharged versions of the iron-block BDA were fitted to racing Escorts in the mid-1970s. By 1978, a 1.4-litre development of this engine was producing 380bhp, and by the end of 1979 that figure had risen to 460bhp, developed at 9000rpm.

Zakspeed's own design included a KKK turbocharger, Garrett intercooler and blow-off valves, and Kugelfischer fuel-injection, but retained many Cosworth-developed components too – it was a very effective hybrid. Before long, Zakspeed had also developed a 1.7-litre version, this pushing out 600bhp, on 1.5 bar boost. These engines never officially carried a Cosworth type name or number.

The next turbocharging impetus came from Boreham, where Ford's rally team began the design and development of the Group B Escort RS1700T in 1980. Much of the concept work was carried out 'in house' to Peter Ashcroft's direction, by John Griffiths and ex-Cosworth design engineer Graham Dale Jones, on a 1.78-litre alloy-block version intended to produce 200bhp in 'homologation special' road-car trim, and about 350bhp in its initial 'works' rally trim. To meet the regulations, 200 of these engines were to be made.

Cosworth was then contracted to supply all the major components (Brian Hart was delighted to confirm that Cosworth produced its own version of the light-alloy block which he had 'invented' in 1971/72, using modified versions of the 'Hart' pattern equipment), and at one time hoped to place assembly of the engines into Swindon Racing Engines. In the end, however, Ford chose JQF Engineering of Towcester to assemble the engines instead. John Dickens, of Cosworth, notes that there was considerable confusion over an engine title:

"We had to designate the project in some way: originally we chose BDP, since 'P' was the next available letter, but since BDT had already been established at Boreham by that stage, we quietly dropped BDP and later re-used that for our Midget-racing specification."

As every Ford enthusiast now knows, the RS1700T project was cancelled after the engines had been assembled, the engines then remaining in store for more than a year, before the four-wheel-drive mid-engined RS200 project was finalised to succeed the RS1700T. In time for original assembly of 200 cars at Shenstone, in the winter of 1985/86, the existing engines were all stripped out, with the blocks going to Mahle for re-boring to a 1803cc dimension. Although many parts had to be renewed, many could also be retained, and RS200 project manager Mike Moreton estimated that more than £5000 was saved on every engine, by comparison with starting afresh.

This engine produced 250bhp in 'road car' form, 300bhp or 350bhp in Ford 'conversion kit' form, and 420bhp (later 450bhp and more) as used on fully-tuned 'works' rally and 'rallycross' cars.

Lastly, there was the mighty BDT-E engine, where 'E' stood for 'Evolution.' This was a much-modified BDT, produced entirely for Ford, by Brian Hart Ltd. As Brian later recalled:

"Stuart Turner of Ford approached us, with what promised to be a five-year programme. His 200-off RS200s were built with 1.8-litre engines, but he was looking for a lot more power in his 'Evolution' cars. Before FISA's axe fell on Group B, we had work planned, on contract, for several years, and there's no doubt that the killing off of Group B was a major blow to us. We had carried out a complete internal redesign of the cylinder block, and we had pushed out the capacity to 2.1-litres (that was equivalent to 3.0-litres with FISA's turbocharger "factor" applied). Ford asked for 500bhp, and after the FISA axe

The first time the BDT engine, intended for use in the Ford RS200 Group B car, was tested, it was observed (left to right) by Boreham engineer Graham Dale-Jones, Keith Duckworth, Peter Ashcroft and Dick Scammell. The manifolding would be tidied up remarkably when the in-car installation was settled.

The ultimate development of the BD design was the turbocharged BDT (and the even more specialised BDT-E), fitted to the 200 four-wheel-drive RS200 Group B cars built in 1985-1986.

fell the very first engine we ran up to power produced 530bhp.'

In the end, Brian Hart's business produced 25 complete engines, another 25 sets of parts, and carried on making replacement items to service and rebuild the engines into the 1990s. Rallycross cars were soon using more than 600bhp, and the very special 2.3-litre units produced by the Norwegian, Martin Schanche, produced more than 650bhp.

across the road from the original site, and when several very bright young men joined the firm to make sense of the new machinery. Graham Dale-Jones, who later moved to Ford at Boreham, and eventually became Terry Hoyle's partner in the well-known engine building business in Essex, was one of them:

"I did a mechanical engineering course at Portsmouth Polytechnic, and as I had always been interested in motor racing – I'd always wanted to be a designer – I wrote to Cosworth, saying that I'd like to be the tea boy!

"I joined in 1970, as an engineer – but no particular type of engineer, that wasn't specified. Neil Lefley, Paul Morgan, John Hancock and I all arrived together. Ben Rood interviewed me, I remember.

"There wasn't any formal training. The training, such as it was, consisted of: 'Here, start making these.' I was given various drill jigs and told to get on with it.

"After making valve guides, drilling bearing caps, and little things like that, I ended up running a CNC (Computer Numerically Controlled) machine tool. At that time we were still on the south side of the road – the new extension hadn't been built – and we used to meet all the 'stars,' all the bosses, at tea-break time. All the time, I had an ambition to get in to the drawing office, so after 18 months in the machine shop I was allowed upstairs to start drawing jigs and fixtures. But it was another year before I started designing anything."

A young man called Geoff Goddard, who later went on to become Chief Designer (Racing Engines) had a similar informal introduction to Cosworth:

"I started out by doing an engineering sandwich course at Lanchester College, Coventry. In my first job, I worked for Rolls-Royce in Derby as an ex-University apprentice, on aero engines of all sorts. Towards the end of my time at Derby I wrote a dissertation on why I thought the RB211's carbon fibre blades wouldn't work, gave it to various directors, and got criticised by them for writing such a thing!"

[In 1971, one of the reasons for Rolls-Royce's financial collapse was that the RB211 was in all kinds of development problems, connected with the turbine blades …]

"The beauty of Rolls-Royce as a training company was that afterwards you could go anywhere, I did a stint in marine and industrial turbines at Ansty, near Coventry, I did a stint in rockets, I even did some work at Shrewsbury, which was not only building diesel engines, but was making combustion cans for gas turbines. I never had a single thing to do with Rolls-Royce cars, though.

"When Rolls-Royce went bankrupt, I was at the end of my apprenticeship, and I was soon told that all of my year's intake was redundant. The company set up a wondrous system to help us find jobs – and I remember being sent for interview to a company in Glasgow which was making sausage skins! Somehow I didn't think that fitted the bill at all.

"I thought that was a huge joke, so I did my own searching. I decided on two companies – one was McLaren and one was Cosworth. Then I looked at the different house prices, decided I didn't want to work for McLaren after all, and concentrated on Cosworth.

"One day I came to Northampton, marched up to the sales counter, and asked for a job. That threw everybody, but eventually Keith gave me a brief interview. Like most of Keith's brief interviews, this went on for hours. In the end he took me on as a Project Engineer, and I joined in February 1971. At the time Cosworth had just bought its first CNC machine tool, and the conversation with Keith went something like this:

'Can you programme an NC machine?'
'Yes, I'm sure I can.'
'Have you ever programmed one?'
'No.'
'I admire your confidence – go and get on with it.'

"So I had to do it, and make a good job of it. Graham, Neil, Paul Morgan, John Hancock, and now me, we all had similar responsibilities. If Keith wanted a particular rig running, he would pick out one of us, or if he wanted a new programme writing, one of us would have to do it. The point about Cosworth, I soon learned, was that there were so many incredibly talented people around – Keith, Mike and Ben all had overlapping talents. It was different at Rolls-Royce where only one person in a department tended to be technically competent.

"Keith soon got me onto camshaft design, which I've been interested in ever since. He soon proved to me what an amazing applied mathematician he is. He'd go away with a particular problem to solve, and apply his withering concentration to it. It might take him weeks to solve the problem, but he would have examined all the ideas, all the possibilities, before settling on the right one; Keith never stops until he is 99 per cent sure he has the solution. I learned a lot from Keith that way, in the 1970s. Nobody at Cosworth ever sat down to teach us anything. Everything was

Although it looked like a normal BDT, Brian Hart's BDT-E (which he designed, with Cosworth's approval though they were not involved) was 2.1-litres instead of 1.8-litres, had a longer cylinder block and larger cylinder bores, and was rated even in 'basic' form at 500bhp, with up to 650bhp available in fully-tuned form.

learned by: 'I see this has failed. I wonder what failed first, and how did it happen?' Then one tended to get a lecture around the problem.

"Nowadays, in the late 1980s, we tend to take in graduates and move them around a lot, but they still have to learn by example. Eventually everyone comes back and tells us which department he would like to settle in, and usually he will be quite brilliant there ...

"One of my first major jobs was to help set up the big machine shop on the north side of the road. But obviously I'd already been drawing things at Rolls-Royce – bits of RB211s and things – and eventually I went full-time in the drawing office in 1976/77."

Both Geoff and Graham recall that the drawing office was still very small in the early and mid 1970s. Graham Dale-Jones: "Keith used to do all his own drawing, designing, and thinking, at home. Mike Hall was chief designer, and he had his own office. There were only eight drawing boards upstairs in the main office – one was a design board, one was for copying, three were for detailing, and three for production engineering. I gradually wheedled my way in there and started drawing engine bits. I suppose because I was slightly mathematical, I ended up working on balancing, crankshaft design, crankshaft flexing, that sort of thing."

Geoff Goddard: "None of us specialised at first. All projects were run by Keith, or by Mike Hall. Keith, though, was a great arguer. He would usually start by arguing against a particular proposal at great length, because he hadn't thought of it first. You had to be sure of your ground, for he would never give in.

"On one occasion, we had been arguing something out from lunchtime on, I knew that my solution would work, and this led to quite heated debate. When that happens, with Keith, the volume tends to go up! It was well into the evening when he said 'Go home,' and more or less threw me out of the office, he wouldn't discuss the subject any further. Then, when I got in the following morning, my desk had been swept clear of all its paper, and Keith had written a short note, agreeing to my views, and finishing: 'Yesterday I talked rubbish – DKD'!

"He can be gracious sometimes, and if ever he had a real row with someone, within 20 minutes the slate would be clean, that would be forgotten, and we could get on with it. He always worked on logic, and reasoning, never on emotion."

Both agreed that Cosworth was, by definition, Keith Duckworth – and that it remained so until the 1980s.

Unless he was totally uninterested in a project that was taken on, Keith would produce the concepts, usually on his own drawing board at home, a few miles from the factory. There would be a brooding silence for some weeks then, after a time, he would reappear (as Geoff Goddard quips: "like Moses bringing the tablets down from the mountain"), discuss the whole thing at length with the two Mikes – Costin and Hall – and usually leave Mike Hall to get the whole thing designed in considerable detail. More discussions, arguments, and redesign would then take place, and it was only then that the detail designers would be brought in.

Ben Rood, in the meantime, was adding to his formidable reputation as the man whose machine shops could do anything, given time. Not only did he design the jigs and tools to do the machining work, but it wasn't long before he was designing the machines (or, rather, completely rebuilding old machines) as well. Like Keith, he "spends a lot of time sitting down, and thinking."

"One day I was driving down the M1 to London – I get a lot of ideas when I'm just sitting there, in the car – when a picture of how to produce cam masters suddenly blossomed in my mind. I came home, we made that machine, and we've been using it ever since. I don't often need a CAD/CAM video screen when I'm designing tooling, because I've already got one, in my head."

By the mid-1970s, indeed, Cosworth's machining capability was so immense that the racing car industry, and later the production car industry, was already offering a lot of business to Cosworth. There was little, it seemed, that couldn't be tackled ("We've even tackled crankshafts for Wankel engines. But not the rotors, though that would be interesting – I'd like to have a go at rotor machining."), and, as Ben Rood told me when I was first preparing this book: "If you want someone to do a job right, to do it first time, and to do it without tears, Cosworth is probably the only company who can deliver.

"Look at one of our F1 crankshafts, for example. We're the only people who can grind with the degree of finish, and control of radii, that's really needed. Yet some of our rivals [Judd and Ilmor weren't actually mentioned, but the inference was there] seem to manage. I don't think that's fair, somehow."

Life at Cosworth, however, has not always been logical, as the list of odd-ball projects, cancelled designs, and whimsical diversions proves. That's a subject, now, which deserves a chapter all of its own.

6: DIVERSIONS – CARS, MOTORCYCLE ENGINES, AND AUTOMATIC TRANSMISSIONS

"The best way to avoid going broke is to spot that you are well on the way to this state, then call a halt ..."

"Nobody can recognise a phoney at a greater distance than Duckworth! He has this early bullshit detector ..."

In October 1967, someone 'leaked' a sensational rumour to the press — that Ford was considering designing a Grand Prix car. Or, rather, that Cosworth was designing it for Ford. Or rather, that — well — let's just say that it made a good story at the time, even if it wasn't all true.

Never let the facts get in the way of a good story! At that time, for sure, the 'car' only existed in Keith Duckworth's fertile 'why-don't-we-do ...' mind, and in any case it wasn't to be Ford-badged at all. For once, however, here was a Cosworth rumour which did, eventually, come true.

It was the first of several diversions that Keith Duckworth allowed himself in the years when the DFV and BDA engines were underpinning the company's finances.

There are some projects which Keith and Mike would never talk about, even today, but the list of those admitted to makes fascinating reading. There might, for instance, have been a Cosworth Grand Prix car, an automatic transmission for Formula One use, a V6 F2 engine, a V8 F2 engine, fuel-flow limiting valves for the F1 scene, desmodromic valve gear for F1 engines, a gas-turbine engine for light-aircraft use, and, of course, there was the little-known Cosworth motorcycle engine, which would surely have been a world-beater if its sponsor had not gone spectacularly broke in the mid-1970s.

With the DFV safely launched, and with BDA design forging ahead under Mike Hall's direction, Keith Duckworth could afford to indulge himself a little. Even though the DFV still had many development problems to be sorted out, Keith allowed himself a diversion – and this diversion turned out to be the design of a complete four-wheel-drive car.

Even so, the motoring press know-alls only got hold of half a story when the first rumours began to spread. *Motor* was guarded about the rumours, while *Autosport* merely commented that hearsay was growing all the time. *Autocar*'s sports editor, Innes Ireland, suggested that the new car would be a Ford, and would not appear until Ford's contract with Lotus expired at the end of 1969, but Cosworth's name was not even mentioned.

Two pages later on, in the same issue, Eoin Young's 'Straight from the Grid' column asserted that: "The newspaper leak that Cosworth was building a four-wheel-drive Formula 1 car raised a storm in several quarters: although talks on the project have taken place, no firm decisions have yet been made, and plans were certainly not ready for public airing. People wondered what Ford [which really meant 'Walter Hayes'] was thinking about, getting Mike Costin and Keith Duckworth to design the complete car. An engine, certainly, but the transmission and chassis as well?"

Eoin Young's column, at least, attributed the project to Cosworth, which was correct, but both were wrong in one major respect – that Ford was not at all involved. The truth was at once less exciting, and more exciting, than this.

"Mike and I were both quite keen on cars," Keith told me, "and I was quite keen on structures. I also think that one of the advantages I had, as an engine designer, was that I soon appreciated that the important thing in racing is that it is really all about the proper utilisation of rubber. The proper use of the tyre was 'Number One' priority. How you applied the tyre to the ground, how you trimmed the aerodynamics, and how you built the chassis was next; the engine and the driver came along behind that.

"Well, with the DFV it was certain that we had produced more power than the chassis of the day could cope with. It looked to me as if four-wheel-drive must soon be coming in, and that would be a complete breakthrough.

"Once we had established that we were going to be completely fair with everyone when it came to engine supplies, we felt we could even get away with running a complete Cosworth car, or at least experimenting with it. Not only that – by going to 4WD it looked as if we might be able to catch up with the technology, whereas to mess about with a two-wheel-drive car starting from scratch might take too long. I thought we could at least start equal in a 4WD situation.

"I felt that I had a fair idea as to the requirements for a 4WD car. So in 1967 we decided, I suppose just for fun, really, that we would have a go at building a car. We needed a designer, and I heard that Robin Herd wasn't very happy with McLaren at that time."

Robin Herd, indeed, was not completely happy with McLaren ("I thought I was really living off the back of other peoples' experience"), but an approach from Keith

Duckworth, muttered as an aside in the paddock of the Italian GP of 1967, at Monza, was a real surprise. Unlike many people who went to work at Cosworth, Robin did not complete any type of apprenticeship, but went smoothly from Monmouth School to Oxford University (where he gained a brilliant first in engineering), and then moved straight on to work in the National Gas Turbine Establishment at Farnborough, where he eventually worked on supersonic nozzle studies for the Concorde airliner:

"I went there as a scientist and an applied mathematical engineer in 1961, but my first love was motorsport, and I soon persuaded them that I ought to spend some time 'training' at Lotus! I was there for two months, sweeping the floors, making the tea, and learning. Then, through Alan Rees and Howden Ganley, I got to move to McLaren, where I became Bruce's chief designer, even though I hadn't then designed anything in my life."

At McLaren, Robin went on to design several successful McLaren racing cars, including the M5 and M7 single seaters, and the M6 and M8 sports racing cars. He also delights in claiming that he and Bruce were the first to try wings on single-seater F1 racing cars, but was ashamed to admit that neither had the courage to follow up successful tests by fitting them to race cars.

"On its first time out at Monza, in September 1967, the BRM-engined M5 was on the front row of the grid, which was very pleasing. It was there that I talked to Keith, who asked me to go along and talk to him about designing a car. Two weeks later I called him, we met one evening in a pub, and discussed everything. He assured me that he didn't have a master plan, that he certainly wasn't going to build three cars and a team, but that he was just going to build one car to start with.

"He made me an offer I couldn't really refuse. I'd only been earning £35 a week at McLaren, but he offered me a lot more – £2750 a year and a car, or permutations around that. Not only that, but he wanted me to join Cosworth as 'Chief Chassis Designer.' Keith proposed to fit me in, with a drawing board, in his office.

"I was very flattered. This was a real education, a real chance to learn, to sit at the feet of Keith and Mike.

Robin Herd lent me his original letter of appointment to Cosworth, which shows just how serious Keith Duckworth was in designing his 'own-brand' F1 car.

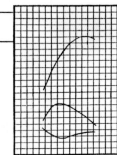

COSWORTH ENGINEERING LTD.

ST. JAMES MILL ROAD, NORTHAMPTON

Telephone: NORTHAMPTON 51802 & 51803
Telegrams: COSWORTH, NORTHAMPTON

Directors: D. K. Duckworth, B.Sc., A.C.G.I., M. C. Costin, W. Brown, B. W. T. Rood

RACING ENGINE DESIGN, DEVELOPMENT & MANUFACTURE

OUR REF. DKD/VL   YOUR REF.

27th October 1967

Robin Herd Esq.,
18 Long Close,
Farnham Common,
Bucks.

Dear Robin,

Further to our meeting last Thursday when we discussed the possibilities of your joining this firm to design, for a start, a four wheel drive Formula I car, I now enclose our formal offer.

I would definitely like you to join us, as I feel we think fairly similarly about design and engineering, and should be able to make a good team.

We would offer you the newly-created post of Chief Chassis Designer - or some title that appeals to you! You would be directly responsible to the directors only.

I confirm that:

a) The beginning of January would be acceptable for the start of full-time work.

b) That some preliminary discussion and part-time design should be done during December

c) That during the intensive design stage, you can work at home, with periodical meetings to report ideas, discuss schemes etc.

We are hoping that should you join us, we would have a long association. We feel that our good position is largely due to good design and engineering and that by maintaining good engineering standards and equipment, we should survive even if motor racing should fall into difficulties.

I hope I have managed to make our intentions clear, but should you have any queries I will be pleased to discuss them at any time.

Yours sincerely,

D.K. Duckworth
Managing Director

Although Robin Herd was only at Cosworth, designing and developing the new four-wheel-drive Cosworth F1 car, until 1969, he then moved on to found March Engineering (he was the 'H' of the acronym which made up the brand name ...), which became an enthusiastic user of DFV power units.

"Now Robin, at Cosworth we do it this way ..." – Keith Duckworth and 4x4 F1 car designer Robin Herd in jocular mood at Cosworth in 1968.

Keith, incidentally, must have been shocked when he learned the depth of my ignorance, for I was only 28 at the time. I wasn't just confined to designing the car, either. There was always a chance to get involved in policy discussions, financial planning, and the other projects which were going on. It was a real education, and a joy to be there.

"At the time, I think Keith had a slightly romantic idea of what he wanted to do. Compared with his expertise, I think he felt that most chassis designers were second class. He also had an ongoing love-hate relationship with Colin Chapman of Lotus. But he obviously thought the world of Jim Clark, I'm sure that the original romantic concept was that here would be a Cosworth car, with a Cosworth engine, and a Cosworth transmission, for Jim Clark to drive."

Keith and Mike realised that it was not going to be easy to be competitive right away and Keith was determined not to let his car project bankrupt the Cosworth business. Robin recalls that the whole project eventually cost about £30,000, which was a great deal of money for one car in the late 1960s.

The concept was settled between Keith, Mike and Robin Herd, with speedy agreement to use the same tyres and suspension geometry at front and rear, and 50%/50% weight distribution front-to-rear. Keith, Mike and Robin would meet at least every week to discuss progress, but Robin worked up the concept, including the layout of the four-wheel-drive transmission, and drew most of the car. Keith designed the centre gearbox, the torque splitting differential, and the road wheel design, which he later claimed was stolen by Robin Herd for use in the original March F1 cars – Robin, by the way, cheerfully agreed with him!

Although Robin had used aerospace-type Mallite honeycomb material in some of his McLaren designs, the new Cosworth car was a conventional, but nicely detailed, aluminium monocoque. There was also a fairly serious stab at getting the aerodynamics right – and this, please note, was immediately before wings began to sprout atop other F1 cars.

Several other people were involved – Mike Hall drew the gearbox and the casings for the centre box, while Alistair Lyle (who went on to design a 5-valve cylinder head for Tickford) was also involved. Cosworth built and machined as much as possible, but some Hewland gears were used in the main casing. There were endless discussions about the torque split, and a gear consultant, Dr Merritt, was brought in. At first the view was that a 40/60 per cent torque split (biased towards

the rear) would be ideal, though some thought was given to a 30/70 split, as Keith later recalled:

"But no more extreme, on the grounds that we couldn't possibly justify having all that weight around unless we were actually putting a fair amount of urge through the front wheels. Some people eventually put so little power to the front that there was really no point in having four-wheel-drive at all."

Robin started work on the car at the beginning of 1968 (which confirms that the October 1967 leaks had been about a phantom car which only then existed in the mind of Keith and, who knows, Walter Hayes?) Everything went ahead well until that tragic day in April 1968 when Jim Clark was killed in a Formula 2 race at Hockenheim, in West Germany. After that, Robin Herd told me, the impetus was gradually lost:

"The problem was that it was always a very technically elegant piece of design, and Keith came to love it, for its own sake. Once Jim had been killed, somehow, it became more of a design exercise than a serious race project. After about a year, by the end of 1968, I sensed that Keith had begun to lose interest, and the building of the car went into the back shed."

The back shed at Northampton, in fact, was also known internally as the 'toy shop,' or the 'hobbies shop,' where Keith kept his Brantly helicopter, Bill Brown kept his boat, and where Ben and Mike could house their gliders. The Cosworth car, therefore, was gradually built up by John Thompson, who had moved north from McLaren at the same time as Robin joined the firm, and by Keith Leighton, who had previously been building F1 DFVs. John fabricated the tub, while Keith looked after the mechanical side of things.

In the end, the one and only Cosworth F1 car took to the track in the spring of 1969, with the general intention of making it competitive for Trevor Taylor to drive at Silverstone in the British GP of that year.

Right away, however, there was a great deal of trouble with the transmission, all centred on the behaviour of the front limited-slip differential, and breakage of the front disc brake bells didn't help either. Mike Costin did the initial shake-down driving, and Keith's interpretation of his views are fascinating, and rather chilling:

"Mike said he'd go down the straight, the car would gradually be trying to go off one way, to one side, and he'd be winding on more and more lock to stop this. Suddenly it would all let go, and dive the other way, but he couldn't get the lock off fast enough to catch it! Then it would do it all over again."

Mike, Trevor Taylor, and even Jackie Stewart all observed the same phenomenon, which Keith put down to the effect of slightly different tyre diameters on the limited-slip device. Cosworth eventually modified its limited-slip mechanisms so that they did not work on the over-run, and in that way the car's behaviour, and its into-corner characteristics, were much improved. Even so, Keith was concerned that in its current state of development, the car was altogether too difficult to drive fast, that it would impose too much stress and physical effort on the driver, and that it might exhaust him before the end of the event:

"I looked at all this, looked at the diff problems, noticed that wings had become dominant since we had started designing our car, and thought that we really were wasting our time, and that we should stop before we began to look even more foolish. There was no way that I was going to compromise, by using only about 20 per cent torque on the front wheels and 80 per cent on the rears.

"At the time I didn't want much strong differential action at the front wheels, and I simply couldn't come to terms with the efforts needed. Looking back, now, perhaps I was wrong to a certain extent, because front-wheel-drive cars with limited-slips are doing a whole lot better than they ought to be. You would have thought that my 'wearing out the driver' problem would still be there, but no doubt the new generation of viscous couplings, or 'sticky diffs' have helped enormously.

"No sooner had we got the car running than wings began to come in. That caused the first great deal of doubt. When we built ourselves a wing, we found that we could get substantial downforce, and we could eliminate wheelspin, so there was really then not much point in driving the front wheels any more. So, when the crunch came, I killed off the project. We were about to go on throwing good money after bad in this manner, and I wasn't having that. The best way to avoid going broke is to spot that you are well on the way to this state, then call a halt!

"I think I allowed the Cosworth car project to go on for too long. In fact, we really shouldn't have started it. This was one of those cases where we built something, but which, with a bit more thought before starting, we would have been able to see where the problems were.

"Generally speaking, I think I have saved more money for the company by analysing on paper, and not starting things, than in any other way. The car *was* a mistake, of a failure to analyse the problem."

Even before mid-summer 1969, Robin Herd realised that the car would soon be cancelled. Keith, he says, had lost interest, the car had gone on to the back burner, wings had come along to change the shape of F1 cars, tyres were a lot better, and the basic need for any sort of four-wheel-drive had become questionable. When Cosworth saw that no other four-wheel-drive F1 car was working well, it was the end:

"Keith was very kind about everything, and offered me the chance to stay on at Cosworth. He even offered me shares in his company, which was a rare honour. Keith was very interested in building a small gas turbine engine for jet aircraft. Obviously I knew a certain amount about those, the theoretical and thermodynamic problems. He offered me the chance to get on with a design, and I was sorely tempted. We went along to see the gas turbines people, and talked it all over, but in the end I decided I wanted to stay in motor racing.

"That was when I started to get approaches from other people (including the chance to set up in business with Jochen Rindt and his manager Bernie Ecclestone), but in the early autumn of 1969 I left, to found March.

"I thoroughly enjoyed my time at Cosworth. Even though I was there for less than two years, it taught me a lot about engineering. Even though Keith could be very difficult at times, very stubborn, I thought the world of him."

Occasionally, in the 1970s and 1980s, Keith thought again about building a Cosworth racing car, until he became thoroughly disillusioned about the way the sport was developing:

"I think this business of grovelling around an inch from the ground is ridiculous; the whole thing has become an utter farce. Unless we can get racing cars up to a sensible ground clearance – say about three inches off the ground – I think racing has become a complete waste of time.

"Now what would be fun, would be for race organisers to corrugate some of the track, overnight, or put a lump on the road 'on the racing line' – now that really would be demanding, wouldn't it?"

In the next few years, Keith spent a lot of time thinking and planning, but very little time actually designing, new products. At one time Graham Dale-Jones recalled spending some time working out schemes for a 2-litre 120-degree V6 engine, which was intended for use in the 2-litre Formula Two category – "It was a private venture idea, but because

The DFV of the Herd-designed Cosworth F1 car was fitted 'back-to-front' (the clutch was immediately behind the driver's seat), with the various drives to front and rear wheels on the left side of the structure. Fuel tanks were mounted to the left and the right, alongside the seat, and the overall body shape was intended to provide downforce as speeds built up.

Several noted race drivers tried their best to make the Cosworth F1 car superior to its rear-drive rivals, but failed. One of them was company founder Mike Costin, here seen at Silverstone in 1969 when the company's patience with the chassis was coming close to the end.

nobody was prepared to pay for the development, we abandoned it."

Cosworth started work on this F2 V6 in 1972, when it became clear that BMW's 2.0-litre 'four' was likely to be more powerful and more durable than the Cosworth BDG unit. Renault had also come on to the scene with its own purpose-built V6, but since Keith was not willing to go further than designing the engine (but not actually building prototypes) unless he could see a market for 20 or 30 sales, the project died there.

This also coincided with the frustrating period in 1973, when Keith had just suffered a heart attack, and was confined to bed for several weeks. It is typical of Keith that he took the trouble to learn all about the plumbing of his body, and all the appropriate fluid flow engineering, which affected his health, but there is no doubt that he was frustrated by the need for inactivity:

"In those days one was supposed to do nothing for about three months. Well, I wasn't having that. So, I got hold of lots of paper and pencils, and spent a lot of time working out the balancing of every possible V8 layout, then I had lots of arguments about the balancing of the 60-degree GA V6 – some with myself, and others with Graham Dale-Jones who was designing the crank. I also sat up and designed the small 2-litre V6 engine, which would have been ideal for use in Formula 2. Then I also sketched up a 2-litre V8, which had cross-bolted bearing set-ups, and I got as far as arranging the crankcase. I sorted out a fair bit of the detail, but that was all. But we never actually started to make either one of them."

It was after this period, which is covered in more detail in the next chapter, that Keith persuaded Alf Vickers to join the company, first as a consultant, then as his managing director. Alf released Keith from many day-to-day administrative jobs, which directly led to two more Cosworth projects – the automatic transmission and the motorcycle engine – taking shape.

By the early 1970s, Keith had also come to know, and to respect, Howard Hobbs, a very capable designer, and specialist in automatic transmissions. Hobbs spent a lot of time working on a variable kinetic drive transmission with Ford, but that project was eventually cancelled:

"I was then talked into putting some money into his company, Variable Kinetic Drives Ltd, and I bought some shares. I looked at his design, and thought it had all the fundamental making of a viable racing automatic transmission. Because it was automatic, it would be able to allow a racing engine to run at almost constant speed, you could run it as an infinitely variable gear. It was stepless, with a wide-ranging torque converter."

The design was complex, and although work on it began in 1973/74, it dragged on for at least three years without ever coming to fruition. It took the first two years to get the transmission designed in its vastly larger 'F1' size, and for all the prototype parts to be manufactured.

To try to describe its technicalities here would not only show up the author's ignorance, but it would fill out the rest of the book. Keith summarises that: "you recirculated some of the torque back to the flywheel. There was an epicyclic gear set in the middle of the flywheel.

"Well, we decided to have a go at making a proper Formula 1 transmission out of this idea. I couldn't spare the time to do all the work – that was where I went wrong – so we hired a man from Borg Warner called Cecil Schumacher, to be our specialist designer. Once Cec had begun to churn out schemes, Graham Dale-Jones and John Hancock, who would normally have been working for Mike Hall, were brought in to design many of the detail pieces.

"Well, we kept on blowing it up on the test beds. One of the major problems was that we got cavitation around the blades, and this eventually damaged the torque converter. It was always very difficult to run this transmission for more than about five seconds at 'stall,' which was at about twice the usual rpm for a normal automatic.

"We were trying to transmit about 500bhp, no automatic transmission had achieved that before, and trying to turn that into thermal energy was a tall order. There were several mistakes in the design, and I blame myself for not being able to keep on top of them. One was the way in which the oil was fed through the centre of the converter, the lack of pressure at the right points, and other details like that.

"If we could have solved the torque converter pressure problem – and at the end of the project I discovered what was wrong with the design – we could have been competitive with a box of mangle gears. It was all going to hinge on the efficiency, whether it would have been high enough to compensate for other losses. The fuel consumption wouldn't have had to matter though – we were proposing to stick the engine on full power a lot more often than you use full power with mangle gears.

"We hadn't even got to the position of fitting it to

a car, and we hadn't committed ourselves to make any more boxes – though we had talked a little to Hewland about the supply of some components – so I then took the decision that, as we didn't have a sponsor to fund us to the tune of a million pounds or so, we should cancel it.

"I think that, on reflection, the gearbox came to grief, and it was always going to come to grief, because it was too complicated, a real bag of tricks in the end, a bit big and too heavy. But maybe I should have gone out, looked for someone to give us some support, and then carried on."

Cecil Schumacher left Cosworth soon after this project was cancelled, and later carved out fame, and considerable fortune, in making $\frac{1}{12}$th scale radio-controlled model racing cars ("he's a very successful maker of model racing cars, he's a good engineer"). Graham Dale-Jones remembered just how much time Schumacher put into this project, which dragged on into 1978:

"It really was *very* complicated. Nowadays, with the help of electronic controls I reckon it could have been made to work, but just to try to make it work with fluid pressure was probably impossible. It really was *very* complicated."

Geoff Goddard told me that although it was no larger than a normal Hewland gearbox, "the amount of metal inside the casing was mighty impressive." There was also the complication factor:

"I once saw Cec carefully drawing a cross-sectioned layout of the assembly. He was cross-hatching the various bits – but at one point he was cross-hatching metal, and at the other end he was cross-hatching fresh air. It had so many bits, one inside the other, that it was very easy to lose track of which bit was connected where …"

Once he had cancelled the project, Keith clearly had no regrets. He told me that only one complete transmission was ever built, although there were sufficient parts to make two complete transmissions. When I asked him if the transmission had been preserved, if only in a dark corner of the factory, he confessed not to know, and I got the distinct impression that he no longer cared.

The problem, I am sure, is that this was one of the rare engineering projects which defeated all his good intentions. As Keith emphasised, so often, and at such length, there is invariably an answer to every technical question – but in the case of the automatic transmission it was never found. The motorcycle engine, on the other hand, proved itself in the end, though success came years after it had been designed. Until 1988, Cosworth was afraid that this was going to be one of the few racing engines it designed which would not win a race – but the 'Battle of The Twins' race, at the Daytona Speedweek in 1988, changed all that.

The story starts with Norton, the famous British motorcycle manufacturer, which had persevered with its own design of air-cooled vertical twin-cylinder engine for decades. As motorcycle historian Roy Bacon related in his book *Norton Twins*:

"By the early 1970s it was very apparent that the old twin … was rather long in the tooth, and stretched to the limit of its road racing and street development. Something new with the old problems removed, unit construction and a five-speed box was needed, but that something had to fit Norton's image, and their budget. At the time a big twin still seemed to be a successful base for both a road and a race machine.

"Rather than try to develop a new power unit from scratch themselves, which was a very time-consuming job, Nortons commissioned Keith Duckworth, the man behind Cosworth Engineering, to design and build them a 750cc twin, in 1973."

The approach came direct to Keith Duckworth, from Dennis Poore. He was a well-known businessman, had been a successful racing driver in previous years, and was the chairman of Manganese Bronze, the company which then controlled Norton and Triumph. Keith told me that:

"He came to us and said: 'We need a new motorcycle engine, for a new bike, to replace the Dominator.' It was to be a road motorcycle engine, with water cooling, but as he thought that future bike racing was going to be production-based, and that two-strokes would be ousted, he thought we would be interested in taking on the job.

"He wanted us to design him a racing-plus-production engine, and the proposed deal was that we would build and sell the racing engines, while his companies would be able to use the designs in production bikes."

As far as Cosworth was concerned, this was the JA project, but for Norton there was a dramatic new name for the engine – the 'Challenge.'

"The contract was that we should design it, develop it, produce 65bhp for the road bike, and get up to 90bhp, or whatever we could get out of it, in racing form.

"Norton would make all the production engines, but

The Cosworth-designed Norton motorcycle engine was designed in the 1970s, but did not gain success until 1988. The cylinder head layout had much in common with the DFV, there were two 'Lanchester' balancer shafts, and the gearbox was an integral part of the entire concept. This was the original power unit, complete with Amal carburettors.

we were contracted to build 25 racing engines. That was to satisfy an homologation requirement for the eligibility of production bikes in the States. Of those initial engines, we would be allowed to keep five engines, the other 20 were to go to them.

"He'd done his homework very well. He wanted a parallel twin – that would fit the sort of bike that his designers had in mind – and he wanted a 750cc engine. Well, if you took two cylinders off one bank of a DFV, that looked to be a sound basis on which to work, for it had been proved to work well.

"The bag of gold that was offered looked very reasonable, and since this was some time after my heart attack, the DFV was building itself, Mike Hall had done the Ford V6 GA, and Cec was going to design the automatic transmission, I thought I would have a go at it myself. So I took out a piece of paper and started.

"We had to produce a 750cc vertical-twin water-cooled engine. Dennis Poore had done the concept, but there was still a lot of thinking to be done. After all, the biggest problem was that it had to be balanced properly. I did an awful lot of work on crankshaft weights – Dennis Poore wanted the engine to be narrow and low – and therefore I chose a very peculiar layout, where I placed two balancer shafts, Lanchester fashion.

"There was one at each side of the crankshaft – which, as the engine was transversely installed in the bike, meant that there was a shaft at the front, below the head, and another behind the block. One was driven by the camshaft drivebelt, the other by a gear from the crankshaft.

"In addition, the crankshaft had to allow 360-degree firing – most parallel twins were like that – so that the carburation would work properly. One of Dennis Poore's forecasts was that pollution control would soon be applied to motorcycle engines, and that the best solution would be to go for a single carburettor – I decided that unless the intake 'sucks' were equally spaced, the carburettor simply wouldn't work properly. It had to be a 360-degree twin.

"For the original racing setup we chose two motorcycle-type Amals, then we also had a fuel-injection scheme as well. I also had to get some flexibility, some 'give' in the transmission. In the end I had a crank gear driving the balance shaft, a long quill shaft going right through the centre of the balance shaft, and then I used a Hi-Vo chain to drive the gearbox from the other end of that quill shaft.

"The problem was that where the engine was wide, it was also high up, so the centre of gravity was quite

high. Incidentally, the engine was also designed to be a part of the frame, so that part of the motorcycle frame would bolt on to the head, while the bearing for the swinging arm rear suspension was built in to the integral gearbox casing too.

"Originally, Norton had designed the gearbox, but we ended up redesigning it. I can remember doing reams of dog calculations, gear drawings, and getting involved in the amount of backlash which was desirable. I was responsible for a lot of the layout of the engine, the concept, its installation angle, how it was going to go into the frame, the positioning of the swing axle pivot, and the geometry to minimise chain length from bump to rebound, but most of the actual drawing work was done by Mike Hall."

So far, so good, but Keith then had the grace to admit that he was human:

"It also embodied one of my biggest mistakes! I didn't see why the water pump should not be placed where the water was leaving the head, driven off the end of a camshaft. It was the easiest possible place to put it. But it didn't work, and when I designed it like that my mind had obviously taken a holiday. I had forgotten that after a hot engine is stopped, the water in the head then boils. In my original design this steam then got through into the pump, and the pump never worked again …

"I didn't even realise this before the head design was finished, and the castings already done – which explains why all the 25 prototype engines Cosworth built had some wonderful welding, fabrication, and bits and pieces, to make sure the water went through the head and then into the block."

Unhappily for Norton-Villiers-Triumph (NVT), the engine was ready, and power-tested, at almost exactly the same time that the company descended into bankruptcy, into a workers' sit-in, and into an ill-judged attempt to set up a workers' co-operative at the Meriden factory near Coventry. The production motorcycle designed to use the Cosworth engine was cancelled, and the racing programme was under-funded and ended in failure.

Cosworth later developed very trenchant views on what Keith described as the "stupidity of government, the pie in the sky and the political ideas of those running the co-operative," but at least the 25 engines were completed, and the company was paid for its work. For Paul Morgan (who later went on to co-found the Ilmor racing engine concern), it was no reward for all the work put in on test bed running, and development. The racing engine was finally refined to produce at least 110bhp at 10,500rpm.

And so, for several years, the Norton/JA engine disappeared into limbo. Then, in July 1984, an ex-road racer, and newly appointed Cosworth director Bob Graves, whose Quantel company had joined Cosworth's controlling company, UEI, was shown round the Northampton factory by Keith Duckworth. Bob spied a few dusty engines on a shelf, asked what they were, and learned the sorry saga from the Chairman, who ended up by saying: "You're looking at the only engine we have ever built which has never won a race."

Keith was happy to get rid of a couple of engines, but wanted no more to do with this failed project. The story is that Graves then spent four years – and £100,000 – to prove him wrong. In 1988 he made his point – not only did Roger Marshall win the Daytona 'Battle of the Twins' on his Cosworth-Norton engined bike, the Cosworth-Quantel, but the machine then went on to win major events at Spa (Belgium) and Assen (Holland) later in the year. Then, as Keith told me:

"After the Daytona win we had the chance of taking more orders for this old engine, but by that time Cosworth was far too big to be playing around with things like that."

Once Cosworth's finances were underpinned, and its reserves continued to mount, year by year, there was always enough money to back any other flights of whimsy that Keith and Mike Costin wanted to pursue. The problem, though, was that logic (the stuff which seeps out of every pore at Cosworth) usually intervened. Keith analysed his standards like this:

"The reason we've survived in the business of making racing engines was that we didn't try things which weren't likely to work. We always thought very hard about everything, hoping to make sure that things would work with the minimum of development. I think that that was essential for the company in the early days. As we became better off, and more soundly based, we could have been able to take on more projects, and perhaps been able to achieve a lot more, if I had allowed things to be done in the fashion that they were normally done – in a fashion less like my purist approach, with design, manufacture of prototypes, appreciation of the problem and the snags, then the redesign, then the normal development/redesign process ...

"I think that's one of the reasons we never made W12s, and things like that, though we certainly looked at W12s, and decided not to make them. We also

The Quantel Cosworth was a fascinating and competitive motorcycle fitted with the near-unique JA Cosworth engine.

Although the Quantel racing motorcycle was hampered by a lack of finance, and of company direction, in 1986 it certainly did not lack horsepower from Cosworth!

looked at rotary valves, and decided not to make them either ... I would say that I have ranged fairly widely over all the possibilities of piston engines, and the reason why I haven't done anything outlandish is that I have conducted an analysis of their problems, and come to the reasonable conclusion that none of them stood a chance."

The nearer I came up to the present day when originally researching this book, the more difficult it became to squeeze admissions out of Cosworth staff. Occasionally, though, I would mention things like Jaguar V12 engines, desmodromic valve gear for F1 engines, or massive contracts for North American manufacturers, and get hints, enigmatic smiles, or even the hasty closing of doors or covering up of drawings. Geoff Goddard even let slip that he had once been asked to design a 38bhp flat-twin engine, but would say no more on *that* subject ...

There is always something going on at Cosworth, and always plenty of closed doors, or locked filing cabinets, to muse over. One day we may know more. One day ...

7: THE WORLD'S MOTOR INDUSTRY COMES SHOPPING

"The next breakthrough came in 1980. It was Daimler-Benz, straight out of the blue ..."

Mike Costin was quite sanguine about the continuing growth of Cosworth:

"My view is that we are a very different company now, from what we were in the 1960s, and this would have been so whether or not we had merged with UEI. Although our policy in the 1950s and 1960s was that we would never expand, in fact we continuously expanded. We kept on saying 'We are big enough, we can manage as we are ...' We said that when we were employing 50 people, we said the same when we employed 100 people, then 150, then 200 ..."

Keith Duckworth agreed that for some years the company was almost run as a co-operative – even if it was run on strictly capitalist lines: "I think that sometimes, when we were totally bound up in some racing crisis, then Cosworth was being run by its second-line management."

"I actually tried to control the growth," Keith confirmed. "Originally when we took on F2 engines, we immediately decided to stop selling complete F3 engines, but merely to supply pieces, and kits. When we moved up to F1, that was the time to drop F3 all together.

"At one stage we actually set up Cosworth Components, to look after the old engines, but we found that that distracted the main team from its endeavours. What we ought to have done was to make it a separate limited company, and I should have made someone else responsible for it – and to forbid too much movement from one company to the other. But that didn't work out, and we find that we're still making a large number of pieces for obsolete engines, which tends to clutter up the machine shops, which ought to be doing something else.

"On the whole, I would far rather run a small, efficient, business, than a large organisation. I always worried about expanding too far, to be able to cater for a maximum demand that you could forecast, but perhaps never see.

"If demand slumps after you have expanded, you are in terrible trouble. I've always thought that we should put excess demand out to sub-contract. In fact I think we should have sold off the BD engine to another company years ago."

Keith, being a Northerner, had a healthy respect for money, understanding from an early age the fundamental principle that if you commit yourself to paying out, it must be balanced by income. Keith recalls Colin Chapman of Lotus and his colander theory: "You liken your business to a colander – with water spouting out of all the holes, those are the costs, while the profit is the water that overflows from the top.

"Colin pointed out that there were two ways forward – to pour more into the colander, to increase the turnover, or to go round plugging some holes, to make yourself more efficient. I was always in favour of plugging holes and making sure that more flowed out at the top."

By the mid-1970s, Cosworth's 'we really don't want to expand any further' strategy was in tatters. Companies asking the company to design new engines were welcomed, but it was becoming more and more difficult to convince Europe's motor industry that Cosworth could not, or would not, then build the engines in quantity. It all depended, Cosworth found out, on what was meant by 'quantity' and 'production.' Ben Rood's machine shops could certainly tackle the manufacture of BD, or even GA, parts in batches of 100 or more, but there was no way that space could be found in the cramped assembly shops for building to take place.

Even so, as company expansion continued – 1973's turnover of £1.15 million rocketed to £1.64 million in 1975, and to £1.88 million in 1976 – the directors were reluctant to turn away new business. This, incidentally, was achieved with minimal increase in staff: from 147 in 1974 to 155 in 1976.

Then, it seemed, the company engaged overdrive, and business really rocketed. Turnover in 1977 was £2.23 million, in 1978 it was £3.46 million, and in 1979 it pushed ahead to £4.1 million. The business was healthy, and profitable, too – after-tax profits in 1973 were £170,294, in 1975 they were £207,060, and by 1979 they had surged ahead to £607,962.

As ever, Keith invested most of the company's profits into machinery, which caused something of a virtuous circle at Northampton – more profits = more machinery, more machinery = more work needed to keep them busy, more work = more profits, more profits = more machinery ...

Along the way, Keith, still by far the largest shareholder in the business, became a rich man, but as he spent most of his time working, and some of his so-called leisure time thinking, his only indulgence was to fly his helicopter, for business and for pleasure. Throughout the 1970s, Mike Hall ran the design office for Keith (who, in any case, spent much of his time working at home):

"We didn't expand much; we were only taking on about one new project a year or two years. Geoff Oliver arrived in the early 1970s, then Geoff Goddard, Graham Dale-Jones and John Hancock. We were still in the old office then, bursting at the seams.

"Companies would come knocking on our door saying: 'We can't get our engine to go, will you have a look at it?' We didn't often take things on, because we didn't want to give out our secrets without getting very well paid for it. Even today [this was said at the end of the 1980s] we are very selective about the type of work we do …"

General Motors was the first company to knock on the door at Northampton, offering a major design job based on the light-alloy blocked Chevrolet Vega engine. Ford was next, asking Cosworth to design an 'homologation special' for its Capris. Soon after this, Vauxhall would ask the company to bail it out of trouble with the Chevette HS engine project, Opel would ask for advice with the development of its 16-valve rally unit, and Mercedes-Benz was not far behind. By the 1980s Cosworth was actually having to turn work away.

Each of these projects, in its intricacies, its political implications, and its design details, was handled by Mike Hall's design office, rather than by Keith Duckworth himself (who was still heavily involved with DFV developments, and on the various 'new-product' schemes already described).

By the early 1970s, Cosworth's reputation was firmly underpinned by the enormous successes chalked up by the DFV, the FVA, and by the BDA engines. Other manufacturers, clearly, wanted to 'drink from the same well,' and each new product, in its own way, enhanced Cosworth's standing, and made the pressure on its factories even more intense than before. First in line was Chevrolet of Detroit, the largest individual marque in the mighty General Motors corporation, which had revealed the four-cylinder 'XP887' Vega engine in the summer of 1970. After the debacle of the rear-engined Corvair of the early 1960s, it was a miracle that Chevrolet was still allowed to dabble in engineering that was advanced by United States standards.

Not only was this much the smallest engine that Chevrolet had ever made – in standard form it was a 90bhp/2.3-litre unit – but it was technically strange, having a cast iron cylinder head but a light-alloy cylinder block. The block had no separate cylinder liners, but had specially-treated cylinder walls, and the cylinder head had a single overhead camshaft, driven by a cogged belt.

Chevrolet engineers, led by its president, Ed Cole, and by publicity-seeking John DeLorean, were proud of their new toy, though by Cosworth standards it was nothing to get too excited about. Single-cam engines, as far as they were concerned, were old hat, and as for cast iron cylinder heads, well …

"GM came along to us, and offered us the Vega engine as the basis of a racing unit," Keith Duckworth told me. "I can only think that they had heard of us because of our DFV and BDA racing engines – I didn't know anybody at GM in those days. In theory, of course, GM's policy was not to get involved in motorsport, but the definite intention with the Vega was to make a shorter-stroke 2.0-litre F2 engine out of it, and a sports car racing engine too.

"Well, because the engine was already a 2.3-litre, and the cylinder block was an aluminium die-casting, at first I thought this was a very good idea. We certainly got a lot of power out of it, more than we could get from the BD at the time. That was before we found out about the weaknesses in the block …"

Mike Hall related this story, more in sorrow than in anger:

"It was intended to be a very light F2 engine which Chevrolet sponsored. We designed the full-race conversion – new head with valves at 40 degrees, just like the BDA, dry sump, all the pumps, everything. It was all very encouraging, and it all went extremely well, performance-wise, but then we had an awful lot of trouble with the cylinder block. They suffered from porosity, quite a lot.

"That was the only Chevrolet part left in our EA engine! The problem was that it was a high-pressure die-casting, which meant that it wasn't possible to fiddle the cores to stiffen up the block. The blocks used to split the bores, from top to bottom. Chevrolet tried very hard though – they changed the material for us, they changed the heat treatment, in fact they were quite open about their own problems, and that was with an engine only producing 78bhp!"

If only they could keep the block in one piece, Cosworth engineers reasoned, the Chevrolet EA had the potential to take over from the Ford BD design, to save weight and to be more powerful. A great deal of detail work was carried out, as Keith reminded me:

"It got to the stage where John Dickens (who was chief quality engineer at the time), and Mike Costin were spending a lot of time looking at every block, and looking at X-rays of every block, to determine whether or not we dared to use them. Not only that, but those blocks which were accepted were then subjected to high-pressure water testing of the bores to see if they would split."

One of the problems seemed to be that some engines detonated, and Keith now wonders if Cosworth was a touch too ambitious regarding compression ratios. What completely mystified Cosworth – and neither Keith nor Mike liked to leave a problem unsolved – was that some engines would run and run. Everyone at Cosworth recalls Tommy Reid's 2.0-litre sports car engine, which never gave trouble, won a lot of races, and even a championship or two. But, as one of them later quipped: "We couldn't take it back and cut it up to see what we had been doing right. We might never have been able to build another engine which was as good!"

It was when the X-ray and pressure test treatment was at its height that Keith called a halt to the programme. He simply could not see the logic of using high-calibre staff on work which should never have been needed. Chevrolet, though unhappy about the race potential of its engine, then decided to turn it into a 2.0-litre production car unit. Managers with experience of European cars had seen the impact made by cars like the Escort RS1600, liked what they had seen, and determined to repeat the trick in the USA.

"Of course," Keith snorted in an interview, "they did it all wrong. They actually took the racing engine, with all its big valves and its biggish ports, and tried to make a road engine out of it. We wouldn't have tried to do that."

In August 1973, Chevrolet released provisional details about the Cosworth-Vega hatchback. This, by the way, was the very first production car to carry the name of 'Cosworth' as a part of its title. By chance, the timing of this launch was all wrong, for within weeks the world was plunged into the energy crisis which followed the short-lived Arab-Israeli war. Initial plans were for 5000 cars to be produced. Everything then went quiet, until the spring of 1975, when the car was re-launched, and it was stated that engines were being built in Chevrolet's Tonawanda plant, where 30 engine builders could assemble 25 engines a day. It was claimed to be the first American twin-cam 4-valve engine since the days of the Duesenberg of the 1930s.

By this time, as with many such much-delayed projects, it was all a bit too late, as ever-tightening exhaust emissions laws had emasculated the peak power to a mere 122bhp. The car was only in production for 16 months, and just 3507 examples were produced.

In the meantime Keith, and Cosworth, were severely shaken when he suffered a heart attack in 1973, and was confined to a hospital bed for several weeks. It was this shock – Keith actually felt quite insulted by it – which caused a big sea change in Cosworth's organisation for the mid-1970s:

"Perhaps I had been getting uptight in the early 1970s. We'd got the DFV done, and winning, we'd done the BD, we were still working away on the Chevrolet EA engine. But our organisation wasn't capable of defining priorities, and we seemed to have little idea of our capacity, or our capabilities. I'd always thought of myself as a cheerful, well-adjusted, chap, and I didn't regard myself as a significant worrier. But I was smoking quite heavily, and I suppose I must have developed some sort of heart disease. There must have been something, some crisis which brought it on, because suddenly I had a heart attack, and was carted off to hospital."

Keith, still smiling, and still pulling his own leg, more than 15 years later, could afford to be flippant about cause and effect:

"It wasn't a very bad attack, just a standard coronary, a blood clot: it didn't seem to cause much heart damage, and I seemed to be OK afterwards."

Nevertheless, it was this rather serious warning which caused Keith and his fellow-directors to think rather deeply about the future. Keith decided that more, and more highly-experienced, management, was needed:

"This was where I went out to find someone to assist me as a consultant. I ran into Alf Vickers at an *Autocar* 'Thursday Club' dinner at the Saxon Mill hotel, near Warwick. Alf had been managing director of Jensen for some years, and he'd just had a heart attack too, and he was away from his office, so you could say that we had a mutual interest.

"I set him the test I gave to all new graduates – about bolt stretching. I was mighty impressed. He answered it there and then, over the dinner table ...

"He agreed to come and have a look round at Cosworth during 1973, and the first things he did was to assess our machine capacity, then to establish a sensible costing system. That, by the way, was the first costing system we had ever had!

"We needed Alf's skills very much. We already had one Milwaukee NC automatic machine, which I'd bought for tax reasons, and I wasn't really worried whether it was being used, or not. There was another one on order. By that stage I was so appalled by the unreliability of NC machines, that I decided I couldn't make do with one, I needed two, with the same control systems, and the tapes usable on either machine.

"In addition, I wasn't able to spend enough time doing what every sensible engineer should do – which was to design carefully and cheaply. A good engineer is definitely someone who can do for a bob [5p] what any idiot can do for a quid [pound]."

Alf Vickers, who was already past what you or I would call a desirable retiring age, joined Cosworth as a consultant in 1973, but became a director from October of that year, and soon rose to become managing director, from the end of 1975. Keith, to this day, regrets that the inevitable result of this appointment was that his old college chum Bill Brown would feel left behind. Bill drifted away from Cosworth in the mid-1970s, though he was still a director of Cosworth when it was sold to UEI in 1980. At that point his final links with Cosworth were severed, he spent more and more of his time involved with his powerboats – after which he was no longer connected with the UK motor industry. It was all rather sad.

"After Alf arrived," Keith reminded me, "we were staggering on, getting bigger, and doing fairly well. I only ever talked occasionally to Alf about matters of significant business importance. Generally speaking, he was running the whole place, in a dictatorial fashion."

It was in this sort of busy, entrepreneurial atmosphere, that Cosworth received its next approach from GM. GM, in fact, had been delighted by Cosworth's design work, by its high standards, and by its remarkable ability to make much out of little. The frustration of the Vega project was not wasted, for in the next few years two other GM projects – one for Vauxhall, and one for Opel – came to Northampton.

Vauxhall announced a new high-performance Chevette, the 2.3-litre 16-valve HS model, in November 1976. To the astonishment of everyone except, it seems, the authorities in the RAC MSA (who were responsible for its homologation), the car was immediately granted sporting homologation, and began to win rallies, using Lotus Type 907 16-valve heads, well before a single HS road car had been sold.

Vauxhall's credibility was strained even further in the spring of 1978, when road car deliveries finally

Cosworth successfully manufactured hundreds of the 16-valve cylinder heads for the Vauxhall HS road car when other contractors had failed to tackle the task. They were also highly successful rally cars ...

... as seen in this Chevette HSR (Terry Kaby driving) on the RAC rally of 1983.

began in numbers, with an entirely different cylinder head from that which the rally cars had been using for 18 months. An homologation scandal followed.

Vauxhall's problem was that its sporting fervour had run well ahead of its production facility. Its own cylinder head design was ready, but the company was not able to manufacture these at Luton. Original contract arrangements – to have it machined and assembled by Jensen – also fell through.

This was where Cosworth had become involved. Vauxhall cast around, looking for another specialist concern to help it out of the mire, and discovered that only Cosworth had the know-how and bustling enterprise, and was flexible enough, to do the job. In a great hurry, and a high state of embarrassment, Vauxhall came to Northampton – could Cosworth take on the machining, and assembly, of 400 Chevette HS cylinder heads? And, by the way, could it please do it now?

Not even Cosworth could produce machined and assembled heads at once, but Ben Rood's machine shop set to, the already busy assembly shops somehow found space (and manpower) to build the head assemblies, and by early 1978 the job was done. It was only after the heads were fitted to cars, the

cars were sold, and the motoring magazines noticed the difference, that the scandal broke. Ben Rood was quietly proud of his machine shops:

"We can virtually do anything. We've always seemed to have fairly good capability. We could always do a good job, just as long as we didn't have to make too many of anything. Quite a few people can make one, two, three, or maybe half a dozen of anything – the real trick, in my opinion, is to make up to a thousand all the same, that's a lot more difficult. Anyone can make two, and anyone can make a million. With two you can do it by hand, and to do a million you can afford to throw so much money at it that you can solve any problem. But between 500 and 10,000 of anything, that's the most difficult production problem, where you can't afford to get anything wrong. I like to think that Cosworth is in that market and, yes I'm boasting, we're the best in that market, because we can always tackle it without a lot of hesitation."

It was Cosworth's success in saving face for Vauxhall, and its growing reputation as a limited-volume manufacturer, which then prompted an approach from Opel. Like Vauxhall, Opel was in trouble. In the mid-1970s the German concern (which, like Vauxhall, is owned by General Motors), had designed a 2.4-litre

When Opel of Germany could not make sense of its 16-valve engine programme for the Ascona and Manta 400 models, it turned to Cosworth to make it into a technical and commercial success. This was the Manta 400, as rallied successfully by Russell Brookes in the mid-1980s.

Cosworth's remedial work on the Opel Ascona 400 engine, coded KAA, was completed in 1978, that unit being a successful rally car at World Championship level. It was later used in the Opel Manta 400 model too.

Cosworth completed the design of the smart, effective and powerful 16-valve engine for Mercedes-Benz – this being the WA power unit – then went on to build thousands of such engines at Wellingborough.

4-valve, twin-cam conversion of its mass-production Ascona/Rekord unit, originally aiming it for Formula 2 racing, where BMW was dominant.

The engine had originally been designed, in Germany, in the mid-1970s, and was unveiled in September 1975, with the intention of homologating it as the alternative engine for use in Group 4 rally cars. Unhappily for Opel, it was not an immediate success, as several well-publicised blow-ups at major rallies proved. Because of GM's standing in the world of motoring, this was one of those occasions where Cosworth accepted a 'Please have a look at this one, and make it work' proposal, as Mike Hall confirmed:

"It was Manfred Tholl of PEK (Opel's design/development centre at Rüsselsheim), who dealt with us. What swung the decision was that Opel were also interested in productionising the design after we had made modifications.

"The engine, as delivered to us, wasn't a howling success: it kept blowing up, the rods broke, and various other things went wrong. The basic head design was already frozen, as was the chain driving system up the front. It had a very narrow valve-included-angle, even by our standards – it was only 20 degrees. We modified the ports, changed the camshaft profile, did a lot of development work, and made it reliable.

"Opel had already designed the manifolds, so that the road car would have long manifolds sweeping across the top of the engine with fuel-injection, though the rally engine would have short stub manifolds and Weber carbs. We only did design work on the rally engine but we advised on the road engine, and were able to improve it significantly."

Alistair Lyle and Geoff Goddard did most of the work to Mike Hall's direction, and the revised engine was 'right on the numbers' as soon as test bed running began. Opel was so pleased with the rescue job carried out at Northampton, that Cosworth was then asked to machine and assemble cylinder heads. Opel supplied unmachined head castings from Germany: Ben Rood's machine shops and the assembly shops then did the rest.

Cosworth built 400 Ascona 400 engines in 1978/1979, then followed them up in the early 1980s with a further 400 engines for use in the Manta 400 coupé. At the same time the rally engine was completely redeveloped, and, before the Manta 400 ran out of development, the engine had been pushed up to 275bhp, significantly more than had ever been achieved on BD-type engines intended for the same rallying Group.

All in all, Cosworth built between 1000 and 1200 production cylinder head assemblies, and also supplied all the 'works' rally engines, many of them through Swindon Racing Engines, a company profiled in more detail in the next chapter. The real accolade, however, was still to come, as Mike Hall recalled:

"The next breakthrough came in 1980. It was Daimler-Benz, straight out of the blue. They wanted us to design a 4-valve rally engine based on the bottom end of their new 2.3-litre M102 single-cam four-cylinder unit. They had already done their own 4-valve twin-cam design, but they were happy to admit that it wasn't good enough. They came to us because of our size, and our capability. If they had just wanted a design, and the odd prototype, several other companies (like Porsche) could have done that.

"However, where Cosworth is totally unique, is that it can start from a clean sheet of paper, design something, detail it, test and develop it, cast and forge the major items, then manufacture it in reasonable quantities. I don't think there is any other business which can do this – certainly not in the UK, probably not at all in Europe.

"This was fascinating, because they gave us a completely free hand – they were super people to work with, and it was almost like getting the Royal Warrant. Although we had to use their cylinder block, they wanted a no-holds-barred race/competition engine for a special Mercedes-Benz model.

"Their engine had a chain-driven camshaft, so we stuck with that, and for the first time I decided that we had to go for one-piece cylinder heads. The fact that we had, by then, the Cosworth foundry at Worcester, which could make much better complex castings than anyone else, helped enormously.

"Our first target for the rally engine was 270bhp, in driveable 'forest' trim. For tarmac use, or racing, we were looking for more than 300bhp. In both cases, we were to use Kugelfischer injection. We didn't ever run one of those engines at Northampton. Two fitters came over from Stuttgart, and between us we built up an engine to make sure that all the parts fitted together, then shipped it over to Germany. I was asked to go there, we started it up on their dyno, ran it in, put it on power, and on the very first run it produced 267bhp. They were fairly impressed – and I was quite proud of that.

"By that time we had so much experience that we could target an engine, specify it, and predict fairly accurately what we could produce.

"We built the parts for a few engines – about a dozen, if I remember correctly – and the idea was that we would eventually build a few hundred so that a car could be homologated."

By this stage, however, Daimler-Benz had discovered that dominance in rallying was hard to achieve. A costly 1980 programme had been highlighted by failures and humiliations, for, at that time, the cars chosen (450SLC/500SLC coupés, with V8 engines, but no Cosworth input) were far too heavy and unwieldy. After signing Ari Vatanen and Walter Rohrl, in preparation for 1981 (with a never-revealed new car), Daimler-Benz abruptly cancelled its motorsport programme, and all Cosworth's work seemed to have been wasted. But not for long. According to Mike Hall:

"This was the best thing that could ever have happened to us. Instead of doing 200 sets of racing bits, we were then commissioned to do 5000 production head assemblies every year. I had to modify the head a little bit, to make assembly easier – this was the first time we had ever had to think about production in such numbers. I'm sure Daimler-Benz could have tackled the job themselves, but the numbers were really too low, and in any case the link with Cosworth gave them a certain amount of prestige."

The result, unveiled in September 1983, but not entering production until 1984, was the Cosworth-designed road-car engine for the 190E 2.3-16 model. For Cosworth, it was their very first volume-production road-car engine contract, where the heads were cast at Worcester, then machined at the new Wellingborough factory, where Cosworth also produced complete cylinder head assemblies before shipping them to Germany. Cosworth, which had signed confidentiality agreements with Daimler-Benz, was delighted when the German firm leaked the source of its new engines, and there is now no secrecy about the arrangement.

Five years on, that arrangement continued, although for a time Daimler-Benz itself also machined a series of heads. In the late 1980s the engine was enlarged to 2.5-litres, and in 1989 an 'Evolution' type was also produced, to allow the 190E 2.5-1.6 to be competitive in touring car racing. Cosworth also produced the specially gas-flowed cylinder heads, and some of the competition pieces, for the racing versions of that car.

GM, having relied so heavily on Cosworth for its Chevette HS and Ascona/Manta 400 cylinder heads, came back again in September 1983, this time asking if Cosworth would produce a new 4-valve twin-cam

Mercedes-Benz was especially impressed by the detail, and the complete development package that Cosworth produced for the 190E 2.3 16 engine of the 1980s.

engine for use in road cars. In terms of projected numbers, the GM contract was as important as that from Daimler-Benz, for GM was proposing to use 16-valve engines in Kadetts and Astras, Vectras and Cavaliers: some with front-wheel-drive and some with four-wheel-drive.

"We designed and made the prototypes," Mike Hall told me, "then we went on to produce several hundred pre-production heads, for test and proving purposes. It was always envisaged that we would then manufacture the first few thousand, but that if the project was a success, GM would also make heads in Germany, too."

Which is precisely what happened. From 1987, Cosworth's production factories were busy casting, machining, and assembling 16-valve heads for GM – but before long GM's own factories were outstripping them. Strangely enough, GM was very reluctant to admit to any Cosworth involvement at first, and it is still rare to see the Northampton concern credited with any of the work.

Cosworth, incidentally, developed, and made, many Group A parts for this engine, while the Swindon Racing Engines concern (once controlled by Cosworth) held the contract to prepare and rebuild 'works' engines in the late 1980s.

The Mercedes-Benz 190E 2.3-16 was the German company's first four-valve/twin-cam road car, for which Cosworth provided design, development and manufacturing facilities in the mid-1980s.

When Mike Hall retired, this charming montage was created, showing the most important Cosworth engines for which he was mainly responsible.

Other projects

Several other projects are listed in Appendix 2, and it is certain that others have been carried out, if not widely publicised, over the years. Here are a few examples:

The MG Metro 6R4 90-degree V6 engine was, in concept, designed by David Wood for the Austin-Rover Motor Sport division. It had, shall we say, certain obvious likenesses to existing Cosworth designs. When the press first saw the engine, in 1985, several observers likened it to a more modern version of Mike Hall's Ford GA design. Mike Hall, however, corrected this impression:

"I did quite a lot of consulting with David Wood, who had once been an engine builder with a great deal of BD and DFV experience. He wanted to use as many proven parts as possible. In the end, we supplied all the valves, the springs, guides, and so on – they were straight DFV parts – as well as pistons. We also cast and machined all the cylinder heads – in layout these were almost three-cylinder versions of the Mercedes-Benz design, and they used DFV type ports.

"There was a certain amount of trouble with timing belts, but we had nothing to do with that, or with assembly of the engines."

Geoff Goddard confirms that the whole of the engine's breathing arrangements were near-identical to the DFV, and that this was arranged with the agreement of Cosworth.

There was also the rather more 'arm's-length' involvement with the TWR V12 Jaguar engine, so successfully developed during the 1980s, for use in XJ-S Group A cars, then in the XJR-series of Group C and IMSA racing sports cars.

At the time, TWR was always very reluctant to spell out its links with Cosworth. The fact is, however, that Cosworth was first approached in regard to the XJ-S Group A engine, producing camshafts, and pistons. TWR's own engine design engineers were always ultimately responsible for the unit, though Cosworth's race-engine designer Geoff Goddard was certainly involved in camshaft design, while marketing manager Jack Field confirmed that he also supplied many machined parts to Kidlington.

Cosworth was also involved in the machining of some parts for TWR's newly-developed twin-turbocharged V6 unit, which was unveiled in the spring of 1989, and was really a totally re-engineered and redeveloped version of the MG Metro 6R4 power unit.

Marketing manager Jack Field admits that in some

cases he machined and supplied parts to 'middle men,' and is not at all sure where they eventually go:

"People tend to discover a use for things. Take a little fuel filter we did for the DFV. We decided to sell it to other people, had it anodysed gold, called it the 'Gold Filter' – and now we sell them 50 at a time.

"The original oil pressure and scavenge pumps we designed for the DFV are now being used by almost every V8 engine running in IMSA, or NASCAR racing, in a DFX, a Chevvy, a Buick or whatever. We get orders in batches of 20 sets, at £5000 a set! Sometimes we have had orders for water pumps, and discovered that they were going into turbocharged marine engines. Then, of course, we get people coming to us, asking for Cosworth to machine a camshaft profile onto the customer's cams. If they didn't mind using one of our range, from DFVs, BDs, YBs, and such-like, we don't mind that either. We certainly make pistons, we don't

mind making connecting rods, though we don't like to do crankshafts."

If, indeed, this wasn't such a high-technology, high-turnover, business, one would be tempted to call this the 'jobbing engineering' side of the business. No wonder that Keith Duckworth set up the ostensibly separate Cosworth Components for a time.

Other companies, on the other hand, think they need only buy a Cosworth head from another engine, copy it, and save themselves many thousands of pounds. Keith Duckworth, however, chortled merrily for some time when I raised this point with him:

"The easiest way to get a fair performance out of a new design is to do a good copy of what is known to work. That is, if you do a fair copy, and not try to improve it. It is the so-called improving of our designs that has wrecked some other designs! Negative improvements have occurred on a number of occasions."

Cosworth's contribution to the engineering of the Group B MG Metro 6R4, was to see the elements of the DFV engine's combustion chamber, the valve gear, and many other 'top end' components.

During the 1980s, Austin-Rover developed the four-wheel-drive, mid-engined, MG Metro 6R4, for World Championship rallying. Although the engine was basically ARG's own design, the heads were cast, machined and assembled by Cosworth, with most of the architecture being 'lifted' from the DFV power unit. TWR later bought the manufacturing rights in 1988, turned the engine into a turbocharged racer for its XJR machinery, and used the same engine to power the Jaguar XJ220 super car.

The basic design of the MG Metro 6R4 was carried out by Williams GP Engineering, but Austin-Rover's David Wood designed the 90-degree V6 engine. The heads were cast, machined and assembled by Cosworth, while most of the valve gear and many of the cylinder head porting dimensions were 'lifted' from the DFV. TWR then bought the manufacturing rights from Austin-Rover in 1988.

COSWORTH – THE SEARCH FOR POWER

8: DFV DEVELOPMENTS – COSWORTH'S AMAZING V8

When Ford asked Keith Duckworth to design the DFV, the original agreement did not specify the car or cars in which the engine was to be used. The agreement actually stated that: "The choice of team will be at Ford's discretion, Cosworth being available in an advisory capacity if required."

Even so, Keith designed the DFV around the new Lotus 49 (and, specifically, the rear engine mountings were placed a mere nine inches apart "to suit the structure, and the size of Jim Clark's bottom …"). It was always understood, though never specified, that only Lotus should have the use of the engines in the first year. Walter Hayes summarised this concisely:

"Well, we could have given them to other people, but since the engine and the car were being developed together, and since we were all part of this great enterprise, it would never have occurred to me to give them to anyone else."

Cosworth's contract, as it stood, merely obliged it to produce a total of five engines by the end of 1967, and to maintain them until the end of 1968. Ben Rood, certainly, did not plan a production run:

"In the late 1960s I never even stopped to think about 20 years on. We never envisaged the DFV going on for that length of time. We only changed the way that we made the DFV in the mid-1980s. I think we should have tackled that job a lot earlier than we did. Originally we just organised ourselves to build a few – and now I'm talking about less than 20 engines – then we had to carry on making batches, a few at a time, for year after year. The tooling, such as it was, was almost non-existent." By the autumn of 1967, however, Walter Hayes could see that the DFV had already changed the face of Grand Prix racing:

"It soon became evident that this could be Lotus-Ford, Lotus-Ford, for ever. Although this sounds a bit like evangelism, I had always thought that the important thing for Ford in motorsport was for motorsport to be successful, and to encourage more and more people, not necessarily for one team to be supremely dominant.

"At dinner, one evening, before the German GP, I said to Colin Chapman: 'You do realise, don't you, that we're going to have to let other people use this engine?' Colin, without any argument at all, said: 'Yes, I can see that.' No argument, no histrionics, nothing.

In later years I used to wonder about that – was he so supremely confident in his ability, or whether he had the same sort of vision as me?

"We were very confident with the DFV, even by that stage. It had really not been tuned, or developed from the very beginning, but people were queuing up to buy it. It was an amazing engine, much better than its competitors. Jim Clark used to say: 'You start with one engine, then you put your foot down, and above 6500rpm it's like getting another engine as well!'

"It became obvious that if we, and Cosworth, did it right, we could become purveyors of DFVs to the whole world. I know people began to call it Senior Formula Ford, but I know of no period when Grand Prix racing was more appreciated than it was in those days."

The records show that Cosworth built its five contracted engines by the summer of 1967, but that by the end of that year a total of ten had been delivered. Then the rush set in – by the end of 1968 a further 22 were delivered, and the 50th engine was completed before the end of 1969.

Not that there was ever a surplus of DFVs to go round. A few, for no very good and obvious reason, never performed as well as they should, and although Dick Scammell's experts took them apart, even cut them up, to find out why, it was never obvious. Walter

Jim Clark's victory in the 1968 South African GP was the final F1 victory (his 25th) in his stellar career.

Jackie Stewart, driving Ken Tyrrell's DFV-engined Matra MS80, won the World F1 Drivers' Championship in 1969.

Walter Hayes had spotted the precocious talent of a beady-eyed young Scot called Jackie Stewart, and it was almost inevitable that he should steer the first 'customer' supplies of DFVs towards Jackie, and the Tyrrell team:

"My first contact with Jackie was at an Earls Court Motor Show in the mid-1960s. Jackie was driving BMC-engined F3 cars at the time, and I heard that BMC had just refused to lend him a road car. I talked to Jackie on the stand, showed him a big Zodiac on the turntable, and asked him if he would like to have it? 'Yes, obviously,' he replied, so I said 'Well, if you would come to do some driving for us, I will give it to you …' In fact, we gave him the car even before he could drive for us, but I knew we were going to need him soon, and at that stage I just wanted to make sure that he was ours."

In 1968, the other lucky recipient of Cosworth DFV V8s was McLaren, another team personally chosen by Walter Hayes. His talent spotting was uncannily accurate. In 1968 there were 12 F1 GPs, of which Lotus won five races, McLaren won three, and Tyrrell-Matra won three. Hayes later insisted that he never wanted to see Ford making big money out of the DFV programme:

"I thought it important that Keith should price the engine, and then he should sell them all. He would keep all the money he made – none would come to us – he would sell all the spare parts, and he would keep all the money he made from servicing and rebuilds. I hoped, I sincerely hoped, that this would make him rich enough to invest in a much more comprehensive facility to go on, and to do even greater things. I wanted to make Cosworth bigger, more powerful, and I wanted it to have more resources.

Hayes told me that there was one occasion when one of his teams had a shortage, but that on a visit to Northampton he noticed what looked like a spare DFV sitting in a corner. "Why can't we use that?" he said. Keith, in a single, throw-away remark, merely commented: "Oh no, you can't have that. It's a bad-tempered engine."

At first it was Ford that vetted the customers, and decided who should use the DFV, but by the early 1970s Cosworth was set free to market the engines in almost any way it wished. Several years earlier,

The start of what became a legendary partnership came in 1970, when Ken Tyrrell (centre) commissioned Derek Gardner (right) to design the brand-new DFV-powered Tyrrell 001 for Jackie Stewart (left) to race in F1. The result was that Jackie won the World Championship in 1971 and again in 1973.

"My ulterior motive? Well, my experience is that you get better work from rich people than from poor people. If an engine builder cannot afford the money to do his own tinkering, and further development, you lose the opportunity of his continuous efforts. When I saw that Keith had bought his first helicopter, I knew that everything was working out!

"In the end, too, I had another motive. When Keith, Mike, or whoever would come back to me and say: 'Look, we were screwed, you got all this publicity for only £100,000,' I could always reply that we had helped him to have a product which had enabled him to make a great deal of money …

"On the other hand, too much money spoils some people. I always said that the decline of a Grand Prix team began when it got its first motorhome. Certainly

I always began to worry when they bought their first executive jet!"

The DFV story has been told, and told well, by any number of people, but not all of them have realised just how much Keith (and to a lesser extent, Walter Hayes) treated it as a personal 'pet' project. Keith, perhaps not by work, but certainly by attitude, always let it be known that he had designed the DFV, and that he would decide what was needed to make it go even better in the future. At Cosworth, therefore, the DFV engine revolved around Keith, around Mike Costin and Dick Scammell, who carried on the development of the year-on-year improvements, and on Jack Field, who had the demanding job of balancing demand against supply. Throughout the 1970s Cosworth was in what economists would call a 'monopoly situation,' for it always had more people wanting to buy the engine than it could satisfy. From time to time Keith would let Jack Field know who was 'in' and who was 'out' of favour.

This, of course, only applied to delivery priorities, for it was one of Keith's axioms that as far as possible everyone should get the same engine specification. The engine, if correctly installed, and correctly plumbed, should perform in the same way for every customer. As an example, therefore, an up-and-coming chassis manufacturer like Williams could be sure in the late 1970s that it ought to beat Lotus or Tyrrell, if its chassis, and its drivers, were superior.

"An important part of Cosworth's ethics was that we succeeded in business because we standardised pieces, and made everything so that outside people could buy bits, and they would automatically fit together. That was an important difference between us and most of our competitors.

"That was one of the reasons why the Gurney-Weslake V12 engine didn't work properly, because the bits weren't made well enough, and the amount of hand-fiddling and fettling was horrendous.

"Coventry-Climax was supposed to have a philosophy of interchangeability, but from my personal observation they didn't carry that out. In the beginning, when I was rebuilding Coventry-Climax engines, most of the problem was in actually making the new parts good enough to fit the old engine. The old FPF twin-cams, in particular, were real 'knife-and-fork' jobs."

"Bill Brown was the proponent of this straightforward approach. We rarely upset people in this way, or over delivery dates. We rarely quoted delivery dates, but on the other hand we always said we 'would use our best endeavours' to get things ready.

Jackie Stewart twice won the F1 Driver's Championship (in 1971 and 1973), using DFV-powered Tyrrells.

"We always decided we would be dead honest about our power outputs. If we said our engines were going to give 'this much,' every engine we sold was going to have to give that much on our test beds. We stated a figure that, in general, we thought would be fairly easy to achieve. Because of the scatter we didn't want to have too much aggravation – but sometimes

James Hunt burst into F1 in 1973, using DFV-powered cars for Lord Hesketh. This was his Hesketh-Ford which he drove in 1974.

WESLAKE'S V12 RIVAL TO THE DFV

Walter Hayes commissioned a 3-litre V12 race engine from Weslake in 1970, ostensibly for long-distance sports car racing, though he also thought that it might rival the DFV. The Weslake engine, in fact, was a major disappointment, and was never used in sports car racing or F1 before being cancelled in 1974.

WALTER Hayes later confirmed that although he was completely happy with the performance of the Cosworth DFV: 'When I was involved in the Ford GT40 project, I got to know Harry Weslake very well. He did some amazing work on GT40 cylinder heads when the team was in trouble. Soon after that, Harry Weslake tried to sell me the idea of a new F1 engine, which was a 3-litre V12. Well, I didn't really want to set up a competitor for Cosworth, we didn't need that, and, as we had a very happy relationship, why should I want to break it?'

Weslake, helped along by his consultancy agreement with BRM, and Aubrey Woods, had produced similar V12 engines for Dan Gurney's AAR Eagle team in the 1966-68 period, for which 410bhp-plus was claimed. Although there were several engines, all were hand-built with virtually no interchangeability, unit to unit. There was one major success for the Eagle-Weslake V12 – the Belgian GP of 1967 – but Dan Gurney became disillusioned, and mainly because of a sponsorship crisis at AAR, pulled out of the project in 1968.

In 1970, however, Walter Hayes and Stuart Turner of Ford encouraged Weslake to design another 3.0-litre V12, ostensibly for long-distance sports car racing, though it was always understood that if it was to be competitive in output, then Ford might consider it for use in a Grand Prix car.

The new Weslake-Ford V12 used the bore, stroke, crankshaft and other details of the Eagle unit. The 4-valve, narrow-included – angle, pent-roof combustion chamber looked superficially like that of the DFV, though this time there were swirl-inducing lobes in the chamber profile, a Weslake favourite, as also used in the famous BMC A-Series engine (and as distrusted, on 'masking' grounds, by Keith Duckworth). The initial power target was 440bhp, which would have made it immediately competitive with the DFV.

The engine ran for the first time on 20 December 1971, and according to Weslake's own test bed it actually produced 460bhp, with a later engine working up to 470bhp – 20bhp more than that shown by a then-current development of the Cosworth DFV on the same bed. Tests in Gulf-Mirage prototypes were encouraging, but all manner of problems – financial, political, and development – meant that it would never be raced. Legal action followed, with Weslake being awarded damages against Gulf-Mirage. John Dunn, of the Cosworth-controlled Swindon Racing Engines concern, also tested an engine and recorded 465bhp, thus proving Weslake's claims, but it never seemed to deliver the goods in a racing car. In 1973, BRM tried one in a P160, while Brabham also fitted one in a BT39, but neither installation was a success.

During 1974, the Weslake V12 project was cancelled completely, having cost £150,000 to develop to that stage, and Weslake had nothing to show for it. The problem seems to have been two-fold – a lack of reliability, and a lack of mid-range torque. Keith Duckworth's race engine design philosophy, once again, was completely vindicated – there was no point in having record-breaking peak power if the engine was not also flexible further down the range.

James Hunt became Formula 1 World Driver's Champion in 1976, driving the McLaren M23-DFV.

we needed rebuilds of engines that didn't quite make the targets. When we had a real demon engine, we often tried to find out why it was so good, but we never made it."

This, of course, was an astonishing breakthrough for what had become the 'Grand Prix industry.' New customers took time at first to accept what they were told, and because the figures quoted were minimum ratings, rather than average ratings, a few people thought they were being honoured by extra-special units. In truth, Cosworth rarely set out to build screamers, and in a few cases actually delivered top-rated engines to the customer without telling him! On the other hand, Cosworth – Keith in particular – expected customers to be honest with them:

"We must have had one of the best experiences of low bad debts, of any firm, ever. We did insist on getting paid promptly for new engines. New engines didn't leave the place until they had been paid for. But we could be fairly generous, by not pressing too hard for prompt payment from customers who we thought were struggling hard, but honest – we were always as reasonable as possible to people like Frank Williams. Frequently, we got paid somewhat late, but we usually got the money in the end. We always got paid by Frank.

"If payment tended to be rather late, and rather slow, we could often fall back on the fact that another of that customer's engines was in for a rebuild. It tended to be fairly difficult to get those engines back to them if they hadn't paid their bills."

"We didn't approve of people going broke on us. Actually there have been teams which went strategically broke, but we've seldom been caught by those people. In a lot of cases they would want to start up in business again, and therefore they could do well without having us as creditors!"

In the early years of the DFV project, although the engine powered a lot of race-winning cars, the DFV was not always as reliable as Keith and Mike would have liked. The engines were always as powerful as claimed, but from time to time breakages occurred. The oil circulation problem was soon solved, but the two most irritating failings were to timing gears, and to crankshafts.

"We had very few DFV problems, really," Keith later recalled, "but solving the gear train torsional problem took us a long time. It was a pure torsional, which we chased from one end of the engine to the other. We eventually found that the torque causing our timing gear failures was far higher than the output torque from the crankshaft. So it wasn't surprising that the fairly flimsy gears failed under it. I had to get more material into a very limited amount of space, so that existing engines could be converted. It was nearly an impossible problem – I was aiming to reduce the instantaneous torque to about an eighth of what it originally was."

In the end, and after a great deal of the 'withering concentration' for which Keith had become noted, the famous multi-quill shock-absorbing gear was developed.

It looked flimsy, it looked complex, and it looked fussy – but it worked. [Significantly enough, when Mario Illien and Paul Morgan left Cosworth to set up Ilmor Engineering, their DFY 'clone' engine was unreliable for the first two years of its racing life. The trouble, they say, was connected with torsional vibrations in the timing gears, which had no quill shock-absorbing feature ...]

There was a short period when crankshafts

Even though Keith Duckworth did not expect his DFV engines to survive in long-distance sports car racing, Derek Bell and Jacky Ickx confounded everyone by stroking this DFV-powered Gulf GR8 to victory in the 1975 Le Mans 24 Hour race.

repeatedly broke, but this was soon traced to a mistake in detail machining. The difficulty was not to solve the problem, but to get new supplies of unmachined forgings to replace the broken items.

By the early 1970s the DFV had come to dominate F1 racing: DFV-engined cars helped Graham Hill, Jackie Stewart (three times), Jochen Rindt and Emerson Fittipaldi (twice) win the World Driver's Championship between 1968 and 1974. Ferrari then fought back, with its flat-12, but James Hunt (1976) and Mario Andretti (1978) went on to show that the DFV was not finished.

The F1 World Championship race successes mounted, as did the number of engines built. Here is a summary of the 1960s and 1970s:

Year	No of victories	Year	No of victories
1967	4	1974	12
1968	11	1975	8
1969	11	1976	10
1970	8	1977	12
1971	7	1978	9
1972	10	1979	8
1973	15		

The whole thing, as Walter Hayes quipped, was getting "bigger than Ben Hur," and:

Could anything have been more strikingly liveried, and so effective? This was Ronnie Peterson at the wheel of the Lotus 72 in 1975.

The elegance of Gordon Murray's Brabham BT49 theme, and the overall excellence of the DFV all helped Nelson Piquet to become World F1 Champion in 1981.

A marriage made in heaven – in 1978 the combination of the Lotus 79 'ground effect' chassis, Mario Andretti at the wheel, and Cosworth's DFV providing the power, was almost unbeatable. This car ran with Olympus sponsorship for much of the season.

The DFV came towards the end of an illustrious career in F1 with victory in the 1982 Austrian GP for Elio de Angelis and his Lotus 91.

"It really wasn't necessary for Keith to do more than sit at home and enjoy it, but he couldn't keep away. I don't think he actively courted this, but, in spite of everything, he soon became famous. Before the DFV he had really been Professor Branestawm, in his own simple workshop, creating his own toys, but all of a sudden he was in big business, he was big business."

Never before, in the history of F1 racing, had so many engines been built by one concern. As the doyen of Formula One history, Doug Nye, once wrote:

"... the greatest compliment that can be paid them is that they put a Grand Prix racing engine into quantity production and kept it at the top of the class for much more than a decade."

By 1973, with the build total of DFV engines well past the 100 mark, the walls were bulging with work. Some changes had to be made. Whereas Jack Field had originally been able to keep track of every engine, and also accept them all back for rebuilds, it was clear that the quality of work would go down unless some work (but not all) was farmed out:

"Until the Nicholsons, the Judds, the Heskeths and the Swindons came along, we used to rebuild every engine. Then we decided that we needed to encourage people outside of Northampton to service all these engines, and that was how they got started."

Swindon was a special case, as founder/managing director John Dunn told me:

"I had been in the States for seven years. I used to be the engines engineer at Shelby American, building V8s, then I went into partnership with a guy called Falconer, setting up Falconer & Dunn Racing Engines." I looked after Keith when he came over to the USA for a week – I remember that we paid a visit to Hughes Helicopters. When I came back to the UK, I wanted

ILMOR

BY 1983 Mario Illien and Paul Morgan were respected and responsible Cosworth engineers. At the end of that year they left abruptly and set up Ilmor Engineering in Brixworth, only a few miles away.

The objective, quite simply, was to use Penske/Chevrolet finance to develop an Indy-racing engine – specifically to rival the Cosworth DFX. This caused a great deal of bitterness at Cosworth, and one can see why. Nothing like this had been seen since a Shadow F1 chassis design suddenly reappeared as an Arrows in 1978. Illien had designed racing engines in Europe before he undertook formal engineering training, and while at Cosworth he had designed the DFY 'conversion' to the DFV, and initiated work on the Sierra RS Cosworth production car engine. Morgan had been involved with the DFX, as a race engineer, since the early days.

In November 1983, no doubt somewhat frustrated by Cosworth's policy of deliberately 'under-employing' people, so as to minimise mistakes, the two decided to branch out on their own. The result was an approach to Roger Penske of the USA, who soon assembled a financial package to allow them to set up shop a few miles north of Northampton.

If the Ilmor engine had been innovative, or significantly different, from anything Cosworth was designing, everyone would have wished them well. It was not, and everyone I have spoken to muttered deeply about the way the years of experience were directly used in the new engine. For obvious reasons, I cannot name the personalities who talked to me, but here is a selection of what was said:

"The Ilmor engine was a near copy of the DFY, with the same head, but turbocharged. It was built to fit the same monocoques as the DFX. Most engine pieces were exact replicas of ours, or 'borrowed' from new designs which Cosworth was considering. Really, it's a straight clone."

"People are going to leave any company, nobody feels hurt about that. If they'd gone off to do a V6, or a totally different V8, Keith would have wished them well."

"I'm sure the Ilmor was just a turbocharged DFY. But they missed out the compound gear with the quills. The cleverest feature of the DFV – and they didn't copy it!"

Instead Ilmor relied on a train of timing gears going up from the flywheel end of the engine, which had a lower torsional component. This was an idea which had been discarded by Keith in view of the tiny flywheels which were being used.

"It took them two years longer than they promised, to make the engine work. Making a slightly updated version of the DFX was a bigger challenge than they had expected, wasn't it?"

The Ilmor engine, however, persuaded Cosworth to drop the 'no-development' agreement it had had with the Indy-racing authorities. Once the Ilmor started winning, Cosworth began to look at new DFX features. The result, for 1989, was the DFS, and the successful new XB followed in 1992.

---

to start my own business, so I went to see Keith. He asked me to give Cosworth a proposal, which I did.

"The result was that Swindon Racing Engines was set up in 1972, a new company and a new building in Swindon, the prime purpose being to service and rebuild DFVs." The deal was that Dunn and Cosworth directors would set up a new company, with Dunn running the business, but with Messrs Duckworth, Costin, Brown and Rood all holding shares in the limited company. In later years Alf Vickers also took a small share. John Dunn made it clear however that Swindon was never a part of Cosworth, although all Cosworth's directors were directors of his new concern. None of this was broadcast, but neither was it kept secret. The motor racing industry soon came to know about the Cosworth-SRE connection, and the Cosworth directors' share interests appear in the annual records deposited at Companies' House.

"It was a completely 'hands off' arrangement. Keith Duckworth has never even been to Swindon – though he told me he had once looked in at the windows as he was passing. There was never any pressure. I used to see quite a lot of him at Northampton, but I was always encouraged to do my own thing. As far as I recall, there wasn't ever an annual board meeting!"

SRE was up and running even before John Nicholson's competing London-based business got under way ("We tested his engines, for him, initially"), not only with the job of rebuilding engines for major teams like Tyrrell, but with specific contracts such as the development of a Formula Atlantic 'package' for the BD Series units, and the building of Formula Super V engines based on the VW Golf engine.

Not only did Swindon prosper by the rebuilding of DFVs, but also from the servicing of other engines such as the Cosworth-developed Opel Ascona 400/Manta 400 rally car engines. Although none of the rebuilders was encouraged to do its own ongoing development, this naturally took place, and some teams stuck closely to one rebuilding concern, keeping their little manoeuvres secret from everyone else. John Dunn is proud of the fact the SRE developed the short inlet trumpet package which suddenly added horsepower to the DFV in the 1975 season ("In South America, Shadow blew everyone into the weeds. By the next race everyone had them.") Nicholson was the first to try an enlarged bore/shorter stroke system, while several tried different cam grinds before Cosworth came back with the definitive DA12 profile of its own.

The various DFV rebuilders were not encouraged to co-operate, each having to pitch for its own contracts, and individual tweaking and development was discouraged. In any case, there was a great deal

FUEL FLOW LIMITS IN F1 – THE COSWORTH SOLUTION

WHEN the Cosworth DFV arrived in 1967, it produced more than 400bhp, and set new standards in F1. Ten years later, Cosworth had found another 100bhp, while Ferrari's best flat-12s were also nudging 500bhp. Surely it was time, the pundits said – and wrote – that this 3-litre power race should be stifled?

But how? Some sort of restriction would be needed – but should it be on engine airflow, or fuel flow? No-one really thought it through except, need I say it, Keith Duckworth.

"Fuel is the thing you pay for, not air, so it only made technical sense to leave airflow alone, and put a limit on fuel flow. As far as I could see, it didn't even matter what size the engine was, as long as the fuel flow was limited. If you restrict air entry you must run the engine rich, so that you use every scrap of air. If you are, in fact, fuel-limited, you must use a surplus amount of air – that's lean burn – to guarantee you use every bit of fuel.

"Therefore your engine would be more efficient if you chose a fuel/second, rather than an air/second, formula. In any case, you could argue that as air is everywhere, and you can't sell it, to ration it would be illogical. Incidentally, I once calculated what size of sonic-flow aperture (F3 style) would do that trick – something like 2.1in/53mm rings a bell.

[Keith's rooted objection to the type of F1 racing which eventually followed in the 1980s now comes through.]

"It would be totally unsatisfactory to have racing based on so many gallons for the race distance, so the only sensible alternative was to limit the maximum instantaneous power. Therefore, some sort of flow-limiting valve, calibrated in fuel/second, was needed. When I thought this through, I calculated that 27cc/second was enough to produce 500bhp, and that this ought to be allowed. In fact if someone developed a two-stroke to use the same amount of fuel, but developing more power, then such an engine should be allowed to win.

"Ideally, you could produce a bigger engine, running slower, because that's the best way to get efficient combustion. The point was that the car would never need to run out of fuel – the car could carry as much fuel as necessary, and the limitation would only be on the rate at which the fuel could be used." It took a lot of talking, but in the end Keith got the authorities to listen:

"FISA actually invited me to make a device, a valve. I did a lot of work, produced a prototype, and somewhere at Northampton it still exists. Then FISA demanded that I make up to 50 of these valves that would all flow at 27cc/second. I said that I couldn't guarantee that – I could guarantee that they would all flow within one per cent of one another, but no nearer. FISA couldn't understand that, and therefore I had to abandon it. To have a valve flowing at exactly 27cc/second, in all temperatures and at all heights, well it just wasn't practical, you would have needed National Physical Laboratory standards of testing kit."

Did FISA pay for all this?

"Certainly not, we – Cosworth – had to pay for it. By the way, I think it would have been possible to cheat, a bit, too. Someone, somewhere, would have found ways of storing some of the fuel flow downstream of the valve, to get more instantaneous power for a very short period."

Keith is adamant, however, that the fuel flow valves would have worked, and would have produced good racing, if all the constructors, and FISA, had really wanted to see it happen. "I showed the device to my main rival, Ferrari, and I still have a letter which agrees that it was theoretically sound, but that there was no way that FISA was competent to calibrate it."

success, not needing to do too much work to make it more powerful, only making sure that the orders could be met, and reliability achieved. Graham Dale-Jones is sure that between 1970 and 1977 (when he finally moved on) there were no changes to DFV ports, valve sizes, or cams though "we changed the trumpets, and gradually we came to let it run faster." Eoin Young, writing in *Autocar* in 1969, summed up the DFV's dominance in this way:

"I have been wondering what Cosworth planned to do when their 3-litre engine starts to get overhauled by more exotic creations from Ferrari and BRM, but Mike Costin doesn't see any immediate problem.

"He idly checked the figures on a slide rule as he talked, and said: 'If we raise the engine limit from 9500 to 10,000rpm, we should get just over 450bhp.'"

By mid 1970, most DFVs had 430bhp, but a few had more than 440bhp at 10,000rpm. If the limit was raised to 10,500rpm, more than 450bhp would be available, and at 11,000rpm this would ease ahead to 470bhp. Even so, teams could put 600 racing miles on an engine before a rebuild was needed, after which a £500 rebuild, and a £200 test-bed check would follow.

By 1974, with inflation biting hard into the British economy, a new DFV cost £9266 (including VAT), and by 1977 it was priced at nearly £15,000 (including VAT).

In the meantime, Ferrari had caught up with Cosworth in the horsepower race, for no significant DFV changes were made from 1973 to 1976 inclusive. The Ferrari flat-12 engine, first raced in 1970 with a claimed output of 460bhp, was rated at 495bhp by 1974, and passed the 500bhp mark by 1976. No-one doubted those peak figures, though the 'boxer' engine was by no means as torquey in the mid-range as was the DFV. Nevertheless, the Ferrari-Lauda combination was a winner, claiming three victories in 1974, seven in 1975, and six in 1976. As Keith Duckworth so succinctly told me, in an *Autocar* interview at the beginning of 1977:

"I don't think the DFV is at its limit, yet, and I do think it should be possible to get 500bhp from it. Anyway it looks as if we've got to try!"

The first effort was to produce a much lighter DFV, by using magnesium castings for the heads and the cylinder block. This produced a 44lb weight saving, but there were innumerable problems over differential expansion as the engine warmed up – if the crank bearings were originally too loose the oil pressure dropped, if they were too tight, then the power would be 10bhp or more down on a nominal figure.

of routine, but profitable, work to be done. John Dunn told me that although a DFV rebuild occupied 120 man-hours, his SRE concern once tackled 130 such jobs in a year.

In the early 1970s, then, Cosworth was happy to let the DFV coast along on the tidal wave of its own

Next, Keith and his team turned their attention to the internals of the engine, to reduce windage, and to the repackaging of the accessories, to make it more suitable for one of the newfangled 'ground-effects' cars. Geoff Goddard, who was later to be responsible for the overall design of the GB (turbocharged V6 F1 engine) and the HB (new-generation 75-degree V8 F1 engine for 1989), carried out most of the 'ground-effect' DFV work, listing it as one of his first major projects. Geoff Goddard recalls how Keith used to worry away at any aspect – every aspect – of race engine design, and tell his designers what was needed:

"He used to supply me with one-phrase headings on paper, then a written discussion – 'Valve Gear,' 'Pumps,' or whatever. Below those headings would be the 'first epistle from the mountain.' I can show you books and books of these. They are fabulous. Keith never throws anything away, and he never forgets anything, either …

"Then he would keep coming in, and saying 'I've just thought of …' and sometimes he would have thought a thing through in total detail. In most cases he would have three avenues he would like explored."

As the 1980s dawned, however, the DFV was under attack from all sides, not least by the increasingly powerful and reliable turbocharged engines from

AUTOCAR: 4 JUNE 1977

IN my survey of the DFV's career to that point, headed "Duckworth's Decade," I opened the piece:

"'**I** don't think the DFV is at its limit yet, and I do think it should be possible to get 500bhp from it. Anyway it looks as if we've got to try!' That is a typically trenchant remark from Keith Duckworth, and followed by a lengthy pause for thought.

"… how else can one summarise an engine which is – quite literally – the most successful Grand Prix design of all time? It has raced more times, won more races, been used by more constructors, been built in far greater quantities, and won more World Championships, than any other engine.

"At one point, too, Keith Duckworth confessed his own limitations:

"'Of course I'm surprised and delighted that the DFV has been so competitive for so long. I certainly didn't plan it that way in 1966, and I certainly didn't design the engine to reach 500bhp eventually. I'm far too ignorant to lay out a design with power improvements locked inside'"

THESE words were written, and spoken, at a time when the DFV was celebrating its 100th GP win. But there was a lot more to follow – between 1977 and 1983 the DFV family won another 55 World Championship GP races, while the turbocharged DFX became the engine to use in North American CART/Indy racing.

To celebrate the DFV's 100th F1 World Championship race victory in 1977, this was the entire Cosworth workforce posed around two of the DFV engines. Keith Duckworth took centre stage, with Ben Rood to his right, and with Mike Hall, Alf Vickers and Mike Costin to his left. Dick Scammell and Geoff Goddard are behind Mike Costin's right and left shoulders, respectively.

By that time the DFV was rated at 495bhp, and the DFY came to the line with 520bhp at 11,000rpm. It was an improvement, and very worthwhile too, but it was not enough. The F1 industry in general was already turning its attention towards turbocharged engines, and the DFY had only one win – at Detroit in 1983.

DFX – 'blowing' the DFV ...

In 1975, a turbocharged version of the DFV – later known as the DFX – first appeared at practice for the Indianapolis 500 race in 1975, won its first major CART/Indy race at Pocono in 1976, and went on to become the standard-setting Indy-car race engine for the next decade. Yet this engine, more than any other in Cosworth's armoury, was evolved by a customer first, and by Cosworth afterwards.

CART/Indy racing, in the USA, had specified 2.65-litre turbocharged engines for some time, and there was no pressure for this to be changed. Once the DFV had settled down, Roger Penske persuaded Cosworth to design and build new short-stroke engines, so that he could produce turbocharged versions for racing in this series, but later he changed his mind, and the project languished. Then, in 1974, the Vel's Parnelli Jones team started to develop F1 cars and CART/Indy cars. By using the new short-stroke cranks, and developing its own turbocharging arrangements, it had prototype engines running before the end of the year. As the regulations allowed 80in of turbo pressure (equivalent to 4.5 bar boost over atmospheric pressure), and the early engines were pushing out 750bhp, it took time to keep the early units in one piece.

The breakthrough came when Cosworth – which is to say, Keith Duckworth – began to take an interest. Keith, however, told me that there was an element of chance in this. It was a time when the combination of Ferrari's flat-12 F1 engine, and Niki Lauda as driver, had started to beat the Cosworth-engined cars:

"I was in one of my 'Well, we don't want to expand' periods. We only went into Indy racing because I thought that our F1 business might be dying. So we produced the DFX. Then, instead of dying, our F1 business stood up well, the DFX engine took off like a rocket, and that caused us to expand rapidly once again."

Several of Cosworth's well-known 'names' got involved in the DFX – Geoff Goddard designed a new top end, Graham Dale-Jones had already designed

Renault, Ferrari and BMW. Keith had fought against the turbo revolution (and lost his case – this is explained in depth in the next chapter), but had set his face against designing such a unit. Instead he authorised one final redesign of the faithful DFV, into the short-lived DFY. This design job, carried out for him by an ambitious engineer called Mario Illien, involved the use of a large bore/short stroke configuration, the latest camshaft profiles, and entirely new cylinder head castings, with an extremely narrow valve-opposed angle of 16 degrees. Not only this, but it was 44lb lighter than the DFV.

Although the DFX engine of the 1970s was demonstrably developed from the DFV, it was a 2.65-litre engine, with turbocharging (the turbo is not yet fitted to the engine in this image), and became Indycar's 'engine of choice' for at least a decade.

the crankshafts for the original Penske project, Paul Morgan became the DFX project engineer, and later Malcolm Tyrrell took up that job. In the early days of the DFX engine, Cosworth actually built up DFXs as low-compression normally-aspirated units, then shipped them out to the USA for conversion and completion. In later years, however, it set up a new company – Cosworth Engineering Inc, at Torrance in California – to build, service and rebuild Indycar engines.

As with the DFV, the DFX went through several stages during its competitive life, notably by the introduction of larger bore/shorter stroke versions, different fuel-injection and different maximum boost settings. It was also sold as a 'Cosworth' rather than a 'Ford' engine, that fact being emphasised by the different badging on the cam covers. Walter Hayes tells why:

"I actually suggested to Keith that he call it a Cosworth in the United States. There were people in the United States who wanted to run it, but who had contractual arrangements which precluded them from going with a Ford engine – for example, it would be very difficult for a Chevrolet dealer to do so."

The DFS was the final turbocharged evolution of the long-running DFV V8 design, and was used in North American race cars in the late 1980s.

Never-ending development

One of the last 'secret' development programmes which Keith initiated for the DFV engine family was to investigate desmodromic valve gear. Desmodromic? This is a 'buzz-word' indicating ways of opening and closing valves by mechanical means, without using valve springs. Mercedes-Benz used such methods on its F1 and racing sports car engines of 1954-55, but at the time no other concern tried to follow suit. Keith told me why:

"We seemed to spend most of our time in valve spring trouble – surge trouble, breakages, and other valve gear malfunctions all due to spring problems. To go to desmodromic valve gear looked to be a way of getting out of this trouble. However, we then found that instead of having valve spring trouble, we had

DFZ – AN 'INSTANT' F1 ENGINE

ON 3 October 1986, FISA made sweeping changes to Formula 1 engine regulations. Turbocharged engines were to be emasculated by the imposition of turbo-boost 'pop-off' valves, while a new normally-aspirated 3½-litre engine alternative was to be introduced for 1987.

As ever, several teams turned to Cosworth for help – as ever, in a great hurry. Before the first race of 1987 – the Brazilian GP on 12 April – Cosworth managed to supply a new type of engine, the DFZ, to Tyrrell, AGS, and March. By mid-season Lola had also joined the fray. Using DFZs, Jonathan Palmer (Tyrrell DG016) won the 'normally-aspirated' World Championship of that year.

The DFZ had been produced in about six months – it was a remarkable achievement, even by Cosworth's own speedy standards. In fact Cosworth, Geoff Goddard, and John Hancock, had been lucky, for there was a great deal of 'stretch' in the original DFV layout. Over the years, a series of 'endurance' versions of the versatile DFV had been built, along with a big bore/short stroke development programme for F1 applications, and capacities varied from 2491cc to 3955cc. Along the way, the bore had gone out, from 85.67mm to 90.0mm, while the stroke had varied between 54mm (DFW) and 77.7mm (3.9-litre DFL).

When the time came to develop a 'DFZ' in a hurry, a few minutes' calculation showed that the largest cylinder bore (90mm – as used in DFLs) could be mated to a new 68.6mm crankshaft stroke. At the cost of designing a new crankshaft, the use of DFX connecting rods, and making changes to the cylinder heads, ports, and valves, the 'instant engine' was made available very speedily indeed.

Geoff Goddard subsequently called the DFZ a "reliable customer engine, to fill the grid." In reality, it was more than that. It was good enough for Tyrrell to dominate the 1987 'normally-aspirated' categories, and it was the engine which allowed no fewer than eight under-financed teams to feel their way back from the dizzy (and expensive) heights of turbo power, to the more sensible 1989 levels. Not only that, but the DFR (the most successful normally-aspirated F1 engine of 1988) was a direct descendant of it.

DFV – THE DYNASTY

OVER the years, the DFV family has grown and grown. Type has followed type, success has followed success, and the total delivered horsepower has reached a phenomenal figure. The first DFVs were delivered to Lotus in 1967, and during 1989 the latest DFVs, DFRs and DFSs were going to F1, F3000 and CART/Indy teams all round the world. In April 1989, Marketing Manager Jack Field provided me with some fascinating statistics about sales of the various types:

DFV (the classic 3-litre F1 engine, and its development, the F3000 engine)

COSWORTH built up to engine number 421. The first seven engines for Lotus were out of the numbering system, and 88 complete engine kits had also been supplied for outside engine builder assembly. 421 + 7 + 88 = 516 total engines and kits. [Many more followed in later years.]

DFW (The 2-litre 'Tasman formula' engine)

THESE were all converted DFV engines, having been F1 engines in the F1 season, and Tasman engines in the winter.

DFX (The 2.65-litre turbocharged engine, for CART/Indy racing)

COSWORTH built 347 engines, seven of which were later listed as DFS, plus 110 kits, six of which were DFS kits. 340 + 104 true DFX = 444 engines and kits.

DFY (The early-1980s development of the 3-litre F1 engine)

ENGINE numbers 2 to 21 were really short-stroke DFVs. Engines numbered 1 and 22-27 had different heads, the integral cam carrier, and different valve angles. Designated as DFY = 27 engines.

DFL (The 'endurance' or 'sports car' engine)

36 engines were built, none of them as kits. These engines were both 3.3 and 3.9-litres. Quite a number of DFVs have also been converted to DFL 3.3s by their owners. Designed as DFL = 36 engines.

DFZ (The 3-litre version of the DFV, for late 1980s F1 cars)

COSWORTH built five complete engines, and supplied 75 kits = 80 engines and kits.

DFR (The 'ultimate' redesign of the DFV family, 3½-litres for F1 racing, used only by Benetton in 1988, but by other customers in 1989)

AT that time, there had been 23 built-up engines, and 37 kits = 60 engines. [Many more would be built up to 1991]

DFS (The 1988-1989 development of the turbocharged DFX)

JUST seven engines, and six engine kits = 13 engines in all.

IN 1989 that made up the astonishing total of 1176 complete engines or engine kits, not to mention the enormous number of major components supplied for rebuilding, over the years.

Jack was then anxious to point out, however, that this was not a complete or final story:

"If I were you, I should 'date' the information on the DFV, the DFX and the DFR. We are still working on the 1989 season order book, and the numbers are a moving target!"

Prices, too, had changed considerably over the years. In 1968 the original price of a 'customer' DFV was £7500. The first DFVs provided for F3000 cars cost £25,000 (plus VAT). The April 1989 price for a built and tested DFR was £46,010 (plus VAT). The original price of the turbocharged DFX, in the late 1970s, was $25,000.

Detail changes continued until the early 1990s, mostly development of the F3000 version of the 3-litre DFV. Major castings and components continued to be made after that, such that complete rebuilds were still possible in the mid-2010s, as the DFV passed its 50th birthday.

In the early 1980s Ford started a Group C racing sports car project, the C100, which used 'endurance' long-stroke DFL engines.

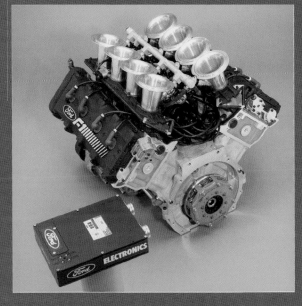

The DFR of 1988 was a root-and-branch redesign of the DFV pedigree, a very effective stop-gap F1 engine for a short period in the company's history.

trouble with all the new pieces, and a fairly difficult manufacturing setup …

"We got a programme going in the early 1980s, it didn't copy anyone, and it was an original concept and layout. We built parts and tested them on rigs. But I stopped the programme, and made myself fairly unpopular. I thought it was all going on for too long, and after I had worked out all the sums for the stressing, I came to the conclusion that we couldn't actually build something of this type that would be strong enough. It kept on failing, and I felt I was vindicated, but some of the engineers thought they could make it work. I thought that my analysis of the problem was reasonable. Either it was never going to work, or it was going to require too much development and redesign to make it work. It was going to need a fundamental redesign, which would throw it right back in time. I wasn't prepared to sanction that …"

The DFV family, in fact, steadfastly refused to die. After winning in F1, it blossomed as an endurance engine (the DFL), then from the mid-1980s it suddenly became the engine to use in F3000. In 1988 Cosworth made more DFV-based engines than ever before, an astonishing come-back when the slump of 1985 is considered. Richard Bulman, Cosworth's managing director since that slack time, was quite unprepared for that:

"I didn't anticipate the F1 explosion, with normally-aspirated engines coming back, and with F3000 becoming so popular, but we were soon in pole position to take advantage of the situation. We went in for a lot of re-organisation of the machine shops – we simply couldn't have met the demand without doing so. In three years we doubled our output of V8 engines, and I believe it cost us no more than £50,000 to make those changes. We were only just in time. Quite a few of the staff were becoming frustrated by having to use the old machining methods, but as everyone had kept on saying that the old engine was going to die out, the changes had never been made."

In that process, Ben Rood's machine shop was able to cut the machining time of a V8 block from 12 weeks to less than a week, and the casting would need to be on only three different machines, rather than the original 30. Even though opposition to the DFV family continued – Ilmor engines for Indy racing, Mugen engines for F3000, Judd engines for F1 – the engine was still alive, kicking and successful at the end of the 1980s. As Jack Field told me, in the spring of 1989:

"At the moment we are still building 110 DFV-family V8 engines a year, or kits of parts to build engines, in four basic forms: DFVs for F3000, the DFRs for F1, the DFX as a 'customer' engine for Indy racing, and the DFS [DFX 'Evolution'] for just two teams in the States. I am building 52 DFRs for 1989 F1 – and I turned down 33 orders! If you ordered an engine today, I would have to say that delivery would be in eight months time, so you've already missed the 1989 season completely. I would immediately want an £8000 deposit to make sure you were serious.

"If you insisted that Cosworth build the engine, well, I would try to do that for you, but a lot would depend on our work on the other F1 engines [the HB, for Benetton, was new at this time]. Otherwise I would have to supply a kit of parts for you to nominate assembly at a company like Mader, Brian Hart, or Swindon Racing. And I couldn't do rebuilds, not at all …"

There will, of course, be an end to DFV sales one day (and manufacture of new pieces, including completely machined cylinder heads and cylinder blocks, continues to the present day, even in the second decade of the 21st century), but no-one is about to forecast the date. Cosworth has been caught that way before.

9: TURBOCHARGING IN F1 – THE FORD V6 PROJECT

"To my mind, the use of turbochargers was always against the rules in F1."

"A turbocharger is a gas turbine which shares its combustion chamber with a piston engine ..."

The new era in Grand Prix racing was born in July 1977, but it made no immediate headlines. The world's first turbocharged Formula 1 car, Renault's V6-engined RS01 model, qualified 21st on the grid for the British GP of 1977 – and no-one thought it significant. Why should they? At the time, the car was thirsty, relatively slow, and dreadfully unreliable – surely the normally-aspirated establishment had nothing to fear?

Not yet, for sure, but the message soon got through. The Renault scored its first points in 1978, its first 'pole position' after practice came in March 1979, and its first win (the French GP, at Dijon) followed in July 1979.

Even so, it took time for other designers to follow suit. The first turbos from Ferrari and BMW followed in 1981, after which everyone joined in. Even though it had already developed a turbocharged engine for racing in the United States, however, [the DFX], Cosworth was in no hurry to follow the fashion. The DFV kept on winning races – lots of them – and the first-generation turbos kept blowing up. Not only that, but Keith Duckworth was convinced that the concept of turbocharging was 'illegal' according to the regulations then governing F1:

"I made myself clear when accepting the RAC's Diamond Jubilee Trophy in 1978. That was the point where I stood up and said that turbocharging was all wrong, and I also took the limit of compounded two-stroke engines, which could have produced any power figure that you wanted.

"Actually, as a result of that, the authorities banned two-stroke engines, but they didn't ban the turbocharger. To my mind, the use of turbochargers was always against the rules in F1, and in any case the 'equivalency factor' defined by the authorities [3.0-litres normally-aspirated, but 1.5-litres with forced induction] was grossly unbalanced.

"What happened, when the rules were being written for 1966, was that 3.0-litre engines were going to be allowed, and the existing 1.5-litre engines of 1961-65 were going to be made obsolete. There were all kinds of complaints – 'We won't be able to get new 3.0-litre engines' – so some bright spark in Paris then said: 'OK, now we're specifying petrol, to give people with 1.5-litre engines a chance to compete in the new Formula, we'll allow them to fit superchargers.'

"Don't forget that between 1946 and 1953, 1.5-litre supercharged cars had been expected to compete against 4.5-litre normally-aspirated machines, though alcohol fuel was allowed in those days. In fact, for 1966 I don't think anyone ever produced a supercharged 1.5-litre engine – I know that Coventry-Climax were asked to do one, but they refused.

"When the rules were written, and published, only the word 'supercharging' was used, and 'turbocharging' was not mentioned at all. At that date, turbochargers were really only for diesel trucks, though I believe GM had fitted them to a few Corvair cars too."

Keith is adamant that there is a vast difference in operation between the supercharged, and the turbocharged, engine:

"In a supercharged engine you can affect the weight of charge getting into the cylinder, albeit at the cost of taking work off the engine to drive the compressor. Then you only have the stroke of the piston to do expansion work, which brings its own limits. On the other hand, a turbocharger is an air compressor driven by a turbine, and the turbine itself is an expansion motor. Therefore a turbocharger not only allows you to 'fiddle the books' on the weight of charge, but it allows you unlimited expansion capacity as well – and that can be a virtuous or a vicious circle. It means that the effective capacity of a turbocharged engine has an entirely different meaning from that of a supercharged engine."

"You could also say, as another approach to it, that a turbocharger is a gas turbine which shares its combustion chamber with a piston engine. That means that you have two engines, which is illegal and – by the way – the rules also state that gas turbines are forbidden.

"At one point Ferrari was actually injecting fuel into the turbocharger, to make it speed up quicker and kill the lag, which rather proves that they were treating their installation as two different engines."

It is no wonder that, at this point in an interview, Keith collapsed into gales of laughter, unable to come to terms with what he saw as the stupidity of motor racing's administrators:

"The limits of the turbocharged engine, therefore, are connected with mechanical strength and thermal problems – the capacity of the engine is virtually meaningless."

Walter Hayes told me that he believed Keith always to be a purist, as far as race engine design was concerned,

Right from the start of the turbo era in Formula 1, Keith Duckworth (centre) kept a careful eye on what rival engine manufacturers were doing. This was Silverstone 1977, where mechanics were working on the 1½-litre turbocharged Renault engine.

and that Keith always regarded the turbocharger as an unnatural and nasty thing, because it was not really an improvement to the engine, but really a crude way of force-feeding it. In the late 1970s, Keith argued, long and loud, that turbocharged engines should be banned, but in most cases he could not even get people to understand what he was saying, never mind to agree with him:

"The telling part of the FIA appeal court, on legality, was that it [turbocharging] was accepted by taxation authorities throughout the world, that the fitting of a turbocharger did not change the capacity of an engine for taxation purposes. Of course, the real stupidity of it all is that it is the world's taxation authorities which are wrong!" It is easy to see why Keith, Mike, and Cosworth Engineering were anxious to get turbocharged F1 cars banned – their future business, after all, was at stake.

No-one, surely, could blame Keith for wanting to preserve F1 as a normally-aspirated formula, when his DFV engines were so dominant? In the Renault turbo's first F1 race, for example, 20 of the 26 starters used DFV engines, these being shared between 11 teams. For Cosworth, F1 was a good business to be in – and the company wanted it to stay that way. Keith lost his fight to ban turbochargers. Being a man of principle, who was not about to change his opinions, it was years before he could then be persuaded to see a new Cosworth turbo engine designed for F1:

"I thought it would all lead to a great escalation in cost and complexity, and I did not think it would be very useful technology for production cars. This problem became worse and worse as soon as we came to special fuels, which compounded the problem.

"If people aren't worried about costs, then I am totally in favour of useful technology, preferably with commercial value, being derived from racing. In fact I don't think that diesel engines, two-stroke engines, turbochargers, gas turbines or even Wankel engines ought to be banned from racing if there is to be a technological challenge. The only thing I object to is to try to equalise everything with equivalencies which are totally meaningless.

"I thought it was against everyone's interests to allow turbocharged engines to continue. There was a lot of talk about motor racing becoming too expensive in the 1970s, and the chances of F1 dying out were regarded as high. Everyone, or so they said, wanted to make racing cheaper, and I was under the belief that this was the serious opinion of the governing body.

"I wasn't totally alone in my views. The whole of British motor racing got together and fought their battles – this being the whole basis of the FOCA/FISA split of the early 1980s. FOCA wanted to ban turbos, but Renault, Ferrari and BMW didn't. It nearly split F1 racing right down the middle. Now we have the Concorde Agreement, as a compromise. It all ended in a very bloody draw, and some fairly daft agreements.

"The only meaningful basis on which all types of car could be made 'equivalent' would be to impose fuel consumption limits. It needn't matter how efficiently each engine uses its air (in other words it needn't matter how large, or small, the capacity is), but how it uses its fuel. Fuel is the thing you pay for, and if you are forced to make an engine – any engine – fuel efficient, then that really is a technological challenge I relish."

By the early 1980s, however, the 'illegal' turbocharged engines had become reliable, and the turbo cars had started to win a lot of races. This was the four-year trend:

1980: 15 races, 3 turbo-car victories, 11 to Cosworth DFV
1981: 16 races, 5 turbo-car victories, 8 to Cosworth DFV
1982: 16 races, 8 turbo-car victories, 8 to Cosworth DFV
1983: 15 races, 12 turbo-car victories, 3 to Cosworth DFV/DFY

The last normally-aspirated Cosworth victory came in the Detroit GP of June 1983, and after that the Cosworth-engined runners were struggling. Yet, even at that time, Keith had not begun to think about a replacement. Walter Hayes, meanwhile, had become vice-president of public affairs at Ford-USA, and thought he knew why:

"I concluded that Keith genuinely thought that he had produced one masterpiece, and he was reluctant to drag himself up to go and do it all again. After all, if you have painted the Mona Lisa, or you have built the Eiffel Tower, it's difficult to repeat yourself.

"By designing the DFV, Keith had already created the one perfect thing in his lifetime, and although it was still a great engine, it had been hit hard by regulations, and by the activities of other people. I honestly think that he was resentful, that although he had probably designed the finest engine in the world, he was going to have to try again. Make no mistake, it was the finest, and if the formula had stayed at 3 litres it would probably still be unbeatable today."

"Once we got a World Championship race in Detroit and I was much involved in that, lots of people were persistent about the need for Ford to do another Grand Prix engine. It seemed to me that the time was ripe to start talking to Cosworth about a new turbocharged engine. But Keith still wasn't having any – whenever I raised the question, he would immediately change the subject!"

That last Ford-Cosworth victory in Detroit, it seems, was an important occasion:

"After Tyrrell had won that race, I took Ken and his wife back to my home in Ann Arbor [west of Detroit], where we gave them a special dinner in honour of the win. I thought that this was the time to start pumping. I actually said to Ken Tyrrell: 'I can't persuade him to do a turbo engine, in fact I can't even persuade him to think about one. See what you can do.' Later on I had a call from Ken, who said: 'I think he's ready to talk.' I wasn't at all convinced, but I invited him out to Detroit, and we started from there." At which point a clever bit of Hayes psychology helped to change things:

"I know enough about Keith, to be able to pull his leg, to get him into the right mood. The way to do it was not to go to fancy hotels, but to have him at my home, where my wife would cook him things like toad-in-the-hole, Lancashire hot-pot and other Northern dishes.

"When I was in the States, and he came over to see us, at first we used to go to dinner in hotels. But my wife tumbled to the secret very quickly. She said to me: 'If you really want to know what Keith's thinking, then you're doing it all wrong. You automatically pick up the wine list, but what you really need to do is to get some beer into him!'

"She was right. Also, at home, we would give him real cups of tea, and offer him as much lager and good British beer as he could drink – after a few glasses of lager, the inspiration really began to flow. Then we would start to have long conversations on the subject ..."

The problem was that although Keith was confident that Cosworth could produce a race-winning F1 turbo engine, he still objected to the whole philosophy, and the doubtful sporting 'legality' of such engines. In any case, the Cosworth company of 1983 was very different from that of 1966, when the original DFV had been designed. As Chapter 11 makes clear, Keith had sold out to United Engineering Industries (UEI) in 1980, the company was vastly larger and less flexible than it had once been, and it was just about to embark on heavy investment in the turbocharged YB-Series Sierrra engine. Keith, as usual, was looking further ahead than almost anyone else in motorsport:

"There was already so much talk of doing away with turbo engines that it seemed unlikely that they would carry on for long. There was talk about changing engine capacities, banning turbos, everything. I really couldn't imagine anyone really settling down to a fuel consumption formula. The entrants were talking about too much power, there were drivers' campaigns as well. Everything looked as if it was about to change."

The pressures, from all sides, eventually paid off:

"There was a lot of internal pressure, to the effect that Cosworth couldn't afford to be out of F1 racing, without a turbo engine. In the end, I said: 'OK, we will have a go at doing a turbo engine. We will need financial support to do this, so I will approach Ford, to get that support.'"

Walter Hayes, in fact, had already persuaded his fellow directors in the United States to provide the backing. Along with Mike Kranefuss, who had moved to Ford-USA at the beginning of the 1980s to rejuvenate the motorsport effort:

"I went along to a much more formal meeting than in 1965, and presented the proposal for a new Cosworth-designed engine, thinking that regulations stability had been achieved. This time, though, it was to be a Ford-USA project, financed from Detroit. The numbers were much larger than last time."

In the meantime FISA's controversial president, Jean-Marie Balestre, had visited Ford's policy makers, and assured them that its turbo engine investment would remain valid until the end of the 1980s. Mike Kranefuss then hatched a 'Five Year Plan' – two years of design and testing, followed by three seasons of racing. Even so, at this time Keith was sure that Kranefuss would favour his fellow-countryman Erich Zakowski (of Zakspeed) for any new engine work, and said as much to Walter Hayes in a transatlantic telephone conversation which Kranefuss (in Hayes' office) overheard!

Keith's decision to go ahead only came after a lot of discussion:

"Mike, Geoff Goddard and I spent a lot of time trying to plot which way the rules were likely to go. Every week, when we had actually decided what was favourite, and what was the sensible concept for an engine, it looked as if the rules would change again. FISA was proposing to change the engine size, they were talking about orifice limitations, fuel limitations, progressively less fuel year by year, and boost limitations – all these things were discussed.

"This was all very well if someone already had an engine – then they would have no option but to do the best they could, with what they had. But to start off, to

Ed Blanch was Chairman of Ford of Europe in 1984, when that company approved the start of the 1000bhp GB turbocharged F1 engine.

Jim Capolongo was President of Ford of Europe when GB development first began.

Mike Kranefuss (centre) was Director of Motorsport at Ford of Europe in the 1980s when the 1½-litre GB was conceived. Here he is seen sharing the victor's champagne with John Fitzpatrick at a saloon car race.

design an engine, to rules that you didn't really think had much chance of still being the same rules when the engine was finished – well that was bloody impossible.

"In the end, we had to design an engine, and hope that when it was running, that the rules wouldn't have changed to mess it all up. Well, in the end, that's exactly what happened – by the time our engine was on the pace, FISA chopped the boost limit, twice, first to 4.0 bar, then to 2.5 bar."

At first, therefore, Keith and his chief racing engine designer, Geoff Goddard, agreed that they needed an engine to be optimised for strict fuel limitations and that, according to Keith's analysis, favoured very small cars, with a four-cylinder engine:

"If we were going to have to run relatively slowly, and with modest power outputs, there was nothing wrong with a four-cylinder engine. So at the end of 1983, that was how we started. We didn't go for an all-new engine, because I thought the aluminium block of the BD, with Nicasil coating for the bores, would be sufficient. We started with the same basic castings for head and block, as with other BDs, but it wasn't long before we re-did the head."

It was not, however, a simple conversion, and was certainly not a specially-prepared version of the BDT which later powered the Ford RS200 model:

"We had just one turbocharger, with a view to it being a divided housing component. At that stage we were proposing to drive it through the crankshaft as well, so that we could cure the response problems. In the end, after an extensive evaluation, we decided to use an infinitely variable drive gear, using the Ford CVT belt from the nose of the crankshaft, along with an electronic engine management system to control everything. We even thought it would be useful as damper for the torsionals."

We were thinking that horsepower was going to be restricted to about 650bhp – by fuel or by air restrictions – and that's what prompted the choice of a four-cylinder.

We thought that our compounding arrangement would help the response and the fuel efficiency. I'd actually thought very deeply about compounding, which wasn't specifically banned by the regulations.

"However, if there was to be a problem with the regulations, I thought we could always fit an over-running clutch in the drive system, so that we couldn't transmit power back to the crankshaft. Now, although all this might sound heavy, the alloy block allowed us still to have a very light engine, all in all.

"We'd actually schemed out a 180-degree six-cylinder engine – a flat-six engine – as well, which also lent itself to turbo-compounding, for we could have fitted this on top of the engine between the intakes ..."

And so it began. Cosworth built the variable speed drive, made epicyclic gearboxes to drive the turbocharger, rig-tested the variable-speed drives and their control systems, and tested driving from one turbocharger to another. Then came the first major setback – the Ford CVT belt was suddenly withdrawn as the programme slipped.

This had been a false dawn for Ford, for Van Doornes were having great difficulty in making suitable belts. Although test bed engines of 1497cc, which ran in 1984, used most, but not all, of the complex turbocharger control gear, original runs, in fact, were done with the aid of an external compressor to provide boosted air.

But there was worse to come. In a series of test-bed breakdowns, so graphically caught in Patrick Uden's Channel 4 TV documentary, the new four-cylinder engine kept breaking its crankshafts when running 3.0 bar boost at 11,000rpm. Cosworth, however, traced this to the rear of the crankshaft, which failed in bending. The crank was redesigned along with the flywheel, and they were on the way to solving all its difficulties.

Stuart Turner, affectionately recalling the work he had done with Keith, thinks that Cosworth underestimated the difficulty of getting back 'on the pace' in the mid-1980s:

"I think you could say that Cosworth had got a bit complacent, and maybe expected to come back in [with a new engine] and resume their lofty stature. But if this was meant to be a 'Royal Return,' they found that there were other royalists already on the scene.

"Cosworth, too, had changed since the late 1960s. Keith commented on this to me at 25th anniversary time – he called in every member of the staff to give them a present, individually, and found that it took him all day to complete the task. Maybe, in the mid-1980s, they were just a bit slow to react."

For many reasons, however, Keith decided to cancel the four-cylinder project completely, and start again:

"We had foreseen which way the rules would go, and we were wrong. Power outputs were well above 650bhp, and rising towards 800bhp, and I didn't feel that our siamesed-bore block would do the job."

Geoff Goddard, who claims not to go to motor races to see what the opposition is doing in case it confuses him, now thinks that Cosworth set its sights too low in the beginning:

"People were probably already racing with more than 700bhp when we started the project, but at that sort of figure, in the first place, the life of our crankshafts could be measured in minutes, not hours. Incidentally, we always worried that if our turbo-compounding worked, and we won races with it, that it might have been banned overnight."

Keith decided on a new approach:

"It was time to start again, and therefore we decided that we would make a conventionally turbocharged V6, very small and light. We had a few early cylinder block problems, but otherwise it was always remarkably reliable."

Even then, the decision wasn't simple, for at the time FISA was still trying to decide whether or not to impose a 1.2-litre limit for 1986. Ford-USA finally gave Cosworth the go-ahead for a completely new design in September 1984, and this was where Geoff Goddard really came into his own. Geoff now had enough design know-how to tackle almost all the work himself, for he had rarely

ignored anything which he had seen, and experienced, since he had joined Cosworth in 1971. Walter Hayes summed up Geoff's character admirably:

"There are several people at Northampton who walk like Keith, talk like Keith, and who behave like Keith! Geoff Goddard is one of them. My wife once spied him at a party and said: 'Who is that chap?' I told her, and she responded: 'I was looking at him from the back, and I thought it was Keith Duckworth.' I thought for a second, then replied: 'Well, it probably is, actually.'

"If you are a successful leader, a successful genius of that kind, then people will clone themselves from you; the manner is adapted. In a way, with Geoff Goddard, Keith reproduced himself."

The new approach yielded the quirk of two project titles – Ford called it the 'TEC Turbo,' while Cosworth decided to call it 'GB.' The Ford acronym stands for Turbocharged Engine, Cosworth. The choice of GB, by Cosworth, had nothing to do with national pride, but was much more prosaic. The original Cosworth-designed V6, for Ford's Capri RS3100 race programme, had been Mike Hall's GA series. What could be more logical, therefore, than to use the next in the sequence – GB – for the next V6 for Ford?

This time, it was decided to produce a conventionally turbocharged engine, one turbo to each bank, and well out at the side where they could be properly packaged in a chassis. Cosworth, as usual, produced the first engine very rapidly indeed. Once again, Keith was spending more and more of his life at home, Geoff Goddard would visit him every week or so to discuss concepts, or agree on layouts, but essentially the TEC/GB was a Geoff Goddard, and not a Keith Duckworth, design.

"The first actual component drawings were released in December 1984, that was the cylinder head, and we first ran the engine on 1 August 1985. We had been doing layouts for a month or so before the start, so it took about ten months to design the engine. The only thing we got wrong at first," Geoff Goddard told me, "was in deciding what power to go for. We aimed for a power level, which we instantly got, we then turned up for the first race, found everyone else disappearing into the distance, and decided that we hadn't been very bright.

"The problem was that we had designed it to run on pump fuel, and we were gazumped right at the end of the design when people started using 'rocket fuel.'" Mike Kranefuss agrees – and disagrees:

"I think there was a degree of ignorance about the opposition at Cosworth. The Honda engine was only on

Designed in 1984, tested in 1985, and raced in 1986 and 1987, the GB was a remarkably small, but immensely powerful, turbocharged V6 F1 engine, which finally produced a reliable 1000bhp. As can be seen, the manifolding was arranged so that each turbocharger fitted in a side-pod of the Benetton.

COSWORTH – THE SEARCH FOR POWER

the horizon, the Renault engine didn't produce a threat enough to frighten Keith, and I think Cosworth should have been sending people out to the races to get a feel for what was happening. Cosworth thought they knew it all by that time. People had started, but only just started, using funny fuels, though the idea had been around for some time."

The difference in potential between ordinary fuels and special fuels was immense, this allowing F1 engine power outputs to double, from 600bhp to more than 1200bhp, in about four years. Cosworth had no say in the choice of team to use the tiny new 120-degree V6, this being a Ford-USA decision influenced right from the top, as Mike Kranefuss confirmed:

"I had already talked to Carl Haas about F1, but I had also talked to Bernie Ecclestone, Frank Williams, and Lotus too. But at first I didn't want to go with Haas – the last thing I wanted was to go with a new team. Then one day the Chairman of Ford, Don Peterson, called me – he was a very staunch supporter of motorsport – and said he had just taken a call from Jim Dutt of Beatrice. Dutt, he said, was going to support Haas, and since Beatrice was not only a big company, but it also controlled Avis, the car hire people, which meant business for Ford and a ready supply of Goodyear tyres for the F1 team.

"Peterson said it was my decision … [but, in effect, that decision was being made for him] … and in the end I signed with Haas, with Beatrice sponsorship.

"Well, it didn't help that the Beatrice thing dissolved when Dutt was ousted from Beatrice, and that was

This stunning cutaway drawing of the Beatrice-Haas car of 1985/1986 shows how the tiny 120-degree GB V6 fitted into the tub, and confirms the position of the turbochargers.

before the Ford engine even ran in a car."

The new Haas car was designed by Lola, and was sometimes called a Haas-Lola, sometimes a FORCE (after the name of the new F1 company), sometimes a combination of all three. Cosworth really didn't mind what the name was – the fact was that the car was not competitive! The team was established near London, with ex-McLaren managing director Teddy Mayer running it. When the new Cosworth V6 turbo first ran in the car, the drivers (Alan Jones and Patrick Tambay) commented on its smoothness, but that it lacked power, which was in the order of 700/750bhp. Only three engines were race-ready by that time. When Alan Jones gave the car its racing debut at Imola in 1986, it was embarrassingly slow:

Mike Kranefuss: "We were way, way, off the pace. It was devastating for me, because I knew there couldn't be an answer overnight – you couldn't just crank up the boost and get more power. We were in dire straits. For Keith it must have been a tremendously painful situation. I would have wished I could be in Alaska. The race was a total non-event."

Keith Duckworth: "We had designed it to run on petrol, with a 6.5:1 compression ratio, but that was miles away from what we could run on special fuels."

For the record, on that occasion, the fastest practice lap, at Imola, was by Ayrton Senna's Lotus-Renault turbo (1min 25.05sec), while Jones's Lola lapped in 1min 30.087sec, and started 21st in the grid. Patrick Tambay was 2.8 seconds quicker in the 'interim' Hart-engined car. In the race the car circulated as high as ninth place, but broke its gear linkage, and suffered a split water radiator.

No-one was impressed by this early showing – Mike Kranefuss described it as Cosworth's "****-up" and suggested they should do something about it, straight away, whereas Keith was critical of the car's preparation. For the rest of 1986 Cosworth pressed ahead with improvements – higher compression ratios, different fuels, modified cylinder heads. The first 7.5:1 compression engine appeared in July, the first 8.0:1 engine in September. By the end of the year the engine was producing up to 1000bhp in race qualifying trim – an improvement of about 300bhp made in less than a season. Even Keith was surprised by this:

"It was all a big multiplying game. For every half ratio [on compression] we went up, the exhaust temperature dropped a fair lump, and the engine went 25bhp better. But it wasn't easy – we needed different pistons and quite a lot of setting-up time every time we made a change. We were feeling for detonation all the time. The peak pressures went up and up, and so did the mechanical loadings." "As we went on, it was almost all good news, because the structure was strong enough – every time we went up on compression, the fuel consumption stayed the same, the inlet temperature to the turbocharger turbine dropped, and we could actually run leaner ..."

By 1987, after less than one year's racing, Cosworth was able to run at the 4.0-bar boost limit which FISA had applied, and although several engines were lost due to failings in the special fuel supplied, at the end of the season it was a reliable 1000bhp engine, as competitive, and sometimes ahead of, the dominant Honda unit. Not only that, but individual engines were running for up to 600 miles between rebuilds. A pool of 25 engines, all owned by Ford-USA, was made available to service one team.

The Haas/Lola team, on the other hand, had never been able to produce properly reliable cars, the loss of Beatrice sponsorship had been a severe blow to the team's finances, and the result was that Ford decided to switch teams. Geoff Goddard summed up, rather bitterly:

"The first year was almost wasted, because it was such a poor team that could never run the car, and we were never able to do much work."

Mike Kranefuss told me how complex the first few months then became:

"Things went sour for Carl Haas. He had been well-funded by Beatrice, then he had to start looking for other sponsors. He started being a bit stingy with the F1 operation. I decided that we had to move the engine to another team. Many of them thought that Cosworth could make the engine competitive, but others wanted money as well as free engines, if given the chance. Keith wanted Cosworth to have the choice of teams for 1987, but politically that wasn't possible."

Then there was the case of Bernie Ecclestone buying the Haas/FORCE operation. Did he really think he could buy the rights to the Ford-Cosworth V6 turbo in that way? Mike Kranefuss heard about this, in a roundabout way:

"It was in Portugal, when relations between Carl Haas, Teddy Mayer and myself were really bitter, that Bernie Ecclestone told men that his driver, Riccardo Patrese, was going to drive our car the very next day! Nobody had told me – not Carl, not Teddy, nobody. I was really pissed off, the car was still breaking things, and I just didn't want that to happen. I found out, later,

that they had started talking to Bernie about selling the team as early as May 1986.

"I had already got to know Peter Collins, at Benetton, and he then told me that Bernie had told Luciano Benetton that he would soon control the Ford V6 engine. I liked Collins, and I liked Benetton, so I recommended to Ford in Detroit that we either pulled out of F1, or that we looked for a new team, and that it should be Benetton.

"Keith was very good. Although he was very unhappy with what had happened in 1986, he told us that he wanted Cosworth to stay in F1 with this engine."

The last few months of 1986 were traumatic for many companies, teams, and individuals. Haas had a three-year agreement with Ford, which had to be dissolved (and in the end, Ford had to make a financial settlement), Ford's 'top-brass' had to be mollified, while Mike Kranefuss and Keith Duckworth had to rebuild a relationship which had gone wrong.

Keith had been disappointed, and very vocal, about the failings of the Haas-Lola team, while Mike Kranefuss says that he had found Keith, at various times, cynical, sympathetic, cold, supportive, and enthusiastic. Keith, in fact, was a normal, warm-blooded, human being who could not accept the way that his designers' best efforts were at times being negated by failures at the race track.

By mid-1987 the Cosworth-engined Benetton B187 was almost on the pace, regularly qualifying on the second row of the grid, and (in the hands of Thierry Boutsen and Teo Fabi) regularly finishing in the points. The problem was, that although Geoff Goddard was sure that in 1987 the Cosworth engine was racing with the same horsepower as the omnipotent Honda V6 turbo, if not slightly more, the Benetton car itself was not as finely honed, or as effective, as the all-conquering Williams-Hondas.

The engine, which had started life in 1986 with a 10,500rpm limit, was now regularly running to 12,000rpm, but if drivers missed gears when changing down for corners, read-outs sometimes exceeded 16,000rpm, and according to Goddard no engine ever dropped a valve.

Then, late in 1987, FISA broke yet another of its promises about technical stability, performed yet another of its somersaults, and issued two decisions. One was that turbocharged F1 engines were to be reduced to a maximum of 2.5-bar boost in 1988, and the other was that turbocharged engines would be completely banned from the end of that year. Just as the

When the original GB-powered Beatrice-Haas F1 car was complete in 1986, it tested at Ford Motorsport's Boreham airfield. Here, posing with the car, are Patrick Tambay (in the car) and (left to right) Teddy Mayer, Walter Hayes, Keith Duckworth and Alan Jones.

The Cosworth GB was a complex but very compact 1½-litre V6, with a 120-degree vee cylinder block, and two turbochargers, one for each bank of three cylinders. As the engine fitted ahead of the transmission/rear axle, this was the rear view. Fresh air trunking from the air intake to the inlet manifolds is yet to be added.

Cosworth V6 turbo had made its reputation (and, make no mistake, there was a queue of hopeful customers forming at Northampton at this time), FISA proposed to kill it off.

This was a body blow to Cosworth, where spirits had been rising as the engine showed its worth. Was it worth redeveloping the engine? Ford, frankly, was not happy to finance another upheaval, as Mike Kranefuss told me:

"By this time the F1 programme had less than total support from my management. We had two alternatives for 1988 – either to continue with the V6, spend a lot of money, and use all available engineering and design capacity, or we could start again with a normally-aspirated engine.

"With the Cosworth V6 turbo, we could certainly match the Honda, but the total picture was that we didn't have the best total team. We would probably have been on pole a few times, maybe even won a race or two, but we would not have been able to focus on the future.

"At that point we thought that we had a viable 5-valve Yamaha alternative to the DFZ. So we had discussions with Benetton, asking them what they wanted to do. Some of them wanted to continue with the turbo, especially as we had made such great improvements towards the end of 1987, but others were saying, let's get on with the future."

Cosworth's then managing director, Richard Bulman, reminded me that Cosworth's commitment to the V6 turbo was, in any case, as heavy as the company could bear:

"We were very stretched with the V6 turbo. It was a very demanding programme. At peak we had more than 100 people working on that project alone, to catch up on the years of lost development, and that was just to supply one F1 team. That was to keep up with just 25 engines. Honda, at the time, was reputed to have 400 people to supply two teams, their budget was 10-20 times higher than ours, and we know they built 135 engines in that last year!"

Keith Duckworth was happy to kill off the turbocharged F1 engine:

"We were not big enough to waste further technological effort on a dying art, on something which I did not think had any relevance. It was a waste of scarce mind-power, to do something as frivolous as that. In any case, if we had tried to drop the boost to 2.5-bar, the engine needed to run faster, but our engine wasn't designed to run faster. I simply didn't want to do it.

"Even so, among the designers there was a vast enthusiasm for keeping going, a frustration that the engine had been designed, but not actually proved. Let's face it, we had come up, on a par, with the Honda in less than two years. Someone had a half-hearted go at making one run with 2.5 bar boost, but it was never a serious effort. By the end of 1987 it was all over, really."

Cosworth, therefore, repossessed all the engines, and stored them away in Northampton, where some of them still remain. As far as I know, no-one outside Cosworth has ever seen such an engine stripped out, and all knowledge of vital details like bore/stroke ratios, port shapes, cylinder head fixing arrangements, and all other structural details, remain secret. Richard Bulman took an upbeat view of the programme which was, let's not forget, totally funded by Ford:

"I think we learned quite a lot from it. In the end, we had the best turbo engine in F1, I don't think there's any doubt about that. The engine was extremely sound, though we simply didn't have the manpower and the budget to meet Honda head-on."

Mike Kranefuss, practical man though he is, certainly didn't want to see the engines locked away for ever:

"It would be stupid to throw them away. I gave a couple to Ford's Engine Design/Engine Engineering divisions in the USA and in Europe. Bernie Ecclestone wanted one or two for the Haas-Lola cars he bought in the takeover, and Peter Collins of Benetton would like one or two.

"One day, maybe, there will be a formula which suits them, or maybe we could use the block and the heads."

One day, who knows …

With the new turbocharged GB F1 engine now on its way to full development, and developing 1000bhp in race trim, this was the layout of the new Benetton B187 which was designed around it. By comparison with several other turbo engines of the day, this engine was very small – and the B187 was probably the most powerful car on the grid at that time.

10: COMPANY INTO GROUP – WORCESTER, WELLINGBOROUGH, UEI AND CARLTON

"It was Alf who originally said to me: 'We'll be in a hell of a mess if you die.'"

By the mid-1970s, Cosworth was still expanding rapidly, and before long it was to open a new high-technology foundry at Worcester. In the 1980s a large production and assembly plant was to be erected at Wellingborough, and, before the decade was over, both facilities were being doubled in size.

An independent Cosworth company might have been able to finance such a massive expansion, but it would never have been as simple as it looked, especially as Keith and Mike were not obviously grooming a successor to take over from them when they retired. In the late 1970s, I had asked Keith why he had not begun to expand Cosworth into a broadly-based consultancy concern, effectively as a British-based rival to Porsche, which was doing the same thing at the same time:

"I don't think that's possible, at this stage. There aren't enough really bright people around, in England, for us to do that."

Mike Costin later countered this statement, in the down-to-earth way that balanced Duckworth so much in 30 years, by suggesting that:

"The geniuses, like Keith, can't do all the work. Most of it has to be tackled by lesser mortals. There is usually a supply of what we might call lesser mortals. Young British engineers are knocking on our door all the time."

Later, Keith would modify his views, as Cosworth took on more and more work on engines, though neither he, nor UEI, was tempted to move into other automobile-based activities. There was quite enough to learn, Cosworth decided, and quite enough business to be won, by concentrating on engine work.

There seemed to be little doubt that Cosworth was much the most capable engine-design company in Europe, and, arguably, the world. As one seasoned Cosworth-watcher told me, Honda would need 200 people (and probably *had* 200 people) to get the results regularly achieved by ten designers at Cosworth. The ever-confident Geoff Goddard, when asked where a customer would go if he didn't like the look of Cosworth, quipped:

"Well, you're in big trouble, aren't you?"

One ex-employee, who had better not be named, remembers one significant occasion at Northampton in the 1970s:

"There was one time when the staff wanted to get a union into Cosworth. Keith heard about this, gathered everyone into the canteen, and calmly stated: 'If the union comes into Cosworth, I'm leaving, I'll close it down,' and that was the end of that little episode!"

From the first 20 years of its existence, Cosworth was purely a design, development, machining and assembly concern. Its premises were always full of work, its facilities overcrowded, and it relied, to a great extent, on its suppliers. The suppliers did their best, but by Cosworth standards this was often not good enough. In particular, the company suffered badly from the variable quality of castings and forgings which had to be bought in.

The forging issue was dealt with by setting up a forge in Northampton. This was needed to produce pistons, and the problem was eventually solved by purchasing redundant plant from Hepworth and Grandage.

Cosworth is famous for many reasons, but it is not generally known that the company shared with Mahle of West Germany a peerless reputation for piston manufacture, in all sizes, all types, and for all manner of cars. Annual sales were measured in tens of thousands, with Cosworth pistons being supplied for engines as diverse as TWR Jaguar V12s, Austin-Rover Metro 6R4s, and NASCAR V8s, and as replacements for almost every competition engine in the business – Toyota, Nissan, Mazda, Yamaha, Suzuki, and Honda among many others. But initially the casting problem was difficult to resolve, as Keith confirmed:

"Our experience of purchasing complicated castings, like 4-valve cylinder heads, was variable to say the least. Some batches would be good, and others would be seriously porous. The foundry we were using – Aeroplane & Motor – was very good, but it couldn't control the porosity. Sometimes we'd be well on with machining something when we struck trouble, and unless we had large reserve stocks we would then be in terrible trouble with deliveries.

"It was the early DFX heads – those used where the engines were boosted to 80in of mercury – which gave most trouble. If there was any porosity around the valve seats, we used to get heads back looking as if they had been flame-cut. We were getting a bad name for having heads that could hardly survive. I was fed up with that. My view was that if it was possible to supply good castings some of the time, it must also be possible to supply good castings all the time. There must be a set of circumstances which would guarantee good castings.

"Foundries would admit that they had a 'housekeeping' problem, and that a lot of 'black art' methods had to be employed. These were old skills, and, as the old craftsmen retired, those old skills were dying out; supplies were getting progressively worse. Therefore, I decided to set up a foundry, to prove that it was possible to cast such things. If, by rigorous measurement, and control of the parameters, we could cast something right, we ought to be able to do it the following week, the following year, or whatever."

What followed was a typically enterprising Cosworthian manoeuvre by Keith and Mike, which confounded the rest of industry. Not only did they decide to start it without expert foundry people ("otherwise they would convert it back into a black art situation again ...") but they decided it had to be remote from Northampton.

Keith and Mike wanted it to be far enough away from Northampton for it to be an awkward trip, so that no-one from Northampton would have a good excuse to "just nip over to the foundry for a while."

"We consulted experts, and this produced the name of Dr John Campbell, who had spent his time researching into porosity and other things in foundries. He struck us as having a fair idea of the problem [that is Duckworth-speak, to say that he was impressed ...], he said he had a cure, and he introduced us to zircon sand and a few other features.

"I then made one of my own contributions: 'There is this pump that appeals to me, it looks right to feed metal from the furnace to the moulds, it allows you to fill how you want, and it should be programmable because it is electronically controlled. We should be able to fill up from underneath, to hold the "head," and that looks like what we need.' John Campbell had an urge to live in the Worcester area because he loved the Malverns, so that is where we set up shop. John installed a pilot plant, gathered a few research people round him, and started out. Alf controlled it, and we hoped it would produce good castings."

Cosworth looked afresh at every aspect of casting technology, not least that of correctly assembling and designing the cores:

"In those days core locations were too sloppy. You got highly individual castings, therefore a lot of averaging had to be done at the machining stage. It was always a big problem, and very time-consuming. We decided we had to get core locations absolutely right, and we also wanted repeatability. We also wanted to turn Worcester from something of a 'boffin' establishment to one which could produce a pile of heads. This meant that Mike [Costin] had to spend a lot of time over there.

"The problem was that soon it was eating its head off financially and there was a limit to how much money I could afford to lose there. We were already into electron-beam microscopes, research laboratories and a lot of kit, but we weren't actually making many heads. It needed a real energy pill ..."

This, then, was the point at which Keith and Mike looked round for a managing director to turn round the Worcester operation. It was typical of Keith and Mike that they chose "brightness, rather than experience," which is where Bob Smith came in:

"The foundry had been set up in the late 1970s, but I arrived in November 1982. I didn't have any previous castings experience, in fact I had been running my own printing business. I already knew Peter Michael [UEI's chairman], and coincidentally I also knew Alf Vickers.

"When I arrived at Worcester, there were 30 people on the payroll – four of them having PhD degrees – but we were making almost nothing. Just a few castings for the racing team and the Rolls-Royce Gem helicopter air intake (they used it in Lynx helicopters) – but the Alvis gearbox casting we were tackling was a bit of a fiasco.

"Alf wanted to get management, and he wanted to get system into Worcester. The Mercedes-Benz head contract was looming up too. All in all, it took nearly three years, a big struggle, to get the business working properly. The problem was that we couldn't get many outside contracts at first, as the whole of the motor industry was in deep recession there were old established foundries going out of business everywhere, and others were selling at cost. "In addition, the company was still called Cosworth Research and Development Ltd, and it had absolutely no track record at this time: it was absolutely unknown. The final problem – the critical problem – was that we still had an extraordinarily high cost base. The new process worked in concept, but it was only a research facility, extremely cumbersome and very slow. This was what we now call Foundry 1. There was no flow line that we could show customers; in terms of commercial exploitation it still had a long way to go."

Cosworth then decided, not only that it would take

the 'brave pill' and install a medium-sized production foundry (Foundry 2) at Worcester, but that it would like to licence the process to companies around the world. Foundry 2 was to be capable of making about 30,000 cylinder heads every year. A deal was struck with GKN Contractors, whereby it would inject capital, and would sell the process all round the world. It would help with the production engineering, and its money would help to produce the production process at Worcester.

In the next couple of years, its small team must have generated up to 200 serious enquiries, but in the end only one of these – from Austin Rover – looked as though it would lead to a licencing agreement, and this finally disintegrated. Even that led to all manner of disagreements, both financial and commercial. Until the large expansion to build Foundry 2 was complete, it was impossible to convince customers that the slow process demonstrated in Foundry 1 was ever likely to be commercially viable. Then, in 1983, at exactly the wrong time for the development of the business, GKN re-appraised its entire business strategy, and decided to close down its 'Contracts' division. As Bob Smith recalls:

"It was 'deep breath' time. Suddenly, we were on our own. We employed two of the GKN engineers who had been made redundant – Simon Wilkins and David Tomlin – and with UEI finance we set about spending £750,000 to build the serious foundry, Foundry 2. The submission for finance went in for approval in May 1983, we began commissioning in July 1984, and it was formally opened in September 1984. We started making Mercedes-Benz heads, in numbers, even before Foundry 2 opened, then started using Foundry 2, and things started to get better after that."

Although the evolution, and the expansion, of the Worcester foundry facility was never straightforward, from 1985, when the Sierra YB heads began to come on stream, it began to fill up, and then became a profitable part of the Cosworth scene. In spite of the heavy spending originally needed on Worcester, Cosworth's finances stayed healthy. In 1976 turnover was £1.9 million, in 1978 it had risen to £3.46 million, and in 1980 it rushed ahead to £5.36 million. After-tax profits, in the same years, leapt ahead from £152,000 to £329,000, and then again to £1.02 million. By 1980 the company's capital reserves stood at no less than £4.17 million.

In 1980, with DFX sales leaping ahead, and with other overseas work also adding its contribution, the balance of Cosworth's business was changing. In 1976 only 20 per cent of Cosworth's sales were to export territories, but by 1980 this figure had risen to 42 per cent. These commendable figures, by the way, had been achieved with a very limited workforce. In 1976 the workforce totalled 155 people, which rose to 184 in 1978, and to around 200 in 1980. Boring statistics? Not at all. They all bear out two of Keith Duckworth's most famous remarks:

"Over the years we've been doing things with a standard of reliability which is totally non-human. I'm one of those people who would rather do a few things very well – extraordinarily well – than what I see at the other extreme, in other companies, of making an average mess of doing a lot of things. It takes an enormous effort to get the last little thing right."

To the outside world, and measured by any sensible standards, Cosworth was on the crest of a wave as the 1980s opened. The DFV engine was still supreme in Grand Prix racing, North American motor racing had taken the DFX to its heart, and the Cosworth-produced Ford BDs, Opel KAs and Vauxhall Chevette engines powered hundreds of competitive race and rally cars. Keith, on the other hand, was looking ahead in a rather pessimistic manner:

"Obviously Alf Vickers was fairly old, and I was petrified as to what might happen if he died, because I didn't want to have to run the place again. I certainly didn't like the thought of running a company of the size we had then become. But then it was Alf who said to me: 'We'll be in a mess if you die,' because I held 85 per cent of the shares. That made me think. I wasn't being morbid, but it made me think. The family would have been in a forced sale situation, and the death duties problems would have been awful. By the time death duties had been settled, quite a lot of the company's shares would have had to be sold off, into odd hands, or there would be an enormous amount of debt to service. Quite simply, Cosworth couldn't have gone on being run by the family. I decided, therefore, that the best thing for all concerned was for Cosworth to be sold into the hands of somebody who looked sensible, and ongoing."

As I continued my original research to write this book, I found that statement astonishing. Earlier, I had been certain that I would uncover any number of takeover approaches for a prestigious concern like Cosworth. Amazingly enough, there appear to have been none.

In the early days, for sure, Ford had every reason

to bid for Cosworth. Walter Hayes, indeed, certainly considered this in the early days of the DFV, but:

"I decided that you must be very careful of taking over anything which really depends on one or two men. Taking over Cosworth, from our point of view, would have been to take over Keith and Mike. On that basis I felt sure it should never happen, because it seemed to me that Keith, without his freedom, would lose his edge."

Walter Hayes, who retired in 1989, must have known that all those fears were justified in the 1980s:

"When we started to get into high volume production with Cosworth, Ford certainly had discussions about controlling Cosworth. I talked both to Keith and to UEI. Ford's concern was not our wanting to own them, or to take them over, but to ensure the integrity and security of Cosworth. We felt that if they belonged to us, then nobody else could take them over.

"We were satisfied that this cannot happen, even though UEI sold out to Carlton. We have an adequate agreement with them, which gives us all we need, and secures their independence.

"Even so, in the 1970s – and especially after his first heart attack – I talked to Keith about the necessity of him establishing a 'going concern' that could operate without him, and which in future years would talk with reverence about 'our founder.' You always have to hope that what you've built will be better after you've departed. We've all seen examples of firms that disappeared when the founder was gone – Lotus was a very good example, and I would argue that Jaguar would have fared better if Sir William Lyons had prepared it for life after him."

Although Keith thought a lot about his company's future, he had never troubled to talk to other and larger companies before the end of the 1970s. Nor had he been more than mildly tempted to 'go public:'

"All that happened was that Alf Vickers began looking around for a suitable company to sell us to. It was felt that the City of London wasn't really interested in people who were involved in racing engines. I'd already had some fairly weird financial advice – setting up companies in the Bahamas, that sort of thing – but the fundamental dishonesty of most the tax schemes I was shown, well I didn't like that. I thought one was always likely to come unstuck, somehow. [This was the occasion for Keith to launch into one of his celebrated tirades, this time against the strange methods which have been developed for keeping money out of the hands of central government.]

"I really did object that the government, while appearing to be hard on those who were earning a lot of money, with taxation very high, always seemed to leave loopholes – so that providing people had minds that were warped enough, they didn't actually have to lose their money.

"It was those years, of course, which encouraged such ethics, and the death of the morals of the City of London. It was the 98 per cent taxation on investment income that caused crookery, that caused an irreversible change in the mentality of the people who operate those systems.

"It was the high taxation system which caused Cosworth to expand, by buying machinery instead of paying out profits as dividends. We kept on stirring the money back into the pot. The planners may say that that is what they intended – but they might say all sorts of things.

"It was crazy to pay high dividends, because that would have been called 'unearned income,' and we had 98 per cent taxation on such earnings in the 1970s. The great advantage of having just one bloke – me – running a company, and not primarily being interested in money, is that any money that was made was just ploughed back. That way, we generated our own capital, and bought a lot of capital equipment – we kept Cosworth going as a self-financing, self-expanding, outfit, and nobody could argue about that."

"I am still staggered by what other people get up to. I do still speak, occasionally, to wealthy people who, I would have to say, are guilty of fraud. But they cannot understand that they are guilty, because they're only repeating something that has been done many times before." Mike Costin, after he became Cosworth's chairman in 1988, commented that Keith had put in a systematic search for companies of the right type to purchase Cosworth. The object, Mike says, was to find a Group which would not indulge in asset stripping, but which would understand the company and let it carry on being run by the people who were already running it.

Richard Bulman, who became managing director in 1985, in succession to Alf Vickers, said that Keith simply wasn't interested in 'going public,' to dilute his shareholding, and to get a USM (Unlisted Securities Market) quote.

Except to his fellow directors, Keith kept his thoughts to himself and nothing leaked to the public. Suddenly however, in February 1980, the deed was done. *Autocar* reported it thus:

"Cosworth are to be taken over by UEI [United Engineering Industries], a Manchester-based engineering firm. The change will in no way affect the supply and servicing of Cosworth racing engines – but it does show how lucrative this business has been. The deal comprises £3.4 million in UEI shares, £2.4 million in loan bonds, and a further £425,000 in loan bonds at the conclusion of a satisfactory year's trading.

"Keith Duckworth, whom many people have been surprised to find owns 85 per cent of Cosworth shares [But why should they? It, was, after all, his company, and he had founded it ...], will be the main recipient of the purchase.

"He will now be left alone to concentrate on the design of new components ..."

In fact Keith had rarely done anything other than design new engines. For the first few years he had had to do almost everything in the business, but Bill Brown had been a very able general manager until the mid-1970s, at which point he drifted away and Alf Vickers had been a very effective, and pragmatic, managing director, after that:

"Alf did a great job running the place on the basis of a few conversations with me from time to time, and odd joint meetings until about 1985. He was responsible for the total running, the administration, and he produced the methods of working out the strategy that he and I devised between us."

Early in 1980, Keith was happy to sell Cosworth to UEI, though in later years he came to realise that he might have got a higher price:

"We sold ourselves for what turned out to be a very modest figure, at a not particularly good time to sell, to an outfit which looked like a club of entrepreneurs, with the board consisting of the founders of those companies which had joined it. It looked like quite a good environment. In the end, I'm positive that we sold out too cheap, and I reckon that Cosworth is one of the best firms, for the money, that has ever changed hands. As we were consistently under-employing people, our latent competence and our capability for expansion, meant that we were really worth a bomb. There were no skeletons in the cupboard for the new owners to discover.

"But I still don't want to be seriously rich. I'm still quite amazed that some people who have some money actually seem to want a lot more. I do not think that it is a great measure of one's life to have made a lot of money.

"Self-esteem, yes, that does come into it – it's really the only thing that comes into it. Incidentally, neither am I interested in external honours, or prizes, or being given fellowships. However, if someone pushed them on to me, it would be unreasonable to refuse. Having had a go at beating the world by building racing engines, and having managed to be responsible for the design and engineering of engines which have been successful, world-wide – I do like that. That's a reasonable accolade."

With the takeover by UEI, all manner of personal and financial upheavals became necessary. [Motorsport enthusiasts, not interested in this, should skip the next few paragraphs!]. All the original directors of Cosworth were obliged to sell their interest in Swindon Racing Engines, which left John Dunn with the tricky job of financing the loans he needed to buy them out:

"We'd never made a lot of money, and I certainly wasn't rolling in it. I paid off the others very quickly, but Keith's holding took longer. Keith, personally, still owns the building and the one next door, but the actual business is now my own."

Soon after the takeover, Ursula Duckworth (Keith's first wife) and Bill Brown resigned from the Cosworth board, and at the same time the nominal share capital was raised from a derisory £1000, to a more sensible £100,000. Two UEI board members joined the Cosworth board at the time, Harvey Fox joined them a few months later, and naturally enough Keith also became a member of UEI's board.

In the next few years Keith gradually, but perceptibly, began to distance himself from front-line management at Northampton, while becoming more and more closely involved in the activities of the parent company. Eventually Richard Bulman, whose family once owned a company making exotic tunnel-boring machinery, who had known Alf Vickers for many years, and who had spent some years at Hawker-Siddeley, joined Cosworth to become managing director. Along the way the company had effectively been split, with Alf Vickers running the operations side, and Keith the engineering and racing side. By this time Keith was visibly less happy working in a larger company, though Mike did not show as much impatience with the way their little company was growing so large, so quickly. Keith, in particular, was having to deal with more and more 'big company' men whose habits irritated him:

"They all speak in a particular way. They all speak like politicians. It is a characteristic of me, and proper Cosworth people, in general, that if you ask something, then there ought to be a certain amount of delay before anyone replies. The next best thing would be for people to admit that they did not have an answer, but that they would find out, or that they would think about it. To me that's a perfectly satisfactory response. In a big company, as far as I can see, that last thing you can afford to do is not to start replying immediately. People must start saying something, anything, immediately, words vaguely connected with the question, hoping that this might constitute an answer. What those people do is to learn to waffle. It is actually known in the dictionary as 'equivocation' – the use of misleading words to conceal the truth. I actually feel mentally ill when people state things that have no meaning. It completely buggers me up, I have to follow it, and worry about it. I've lost the next ten sentences. I don't think I should be paid to suffer the company of people who are waffling!"

[A set of crisply stated opinions which then led Keith to recall one of Ben Rood's most famous Cosworth moments.]

"Ben once listened carefully to a visitor, then said, 'You and I understand English, and therefore I know the meaning of every word you use. Unfortunately, when you string more than two of them together, to me they become entirely meaningless.'"

In the meantime, Cosworth, its future, and its finances, thoroughly underpinned with the backing of UEI, was gradually growing larger, and larger. From the outside, growth looked unstoppable. Cosworth was allowed to go ahead, freewheeling, with little influence from above. There was no attempt, fortunately, to send in teams of grey-faced accountants, to milk Cosworth's name for all that it was worth.

By 1984, and ahead of the public announcement of the cylinder head assembly contract from Mercedes-Benz, annual turnover was up to £8 million, and a new engine assembly factory, at Wellingborough, was already partly built. Details of this major project, closely linked to the Sierra engine programme, are included in the next chapter. Two years later, in 1986, turnover had doubled to £16.1 million, and in 1988 it had doubled yet again, this time to £33.3 million.

Richard Bulman admitted that the company had grown even faster than he expected, much of it due to the way Sierra RS Cosworth engine assembly had gone ahead. He also insisted that motor racing was, is, and will remain, a very important part of Cosworth's activities:

"Racing is a superb vehicle, a great catalyst, for really stretching the technology. The time scale forces the issue like no amount of R & D, trials and endurance testing can ever do. We want to sustain the racing position, in several areas, as key players. I'm absolutely determined about that. Look what happened to Coventry-Climax, look at Aston-Martin, which was bailed out by Ford."

By the 1980s, perhaps, it was high time that Keith began to think seriously about his personal future. Whereas his co-founder, Mike Costin, always appeared to be affable, relaxed, and well able to float calmly over the stresses of running a fast-growing concern, Keith was visibly serious, and closely involved, in everything which he tackled.

Mike seemed to rise above all the increased 'politicking' which crept into the much expanded company. He had never been unhappy at Cosworth, he told me in 1989, and he had never been tempted to leave, for another firm – "maybe because nobody thinks I've been worth poaching!"

Ben Rood, too, was still running all the machine shops with obvious enjoyment. It was rarely possible to pin him down to talk about his past, as he was too obviously tied up with the future developments. He was always, he said, "thinking six machines ahead" of the last one he had designed. He also admitted that:

"I don't think I will know when to stop, that's going to be the disastrous undoing of me. I'm a bit worried about the day which may come when I've got nowhere to go in the mornings. I hate going on holiday, and I'll tell you why – I'm pretty sure that I could get to like it!"

The traumas surrounding the design of the new turbocharged engine, the break-up of Keith's first marriage, and the sheer size of the Wellingborough/ Sierra engine project, all clearly had an effect. Perhaps his heart attack of 1973 had been too lightly shrugged off. Suddenly, in 1986, the old trouble flared up again. Three years afterwards, Keith was more cheerful, when describing an awful period in his life, than he must have felt at the time:

"Generally speaking I was feeling very fit, and I felt that I might get my helicopter licence back. I went to Harley Street for a check, and there didn't seem to be a lot wrong at first. Then he suggested that I should have an angiogram – great sport, that was, they gave me a great shot of heroin – but the results of that were terrible. I had partial blockages in two of the tubes. As a reasonable plumber, who had been dealing with fluid flow all my life, I was rather offended. Not only that, but there was no way I could get my helicopter licence back! The specialists suggested that I have

After Keith Duckworth retired from Cosworth in 1988, Mike Costin became the company's chairman. This was the ideal opportunity to pose: Mike (in sports jacket), his managing director, Richard Bulman, and a Ford Sierra (Sapphire) Cosworth in front of the famous logo at the Northampton factory.

still to be with us,' and I said that I thought I could see that. By that time I had decided that I would only settle for Magdi Yacoub and a transplant, but when they then told me that a team could be assembled in Oxford, for the following day, I decided to be gracious and accept their kind offer."

The result was that early in 1987 Keith endured major by-pass surgery, not without many problems, and he told me that he still felt thoroughly let down by his own body. He also admitted, incidentally, that his surgeons told him that there was no point in their carrying out by-pass surgery if he carried on smoking:

"I'd tried to stop smoking before. This time I stopped – immediately!"

Although he eventually returned to work and got married again, to Gill, Keith soon retired to 'The Folly,' his comfortable house on a hill top, not far from Northampton, where he continued to dabble in F1 engine design, and: "any technical problem that made me really sit down, and think." Times, and his company, had moved on too far to interest him any more in Cosworth:

"When I was chairman, I felt that I had to be responsible overall for what was going on. I had to be in charge. That had now become unreasonable. I'd always taken the view that any job we took on should have been with my knowledge. If the worst came to the worst, if an engineering job got into the mire, I felt that by abandoning other things, I could apply myself and dig it out of the mire.

"We needed someone like Richard Bulman, to impose some discipline, to watch over all the finances, to implement the strategy. Someone with a normal large-company approach. It was beyond me. As the company got bigger, this became more unrealistic.

"I think I am, always was, unsuitable, to be in charge of a larger company. The whole of my nature, anyhow, was that I wanted to do a few things very well indeed, rather than doing a lot of things only fairly well. Mike is far more capable, by his nature, of assisting in little ways, generally to uplift the standard. I would like to lift all the standards to an unrealistic height. I am really not very good at just assisting things. The problem in life, for me, was that there never seemed to be enough time to do everything right."

'The Folly' was the sort of house you might expect of a 'Professor Branestawm (to use Walter Hayes' apt phraseology), with not one, but two, helicopters in the hangar, a microlight kit being built up, a Sierra RS Cosworth in the yard, son Roger's Sierra Cosworth-

heart surgery, but I ignored that advice. I said 'Sod that, I'm not going through with it.'"

Walter Hayes was really rather angry with him about this vacillation. It was no good, he said, for Keith to carry on acting as the Founding Father of his company if, one day, he might no longer be there to be the Father. Then came the first, embarrassing, race debut of the new turbocharged F1 engine at Imola, in 1986:

"After the race, I had to run through the paddock to catch the Ford helicopter, and I was out of breath, and in a fair bit of pain. So I thought I should get Harley Street to have another look at me, but I wasn't in a hurry, and I did nothing until the beginning of 1987.

"Then I think I must have had another, very mild, heart attack, at home in bed. The following day I went for a check up, was put on a monitoring machine, and it was suggested that I should have another angiogram in Oxford. That was terrible – much worse than the last time. I saw the records, and I sat there, and thought that was Heap Bad News. They said, 'Well, you're lucky engined Escort rally car nearby, and a large and rather untidy study into which Keith regularly disappeared to think out a particular problem.

He had already split Cosworth into two major activities – one centred around the racing engine business, the other larger one being bound up in production engine design and manufacture – but was no longer connected, at ground level, with either. His old friend and confidante, Alf Vickers, died in February 1988.

Slowly, but definitely, the atmosphere at Northampton changed – not deteriorated, but changed. The pressure-cooker, high-technology, university-of-engineering atmosphere dissipated, and a more conventional atmosphere took over. To some of his designers, Keith had been too long-winded, too anxious to argue every technical conundrum, however, minor, to its ultimate conclusion. There were people, let us be honest, who would try to avoid him when that 'let's have a discussion' gleam came into his eyes – life, they said, was too short for that. To others, the crackle in the atmosphere had gone. As one ex-designer told me:

"He was always a very exciting bloke to have around, he had so many ideas, all the time. If that made you tick, it was a happy atmosphere. After he had been with me, at my drawing board, I ended up being quite inspired for the rest of the day."

Mike Costin thought that what followed was inevitable: "He gradually lost interest in the company which he had founded, because he could no longer control all the engineering which was going on. In the end, really, he said 'Stuff it,' and retired. On the other hand, he is still going on consulting, especially on the race engine side."

By 1988 Cosworth had grown to employ 570 people, none of whom were involved in useless, or esoteric, activities. Keith, following his second heart attack, had mellowed, and decided that there was more to life than killing himself in the pursuit of technical excellence.

Mike Costin once quoted from a note which Keith had jotted, after a particularly difficult time: "I have decided that I will join the human race and take no thought for the morrow, let the morrow take care of itself." Or (as Costin quipped, eyes glinting behind his glasses): "He's decided that he can't rebuild the world – stuff it, he'll join it."

The records show that Keith stepped down from the Chair, which he had held since 1958, on 30 August 1988, and that Mike Costin took his place. It was 29

years and 11 months since Cosworth Engineering had been incorporated.

His enormous contribution to everything achieved by Cosworth was formalised in April 1989 when the 'new regime' presented him with a mounted version of the famous DFV multi-quill timing gear, and the following inscription:

"Keith. On your acceptance of HONORARY LIFE PRESIDENCY. With these quills, you wrote a New Book in the History of Motor Racing. THE BOARD, COSWORTH ENGINEERING. April 1989."

Even while the first edition of this book was being drafted, the surprises, and the commercial manoeuvrings, continued. No sooner had UEI announced record profits for 1988 (26 per cent higher than in 1987), with group turnover up by a similar amount, than UEI itself agreed to be taken over. The report in 25 May 1989's *Daily Telegraph* summarised the attitude of the City:

"Carlton Communications, the ambitious television services group led by Michael Green, took its shareholders by surprise yesterday, with an agreed £492 million offer for the UEI electronics-to-engineering company.

"UEI will significantly add to Carlton's strength in the world market for advanced television technology."

There was, however, a rather disturbing paragraph, later on:

"UEI has two other major divisions – including the Link Scientific and Cosworth motor engine businesses – which Carlton admitted yesterday are not an obvious [business] fit. However, Mr Green insisted that: 'No companies are for sale.'"

The Times took this on board without much comment, except to suggest that: "Cosworth is likely to attract offers, particularly from suppliers to the motor industry."

In the autumn and winter of 1989/1990, in fact, Britain's 'rumour factory' decided that Cosworth was for sale, and linked its future with several different concerns. For obvious reasons Ford, General Motors and Daimler-Benz were all quoted as possible buyers, with Fiat also thought to be a strong contender. Since Cosworth's 1989 profits had reached £14.2 million, the company was obviously very attractive to predators.

In March 1990, however, almost everyone was surprised when Carlton agreed to sell Cosworth to the Vickers Group, the deal going through with the minimum of disruption. Vickers, which already owned

The caption says it all: "Keith. On your acceptance of HONORARY LIFE PRESIDENCY. With these quills you wrote a new book in the history of motor racing. THE BOARD, COSWORTH ENGINEERING, April 1989." This was Keith's memento of his famous DFV engine, the complex timing gear of which solved all the vibration problems of that power unit.

Mike Costin became Cosworth's chairman in 1988, and finally retired in 1990. He had already been connected with the company for 32 years, and, even in retirement, has never lost touch.

COSWORTH – THE SEARCH FOR POWER

THE HART-COSWORTH PARTNERSHIP

BRIAN Hart set up his own engine building business at the end of the 1960s, designed the aluminium block for the BD engine in 1971, and went on to produce his all-new Hart 420R F2 2.0-litre engine, which was announced in 1975:

"I spent a complete winter designing it, and there was only one proviso. Stuart Turner, of Ford, wanted to be sure that it would fit into the engine bay of a Ford Escort, just in case it might be turned into a road car engine!"

The 420R started winning F2 races in 1977, first won the F2 European Championship (with Toleman) in 1980, and was then converted to 1.5-litre turbocharged power (as the 415T) for Toleman in 1981. In normally-aspirated, 2.3-litre, form, it was also proposed as an engine project for use in Ford's still-born RS1700T rally car.

For the next few years, the small and admittedly underfinanced company struggled to make the 415T engine competitive and reliable against the might of Renault, BMW, Ferrari and TAG-Porsche. It was a losing battle. At best the 415T could race at 4-bar boost limits with 800bhp, which wasn't enough. The last team to use Hart F1 engines, as a temporary measure, was Beatrice/Lola, prior to the delivery of its Cosworth GB V6 turbocharged units.

The F1 programme cost Brian Hart Ltd a great deal of money, and he was only able to stay in business because of the other work which came his way, not least the Ford 'BDT-E' RS200 project. When that engine, too, was killed off by a change in regulations, Brian felt very downhearted. His design staff, after all, consisted of himself and his brother Tony, with John Lievesley working on a consultancy basis, and there was also a 29-man workforce to feed:

"We were then approached directly by Keith Duckworth in November 1986, wanting to take us over. At the time Cosworth had more work on racing car engines than it could foreseeably cope with. We, on the other hand, had designed a very promising twin-cam conversion of an established road-car engine, but were not capable or interested in putting it into production.

"Since we had already said to the client: 'Look, we're only small, we can only build prototypes, you'd better go to Cosworth for production engines, there's no-one else in Europe who has the same kind of facility,' I suppose the solution was obvious. Of course, Ford and Cosworth already knew this, because they had just got the Sierra engine into volume production."

In Richard Bulman's own words: "We were so stretched with the turbocharged F1 engine that we couldn't look at anything else. We both needed each other." The result was that Keith had a close look at the projected road-car engine and wanted to acquire it, offered a great deal of racing design and development work for BHL's future, and made a bid for Brian Hart Ltd. Brian, who was the sole shareholder of BHL sold 75 per cent of his holding, and his company then became a subsidiary of Cosworth Engineering. The road-car engine project was moved to Northampton, was redesigned, developed and tooled for production, and was due to go into a fast and prestigious car in 1990. It was later known as the 2.9-litre FB V6.

The deal was made public in February 1987 when it was suggested that BHL "will take an important role in the design and development of the 3.5-litre Ford engine for F1." Unhappily, the fine words were never translated into worthy actions. Within a year the relationship between Cosworth and BHL had soured, for neither party found that it was gaining any benefit. BHL had been given very little design and development work on the interim DFR, and had not been consulted on the layout of Geoff Goddard's all-new HB V8 F1 engine for 1989. Cosworth, on the other hand, was not content with the profits earned by its newest subsidiary. Cosworth managing director Richard Bulman puts it this way:

"We found that the opportunities for BHL in F1 were, to a certain extent, inhibited by Cosworth, because teams felt that their particular technology would be spewed around within Cosworth."

Brian Hart was more direct:

"We didn't get the work in exchange that we had been promised. We were never asked to give an opinion on the 5-valve/Yamaha dilemma, in fact we were never taken into Cosworth's confidence over that. Two things then happened. Dear Alf Vickers, who had done all the negotiations with us, died. Keith had his heart operation, and for a long time in 1987 that prevented work coming to us. When Keith stepped down from the chairmanship of Cosworth, Richard Bulman came to see us, and it was fairly clear that Richard thought we were something of a corporate irritation. He wanted us to be much more profitable, and told us so.

"Soon after Mike Costin took over as Chairman, he came down to see me, and we discussed various solutions. It was clear that we weren't going to get any new design work from Northampton, so one of the alternatives – that we dissolve the marriage – seemed to make sense. So, we accepted that, and after a protracted period, I bought back my 75 per cent. Now we operate on a purely commercial basis – supplier to customer – with Cosworth, no more and no less than that."

After squeezing even more power out of DFRs, DFZs and DFLs, Hart then designed a completely new F1 V10 engine of his own, a compact and powerful 3.5-litre unit which was used by the Jordan team in 1993 and 1994. Further F1 3-litre engines were promised for 1995 and beyond.

Brian was the chairman, the chief designer, the chief development engineer and – on the evidence of a visit I later made to Harlow – the storeman and marketing chief as well. Which, I suspect, is what he preferred to be …

Rolls-Royce Motor Cars, agreed to pay £163.5 million for Cosworth.

There was a brisk re-shuffle of names before Cosworth settled down under new ownership. Mike Costin vacated the Chairman's post, stepping down to become Deputy Chairman for a time, as Vickers appointed Rolls-Royce Engineering Director Mike Dunn as the new (part-time) Chairman.

A few months later Dr Peter Nevitt became Cosworth's new Chairman in place of Mike Dunn, and Mike Costin finally retired. Cosworth, under new direction, faced up to major expansion in the 1990s.

11: THE SIERRA PROJECT – A QUANTUM LEAP INTO THE FUTURE

"We think there's a market for 200 conversion kits a year, so we thought we'd do one."

"You know, we could put that engine in a Sierra, with a turbo, and there's no way anything would beat us on the track."

When a new project is successful, any number of people are happy to take credit for it. Cosworth's famous turbocharged YB-series Sierra engine is a case in point. Not only did it become a race and rally-winning unit in the late 1980s, but it was also the main influence behind the company's huge expansion. Consider these simple facts – in 1982, before the YB was designed, Cosworth's annual turnover was £5.2 million, and its after-tax profit £943,000. Five years later turnover had rocketed to £33.4 million, and profits to £3.3 million.

The story of this phase of growth really began in the early 1980s, when Keith and Jack Field began to study the needs of the specialist manufacturers, and the 'engine kit' market. The BD series, they decided, was getting old; block supplies could not be guaranteed indefinitely, and in any case the cylinder head was considered too expensive to produce.

In a private venture, they decided to use Ford's long-established T88/'Pinto' cylinder block and bottom end, and to develop a new normally-aspirated 16-valve twin-cam cylinder head conversion for it. Mike Hall recalled that: "It could have been a bolt-on goody for private owners. We even thought we might sell a few to Ford RS dealers."

Cosworth was not the first company to try a 16-valve/Pinto combination. Holbay had attempted a more basic conversion in the 1970s, and Ford had actually commissioned Brian Hart Ltd to produce an engine at the same time, but neither came to anything. By 1983, the first Cosworth-Pinto engines – what we now know as the YAA types – were built, but no serious testing had begun.

It was at about the same time that Ford's European Motorsport division experienced an upheaval. Karl Ludvigsen, who had been running things, moved out, while Stuart Turner returned from a long sojourn in the Public Affairs division. Within days, Turner had killed off the C100 sports car project (complete with its 3.9-litre DFL engine) and the rear-wheel-drive Escort RS1700T rally car (complete with its BDT engine). He needed new projects to take their place.

The coincidences then began to build up:

"The week after I came back, in March 1983, Walter Hayes and I went to a Silverstone touring car race, and watched the Rover Vitesses winning. I recall saying

something like 'It would be nice to see something of ours that could beat them.' Jim Capolongo and Ed Blanch, who were president and chairman of Ford of Europe, were discussing the 'Shall we design a new F1 engine' question at the time, and felt that they should visit Cosworth.

"I took them both to Cosworth in Northampton, and as we were walking round, there was this T88 block, with a 16-valve head on it. I asked Keith what it was, and he told me: 'We think there's a market for about 200 conversion kits a year, so we thought we'd do one.'

"Then we all went to the local pub and had a ploughman's lunch. Over lunch I distinctly remember saying:

"'You know, we could put that engine in a Sierra, with a turbo, and there's no way anything would beat us on the track.' Really, it all began to roll from then. Make no mistake, we were incredibly lucky with our timing, just to see that engine there, at the right time. Don't run away with the idea that Ford is all about computerised planning."

One famous document, produced by the dynamic Turner in his whirlwind return to Motorsport, listed a "Ladder of Opportunity" for the division. It started, at the bottom, with "Posters for Motor Clubs," and finished, at the top, with "New F1 engine?" Near the top were three other queried projects: "Escort Turbo for rallying?", "New Group B car for rallying?" and "Turbo Sierra for Group A racing?" Stuart asked for all three projects to be approved, expecting at least one to be refused, but was astonished to see all three get the go ahead.

The project was formalised in 1983, the prototype Sierra RS Cosworth was unveiled in March 1985, and engine deliveries to Ford began before the end of that year. It was necessary to build 5000 engines (and cars) to achieve sporting homologation, and the initial production contract was for 15,000 YBs of all types. Stuart thinks the gods were on Ford's side in 1983:

"Had we had to start by creating 16-valves, then turbocharging, it would have taken too long. It was only because Cosworth had already designed the engine as a private venture that it could be done so quickly."

These things are never quite as cut-and-dried, or as romantic, as they seem. One experienced engineer, with

Ford SVE connections, assured me that Cosworth had already offered the normally-aspirated YAA engine to Ford for appraisal before Capolongo, Blanch and Turner saw it, and that Cosworth had been told: "it will need turbocharging to be competitive."

The vagaries of FISA's new Group A regulations had to be taken into account, particularly as to what could and could not be changed when power-tuning took place. The new engine needed a steel crank and steel rods, the road-car camshaft profiles were carefully drawn so that a revision for Group A events would be feasible – the result being that the cylinder block was the only standard Ford item left over. Mike Hall, too, of Cosworth, told me that:

"Ford originally talked about taking several thousand of these, but in normally-aspirated form. I think it was a bit of a surprise to us when they came back and said they wanted a turbocharger."

Mike also remembered, with a smile, that it was work on this new project which caused him to have a heart attack himself:

"We were terribly busy, but I didn't think I had so many hassles that it would affect my health. We were right up against it with the Opel [GM 16-valve 2-litre] job, and I was also having to pick up the Sierra YB work. Mario Illien had actually done most of the design, but he had just left to set up Ilmor, and soon after he had gone, one of our best draughtsmen, Geoff Oliver, also left. So suddenly, I was right in the thick of it, I had too much on, and my body let me know about that."

The new engine, when first built at the end of 1983, worked well immediately. As Keith once commented, on another matter:

"There's one major difference between Cosworth and anyone else. As far as we can see, we're the only people who expect a prototype to go together straight away, and definitely I think that disgust is felt when the pieces don't actually fit together."

Geoff Goddard also made the point that: "With road engines, we're actually able to dial in, within the odd horsepower, of what was requested. With the Sierra though, well we didn't get the 200bhp as requested, we just couldn't get the engine down to that!"

The YB project was to be much the biggest and most ambitious that Cosworth had ever tackled, and much of the liaison work was carried out by project engineer Paul Fricker. If the company had still been privately owned, perhaps the offer would never have come – for Ford not only wanted an 'homologation special' engine designed and developed, but also wanted to

see Cosworth manufacture the production engines, too. Because Ford's own prestigious new product was involved, it gave a great deal of help to Cosworth in planning the project, to make sure that its finances were always on an even keel. A huge multinational company like Ford could visualise itself building a handful of engines every year, or building hundreds of thousands a year, but would have found it difficult to build just 5000 to 8000 engines a year. For a company of Ford's size, it didn't make economic sense.

On the other hand, there were very few companies in Europe that would be comfortably set at those sort of rates. To meet all the targets, the engines had to be built quickly. Cosworth, for sure, was an ideal candidate. For Cosworth, indeed, the offer came at exactly the right time.

Keith Duckworth agreed that "it wasn't worth my time even going to a drawing board, unless I could see an end product to keep my own machines busy." Once Alf Vickers had explained the problems, and the possibilities, UEI, Cosworth's parent company, gave enthusiastic support. A new assembly plant would be needed, but this would become necessary soon anyway, to look after Mercedes-Benz and GM 16-valve cylinder head assembly in the years to come.

As YB development got under way, Alf Vickers looked around for a site to build a factory to assemble the engines.

There was no space alongside the Northampton or the Worcester facilities, and, in any case, Mike Costin reminded me that it was desirable that the plant should be situated far enough away from corporate HQ "so that people don't always have the excuse to nip off and get involved in production problems."

Fortuitously, because there was an unemployment problem at Wellingborough, with the local authority offering financial incentives and plenty of space for firms to set up shop on the north of town, Cosworth decided to build a new plant, just ten miles from Northampton. Building work started in 1984, and the first engines were built before the end of the following year.

The old hands – Alf Vickers, Ben Rood, and Mike Costin – all had much to do with the layout of the Wellingborough facility. The original consultants' report suggested such a high capital cost of installing machinery, that Cosworth "would have gone broke trying to set it up." Ben Rood then suggested ways of doing the job, and although his original ideas were partially rejected, the late-1980s re-equipment and expansion saw several pure 'Rood' machines installed.

The elegance of Gordon Murray's Brabham BT49 theme, and the overall excellence of the DFV all helped Nelson Piquet to become World F1 Champion in 1981.

Although the Sierra RS Cosworth was fitted with the new YBB turbocharged engine, and based on the Sierra three-door bodyshell, the rest of the car was carefully developed to match the engine. On this early (1985-1986) version, note the modified nose, the cooling vents in the bonnet, the special alloy wheels and the massive rear spoiler.

YB-Series (Sierra RS Cosworth) engine assembly at Cosworth's Wellingborough factory in the mid 1980s. One very compact assembly line, where excellent craftsmanship was more important than automation, could complete up to 30 engines a day.

It was Ben, who brought so much machining know-how to Cosworth, who enabled amazing machining feats to be done on machinery which looked as if it should have been ditched years ago. A closer look, however, reveals that most have been extensively redesigned by Rood, originally in his head, then practically, and robustly, on the ground.

"The most I ever paid for a secondhand machine tool was £3250, and the cheapest was just £200. But some of them had solid casting beds which had aged for 30 years, had stopped creeping about – and we could have them reconditioned, and modified for our 'machining between centres' methods for less than £4000. We also work to extremely tight tolerances these days. The limits on production heads, such as for the Mercedes-Benz and the Sierra, well, they're tighter than ever we imposed on the racing engines! Other people may specify tighter tolerances on their drawings, but we keep to ours. I think we probably work to tighter tolerances than anyone else in the motor industry."

The Sierra, too, was significant for being the very first Ford car to carry the name of 'Cosworth' in its badging. Mike Hall, who had been through the politics of this on previous occasions, told me why:

"It was only because we had done the entire project, from drawing to production, testing to delivery, that this was entirely our own engine. It was the first time we had ever manufactured the entire engine for a road car. If we had just done a head for someone else to assemble, then Cosworth wouldn't have allowed its name to go on the car."

In business terms, however, Cosworth had to go out on a limb, and teeter, out there, for some time. Stuart Turner reminded me that the Sierra RS Cosworth car, in its original stages, had a very charmed life, that the big rear spoiler on the tail of the three-door car didn't help some of Ford's bosses to like it, and that Walter Hayes "had it on a life support machine at least twice, before it was finally born."

Mike Costin told me that it was the most cliff-hanging project ever, while Richard Bulman pointed out that even after Ford unveiled the prototype car in 1985, it had still not finally committed itself to go ahead. Mike, cheerful but exuding false modesty for his company, reckons that if Cosworth had made a really professional study of the Sierra project, then it would never have built the factory because:

"There is a world of difference between building 100 BDs a year, and 5000 Sierra engines a year. Assembling heads was one thing, but this was the first engine that we had to manufacture, in total. This time we had to machine, assemble, test and validate everything."

Cosworth's Wellingborough factories (there were two adjoining plants from 1985, and a massive new block, for a still-secret new assembly project, later unveiled as the FB V6, was completed during 1989) were brand new, and built without technical compromise.

A plaque in the sparsely furnished office entrance revealed that the original 29,000ft² factory was formally opened by the Duke of Kent in November 1985, by which time it was already building the first 'off-tools' engines for delivery to Ford in Belgium. Bernard Ferguson, who would later become Cosworth's much-respected figurehead on the company's sales and marketing side in motorsport, started his Cosworth career at this site.

There were delays in getting the Sierra RS Cosworth into the showrooms, none of them due to any hold-ups at Wellingborough. By the beginning of 1986, more than 20 cylinder heads were being cast at Worcester every day, with all the machining being done on multi-purpose tools at Wellingborough. T88/Pinto cylinder blocks arrived, in batches, from Ford, Cosworth machined many other components in its Northampton shops, and final assembly was carried out along one side of the Wellingborough premises.

Even before the public got its hands on the Sierra RS Cosworth, the engine looked remarkable, but once the car's 150mph top speed, and the engine's great flexibility, had become known, it was seen as phenomenal. There had never been a 2-litre engined car like this before.

Ford wanted the Sierra to be a race winner, and its targets had been set very high. Originally it had asked for 200bhp, and Cosworth came back with a guaranteed output of 204bhp. This made the Sierra RS

Cosworth the world's first series-production road car to be sold with an engine offering more than 100bhp/litre – 200-off 'Group B' specials like the Audi Sport Quattro were not really series-production machines, and don't qualify.

But there was more, much more, to come from this remarkable statement of Cosworth's art. In fully-tuned Group A racing form, the YBC version of the engine produced up to 340bhp. Even so, Ford was not satisfied. Group A Regulations allowed 'evolution' versions of cars to be produced – with 500 identical extra cars needing to be built. One of Paul Fricker's tasks was to produce a development of the 'ordinary' engine for such cars, with a lot more power potential locked inside.

Ford had been planning ahead, and actually built not 5000, but 5500 of the original 'whale-tail' Sierras. 500 cars were carefully stored for a few months, then shipped to the Aston Martin Tickford factory at Bedworth, near Coventry, for conversion. Among the many changes then made to convert an RS Cosworth into an RS500 Cosworth, was the removal of the original engine, and the craning into place of the YBD 'Evolution' version of the Sierra engine.

The engines were built at Wellingborough in one continuous run in the spring of 1987, around a much strengthened version of the cylinder block, and with larger turbochargers and two rows, rather than one, of fuel injectors. In standard form, for road use, the YBD produced 'only' 224bhp, but when fully-tuned for circuit racing (and running at the sort of boost which DFX and BDT tuners would be proud of) more than 500 to 550bhp was on tap. Remarkably, little of this power tuning was ever carried out at Cosworth, though much of the hardware, and expert knowledge, was based at Northampton. Jack Field explains why:

"We did a rally spec, and got that off the ground, but other engine builders took over, and some now say

The EB project, carried out diligently for General Motors at the end of the 1980s, was one of the largest Cosworth road-car projects on which Mike Hall worked – however, it was cancelled by GM when development was complete, but before production could be authorised.

During 1986, Cosworth produced well over 5000 YBB engines to power the production run of Ford Sierra RS Cosworths. It was their biggest 'production line' project to date, and would be developed and improved significantly in the years which followed.

COSWORTH – THE SEARCH FOR POWER

Almost every component of the YB engine was Cosworth-designed and developed (the original Ford T88 cylinder block is hidden in this shot), and a brand new factory, at Wellingborough, was built to accommodate the assembly lines. This was the 'inlet' side of the new engine ...

... while the 'exhaust side' view shows the complex layout of the exhaust manifold and turbocharger installation.

that everything is of their own manufacture. In fact we do nearly 100 per cent of all the special pieces used in YBs – everything except the electronics – but don't trumpet this.

"As far as the RS500 racing engine was concerned, we did some development, but much of the work was done by people like Eggenberger, Hoyle, Andy Rouse, and Dick Johnson (in Australia). We have tried to work closely with them. The engine builders all like it that way. They're in the business of preparing, and rebuilding engines. They need a ready supply of good pieces, but the last thing they want is to see Cosworth building engines. It's far better if they can buy a full kit from Cosworth – and they can.

"We like to keep abreast of what is going on out there at the engine builders – but you'd be amazed, some can be very difficult, very secretive. I don't know why: The last thing we want to do is to build engines which compete with those produced by our best customers."

Leading engine builders like Terry Hoyle Ltd, however, do a lot of their own work. The relationship with Northampton is open, and relaxed, but partner Graham Dale-Jones was not anxious to pay Cosworth's consultancy rates on too many occasions.

By 1989, on the other hand, Jack Field thought that there was a great deal of scope for the Sierra engine to take over from other, older, Cosworth units. Among his ongoing projects was a normally-aspirated derivation:

"I could offer a much cheaper engine, offering similar performance, to some of the BD types. I'd be able to kill off the turbocharged type, except for supplying spares. The Sierra engine already has the steel crank and rods, as built at Wellingborough, which makes it much simpler than with the original BDs."

The challenge to turn the super-high-performance Sierra engine into an environmentally friendly, 'green' unit, was achieved with almost contemptuous ease in 1987 and 1988. The pundits who knew little about Cosworth suggested that the Sierra's teeth would be well-and-truly drawn by the need to meet clean-exhaust rules, and the need to run on lead-free fuel. Instead, the job was completed without any major redesign, and an engine which was not less, but actually more, powerful than before.

Even when using 95 Octane petrol instead of 99 Octane, the engine produced 207bhp instead of 204bhp. Geoff Goddard, who was involved in the original camshaft profile design of this remarkable engine, told me why:

"We had been designing F1 engines for some years

When the YBD engine was race-tuned, it could produce a reliable 500bhp, making the Sierra RS500 it powered quite unbeatable. This is Andy Rouse at the height of his powers in 1988.

Sierra RS500s built by the Swiss-based Eggenberger team, but backed by Ford-of-Germany, won the World Touring Car Championship in 1987, the European Championship in 1988 – and were then effectively banned from this category because they were too dominant!

The YB engine was intended to turn the Sierra Cosworth into a race and rally winning product, which it did with great success. This was Didier Auriol, on his way to winning the Tour de Corse rally in 1988.

which had extremely efficient combustion. To go 'green,' all that was necessary was to know what octane number was going to be available, to decide what compression ratio could be used, then look at valve seats and valves, and the job was nearly done. The Sierra's burning was so clean, in any case, that we were almost there at the start."

Cosworth's people seem to have retained that amazing 'can-do' attitude of its founders, that other less-accomplished firms did not even approach. Keith Duckworth told me, rather fondly, of one of his design engineers:

"He always sees things as simple, he seems to know so much, and he always promises speedy deadlines for anything. His ability is colossal, even though some such things are not simple to other people."

The company, on the other hand, became progressively besieged by the motor industry, some existing customers, and some old and new. By the end of the 1980s, the original Worcester premises was bursting at the seams, for Cosworth had started to make 4-valve cylinder heads for the Chrysler TC-Maserati turbocharged engine, cylinder blocks for Mercury Marine outboard two-stroke V6 engines, and several mysterious prototype block and head castings for destinations which I was not encouraged to discuss at the time. All this with a workforce of 125 people, and a wastage of the precious Zircon sand of only one per cent. Meaningless? In that case, consider that the sand could be used up to 100 times – how many of the world's other foundries can achieve that?

By 1989 Worcester was sending 450 cylinder head castings to Wellingborough every week, and another 120 heads to outside customers, in addition to another 40 castings for miscellaneous customers. With a doubling of Cosworth's engine assembly planned for the early 1990s, the castings facility needed to be expanded, so a brand new factory block was built, in Warndon, at the other side of Worcester. Cosworth, of course, would always use 'own-make' castings to machine and build into its own engines, but why shouldn't other companies, some of them rivals, do the same? Bob Smith had a ready answer:

"We're so much more accurate than most people, and our consistency allows us to cut down on spare metal, and therefore on machining. This is more important as castings (such as for a 4-valve head) get more and more complex."

He was delighted to confirm, too, that both Ilmor

Discovered in a Ford-UK 'Find a Lady' competition in 1984, Louise Aitken-Walker eventually went on to become World Ladies Rally Champion, and drove four-wheel-drive Sierra Cosworth 4x4s in the early 1990s.

When the YBD engine was race-tuned, it could produce a reliable 500bhp.

and Judd had approached Cosworth to have major castings done at Worcester, but that Keith Duckworth had emphatically turned them away. Just as Worcester was getting larger, so was Wellingborough. By the early 1990s, instead of being instructed to go round the eastern ring road, and "to look for Mothercare's factory, we're just beyond that," it was possible to see a massive new factory block, some distance away, well before one reached it. This time, perhaps for the first time in Cosworth's illustrious 30-year life, there was more than enough space for the next phase of expansion.

But where would the limits be? Was there a lot more to come in the next few years?

12: A NEW 'ATMO' ENGINE FOR THE 1990s

"I sent a Fax back to Japan saying: 'Please arrange a search party, we appear to have a leak on our dyno, there must be a big puddle of horsepower on the floor.'"

"The first time they put an HB engine together, and took a power reading, we got significantly more power than the DFR ..."

Cosworth's last F1 victory had been recorded in 1983, and normally-aspirated engines were totally banned from the end of 1985. Had the 1.5-litre turbo engine won the war? Keith Duckworth had always been adamant that an all-turbo formula was a mistake, and within two years he was vindicated. By 1986, FISA, horrified to see the way that turbo horsepower, in 'race trim,' had leapt to more than 1000bhp, turned one of its well-known credibility somersaults. For 1987 normally-aspirated engines of 3.5-litres would be allowed as an alternative to turbo engines, and for the 1989 season these would be compulsory once again, while turbos would be banned!

Having been double-crossed, maybe even triple-crossed, over engine stability regulations in Grand Prix racing, Cosworth could have made excuses for turning its back on the tight little world of F1. At the time, managing director Richard Bulman, a businessman with no dyed-in-the-wool experience of motor racing, thought this would be ill-advised:

"Although F1 sales volumes are low at Cosworth, the race engine side is a very significant side of our business. We're unlikely to get any larger, in proportion to the whole of the business, but it is the 'driving force' of our innovative technology. We need to keep on racing, to protect our reputation."

In 1987, therefore, Cosworth decided to shrug off the short-lived F1 V6 turbo programme, and try again. This time, at least, it would be with a normally-aspirated engine, a type of which Keith Duckworth and his disciples thoroughly approved. As already recounted in Chapter 8, Cosworth was able to produce the 3.5-litre DFZ at very short notice, a 565bhp engine which at least allowed many teams to stay in Grand Prix racing, but this was only meant to be a very short-term project, a stop-gap solution.

Ford-USA's motorsport director, Mike Kranefuss, weary of the double-talking, the cynicism, and the disappointment of his first two seasons in F1 racing, gained approval for a new Ford-financed programme, with engines originally to be supplied only to the Witney-based Benetton team. There would be two phases. Just over the horizon – or so it seemed to Mike Kranefuss and Cosworth, at the time – there was the promise of a powerful 5-valves-per-cylinder version of the DFV, by Yamaha of Japan, and this was the project which Ford approved for 1988. As the choice of 'DFZ' had dropped the naming sequence off the end of the alphabet, Cosworth was forced to jump back further along the scale, and chose DFR for its identification.

For 1989 and beyond, however, Cosworth would be encouraged to design a completely new normally-aspirated engine, and the DFR would then become the current 'customer' F1 engine.

The Ford-Yamaha connection was first made in the USA, when the Japanese company (hitherto only famous for building successful road and racing motorcycles) was contracted to produce high-performance versions of Ford's road car engines. To follow this, Yamaha decided to get into F3000 racing in Japan, where the main battle of the normally-aspirated engines was between Cosworth's ageless DFV, and a new Honda V8. Geoff Goddard (who, with Martin Walters, would be responsible for the design of the next two Cosworth F1 engines) clearly recalls what happened next:

"Yamaha asked our permission to put their new 5-valve cylinder head, which was totally their own design, on to a DFV bottom end. It seemed to be promising, but it was no more powerful than a 4-valve DFV."

Five-valve cylinder heads, with three inlet and two exhaust valves, are theoretically able to pass up to 10 per cent more air through their cylinders than can a 4-valve head. However, because F3000 engines were limited to 9000rpm by regulation, this advantage never showed up. Mike Kranefuss confirms that Yamaha then proposed that it should supply cylinder heads to Cosworth for use on the interim 1988 F1 engine:

"They discussed a deal with Cosworth. The horsepower numbers they gave us were absolutely convincing – if the engines came out anywhere near close to the predicted figures we would be in good shape. The DFZ had produced 565bhp, we were looking for 600bhp, but they said that 630bhp shouldn't be a problem."

The problem was that Yamaha had merely projected their F3000 figures upwards, to horsepower ratings which looked very attractive. For the moment, at least,

Ford was convinced. Yamaha was already an important commercial partner with Ford, and eventually Keith Duckworth was persuaded that this was the interim way to go. Geoff Goddard, who swore that there was no jealousy involved on his part, was never convinced, and actually wrote a discussion paper arguing that the 5-valve head should not be used. It wasn't long before Mike Kranefuss was very nervous about the whole project:

"Yamaha took a DFZ away, and kept coming back with complaints about the block, that this was flexing, that that was wrong. Cosworth kept on replying 'Yes, we know about that, just keep concentrating on the cylinder head, and the power.' Then, of all things, Yamaha were late. Instead of running engines in August and September 1987, they were months late. It wasn't until just before Christmas 1987 that Cosworth ran up an engine at Northampton. It was disastrous, no power, a very erratic curve, all kinds of things were wrong."

Yamaha, in fact, had built five engines, and all were disappointing. Geoff Goddard, who was itching to get started on an all-new design, was appalled by what he discovered when the Yamaha-developed engine went on to a Northampton test-bed:

"It wasn't even competitive with our own 4-valve engine, never mind ahead of it. I sent a Fax back to Japan saying: 'Please arrange a search party, we appear to have a leak on our dyno, there must be a big puddle of horsepower on the floor,'" – which they did, and were unsuccessful in their search.

Cosworth worked away on the engine until the middle of January 1988, then cancelled the project. Mike Kranefuss (in the USA at the time) remembers receiving a 'phone call from Keith ("It must have been 3.00am in England") stating, quite firmly, that the 5-valve project had been abandoned. Mike then told me, with a fond smile on his face, about the speed of Cosworth's response:

"This convinced me that the basics at Cosworth are still there, and alive. Within a few weeks, all their resources were behind the 4-valve engine, and they soon came up with some pretty good figures, considering the time wasted on the 5-valve engine."

[Yamaha, incidentally, were still convinced that their head was a definite improvement over anything that Cosworth had ever done, and set out to prove it by supplying new F1 engines to Zakspeed for the 1989 season. Unhappily, by mid-1989, no Zakspeed had even qualified to start a race, so the claims were still never proven!]

Whenever I mentioned 5-valve heads to Cosworth personalities, while originally preparing this book, a fair amount of bristling, injured pride, and a dismissive "Well, I was never convinced ..." attitude surfaced. Keith, however, talked all round the subject, and was not prepared to write-off the layout, while Geoff Goddard sagely admitted that there were "certain advantages, certain disadvantages," but also told me with a grin that Cosworth has kept on working, has continued to look at everything in detail, and has continued to test ...

Aston Martin Tickford's engine development division, led by no less a personality than ex-Cosworth engineer Alistair Lyle, produced its own 5-valve heads for the rival Judd V8 engine, but as these featured not two, but three, camshafts, per head, there was yet another factor to be considered ...

Early in 1988, Geoff Goddard was finally unleashed on the definitive DFR, a possibility which he had in any case been studying throughout 1987. While admitting that what Ford really needed was a newer, and altogether smaller, engine, he "went through the whole engine and looked at everything hard, in detail." He was not impressed when I suggested that it had been a routine redevelopment job.

"This was a good example of a major new design that doesn't look like it. The DFR was developed from the old DFV, but we did over 400 new drawings for the new version – that's about 80 per cent of the drawings involved in an all-new engine."

The DFR, as raced by Benetton in 1988, produced a minimum of 595bhp at 11,000rpm as soon as it ran, with occasional engines just creeping above 600bhp – this latter figure representing 171bhp/litre, slightly less than the DFY had achieved way back in 1983. It was good, but in a year completely dominated by turbocharged Honda engines, it was never good enough to win a race. Nevertheless, the Benetton-DFR cars were far and away the most successful of the normally-aspirated runners that season.

During the year, Benetton drivers Thierry Boutsen and Alessandro Nannini took eight third places, and another eight points-scoring positions, while the team finished third in the Manufacturers' Championship, behind the turbocharged McLaren-Honda and Ferrari teams.

Even so, it was not until the DFR was up and running, and already proving itself to be a very satisfactory normally-aspirated V8 – the best of the current bunch – that Cosworth could even turn to the

The 3.5-litre HB, first seen in F1 in 1989, was a neatly-detailed 75 degree V8, which proved to be F1-dominant in the early 1990s.

idea of building a new engine. The new unit, coded HB by Cosworth (but stubbornly not named by Ford when originally revealed in 1989!), only existed in the mind of its creators – Keith Duckworth, Mike Costin and Geoff Goddard – until Geoff took a drawing board home in May 1988, and started the drawing process. Only seven months later, the first engine ran on a test bed in Northampton!

[You want a reason for the use of the HB title? There really isn't one. The previous new F1 design for Ford had been the V6 turbocharged GB, so maybe HB was a logical progression from that? Why not HA instead? Had there been a secret HA project, once? Indeed there had, but Cosworth wouldn't tell me at the time, and finally this was revealed as the code for the still-born 120-deg F2 unit of 1972 ...]

Mike Kranefuss was encouraged by the new engine: "The first time Cosworth put an engine together, and took a power reading at 10,500rpm, which was by no means the peak at which it was to be raced, it produced significantly more power than any DFR had ever done.

"I was surprised. Maybe the whole process of going through the difficulties of the V6 turbo project after so many years of success with the DFV, then the disaster with the Yamaha engine, which never really worked, made it unexpected. Probably this could be the turn-round for Cosworth Engineering, into getting back to the forefront of F1 racing engines again.

"Martin Walters is very cynical, and he thought we'd be lucky if we got the same power, at first, as a DFR. Geoff Goddard, who is a racer at heart, and always very enthusiastic, was always saying that the new engine was going to work well."

Since Keith Duckworth designed the original DFV in 1967, the Formula 1 engine business has become much more specialised, much more competitive, and the various companies have become more secretive. For that reason, neither Ford, nor Cosworth, released bore and stroke dimensions, valve sizes or valve angles, compression ratios, power or torque figures for the HB. What follows, therefore, is merely a summary of what Mike Kranefuss and Geoff Goddard were prepared to tell me. Since the 1960s and 1970s there had also been a fundamental change in the design process at Cosworth. Mike Costin told me that Keith was finding it more and more difficult to design anything new because:

"His experience was such that it was becoming impossible to get him to make decisions. The more he

Cosworth's approach to the design of the HB was to look at all the great features of the legendary DFV, and to make the new engine (based on a 75 degree vee rather than 90 degrees) more compact, lighter, and with even more efficient breathing. It was a remarkable success.

understood about the subject, the more he saw the impossibility of it all."

Mike Kranefuss agreed:

"Keith reached a point where he could talk through a programme, analysing it in detail, which in my opinion is his greatest capability. Then he goes on talking, and analysing, and starts talking about solutions, and problems. Eventually, he then talks himself out of the solutions! He got to the point where he could always see the next mountain of problems."

Keith Duckworth reluctantly agreed with that, and that he had almost nothing to do with the new engine:

"I think I have got over the hill, as a designer," he told me in 1989. "I know too much nowadays, I try to design too many things out. I could see all the problems that weren't necessarily going to occur, or not be serious, and I would try to design them out."

Two examples of what Goddard called the "theoretically impossible problem" to solve, were that DFV cylinder blocks weave by up to 0.022in, while connecting rod compression loads are sometimes as high as 12 tons. Not only that, but something like 50lb/ft of stab torque is needed to open two valves.

"But I'm still a good lateral thinker," Keith said, "These days I tend to write great treatises on head gaskets, cylinder head to block joints, and great elastic diagrams to show how the cylinder block behaves. I worked out what should be a fundamentally reasonable head and block structure. Someone like Geoff can then translate from these principles into something which embodies the principles into the detailed design. I think I'm still very good at concepts, and at the fundamentals of a thing, but nowadays when I get down to the details, I start worrying. I'm now too slow, because I'm still trying to do things too well. There's no doubt that this has got worse over the years.

"Never mind. Geoff Goddard is very good and so is John Hancock, who has now moved over to road-car engine design with a project of his own. They are both quite capable of designing a whole engine on their own. In both cases, if I have to explain some very complicated thing, they understand.

"It's when I have to do something which is different from the normal that I have had difficulty in finding people who understand. John Hancock and Geoff Goddard, well they're both very bright …"

['Bright,' let's not forget, is the ultimate accolade from Duckworth …]

Keith then confirmed the way in which the 1989 HB came to be laid out:

"Geoff was responsible for the total mechanical layout, from concept, to principles of the bank angle [which was 75 degrees, not 90 degrees as one might expect], to decisions on the crankshaft and the balancing systems. Quite a number of the conceptual things were mine, though, and structurally the V8 HB is really the 'son of GB V6 turbo.' Martin Walters did the electronics and the fuelling system, using Ford's system and was helped a lot by Ford's people.

"The HB was essentially a two-man job – Geoff and John Hancock – the major components being shared almost equally. Incidentally, it's always important to get people to appreciate the importance of detail – engines usually only go wrong in detail – but Geoff and John know all about that."

Geoff Goddard confirmed the arrangement:

"In 1988 the racing design office was only seven people. Keith and I had been talking about the engine for some weeks before I started drawing the engine on 12 May 1988. It ran on the test bed for the first time in December 1988. That was only achieved by people spending up to 60 hours a week on design work.

"We don't learn much by looking at what other people were doing. All you can really see, in any case, is installations – fuel systems, electronics, and how you might package things. The really important bits are always hidden away. You never read, in the magazines, of what is going on inside an engine, do you? If someone gave us – say – a complete Honda engine, and invited us to have a look inside, that would be wonderful, but I doubt if we'll ever get the chance.

"If you pick up the motoring magazines, they will all tell you that a 12-cylinder engine is needed, because it can run the quickest, and breathe the most. But when, with Benetton, we started to look at the package, the weight, the fuel consumption, this led us to look at several different types. Benetton wanted the car to be as small and light as possible – down to the weight limit, if possible.

"When we started talking, and thinking, we oscillated between several different layouts. The '12' perhaps, was going to be the best for ultimate power, but fuel consumption was going to count against that. In deciding what engine to make, we also projected what we thought the different engines would be able to achieve, if they were all done to the same standards – you can't argue 10s against 12s against 8s unless they're all designed by the same people, to the same standards."

Mike Kranefuss agrees, entirely, with the way that the concept was settled:

"We all talked to each other. We looked at a V12, but thought it would be bigger, a bit more thirsty, and would need a bigger car. A V10, well, no-one could really warm to the idea. Cosworth then said, 'Well, we know a lot about V8s, we can do a new one very fast, we can do one lighter, smaller …' Rory Byrne of Benetton agreed that the V12 would probably be too large, the V10 was a 'maybe.' Cosworth also thought that they had never ever gone for the 'ultimate DFV,' and now here was a chance.

"I said I wanted a new engine for just one team, two later, maybe. Later on, perhaps Cosworth could supply engines to ten teams if they wanted to. Right now, I said, I want to win some races."

Geoff Goddard, in the meantime, was backing up this process with lots of 'paper engines:'

"We sketched several package shapes in several months – Vees, flats, tens, eights, 12s – showing them all to Rory Byrne at Benetton. Did we need a flat engine now that there were no 'ground effect' structures, or would that get in the way of the 'Coke bottle' body profile – that sort of problem.

"In the end we homed in on a 75 degree V8, a very compact package which hides behind any other engine, from any angle. The difference between the HB and the old DFV, was not only 20 years of development, but the fact that the DFV eventually went out to almost 4.0-litres, where the 3.5-litre HB is almost impossible to stretch."

Compared with the launch of the DFV in 1967, the launch of HB in March 1989 (or, as Ford insisted on calling it, 'the new Ford Formula One' engine) was a very muted affair. Mike Kranefuss made a very short, humorous, and downbeat speech in which he gave nothing away, while the written information was sparse in the extreme. Except that we were told that it was to run on a 12.0:1 compression ratio, and that "in excess of 600bhp" was claimed, almost nothing else was revealed. A side by side picture of the DFR against the HB was more instructive, for the new HB was clearly narrower and lower, but at least as long. The inference was that it had a larger bore and a shorter stroke than the DFR, and that every millimetre of unnecessary size had been squeezed out of it.

Right from the start, it seems, the new HB exceeded its own immediate targets, and on my visits to Northampton I often heard the most exhilarating 12,000rpm wails coming from the test beds at the back of the original factory block. But how much? Even these days, perhaps, we will never know. Some people laughed off ideas of a 650bhp peak though talk of 635bhp was thought to be reasonable. Geoff Goddard, exuberant, confident, and secretive, all at the same time, suggested that:

"Limits are only set by a lack of knowledge. The key measure, the BMEP in the cylinder head, is now very hard to shift – we're only talking of crawling up half of one per cent at a time. The secret is to keep the BMEP curve up, and to make the engine rev faster than ever. All the time, these days, we are scratching around for little improvements – and don't forget that for this engine one per cent is 6bhp!"

Before getting the HB into F1 racing, there were many frustrations. First the Benetton B189 car was completed a few weeks late, and on an early test the first car was crashed. Lengthy tests then uncovered an engine problem which resulted in crankshaft breakages after considerable test-running in cars. The puzzle for Cosworth was that the same problem could never be reproduced on the test bed.

It was not until June that the first race-length tests were satisfactorily completed, and it was not until July

The 1989 specification HB (right) compared directly with a 1988 specification DFR (left). Clearly the HB was more compact – slimmer and lower – this mainly being due to the use of a 75 degree vee angle in place of a 90-degree angle. The horsepower difference? No one at Cosworth, or Ford, ever admitted to any definitive figures.

that the B189/HB combination first appeared in a race. One new Benetton B189, driven by Alessandro Nannini, started the French GP. On the first day of practice it was way off the pace, but on the second day the chassis matched the engine's potential, and Nannini was fourth fastest, just 0.934 sec behind pole-sitter Alain Prost. The Benetton was on the second row of the grid, behind the two 10-cylinder Honda-engined McLarens, and alongside Nigel Mansell's V12-engined Ferrari. [The 5-valve Yamaha-engined Zakspeeds, as usual, had not qualified – they were three seconds slower than the B189.]

At Paul Ricard, where the race was held, there is a long drag down to the first corner. After the lights turned green, the Benetton made a fine start, out-dragging the Ferrari, and jinking around behind the two Hondas. Then Gugelmin's crash caused the race to be stopped.

No matter, the HB's power was proven, once again, at the restart, and before long Nannini was sitting comfortably in second place, behind Prost's Honda-engined McLaren. No other car, and no other engine, could keep up with the HB-engined Benetton. For half the race the Benetton howled around the fast Paul Ricard circuit until, suddenly, a rear suspension link failed at high speed, and the car hurled off the track, to retire. It was a let-down, but at least the engine had proved its point. The Benetton had set the second fastest race lap too.

The second outing, just a week later, came in the British GP. This time Nannini qualified the car ninth fastest, but right from the start he tucked in behind the McLarens, Ferraris, and Williams cars. An early pit stop for tyres dropped him off the leader-board, but in a spirited drive, he soon regained fourth place, spent much of the race catching, then passing, Nelson Piquet's Judd-engined Lotus. The Benetton, and the new HB, took third place in the end, its first 'podium finish,' and an encouraging beginning for the team, and its new power unit.

Neither Benetton, Ford, nor Cosworth could then have been completely happy with the rest of the HB's first season. Although the engines were almost completely reliable (and it was soon clear that they produced at least as much power as every engine except the Honda V10, and possibly the V12 Ferrari), the cars, and sometimes the drivers, let the side down on many occasions.

Many observers, not only among the pundits, but among the rival teams, observed that the 1989 Benetton did not handle as well as the 1988 car – with more than one writer suggesting that it was one of the season's worst-handling cars. Clearly if the car could achieve so much with such mediocre handling, then the engine must be quite outstanding?

In Germany, Emanuele Pirro got up to third place behind the two McLaren-Hondas, then went off under braking; in Hungary, Nannini's gearbox let him down; in Belgium, Nannini finished fifth in atrocious conditions; while in Italy both cars retired. Pirro spun off in Spain, when lying fourth, apparently due to fatigue. In the same period, team manager Peter Collins (who had been the inspiration behind the signing of Johnny Herbert, who was then dropped from the team in favour of Pirro) walked out of his job.

Then, towards the end of the year, it all began to come right, and the HB recorded its first World Championship win. Nannini finished fourth in Portugal, and was all set to finish third in Japan, when the two leading McLarens suddenly tangled with each other. He then took the lead as marshals sorted out the chaos, and although he was later re-passed by Senna's hard-charging McLaren, the Honda-powered car was later disqualified for a variety of offences.

This first outright win for the HB, though unexpected, was none-the-less welcome – and it represented a huge 'loss of face' for the Japanese Honda concern. Nor had Nannini anything to apologise about, for he had backed off the racing pace well before the end

of the race, when secure in third place. Without this precaution, he would certainly have recorded an undisputed victory.

The last event of the year, the Australian GP, was pure farce, for the weather was appalling, and many drivers simply spun off and crashed in the awful conditions.

Alessandro Nannini had qualified fourth and, driving with his head as well as his heart, managed to stay between the walls, settled into second place (behind Boutsen's Renault-engined Williams) at quarter distance, and stayed there to the end. Pirro's car took fifth place – this was the first time both HB-engined cars had been on the leader board in the 1989 season.

In its first half-season, therefore, the V8 HB had recorded one victory, one second place, one third, one fourth and two fifth places. Compared with the DFV in 1967, it was a modest beginning, but in the super-competitive Formula 1 of 1989 it was a solid start. Not only that, but Geoff Goddard's team had already developed an HB 'Mark 2' tune (officially called the 'development engine') which had more power and torque, and which would form the basis of the 1990 engines for the Benetton team.

At the end of 1989, however, it was clear that many people had great confidence in Benetton's future, which was also a real compliment to the performance of the new Cosworth HB engine. There were two totally unexpected moves – one was the appointment of John Barnard as Technical Director, the other was the signing of three-times F1 World Champion Nelson Piquet to drive one of the cars. John Barnard had made his name as McLaren's principal designer earlier in the 1980s, but had later set up the 'satellite' Ferrari business – GTO – at Guildford. It was Barnard's expertise which had transformed Ferrari's chassis performance with a new structure built in the UK, along with a revolutionary seven-speed semi-automatic transmission. Although Ferrari wanted to keep him, Barnard was attracted to Benetton to work on new cars for the 1990s.

His appointment was always likely to make the relationship with Benetton chief designer Rory Byrne rather prickly, especially as the pundits suggested that the 1989 car's chassis had not been as competitive as the HB engine which powered it. Clearly two top men could not remain together for long – this being confirmed during 1990 when Byrne resigned and moved to another F1 team.

Even before the end of 1989, Ford's Mike Kranefuss had started getting requests from other teams, for supplies of HBs for the 1990 season. Tyrrell wanted to know if HBs could replace their DFRs? Lotus asked if HBs could replace their Judds? Ligier made approaches – and there were others.

Mike, for sure, listened politely to everyone, but turned them all down. For 1990, at least, Ford and Cosworth's HB engine would still remain available to only one team. The signing of Nelson Piquet (to replace Emanuele Pirro) was a real surprise, for the Brazilian's 1988 and 1989 record in the Lotus F1 team had been disappointing, and there were those who suggested that he was past his best. Benetton, Ford and Cosworth, however, were all convinced that the problem had been with the cars, and not with Piquet.

Nelson was known to shine when the cars encouraged him to do so, and perhaps to switch off when there was nothing to be gained by grappling with uncompetitive equipment. For 1990 he was given an extra incentive to get results; his contract reputedly included huge extra payments for each World Championship point notched up.

For 1990, therefore, Cosworth's still-developing HB engine was matched to yet another Rory Byrne chassis, the Benetton B190, and to the new driving team of Nelson Piquet and Alessandro Nannini.

Cosworth's race engineers, led by Dick Scammell and designer Geoff Goddard, worked hard on the HB all through the winter, ensuring that the original 1990-spec HB engine was more powerful than the last of the 1989 types – and an even bigger improvement was already being promised for mid-season.

In any case Cosworth had to keep on improving the HB, merely to keep up with the opposition, for technical progress in F1 was as rapid as ever. At the end of 1989 Honda reported that it had squeezed a lot more power from its successful V10 F1 engine during that year and revealed a new V12 unit to be used in the 1991 season. In addition Judd and Ilmor were known to be developing new V10s while Porsche was designing a V12 …

Quite independent of the Cosworth factory, by the way, Brian Hart had been working away on the development of the venerable DFR engine. Somewhere from inside that long-established layout he found more power, and for 1990 guaranteed a peak rating of 612bhp instead of the 595bhp of the 'standard' DFRs of 1989. That brought the specific output of the old design up to 175bhp /litre – better than Cosworth itself had ever achieved with the 3-litre DFY of 1983!

As is usual in this modern security-conscious F1 era, neither Ford nor Cosworth said much about the internal changes made to the HB; certainly there were no obvious visual changes to be seen on the engines during 1990. The only clues we ever had were that the engines seemed to rev faster and faster – and they were usually extremely reliable.

Benetton started the 1990 season with the 1989 cars, and were out-qualified at Phoenix by Jean Alesi's DFR-equipped Tyrrell! Alesi then went on to lead the first half of the race, and finished second, beating Piquet's B189 into fourth place. The new Benetton B190s were ready for Imola, in May, where Alessandro Nannini finished third and Piquet fifth, and the HB engines could be spun up to 12,500rpm.

Benetton, and the still-improving HB engine, was getting better all the time – Piquet picked up second place in Canada (though Nannini wrote off his car), Nannini was fourth in Mexico, and Piquet fourth in France. Before the British GP, where the 13,000rpm Series IV HB engine was available, Nelson Piquet was so confident of victory that he placed a bet to back himself; everything then went wrong however, when he was forced to start from the back of the grid, and he could only finish fifth.

By this time the resurgence of the team was a big talking point in the F1 'circus' The Benettons usually qualified immediately behind the McLaren-Hondas, Ferraris and Williams-Renaults, but in race trim they were often fastest in a straight line, and gradually they were beginning to beat the V10 engined Williams cars in the races themselves.

Benetton's philosophy was to avoid mid-race tyre changes if at all possible (Keith Duckworth with his 'optimum use of rubber' philosophy would have approved of that), which meant that their late-race performance was sometimes marginal. Out on the circuits, though, only the shrill V10 Hondas and V12 Ferrari engines had their measure, and Benetton was closing the gap. Not only that, but Nelson Piquet's return to form – a rejuvenation, no less – was quite remarkable.

At the end of 1990, Ford admitted that the Series IV HB engine produced 'more than 650bhp' (already 50bhp more than it had claimed for the original HB in 1989), though pundits reckoned that it probably peaked at around 680bhp or even more. Certainly, Geoff Goddard's statement that: "the secret is to keep the BMEP curve up, and to make the engine rev faster than ever" was being borne out. Cosworth was still using conventional valve springs, yet the engine was

Ford and Cosworth were always very sparing with the information they revealed about the new HB engine in 1989. The 75 degree vee angle is not obvious in this shot, but the compact pumps layout, and the stubby inlet trumpets are evident. This is the Series V derivative as seen, and winning, in 1990.

happy to exceed 13,000rpm – no other F1 racing V8 could match this.

Benetton's real charge came in the second half of 1990, and the sturdy Series IV HB engine had a lot to do with this. At Hockenheim, in the German GP, Nannini's Benetton took the lead at pit-stop time, and held off Senna's Honda until nine laps from the end. His second place was a truly storming result.

Then came Hungary, and one of those bursts of controversy for which F1 had become noted. Nannini and Piquet qualified seventh and ninth, yet Nannini had moved up to second place by two-thirds distance. Eight laps later, when shaping up to pass Boutsen's Williams, and take the lead, his Benetton was literally shunted off the circuit by Ayrton Senna. As Nigel Roebuck's *Autosport* race report pointed out: "On lap 64 Nannini and Senna touched at the chicane. Which is to say that Senna touched Nannini in a move which had no place in the repertoire of Formula 1's fastest driver … Nannini's car was pitched high in the air and off the circuit."

Feelings ran high, and Senna, acting saintly as usual, protested that it wasn't his fault. Nannini, Benetton and the whole world knew, though, that this should have been Benetton's first victory of 1990.

Two weeks later, in Belgium, the Benettons finished fourth and fifth, while at Jerez, in Spain, Nannini's car took yet another third place after Piquet's car had briefly led the race at mid-distance. All the time this was going on, the two drivers were piling up points and the team was creeping up in the Manufacturers' standings.

In October, everything went wrong – then dramatically right – for Cosworth and Benetton. The likeable Alessandro Nannini was dreadfully injured in a helicopter crash at his parents' home in Italy, and Roberto Moreno had to be drafted in to the team for the last two races of the year. The Italian was not thought likely to be able to drive a racing car again.

Even so, in the wake of this sadness for Benetton, there was a splendid finish to the season. In Japan, at Suzuka, both McLarens and Prost's Ferrari were eliminated by early crashes, which allowed the Benettons to slot comfortably into second and third places. Suddenly, at half distance, Mansell's Ferrari broke its transmission, which left Nelson Piquet's Benetton in the lead, and his new team-mate Roberto Moreno behind him in second place.

That was the way it stayed, with Benetton notching up its first-ever one-two finish, repeating its great

success of precisely one year earlier, and, once again, humiliating the Japanese engine manufacturers on their home territory. Not only that, but Benetton moved firmly ahead of Williams-Renault in the Manufacturers' Championship, headed only by McLaren and Ferrari. For Nelson Piquet it was a triumphant return from the depths of 1989. He had not won an F1 GP since 1987, so it was not surprising that, with an impish grin, he reintroduced himself to the world's media at the post-race press conference!

Two weeks later, at Adelaide in Australia, Benetton did it again. The two Benettons qualified in their customary seventh and eighth positions, once again the cars were seen to be very fast in a straight line, and once again they planned to go through non-stop, in the 81-lap street race.

Nelson Piquet surged into fifth place on the first lap, moved up to fourth two laps later by passing Alain Prost's Ferrari, annexed third place from Gerhard Berger's McLaren-Honda six laps later, then calmly set about reeling in Nigel Mansell's Ferrari to take second place on lap 46.

Was there more to come? Could the beautifully-balanced Benetton overtake Ayrton Senna's McLaren-Honda? We may never know that – for what we do know is that Senna was being pressured so much that he missed a gear and crashed the McLaren.

Piquet's Benetton, with HB engine singing away at up to 13,000rpm on the main straight, surged into the lead, and, in spite of a last-minute excursion, kept that to the end, defeating both the Ferraris, both the Williams-Renaults, and the surviving McLaren-Honda.

In the meantime, Ford – and Cosworth – had decided to increase its F1 involvement for 1991, and to build more HB engines. While Benetton would continue to get every priority, especially with new developments, this meant that it would be possible to supply engines to an extra team.

Even though Judd, Ilmor and Porsche were also bringing new F1 engines to the scene, once the word about HB availability got around (and rumours travel very fast in the Grand Prix business) there was another rush to contact Mike Kranefuss, and all manner of deals were proposed, though several potential customers were reluctant to pay the leasing fees which Cosworth required.

In the end, almost everyone was surprised when Ford decided to supply engines to the newly-formed Jordan team. Who? If you had to ask, you obviously hadn't been looking at F3000, where Eddie Jordan's

DFV-engined team cars had usually been front-runners, and race-winners.

The persuasive Eddie Jordan, who was also personal manager to several up-and-coming F1 drivers, had clearly offered an ambitious package to Ford, which obviously expected his cars to be better than those of any of the other long-established teams that were using Cosworth DFR, or Judd V8 engines.

Yet more fascinating HB developments were promised for 1991. One was that Cosworth develop a Group C (World Championship Sports Prototype racing) version for use in Tom Walkinshaw's two-seater Jaguars. A 'Ford' engine in a Jaguar would have been quite unthinkable in previous years, but after Ford had completed the takeover of Jaguar in November 1989, anything was possible. For 1991 there was to be a new Group C formula, which required the use of normally-aspirated 3.5-litre engines, so, with the Ford HB and the XJR racing Jaguars now all under the same corporate umbrella, this was an obvious marriage.

It was typical of Cosworth, of course, to insist it had not originally designed the HB for endurance races, but, as the modern type of Group C events were much shorter than before, this made reworking of the 75-degree V8 more sensible.

For Cosworth – and for Ford and Jaguar – 1991 was going to be a busy and varied season.

Just for fun, Ford built 'Supervan Three' in 1995, which hid a mid-engined chassis evolved from the C100, but powered by the modern Ford-Cosworth HB F1 engine! Later, that engine was swapped for a modified FB power unit. Both derivatives were astonishingly fast.

In his last-ever drive for McLaren (and, incidentally, in his final F1 victory), Ayrton Senna took this HB-powered McLaren MP4/8 to an outright win in the 1993 Australian Grand Prix. Senna won five GPs in the HB-powered cars during 1993, yet some ill-informed observers suggested that his car had been 'under-powered!'

Not only was the HB engine very successful in F1 racing but, when used by TWR in the Jaguar XJR14 sports car, it won the 1991 World Sports Car Championship, too.

COSWORTH – THE SEARCH FOR POWER

13: NEW BUSINESS IN THE 1990s …

"My mission is to grow the company. We already have a vision – the management team has a vision – for Cosworth until the year 2000."

"I don't feel that anyone else in the Western world can approach Cosworth's expertise in doing what it does."

As the 1990s unfolded, Cosworth changed considerably. The reticent, if not to say reclusive, company of old, gradually gave way to a more open business. In the 1960s and 1970s the company had seemed to expand almost against Keith Duckworth's wishes, but in the 1990s it positively looked around for growth, and new business, at every opportunity.

The master-plan, if that is the way to describe what happened, was formulated by the parent company, Vickers. After it gained control, Vickers installed Dr Peter Nevitt in the chair. To quote a colleague:

"I think Vickers brought in Peter because he could provide good links, and a good understanding of the Ford mind. [As ever, Ford still provided Cosworth with a lot of its business, especially on the road-car engines side]. But he had already retired from Ford, so this was always felt to be a medium-term appointment.

"They were then looking to replace him with a career executive, someone with the ability to look at Cosworth as a business. Vickers was anxious to preserve all the good things of Cosworth, then grow the business. Vickers is a great boss. They sign off an operating plan every year, and a three-year business plan. Generally they give us a lot of autonomy."

Seasoned Cosworth-watchers were astonished to see the changes that followed in the mid-1990s. For the first time, regular factory tours were started, and new race-engine launches took place at Northampton. The company – which had once positively recoiled from public relations activity – now appointed a PR manager, who was immediately inundated with requests for facilities – tours, visits, photographs and interviews.

"In fact, the Cosworth brand name is quite difficult to market," the newly-appointed Chief Executive Chris Woodwark later admitted. "Our best and most famous product today is the Ford Zetec-R F1 engine, which isn't badged as a Cosworth – it's a Ford engine. Because some of our customers want secrecy we can't talk about the excellence of Cosworth without hurting those customers! But for them our ability to preserve secrecy and integrity is vital, and important. For all of them, we have to preserve individual expertise, integrity and knowledge within the group."

Most significant of all was that archivist Valerie

Given collected together so many historic old engines and artefacts, and that space was found for a small, neatly detailed company museum. By 1994 relatively unknown race engines such as the JAA motorcycle unit had gone on display, along with previously secret engines such as the AB Chevrolet V8 conversion – and even an example of the still-born VB V12 F1 engine of 1991/1992.

Chris Woodwark, who became Cosworth's CEO in 1993, explained that: "In recent years Cosworth had been on a plateau. It made reasonable profits, and had reasonable revenues, but the company hadn't been moving forward. The management team then developed a growth strategy – which was new, because there was no aggressive strategy before that! The shareholders wanted to see the company grow. Cosworth had to react to the fact that it was owned by a PLC [Public Limited Company]."

Although it was going to take years to revolutionise the company, by 1994 Woodwark knew what he, and Vickers, wanted to do:

"My mission is to grow the company. We already have a vision – the management team has a vision – for Cosworth until the year 2000. I've worked in British manufacturing all my life, starting in 1964, and never have I seen engineers having such a say as they do here. We want to give them authority, let them lead, and develop the company against that background, its desire to win.

"Cosworth's strategic intent is to win wherever it competes – in any of the four operating divisions – racing, engines engineering, manufacturing and castings. I've tried to give people room to operate, and to give them authority.

"Next we want to expand a fifth division, to gain new business in other areas. We're trying to do that: we've just opened an office in North America, and then we're concentrating on the Far East."

Woodwark's view was that the company had been ripe for change, and that the original founders – Keith Duckworth and Mike Costin – had been very graceful about it when they retired. From time to time they still visited 'their' company in this period, and recognised that Cosworth had become very different:

"A lot of the heritage and ethos they brought to

CHRIS WOODWARK

AFTER working within the Rover Group and its ancestors for 22 years, Chris Woodwark took over as Cosworth Engineering's Chief Executive in 1993. His mission, to expand Cosworth's horizons, would only become obvious to the public in the later 1990s.

Born in Surrey in 1946, he gained a BSc Economics degree at the Polytechnic of Central London, before joining Rootes in 1964 as a trainee. Like many others who worked there, he decided to move on after Chrysler took control of its newly-bought British subsidiary, and in 1971 he joined British Leyland on the marketing side.

By 1978 he was Sales Director of Land Rover, Africa, became Sales and Marketing Director of Leyland Trucks in 1982, and took over as Managing Director, Land Rover-Leyland International Holdings in 1985. Because Austin-Rover (later Rover) liked to shuffle its pack at regular intervals, he then held down seven top jobs in the next eight years, latterly running Austin-Rover Cars of North America, Land Rover, and Rover International.

"Then I was approached by head-hunters. I wanted to get back into the heart of the motor industry, in engineering, to create something. At Cosworth I have to lead the company, to give it a strategic framework ..."

Not only was Woodwark a formidable manager (his career record proved that), but he was also demonstrably a motoring enthusiast too. From the start, Cosworth's racing heritage seemed to be safe with him: "It is terribly important, there is a history of success, and a huge body of expertise in the company."

He was also determined to make it more visible, and more accessible, to the public and the motor industry: "I want to open Cosworth up. I'm very proud of this company. People are now understanding much more about what Cosworth is all about, and how broadly based it is ..."

In spite of a punishing schedule – in 1994 he completed 70,000 miles in a Scorpio 24V, spending a lot of time working alongside his driver, while being whisked from his Buckinghamshire home to the various Cosworth, Vickers and customers' factories – he exuded the sort of enthusiasm with which every young Cosworth employee could identify.

When I met him once again at Cosworth, his enthusiasms shone through – so much so that I was taken on a whistle-stop tour of the design offices, to the consternation of watchful engineers who were busy finalising the new 3-litre F1 engines and the next generation of Indy car units ...

"I'm very proud of this company ..."

Woodwark was appointed Chairman of Cosworth Engineering, and Chief Executive of Rolls-Royce Motor Cars on 1 January 1995, and became a Director of Vickers PLC.

Chris Woodwark became Cosworth's Chief Executive in mid-1993, his oft-stated mission being "to grow the company into the 21st Century ..."

Cosworth is still here, still being developed and built on. I think one of the nicest things is that they understood what had to happen, wished the company well when they retired in the late 1980s, and still take an active interest in how it prospers."

Compared with the 1960s, when the DFV F1 engine was designed, and when there were fewer than 50 people in the entire workforce, Cosworth in the mid-1990s had changed completely. There were almost 1000 people on the pay roll – putting it into the top five per cent of British engineering companies – in more than 250,000 square feet of factory space on five sites (including Torrance, California); these figures, in any case, were set to rise again by 1996, when the large new castings factory in Worcester came on stream.

In 1990, when Vickers took over the business, the balance at Cosworth between road-car engines and motorsport was just about half-and-half. Once the Wellingborough Two plant was up and running, with the Ford FB V6 engine in series production, that all

Scorpio 24V (Cosworth FBA) V6 engines being assembled at the Wellingborough factory at the beginning of the 1990s. The FB family was deliberately under-stressed and built with mainly standard components, because Cosworth had no plans to turn it into a motorsport power unit.

changed. Even though growing numbers of world-class race-winning V8 race car engines – HB, AC, XB, and Zetec-R – continued to pour out of Northampton, the shift to road-car work was noticeable.

By the mid-1990s there was evidence all around. Wellingborough Two, the large road-car engines factory, had taken over from Wellingborough One, whose lease was ready to be released. The second castings factory at Worcester (in Warndon) was already bursting at the seams, the original Hylton Road castings factory was set to be sold off, and a massive 'Worcester Three' building was being built to produce major components for the brand-new Jaguar V8 engine, which appeared in 1996. In Windsor, Ontario (Canada) Ford was already using the patented Cosworth castings process for new generations of engines, and in Northampton more V8 race engines were being built, serviced and developed than ever before.

More was already on the way. On a visit to Northampton in 1994, I saw that the facade of the original (1964) factory building had been enlarged and redeveloped, and that the site of a non-Cosworth business (Bullers), once surrounded by Cosworth buildings in the 1980s, was finally absorbed, and integrated, into the business.

Diggers and bulldozers had already moved on to an adjacent site (the Emissions and Driveability Centre), to prepare the ground for yet another high-tech facility, where the Duke of Kent had just laid the foundation stone. I also saw a Crewe-registered Rolls-Royce Silver Spirit in the car park, which was clearly a development car.

The transformation of a Ford–Cologne pushrod ohv V6 engine to the four-cam FB power unit (right) was remarkable. Conceived and prototyped by Brian Hart, it became a Cosworth 'mainstream' product after Brian Hart Ltd was absorbed by Cosworth.

The FB V6 engine fitted neatly into the engine bay of Ford's Scorpio family car, and was very conservatively rated, initially at 195bhp, matched to a four-speed automatic transmission.

Road car engines

By 1990, Cosworth's principal road-car engine-building project was the YB-Series for the Ford Sierra Cosworth 4x4. Almost at once this was joined by the manufacture of Ford Scorpio 24-valve V6 (FB) engines, while work for Mercedes-Benz and General Motors gradually tailed off.

Mercedes-Benz, having relied on Wellingborough to produce cylinder heads for the 190E 2.3-16, later embraced four-valve technology for its own mass-produced units. GM, having shared KB-type assembly with Wellingborough at first, later began making many more engines in its own plant in Germany. Where high volumes are concerned, transfer-line production is more cost-effective than Cosworth's unique abilities.

Mark Hunt, Manufacturing Director, took up the story: "We had tremendous expansion in two years, but in 1991 we were then hit hard by the British and then the European recessions. Volumes went down to about one-third of what they had been. But it wasn't only the recession – the Escort RS Cosworth was a different class of car from the Sierra, and didn't sell as fast. Even when Scorpio volumes came back, the straight-four [YB Series] volumes didn't come back with them."

The result was that all activities were consolidated into the new site – Wellingborough Two – which was then offering about 30,000 square feet of space:

"We then went out to get new business ... We now

do some sub-contract machining of heads for Ford, and [by 1994] we were fully utilising the new factory and looking to expand again. We actually have a 6-acre site, of which we occupy only about one-third."

At that point, Wellingborough was operating round the clock – three shifts, and employing about 120 people – but there was certainly an ambition to tackle even more. At its peak, Wellingborough was certainly very profitable, and there were signs that clients were wondering if they could do the same sort of job themselves, in house. Even though the 'between-centres' machining system which Ben Rood had devised could not be patented, Cosworth – Woodwark, Hunt, et al – were convinced that there was new business out there, waiting to be won.

Commercially there was a significant difference between the two Wellingborough sites. The original, brand new in 1985, had only ever been leased, and was now redundant. Wellingborough Two was always owned by Cosworth, and was to be expanded, long-term. By 1995 'Two' was producing YBs and FBs – each with its own dedicated assembly line – plus spares requirements for many obsolete Cosworth engines; it was also manufacturing and assembling complete overhead-valve 12-valve pushrod engines for the Ford Scorpio.

This last was the venerable 'Ford-Cologne' V6, which was nearing the end of its life. Ford, having done its sums, concluded that it made more sense for this old engine to be built by Cosworth in limited numbers, for in Cologne this then released valuable space for a new generation of ultra-modern engines to be installed instead. The move was made in 1994 (after assembly was closed down in Cologne, it took only 12 weeks to restart production in Wellingborough), but was not expected to be a long-term project.

Although the grey iron pushrod heads of this design could not be machined by Cosworth's celebrated 'between-centres' tools and fixtures (the cutting forces were too great), this facility nevertheless made Cosworth almost uniquely capable in Europe's motor industry. When I asked Hunt (and one of his colleagues, Rob Oldaker) about this, both claimed that Cosworth was pre-eminent, but that they rated "one or two competitors in Germany and Italy" extremely highly.

The founders, Keith Duckworth and Mike Costin, would certainly be proud of the way their company had developed. Their ruthless ambition to be the best was always evident – as was the policy of not dabbling in fields where unique technology could not be deployed. This might explain why Cosworth, still Europe's most famous specialist piston supplier, has never been tempted to expand into other forging activities (crankshafts, for instance). Gear cutting was once considered, but rejected – Hunt, with previous transmission engineering experience in an earlier job, thought that it would have required a new building, different machinery, and a step change in technology.

Cosworth methods continued to be exported to other customers. In Britain the reborn Triumph motorcycles business at Hinckley used Cosworth 'between-centres' methods to make its engines: "Mike Costin and Ben Rood went into their factory to advise them."

By this time Cosworth was so flexible that it began to advertise its ability to deal with other companies' 'peaks and troughs' problems. Mark Hunt confirmed that the combination of Wellingborough and Northampton could take on the building of mere hundreds of cylinder heads, right up to a maximum of about 60,000/70,000 a year. In a clearly delineated diagram in a brochure, Cosworth proposed a solution to the 'problem zones' – that it could tackle pre-production, the run-in and run-out phases, and to take on what it called 'peak-lopping' contracts, of which the Ford-Cologne V6 was an ideal example. Even so, there was still time – sometimes – to make parts for older 'heritage' Cosworth engines:

"The racing season is very peaked," Hunt reminded me. "So if someone wants a part for a 20-year-old engine, we certainly wouldn't be producing that between November and March. But we would certainly consider doing that in the summer. We still produce BD parts, and some DFV parts." To make sure that there would be a steady flow of new work into the workshops and assembly buildings, Vickers encouraged Cosworth to expand its road-car strengths. Engines Engineering, which had developed the YB and FB types, carried on selling itself to the world's motor industry, and from 1993 Rob Oldaker (ex-Rover Group, where he had been running the entire Chassis Engineering operation) arrived at Northampton to take over from Ron Nicholls. Rob's Chief Engineer, John Hancock, had already moved over from the racing side.

Because work on the Ford Mondeo and Opel Calibra Touring Car racing projects involved the modification of road-car units, Engines Engineering also took development responsibility for them:

"They are good learning projects for the road

engines side – and vice versa – though there's very little true technology transfer from racing to road engines. However, because we've learned a lot about manufacturing, engines like the latest Zetec-R F1 engine are a lot quicker and easier to build than the HB."

Under this new regime, it was logical that Geoff Goddard, who had featured strongly in the design of the HB F1 engine, should be involved in the design, development and proving of work on the Ford Probe V6 engine for use in the 'works' BTCC Ford Mondeo race cars.

Recognising the limits imposed on them by BTCC rules, and the need to use castings from standard road-car engines, Goddard's small team speedily produced a race-winning 290/300bhp 2-litre unit, that could have revved to 10,000rpm if authorised to do so.

"My job is to grow this division some more," Oldaker told me. "We have an interesting list of clients ... [at which point he smiled secretively, and would say no more ...].

"We have a reputation for being able to do things quickly, we are flexible and responsive. I guess another big selling point is that we do our own castings at Worcester.

"In 1994, for the first time, I put a man into an office at Dearborn, near Detroit. His job, at first, was to put together a business plan, to see how we can proceed in North America. We're already doing a job for Ford-America ..."

'That man,' incidentally, was none other than Paul Fricker, who had been Cosworth's project engineer on Sierra RS Cosworth YB development, and was once famously described as "having forgotten more about the YB than most other people had ever learned ..."

Woodwark saw the Dearborn operation becoming very important:

"I can see the company growing in North America: that's why we have moved to new premises in Torrance. I believe we will eventually replicate Costin House in Detroit, or we may enter a strategic alliance, with a company out there. From there we could service Japanese customers on the West Coast too, and obviously we have to talk to Mercedes-Benz and BMW, who are opening up new factories on the East Coast.

"Our next stage is to see what we can gain in the Far East."

By motor industry standards, Oldaker's claim about "doing things quickly" meant taking an engine from concept, through testing and calibration to

mass production in about 3½ years. When the new Northampton EDC facility was in use (construction began in 1994) this was expected to fall by at least three months.

Prototype engines could be running in cars only six months after design work began, which meant that a team of 80 people ("That's from me down to the office cat ...") and an increasing back-up from Computervision's CAD (Computer Aided Design) equipment were working very efficiently: "We tend to recruit selected people from outside to do project work. We're expanding our own operation right now, and we've started to grow the business – in advance of getting the orders!

"We do tend to get a lot of graduates knocking on our door, wanting jobs – Italians, Danes, Germans, Chinese, Americans, as well as Brits – and we're trying to build up a long-term strategic plan."

Chris Woodwark confirmed that for every 100 graduates who applied for a job, only one of them was taken on:

"We set a first class honours degree, or an upper-second, limit on entry. Yes, there's a lot of interest." Oldaker also confirmed that, as larger manufacturers made their own operations more flexible than before, projects like the Ford YB and FB engines might not come along in the same way again:

"What we are now seeing more of is smaller projects, which means the design and development of a cylinder head, or a complete engine, but not necessarily a manufacturing agreement."

So, with so many clients, what happens if one particular innovation is produced for one of them? Could it be offered to their rivals?

"It depends. We do, indeed, have to build 'Chinese

The 2.9-litre Cosworth FB V6 engine, originally conceived by Brian Hart in the late 1980s, was a remarkably compact, though complex, power unit, intended purely for use in the Ford Scorpio 24V model. It was a great success.

For the 1990s Ford needed a new 'homologation special' as the basis of cars to go International rallying. This was done by merging the shortened platform of the Sierra Cosworth 4x4 with a much-modified Escort bodyshell – with power by a modified version of the YB engine described as YBT (and later YBP). It was a great success, more than 7000 would be built, with all engines being manufactured at Wellingborough.

COSWORTH – THE SEARCH FOR POWER

This 'ghosted' view shows the basic layout of the four-wheel-drive Escort RS Cosworth, as unveiled in 1992. In this form, the Cosworth YBT engine produced 227bhp in road-car form, which could be boosted to at least 350bhp for motorsport where the regulations allowed it.

In its final form, when fitted to Escort RS Cosworths built from 1994 to 1996, the YB series became the YBP, complete with smaller (T25) turbocharger), a Ford EEC14 engine management system, and a restyled camshaft cover.

walls' between teams, and every client has to rely on our integrity. If we developed a new 'widget' – well, it all depends on the contract with the customer. Certainly we would not exploit a novelty with someone else unless we were cleared to share it. When clients come to us, they expect Cosworth to be at the leading edge, and they expect to get something which is perhaps different from what they can do themselves."

By 1995, the small-turbo/EEC-IV version of the YB engine had gone on sale in the Escort RS Cosworth, and the up-rated (210bhp) 2.9-litre FBC V6 was being used in the radically restyled Scorpio. But what was due to take over in the mid and later-1990s? Let's just say that there always seemed to be areas of the factory which were out of bounds to me when I made a visit at that time, and that there were photographs on file with very significant company logos on cam covers, which I was asked to ignore "for the time being."

Cosworth celebrated 30 years of life at Northampton at the end of 1994, though most of the staff were too busy to notice. It looked as if the future would be just as interesting, just as exciting, as the past.

Coscast – still a world leader

The first time I ever visited Cosworth – in the 1970s – Keith Duckworth's frustration with the British castings industry was at its height. Subsequently, he encouraged Dr John Campbell to set up a research facility in Worcester, and by the mid-1980s the revolutionary Coscast process had been unveiled.

[I nearly called Coscast a 'mould-breaking' achievement, then realised that was precisely, and absolutely, the wrong thing to do, as Cosworth castings don't need 'breaking' in the same way as everyone else's ...]

By the end of the 1980s, the Worcester factory had become a highly efficient operation, producing tens of thousands of cylinder heads and cylinder blocks every year. In the meantime a new site – in Warndon, on the outskirts of Worcester – was built, at first to support a major contract with Ford at Windsor, Ontario, Canada, where the company was shaping up to build brand new four-overhead-cam V6 and V8 engines.

By the early 1990s, Ford of North America had invested US $150 million in new plant, and had a ten-year operating licence; both engines were in mass production, with the unique Cosworth 'roll-over' casting process providing up to 1.5 million castings a year. The V6, in fact, was the smooth, high-revving 2.5-litre unit found in the then-modern Ford Mondeo 24V model.

"Things then moved on," says Geoff Tupman, the Managing Director of Cosworth Castings. "We then transformed the Warndon factory into a product development centre – It was opened in September 1993 by Sir Richard Lloyd, the Chairman of Vickers – and put in a small amount of plant, the object being to use it for very low production runs, to do a lot of process development, and to develop our customers' product.

"It was the forerunner to what we wanted to do – we wanted to build a new site. That accelerated even beyond what we expected. We negotiated a deal to produce several new major castings for the new Jaguar V8 – that was in May 1994 – and immediately we had to start provisioning a new site."

Months, and many meetings, later (along with a great deal of investment from Vickers, the parent company) a new 10-acre site was found, half a mile away, near the M5 motorway.

Prototype Jaguar castings were already flowing from Warndon in 1994, but, before the new site could be erected, a nearby pond had to be relocated, so that a particular rare breed of greater crested newt could be preserved. No, I am not joking ...

By 1996, when series production of Jaguar V8 castings was due to begin, Tupman expected to see the original downtown Worcester site closed down and sold off ("It's quite a cramped site, and it's no place to have a foundry any more ..."). Several hundred new jobs would eventually be created at the new site, which would easily make up for this closure.

In the meantime, Hylton Road and Warndon continued to deliver an amazing variety of castings – mainly cylinder heads and cylinder blocks – some so carefully and intricately detailed that very little machining would need to be done by the customer. It was this, Tupman claimed, which made Coscast components so easy and economical to work.

A typical week's output would feature much more than quantity production parts to Wellingborough Two for Ford assembly to go ahead. F1, Indycar and F3000 work would be scheduled alongside cylinder head castings for Triumph motorcycles, for Maserati, for Aston Martin, Mercury Marine [engines for power boats], and high-tech aerospace products. Prototype work was always being carried out: when I spotted unfamiliar shapes and configurations and commented, these were studiously ignored by my guides ...

Although the early castings patents weren't as legally strong as Cosworth would have liked, later developments, particularly related to the 'roll-over' process, were well protected. Mainly for that reason, Cosworth still claims to be well ahead of the rest of the world's castings industry:

"There have been several attempts to copy our roll-over process – and most of them don't work! All the other systems, gravity die and so on, have major problems, and fundamental flaws ..."

So, what would happen next? Tupman could clearly see a path ahead, and Tupman insisted that: "We have a phased expansion programme. We hope we will have more new orders, new products coming in, even before Phase 1 [the Jaguar facility] is up and running.

"Then we're going to go back to look at magnesium, on which we did some work ten years ago. Aluminium to magnesium? Yes, there's a weight saving, and it's worth doing. Also there's now a huge trend in Europe to go over from iron blocks to aluminium blocks.

"There was once quite a trend away from metal, to ceramics, but that trend now seems to have been reversed."

Research projects

When it was revealed at the Detroit Society of Engineers' show in March 1991, the new MBA V6 engine seemed to pose more questions than it answered. Was it all-new and all-Cosworth? If so, did it have a customer? What was its purpose? Was it a race engine or a road-car unit? What was new about it, and would Cosworth tell anyone?

Although Cosworth, as usual, was modest rather than drum-beating on the subject, it rapidly became clear that this was probably the company's most ambitious research project to date, for it was the very first Cosworth road-car engine to use its own cylinder block. Rob Oldaker, Engineering Director, Engines Engineering, since 1993, told me that:

"MBA was always going to be the first of a family of engines, should anybody want it, though it was really built as a concept engine to show off our technology.

"It was meant to achieve a platform for displaying a

GEOFF TUPMAN

ONCE Bob Smith retired from Cosworth Castings in 1992, Geoff Tupman took over, to direct the massive expansion scheduled for Castings in the mid and late 1990s. Although he claimed to be a manager rather than an engineer, most of his earlier experience had been with engineering concerns.

Having run his own management consultancy for some years, he joined Vickers in 1979, and began running subsidiary companies, or divisions of companies, in 1981. Having moved to Vickers' corporate offices on Millbank, in London, in 1989, originally as PA to Chief Executive Sir Colin Chandler, he then took on the job of monitoring investments – business investments – around the Vickers empire.

"Then, very rapidly, Vickers moved into an acquisitions programme, so I became the leader of that, and a prime target was Cosworth. I spent a couple of years 'shadowing,' learning about it, and became very interested. But it was always difficult to get to know anything – I had to gather information from the public domain.

"I was involved in the Cosworth acquisition, then became the man who helped integrate Cosworth into the empire. For two years I was a non-executive director of Cosworth ..." Geoff confirmed Vickers' modern attitude to its subsidiary businesses:

"Vickers saw a world-class engineering company which would fit in nicely with Vickers' own engineering companies, not necessarily tightly integrated. From a brand point of view – Vickers is very much into brands – Cosworth was seen as a great brand, very high profile, very high quality.

"For Cosworth, the link with Vickers was to give real stability: it was always going to be more appropriate being linked with a group concentrating on high-class engineering, than in TV or whatever. It was the right type of home."

That was the businessman talking, but there was a glint in his eyes while it was being said. Tupman, like most of the top management at 1990s Cosworth, clearly enjoyed his job.

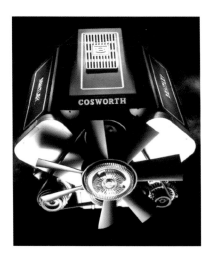

When Rolls-Royce unveiled the Java project car in March 1994, it released this engine picture of a 3.5-litre 75-degree V8 unit. But don't get too excited. Although the press release suggested that there might be a spin off from Cosworth HB F1 engine technology, this was no more than an extremely smart mock-up of an engine which was coded as the LF, but never came to fruition.

number of advanced pieces of technology, particularly the use of port-located barrel throttles (which was coming direct from the racing programme), which in this case were being used to control exhaust gas recirculation, as well as allowing high overlap cam timing in conjunction with a primary throttle to allow a very wide spread of torque, as well as high power and an unusually high rev range.

"It was a high-revving engine, it was light, it was small, and it did show anybody else that they, too, could use a very small high-powered V6. Three years on we're still using it as a demonstrator of technology. We're not trying to sell the engine, as such, to anybody. The view, today, is that it demonstrates technology. We can say: 'Look Mr Customer, you could have a three, a four, a six, an eight, or a twelve-cylinder, incorporating a lot of things that are in here.' There are one or two patents in that engine which we can exploit ..."

Features like the hollow balancer shaft which doubled as a crankcase breather, removing oil by centrifugal force, were all steps forward. John Hancock and Darren Cairns led the project, which was producing full power within 12 months of work starting, but it was not until a prototype was installed in an Audi 80 Quattro 'slave,' and shown in public, that the real advantages were proved.

Compared with the Audi's 2.8-litre V6, the MBA was 80lb/36kg lighter, and was demonstrably smaller than the unit it had displaced. It was 50bhp more powerful, too. Performance – acceleration and top speed – was up, fuel consumption was improved, and, with a tickover of 500rpm allied to peak revs of 8000rpm, is was clearly a totally versatile road-car design.

But if MBA was research being carried out in public, with the intention of capturing interest – and orders – from the world's motor industry, co-operation with Rolls-Royce was much more discreet. It was surprising indeed that the two Vickers-owned companies had not appeared to get together often. One reason, perhaps, was that until the 1990s Rolls-Royce was widely seen as technically arrogant, even though features like its chassis platform dated from the 1960s, and its massive alloy V8 engine had been conceived in the 1950s.

It was only after Chris Woodwark and Peter Ward got together in 1993 that the companies began to work together. This led to the most intriguing, and most secretive, road-car project of all, unveiled at the Geneva Motor Show in 1994. Rolls-Royce showed a new compact prototype, a sleek coupé or convertible named the Bentley Java.

Styled by Roy Axe's Warwick-based Design Research Associates concern, this was more mock-up than running car – *Autocar & Motor* described it as "a model looking for a platform" – this concept car was never seen with the bonnet open.

Both companies – Rolls-Royce and Cosworth – were very secretive about the actual engine used. Rolls-Royce described it simply as a "twin-turbocharged V8, conceived in conjunction with Cosworth Engineering. With four valves per cylinder and a capacity of 3.5 litres, giving it 0-60mph in 5.6 seconds and a 0-100mph capability of 14.2 seconds, this new engine could provide the best solution. A theoretical top speed of 170mph would be electronically governed to 155mph ..." To produce that sort of performance, something

THE ROLLS-ROYCE CONNECTION

NO sooner had Cosworth merged with Vickers, which already controlled Rolls-Royce, than the know-alls gave voice:

"Well, of course, it's obvious. Cosworth will design the next engine for Rolls-Royce. You wait and see."

That was in 1990, and five years later there was still no sign of that engine. Further, in the interim period Rolls-Royce had conducted well-reported talks with BMW and with Mercedes-Benz, all the hard news eventually being that BMW engines, much-modified, would appear in the next generation of cars from Crewe.

Vickers, it seemed, had a more subtle approach to mergers, and to integration. Although Cosworth began to consult with Rolls-Royce almost at once, this was on a more general basis.

Cosworth designed a four-valve/twin-cam cylinder head conversion for the existing 6.75-litre Rolls-Royce V8 engine (the RB project), saw the head briefly shown at a British trade show, then consigned it to history. [When I asked Rolls-Royce for pictures, I was politely, but firmly, rebuffed ...]

Chris Woodwark confirmed that there were no formal links between the two Vickers subsidiaries until 1993, after which:

"Peter Ward and I made it our job to see what synergies there can be ..."

Development work, of an entirely secret nature, then began again, but to no greater priority than for other divisions. By the end of 1994 "Rolls-Royce engineers are working here," Woodwark admitted, "on a project we're undertaking for Rolls-Royce.

"But we do other things for Vickers – including helping the Vickers Medical Division – and we did an audit on a gearbox in the Vickers battle tank! I'm developing this cross-company fertilisation ..."

like 350bhp, with a wide torque band, was going to be needed, not a requirement which was likely to make Cosworth's engineers lose too much sleep.

Autocar & Motor's description suggested that the engine had its roots in the Ford-Cosworth XB Indycar unit, which seemed to be very unlikely, and the picture Rolls-Royce released of the engine showed what was certainly only a mock-up of a likely power unit. Rob Oldaker denied any direct connection with XB or HB: Later seen in the company's project list as the LF, it never enjoyed a serious development programme, and was soon abandoned.

"The engine for Java was based on our MBA, but was a V8. It draws on some racing developments, but it's not a racing engine. The porting and throttling are shared with the XB; throttling developed on the MBA V6 project enables us to run with a camshaft overlap, which fills in the torque curve and gives high top power. It also harnesses our latest thin-wall cylinder block techniques ..."

All of which led me to conclude that Java was more mock-up than motor car, and that there was more wishful thinking than firm engineering in what we were allowed to see. In 1994, whatever it was meant to become, Java was at least five years away from production – if, that is, it ever got the nod from Vickers – and it never did.

By the late 1990s, as Mark Hunt admitted to me, Wellingborough Two was likely to be producing several different – new – products. The famous YB-Series Sierra/Escort engine would be beyond its tenth birthday, the long-lived Scorpio platform which used the FB V6 would also be moving into retirement – but Woodwark and his colleagues were confident that new projects would then take over. Woodwark: "I hope and intend to build another new factory at Wellingborough – Two has got an identical piece of land next to it. As we are opening the company up, and getting far more visitors, people are understanding much more about what Cosworth is about, how broadly based it is, and the fact that it's quite capable of doing business with other customers as well as Ford. Ford are important, much respected and loyal customers of ours: they want to see Cosworth grow outside that relationship."

Oldaker pointed out that he didn't think anyone else in the Western world could match Cosworth's expertise in doing what it did, and Chairman Chris Woodwark summed up like this:

"My vision for Cosworth's future is that our team will remain at the forefront of engineering excellence,

Although the Bentley Java project of 1994 was a very attractive machine, and was supposedly to be powered by a Cosworth LF V8 engine, it never progressed beyond the show stands of Europe.

The YBT derivative of the famous YB engine fitted neatly into the engine bay of the Ford Escort RS Cosworth – and enthusiasts will notice just how similar the layout was to that of the original Sierra RS Cosworth.

around the globe, and continue to succeed across all its racing and business activities."

In the meantime, there had also been a revolution in the company's racing activities. So much had been tackled, and so many victories had been achieved, that these deserve a chapter all to themselves.

14: MOTORSPORT – WINNING ALL ROUND THE WORLD

> **"The 1994 F1 season ... revolved round the amazing new EC-type Zetec-R V8 engine. Here was a remarkably successful power unit. Not a V10, not a V12 – but a classic V8, which did everything very well, and most things superbly."**

In the early 1990s Cosworth's race engine design strategy changed considerably. After years of getting by with a small design team, and the ability only to develop one all-new engine at once, the company took a corporate deep breath and changed its ways. By the mid-1990s several brand-new engines – for F1, Indycar and Formula 3000 – had appeared, and all of them were winning!

New designers, new customers, and intense competition from rival companies had seen to that. Encouraged by Vickers, Cosworth wanted to be winning, preferably dominant, in every category it contested. Ten or especially 20 years earlier, that might have been straightforward enough – but not in the 1990s. Big money was needed to finance the development of new engines – if, that is, they were to be produced quickly, and if they were to be competitive from day one. Cosworth was now confronted by big spenders like Honda, Renault, and GM (later Mercedes-Benz) backed Ilmor, and had to match their methods – and their results.

In 1990 the only truly modern Cosworth race engine on the market was the HB – and even that high-revving V8 unit had been around for more than two years. The DFS (a turbocharged but lineal development of the 1960s-generation DFV) was not a winner, and in Formula 3000 the rev-limited DFV seemed to have reached its peak.

For the time being, though, Ford encouraged Cosworth to carry on developing the 75-degree HB F1 engine. Benetton stayed on as the 'works' team for 1991, while Jaguar got the use of HBCs for sports car racing in its XJR14 models. There was general surprise when Jordan, a new F1 team, also gained a supply of recent-specification HBs, but this was a new and thrusting team whose results soon made everything worthwhile.

Even at that point, though, there were hints of new engines from Northampton. When Benetton's high-nose B191 was launched at a London hotel, in the usual flurry of strobe lights and clouds of dry ice, Technical Director John Barnard agreed that: "We will be using the latest Ford V8 engine 'for the moment.'" Nothing more was said – and no amount of probing made him add to that comment, but everyone assumed that another Ford-Cosworth engine was already on the way. They

were right, and they were wrong. Cosworth had already started work on an advanced new V12 – but in the end it would never be raced! John Barnard, incidentally, was to leave Benetton before the end of 1991, his ego bruised by the number of high-profile bosses and influences with whom he was obliged to interact ...

Benetton's B191 was once described as 'one of the ugliest F1 cars ever built' (it was certainly no beauty), whereas the Jordan was praised for its lissom lines. For Benetton in that year, there was a single F1 victory (by Nelson Piquet, in Canada), while Jordan's best finish was fourth, also in Canada, but the most significant event of that year was the arrival of Michael

The YB power unit was phenomenally successful in motorsport. Here was François Delecour on his way to winning the Rally of Portugal in 1993 ...

... and the 1994 Monte Carlo rally, both times in 'works' Escort RS Cosworths.

The 'works' Escort had a phenomenally successful career in rallying, which lasted for 31 years, starting in 1968 with TA-powered Escort Twin-Cams, and ending in February 1999 with Petter Solberg competing in the Swedish Rally in his Escort WRC.

Only rarely did Ford encourage their Cosworth-financed engines to be rebranded, but for Jaguar's XJR14 sports racing car of 1991 they made an exception. Under the skin, that 'Jaguar' engine was pure HB ...

Schumacher on the F1 scene. Scoring championship points in only his second race, he soon proved that he was the fastest HB driver on the F1 scene.

That was also the year in which Jaguar's HBC-powered sports racing cars won the World Sports Car Championship, where the cars were heavier, and the races were longer, but not that much longer, than an F1 GP. This, though, was a single-season programme, for with the World Sports Car Championship in disarray at the end of the year, Jaguar withdrew from the sport. Once again a great Cosworth engine's career was cut short by motor racing politics. Jaguar publicity quoted the 3.5-litre HB's power output as 730bhp, which didn't sound credible. Cosworth, when asked to confirm that figure, merely smiled and refused comment – it later became clear that it was less than 700bhp. Those engines, apparently, then came back to Northampton, and were used by Minardi in the next season.

All-in-all, the HB was proving to be a remarkable engine. Racing Director Dick Scammell later told me that:

"There was no pre-conceived idea as to how long we could keep using it. We never had a long-term strategy for it – we would keep it as long as we could carry on developing it ..."

There was a further breakthrough for 1992. Not only did Benetton have Michael Schumacher to prove that he was a potential World Champion, but the B192 was a better car than the B191 had ever been. With Tom Walkinshaw now on board at Benetton, the team finished third in the Constructors' series (behind Williams-Renault and McLaren-Honda), while Schumacher and team-mate Martin Brundle were always on the pace. Tom Walkinshaw was once asked

if the team would be trying to sign Ayrton Senna: "Senna? No, why would I want Senna? I've got Michael Schumacher!"

As *Autosport* reported in its annual GP review: "The B192 was one of the most sinfully ugly racing cars ever built – but none could deny it went like hell ... Cosworth continued to do a wonderful job for Benetton ... this lone V8 often showed its strengths, in torque and fuel consumption. Nothing went to the grid lighter than a Benetton-Ford. And not much went faster either ..."

Michael Schumacher won one race, and took a total of eight podium finishes, while Martin Brundle finished second or third five times.

The final HBs were known as Series VIIs or Series VIIIs (there were many detail differences, especially in torque characteristics) and they were known to rev all the way to 13,500rpm. Clearly something remarkable had been achieved:

"The problem with the original engine," Dick Scammell says, "was that we couldn't run it fast enough because of the wire valve springs. Therefore we sat down quite early to make some air valves, and they opened up a whole new prospect. Before then we ran the HB to 12,800rpm, after which we lost control of the valve gear. Once we started using the air valves, we could run to 13,500rpm. But then we started to have problems with other parts of the engine – you go round and round the engine looking for the next weak link. We had problems with the bottom end, and we also struggled with the pistons ..."

Dick insists that the pneumatic valves were totally a Cosworth concept. Because the engineering of F1 engines is now such a secretive business, Cosworth never got a chance to see inside its rivals' products, or to study them, so there was no foreknowledge of other people's technology.

"We had looked at air valve springs right back when the 3.5-litre formula came in," Scammell confirmed, "we knew the valve gear would be the Achilles' heel to us, and we had been developing it for some time. It was a very big development exercise."

Not only was this an intricate design and development job, but manufacture and assembly was extremely ticklish.

Observers who have been walked through the Cosworth F1 engine build shops (where cameras are strictly forbidden!) always comment on the clinically clean environment – where valve gear is assembled, there is talk of tweezers and other medical-standard equipment being used.

It was in this discussion that Scammell confirmed that Cosworth never allowed its HB-users – not even Benetton – to look inside the engines, even after a major problem at the circuits:

"That's why we now lease engines. We started leasing in 1989, and that way we know where all the engines are, all of the time. We have to keep the technology in house. We never see the insides of other teams' engines, and they don't see inside ours. We were more open once, but all that ended with the last DFs – DFY and DFR – and ever since then we have had Cosworth people supporting the teams at the circuits, whether they're customers or the 'works' teams, and we rebuild all the engines ourselves. Other engine manufacturers operate in the same way these days.

"We'd all love to see inside other peoples' engines, wouldn't we, but we can't!"

Although the HB had become a truly remarkable V8 by the end of 1992 (Cosworth never quoted peak power outputs, but unofficial estimates were that a Series VIII HB could produce well over 700bhp, maybe 730bhp or more), there was still little official news of the much-rumoured VB V12 design which was meant to replace it. During 1991 Ford and Cosworth had circulated a sketch of what the new engine might look like, but that was all. By 1993 the engine had still not been seen in public. Nothing official was ever said, but eventually it became clear that the project had been abandoned. So, what happened, and when?

The initial thrust for a compact V12, to take over from the HB, came from Ford's 'works' team, Benetton, which by 1990 was convinced that a V12 was the way to improve on the HB V8. Once Ford approved the investment, Cosworth quickly got to work, and produced a 70-degree (note the intriguing vee angle, which is not one normally associated with V12s, for which 60 degrees is often considered normal) during 1991.

It was an extremely compact design, really quite astonishingly for what must have been a very complex unit. Only about two inches longer than the HB, it pushed Cosworth's knowledge and application to new extremes. The final version of the VB, later put on display in Cosworth's own museum in Northampton, confirms this.

"Possibly we went too far in the steps of trying to make progress," Scammell told me. "We really 'hung it out' in a few places, one of them being the bearing sizes. The engine was very small, so the bearings were also very small. We just overdid it – we went too far in trying to scratch for performance.

The DFR-powered Benetton of 1988 was a useful stopgap until the new HB-powered generation of Benettons appeared in later seasons.

"To overcome some of the deficiencies during the development, we ran it with an external oil supply – the idea was to develop the engine with a slave oil system, and then when we'd worked out what we really wanted to do, to redesign it, and produce a 'Mk 2' V12."

By that time, though, F1 regulations were changing, and the architecture of the cars was changing to suit them. Soon after, Benetton came back to report that the position of the driver had to be pushed back, and that the radiators really needed to be moved, all of which would affect the position of the fuel tanks,

Although a confidentiality clause got in the way of suitable publicity, it eventually emerged that Cosworth had been much involved in the manufacture of special racing components for the V12 engines fitted to the Jaguar Le Mans cars of the 1980s. This was the winning XJR12 of 1990.

which would therefore cramp the space available for the engine …

"In any case," Scammell explained, "because the V12 was set to use more fuel, the car would have needed a bigger fuel tank, and bigger radiators. So we all had to reconsider – should we design the definitive 'Mk 2' V12, and what would the ideal cars look like in a year or two? In the end we cancelled the project." It was a clean break.

Almost immediately after work on the VB was killed off, project work began on yet another F1 engine, which proved to be enormously successful – the World Championship-winning Zetec-R, always known within Cosworth as the EC.

By that time about half-a-dozen prototype V12 engines had been built, at considerable cost in time and material. Prominent Ford personalities once told me that the VB was the best thing that ever happened to the HB, for it promoted healthy 'in house' competition at Cosworth. Scammell insists this was not the case, as some technicians were involved in both engines, but agrees that the HB continued to improve throughout 1991 and 1992.

"By the end, in fact, the VB was producing more power than the HB. It would obviously have gone on from there …"

Accordingly, after a long development period, several V12 VBs were, quite literally, scrapped, and the example shown in the museum was originally labelled as a "1991/1992 Development Project 3.5-litre V12." The only alternative, as with the 1000bhp turbocharged GB Formula 1 engines of the mid-1980s, would have been to loan the VBs to museums and technical organisations, but because the VB was such a modern design, Cosworth decided not to do that.

Cosworth insists, though, that much of what was learned on the still-born V12 was applied to the next F1 engine, the ultra-successful EC (Zetec-R) which followed it, and that it allowed design work to be completed more quickly, and more surely.

In the meantime the HB carried on, enjoying a real 'Indian Summer' in 1993, when the top teams all had cars with semi-automatic transmission, traction control and computer-controlled active suspension. Because traction control operated by cutting the power of the engines as the rear road wheels started to spin, even the best-prepared and tuned F1 units sounded awful at times, but not the HB, for which more sophisticated electronic control of the engine was developed …

Not only did Benetton have the use of 'works team'

engines, but McLaren also became HB users, first as customers for recent-spec (but not up-to-the-minute) engines, then after mid-season with the same spec as Benetton. The end-of-season scorecard showed that HB-powered cars won six of the 16 World Championship F1 events – but only one of those victories went to Michael Schumacher and Benetton. McLaren finished second in the Constructors' Championship, Benetton third. In each case Cosworth set up separate build and development teams, keeping a float of 25-30 engines for each team, which looked after a full race programme and ongoing development. 'Customer' teams such as Lotus or Footwork would use about 15 engines each. Cosworth has heard of major engine builders talking of running pools of more than 100 engines (Honda was supposed to have more than 200 F1 V12s in play for McLaren in 1991 and 1992!), but simply could not see the need for it. Many of those engines, it thinks, would never even have been uncrated, or installed in a car, during their lives …

In spite of what seemed like continuous friction between McLaren and their lead driver, Ayrton Senna, the brilliant Brazilian won five races in 1993, one of them the prestigious Monaco GP. Better yet, for those with short memories, he won the last two races of the season – in Japan and Australia. Perhaps McLaren would never admit it, even afterwards, but the MP4/8-Ford/Cosworth HB combination was eventually far more competitive than they could ever have hoped, even though Ayrton Senna was often out-qualified by Michael Schumacher's B193 Benetton.

For those of us addicted to fair reporting, the antics of those pundits trying to explain away all those victories, while claiming that Cosworth's HB was 'underpowered,' was enough to turn the stomach. Cosworth engineers themselves have no idea how much power their opposition's engines produce – so how could the press know any better?

These days, in Formula 1, an engine's reputation can only be made by its results. Dick Scammell confirms that Cosworth never revealed power outputs or power curve. "No, that would be another useful piece of information to the competition. We would tell people 'ball park' figures, but in fact it would have to be 'sold' on the basis of its performance elsewhere. If a team decided to leave its supplier to come to us, it was because they had seen the way the Benetton had run with an HB in it."

When teams came to make a choice of F1 engines, there was always another factor – money. Well-drilled by founder Keith Duckworth's Northern business ethic, Cosworth never set itself up as a benevolent society. Every team using HBs had to pay leasing charges, and were not allowed to renege on a deal at a later date. In the early 1990s, Cosworth had to resort to the law to oblige Jordan to settle their 1991 programme debts, while Lotus's plunge into administration in 1994 was not helped by its inability to pay Cosworth's bills from 1992 and 1993.

As Bernard later recalled, some years later: "Jordan? Well they didn't really have any money. In fairness, though, I think Eddie had banked his hopes on going with Mild 7 tobacco sponsorship, and Benetton had whipped it away from him at the last moment. We didn't get the cash for which we had contracted, but Vickers had taken over the company by then. In the end it was settled somehow, which included Jordan 'selling' a 1991 F1 car to Vickers, which was purported to be Michael Schumacher's first-ever F1 car. I believe it was one of three such 'Schumacher first' cars, and Eddie got away with a big smile on his face … then for 1992 he went off and made a deal with Yamaha, and those engines were awful.

Money, secrecy, and good old-fashioned F1 politics went a long way to explain why HBs were taken up, then dropped, by several F1 teams over the years. Why did McLaren dump the HB in favour of a new Peugeot engine in 1994 (both of which were supplied free!) – a major error? Why did Jordan, so promising with HB power in 1991, use Yamaha engines instead of HBs in 1992, with dismal results? Why was the Mugen-powered Lotus of 1994 such a disappointment after the promise of the HB-powered cars of 1992/93?

How, on the other hand, could the HB-powered Footwork of 1994 be so effective, compared with its previous Honda/Mugen-powered cars? Most amazing of all – how could Benetton, for whom Michael Schumacher won the 1994 World Championship with Ford Zetec-R-powered cars, discard such a magnificent engine for 1995 – and how could Cosworth then find itself struggling to find a race-winning partner for 1995?

1994, however, was an F1 season to be savoured. For Cosworth, Ford, Benetton and Michael Schumacher it revolved around the amazing new EC-type Zetec-R V8 engine, which took over from the HB as Ford and Cosworth's front-line F1 power unit. Against all the sneering forecasts of the motoring press, here was a remarkably successful power unit. Not a V10, not a V12 – but a classic V8, which did everything very well, and most things superbly.

Immediately the VB V12 project had been cancelled, a team led by Martin Walters started project work on the new F1 design which was initially called the EC. Well before release, however, the EC designation had been dropped, and Ford's publicity-inspired 'Zetec-R' name took over instead.

By 1993, the HB, a remarkable V8 by any standard, had reached its limits. On my assumption (mine, only, please note), the most powerful HBs probably produced about 210bhp/litre, but Walters and Scammell were not satisfied: "We felt the cylinder bore should be bigger," Scammell admitted. [How much bigger? We were never told …] "But we couldn't do this within the confines of the HB block, so we had to design an all-new engine, to carry on the developments which were indicated to us. The HB gave us a lot of clues about the way to go, and fortunately those signposts were good ones."

Work started on layouts in October 1992, detail drawing and CAD (computer aided design) began at the end of the year, and the very first engine ran on the test beds in October 1993. The first engines were delivered to Benetton for in-car testing in January 1994 – and duly won their first race in March 1994. Even Scammell, the dyed-in-the-wool realist, admits with pride that this was very rapid progress indeed:

"A lot of what we knew from the 'works' HBs went into the Zetec-R," Dick told me. "There was a lot more than a bigger bore, a shorter stroke and a longer cylinder block in the design.

"But it wasn't reliable straight away. We did, in fact, have a problem with pistons. That was reasonable [there's that famous Duckworth description again … (AAGR)] because we had bigger pistons, and one of the engine's design parameters was that this new V8 had to run up to 14,500rpm. During the first four months of

Driving Benettons powered by the 3.5-litre EC V8, Michael Schumacher became World F1 Champion in 1994.

Cosworth produced the all-new EC V8 for Benetton to use in the 1994 F1 season, where Michael Schumacher proved to be the dominant personality, and won his first F1 title in these cars. Notice, incidentally, only a modest reference to 'Ford,' tucked in on the rear of the air box, inside the rear wheel positions.

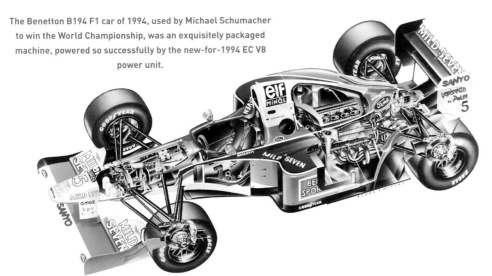

The Benetton B194 F1 car of 1994, used by Michael Schumacher to win the World Championship, was an exquisitely packaged machine, powered so successfully by the new-for-1994 EC V8 power unit.

the engine's life, we probably used 15 different piston designs …"

Once again, this justified everything Cosworth had ever tried to do at Northampton, for the piston forging plant was just 50 yards from the design offices, and when Martin Walters wanted to make changes, he had only to cross the road to consult the technicians in the forge.

"By the time the Zetec-R engine got to Brazil, we had got it to run a race distance on the dyno, but we certainly weren't out of the woods. We were still working on the pistons – and have done so since then …"

Right away, even on early test bed runs, the original EC/Zetec-R was more powerful than an HB. Naturally no peak power figures were ever published, but if Cosworth's philosophy of keeping up the BMEP while letting the engine rev faster was achieved, that alone must have been worth an extra 40-50bhp: it certainly looked like that out on the tracks.

There's no doubt that the 14,500rpm figure was achieved, without affecting Cosworth's quite astonishing low-speed torque and flexibility, for Ford and Benetton often allowed the B194's telemetry readings to be superimposed on the TV pictures published worldwide throughout the 1994 F1 season.

The Zetec-R's most remarkable performance was not a victory, though. In Spain, Schumacher's Benetton gearbox stuck in fifth gear, but the driver elected to keep going. TV-published telemetry showed just how far down the rev range the engine continued to work well – so it was not surprising that Jim Brett was told to sprint to the team's electronic centre and hastily pull the plug to the TV feed …

In later years, when we looked back on the 1994 F1 season, more attention was paid to the personal tragedies, the technical changes which followed, and to the extraordinary political wrangles which affected motor racing. A season which opened with the enthralling prospect of head-to-head battles between the Schumacher/Benetton/Ford-Cosworth combination and the Senna/Williams/Renault, was suddenly shattered at Imola when Senna's Williams crashed, and the driver was killed.

Although Schumacher's Zetec-R-powered Benetton had already won the first races (in Brazil and Japan), this was no way for him to become the sport's leading driver, and later events made it more controversial still. Throughout the year the Benetton was dominant, but there were more traumas to be suffered. For ignoring a black flag at Silverstone, Schumacher was disqualified, and obliged to miss two further races, while his Benetton was disqualified after winning the Belgian GP, when the newly-introduced compulsory 'plank' under the monocoque was found to be worn below regulatory limits. And, in the final race of the year, Schumacher's Benetton and Damon Hill's Williams hit each other, eliminating both cars.

As an understandably bitter Schumacher later commented, he was being asked to win a 16-event World Championship by competing in only 12 events. It says a lot for his gritty character, and for the resources of his team, that in the end he won eight of those 12 races, and became a truly worthy World Champion. After such a successful season, few outsiders could understand why Benetton then walked away from a supportive long-term agreement with Ford and Cosworth, choosing Renault engines for its future. It could only have been money-influenced.

Worse, how could it then be that Ford, and Cosworth, found it so difficult to link up with an established front-line team for 1995? Scammell, Martin Walters, Nick Hayes and their team had already spent months working on a 3-litre update of the Zetec-R theme, before they knew that it would be used in the Sauber chassis. Formula 1 was truly impossible to understand at times …

XB: A new generation of Indycar engines

Although Cosworth had produced the world's most successful CART/Indycar race engines in the 1970s and 1980s, by 1990 and 1991 the final member of that generation – the DFS – had been out-gunned: the Chevrolet-backed Ilmor V8, designed by two ex-Cosworth engineers, had become dominant in this unique type of racing, where engines had to be turbocharged 2.65-litre units running on methanol. The time had come to fight back.

Originally at Cosworth's own cost, a new and specialised engine, the XB, then took shape in Northampton. But there was more. All previous Indycar race engines had been Cosworths, with no overt Ford backing. Now, for 1991, Ford helped to fund the XB unit. When Ford-USA and Cosworth launched the programme at a function in the Indianapolis Motor Speedway in November 1991, Ford made the point that they were returning after a gap of more than 20 years, and that in 1992 this would be the first time that Ford and General Motors had ever clashed on Indycar race tracks.

Even before starting work, Cosworth had made it clear that to make any sense, this had to be a multi-season programme. It liked to produce engines for a minimum life cycle of at least three years ("You need to have it around long enough to learn what's good and bad about it, and to develop it to know where you want to go next …").

For the XB that was a minimum requirement, especially as a 'works' team test, development and engine-building department would have to be set up in Northampton, along with other facilities for the customer teams at Cosworth Inc in California. As with the existing F1 HBs, all engines would be leased, not sold outright, and customers were forbidden to open them up at any time.

By any standards, this was a very serious and ambitious programme. Not content with getting modestly back into the swim, Michael Kranefuss and Steve Miller surveyed the Indycar field, courted, seduced, then won the most successful of all teams – Newman-Haas racing, in which Carl Haas' partner was Hollywood superstar Paul Newman. Newman-Haas, whose star drivers were Michael Andretti and his father Mario, had won the 1991 Indycar series outright in Ilmor-powered Lola T91s, so when the team agreed to defect to Ford, General Motors was not best pleased.

If it had chosen to back any other engine design than the new Cosworth XB, this would have been a high-risk strategy for Ford. In the past, other major engine-builders, like Alfa Romeo, Porsche, Buick and Judd, had all tried to beat Ilmor – and failed. This, however, was about to change, for, when previewed in 1991, the XB looked to be lighter, more compact, and more carefully and delicately engineered than all of its rivals. The new 'works' team facility was up and running in Northampton by 1992, and there never seemed to be any problems caused by the transatlantic chasm between Newman-Haas and Cosworth. Which says a lot for Cosworth engine reliability, and for the efficiency of modern airline freight services …

Unlike the successful old DFX, the new XB Indycar engine was not, repeat not, a conversion of the modern HB Formula 1 engine. Even so, for a time there were people who heard the denials and chose not to believe them, noting a similar vee angle and low, compact, layout – but in fact there was virtually no common ground. By 1994 this was always clear to Cosworth visitors, for HB and XB engines stood side-by-side, on display stands, at Northampton in the company's reception area.

Dick Scammell succinctly outlined the thinking behind the new XB unit:

"Obviously, because Indycar engines have to be 2.65-litres – a lot smaller than the 3.5-litres of the F1 engine of the day – they can be more compact. We designed the XB to take maximum advantage of the rules. We designed it from the ground up, as a turbocharged engine.

"The competition is now so great that unless you optimise the engine totally, you lose out. These days this always impels us to make new engines for different formulae – and we run the place deliberately set up with different teams of people."

It was typical of Cosworth's approach to original thinking that it also decided to fuel the XB in a novel way. Not only were there conventional fuel injectors near each cylinder trumpet/port at the base of the inlet manifold, but there was also a further injector at the outer, upstream, face of the turbocharger compressor. Naturally Cosworth's rivals, Chevrolet-Ilmor, did not like this (maybe because they had not thought of it first …), but officials eventually declared it race-legal. This was yet another instance of the way all Cosworth engineers are encouraged to think, to innovate, and to push technology to its limits. It was also classic proof of that old dictum, "The competition starts when the regulations arrive …"

Although it was always too much to ask Newman-Haas to win the Indycar series in 1992 with a brand-new engine, they came mighty close, for Michael Andretti finished second – very close behind Bobby Rahal's Ilmor-powered car. Along the way, though, XB-powered

Michael Schumacher won no fewer than eight Grands Prix during 1994, and was disqualified from success in another race, all in Ford-Cosworth EC-powered Benetton B194s.

When Benetton deserted Cosworth after winning the Constructor's Championship with EC-engined B194s, the redeveloped EC (then in 3-litre guise because of a change in regulations) was used by Sauber for the 1995 season.

Nigel Mansell raced HB-powered Newman-Haas Lolas in 1993 and 1994. In his first-ever Indycar season, he became Indycar champion, and the XB proved itself to be the most powerful of the series.

Lolas won six of the 16 races, Michael Andretti won five events (more than any other individual), led all but two of the season's races at one point or another, and led more race laps throughout the season than any other driver. Mario Andretti finished sixth in the series.

Then came 1993, the year in which Michael Andretti moved to F1 (and the HB-powered McLaren) with dismal results, while F1's new World Champion Nigel Mansell took his place in the Newman-Haas Indycar team, with quite sensational results. Although Mansell was the 'rookie' in every sense, he soon mastered the cars. After winning the season's first race, at Surfer's Paradise in Australia, he then suffered a high-speed testing crash on the Phoenix Oval. After recovering rapidly from a back injury, Mansell then won at Milwaukee in June.

By the end of the season, with five victories from 15 starts, along with five other podium finishes, the Englishman had won the Indycar championship, with team-mate Mario Andretti winning one race and yet again taking sixth place in the series. It was an astonishing performance in every way. Mansell was known to be brave, the Lola chassis was fully competitive, but above all it was clear that Cosworth's latest XB was the most powerful Indycar engine in existence. General Motors, in fact, was so demoralised by this, that it withdrew its backing from Ilmor, which smacked of the old British schoolboy adage, "If I can't win, I'll take my bat and ball away …"

For 1994 everything looked set for another Ford-Cosworth triumph, which merely went to prove that one must never make assumptions in motor racing. Although the XB was on top of its form, and still acknowledged to be the best Indycar engine, the Lolas used by the Newman-Haas team struggled against the (now Mercedes-Benz backed) Ilmor-engined Penskes. Nigel Mansell did not win a single race, rapidly fell out

of love with the Indycar circus (and they with him …), and returned to F1.

During that season, too, the Indycar establishment shocked the engine builders by announcing major changes to be imposed for 1996. For Cosworth this meant that developed versions of the XB would be allowed one more season – 1995 – but thereafter Indycars would have to run with 2.2-litre engines. However, if the Indycar law-makers thought that this would merely mean the modification of existing engines, they were totally misguided.

Even in 1994, therefore, Steve Miller's Indycar team had to start designing yet another new unit. Dick Scammell confirmed that it would be entirely new, smaller, and more advanced than the XB itself. There would also be a 'customer conversion bit' for the XB – reducing it to a 2.2-litre unit, to ease the transition for them.

"Everyone talks about costs, about saving costs, but one of the biggest cost-savers of all time is stability, so that the same equipment, or modifications of that equipment, can have a reasonable life span.

"Every time anybody changes anything in motor racing, it often means changing the engine to suit. It isn't always changing the engine regulations which we worry about."

Although Scammell was smiling as those remarks were made, he could have been excused for being cynical about the whole process. Faced, in any case, with the busiest race-engine design period which Cosworth had ever known, his engineers were now being obliged to meet yet another unasked-for, unexpected, challenge. It was exciting, and it was enthralling, but one could see that Cosworth would rather have concentrated on other things.

Other formulae, other successes …

By this time, however, Cosworth was so resourceful, and so quick to respond to new opportunities, that it had also found time to have another look at Formula 3000, and at the same time to get back to its roots, as an ace-modifier of other peoples' engines. In 1993, for instance, not only did they produce a brand-new F3000 engine – the AC – but Cosworth also got the task of optimising Ford-Mazda and GM V6 production car engines for Touring Car racing in Britain and Germany.

Originally set up in 1985, F3000 single-seater motor racing had always been seen as the final step up towards F1 competition, with engines limited to 3-litres, and to not more than eight cylinders and a maximum of 9000rpm. At first this was almost tailor-made for the venerable DFV, which was chosen by most chassis builders. Although it was always the most successful engine in this series (DFV-powered cars won eight out of ten International races in 1992), the DFV was by no means the optimum design – and, according to Cosworth's design ethic, this was not desirable.

As the company's promotional literature made clear: "Sales of the old DFV were stagnating, and Cosworth decided it needed to reinforce its dominance by introducing an engine designed specifically for the requirements of Formula 3000."

For 1993, therefore, the company launched yet another all-new racing engine to take over from the DFV – the AC, which was a purpose-built 3-litre 90-degree V8. Cynics who suggested that this was no more than a revamped DFV were speedily re-educated. At 282lb/128kg, Cosworth claimed, the AC was 10.4 per cent lighter than the old DFV, was smaller and more compact, and (very important, this) featured a lower vibration level than before.

It was typical of Cosworth that neither bore and stroke, nor peak power output figures, were released – all that was guaranteed was that race engines would be ready by April 1993, that they would fit into existing chassis, and that they would be competitive. All of which came true! AC-engined cars won seven out of nine F3000 races in that season (the other two races being won by DFV-engined cars ...), while there was also total domination in 1994.

By this stage Cosworth-prepared cars seemed to be winning everywhere once again. The opportunity to prepare engines for Ford's British Touring Car Championship programme (Mondeos using 2.0-litre V6s lifted from the Ford-USA Probe model, which was itself based on the chassis of the Mazda MX-6), as well as for Opel's German Touring Car Championship (Calibras with new-type V6 engines), meant having to modify rather than innovate, and to make production castings stay in one piece when subjected to much-higher-than-planned stresses. For Cosworth it was almost like old times, though few of the 1990s breed of engineers could recall the 1960s period when a much smaller Cosworth company was doing little else!

To make the most of these projects, Cosworth

gave Geoff Goddard free rein to liaise between race and road-car engineers, and to wrap his own particular expertise around the various, sometimes conflicting, regulations. In the BTCC, for instance, the 2.0-litre engines needed to produce 290/300bhp to be competitive. By Cosworth standards this was not difficult – except that they also had to be rev-limited to 8500rpm, a regulation which was strictly and ruthlessly policed by the organisers. All had to use production castings, though in some instances, project leader Len Newton told me, these were really not very suitable for the job.

Goddard, operating a very different programme from that of an F1 engine, rapidly turned the original Rouse-tuned V6 into an even more powerful unit, and only weeks after the Mondeos first raced, New Zealander Paul Radisich used a Rouse-prepared car to win at Brands Hatch (an occasion, incidentally, which notched up Ford's 200th BTCC victory, most of which had been achieved using Cosworth power). More Mondeo wins followed – including victory in the World Touring Car Cup races of 1993 and 1994 – and yet more developments were promised for the mid-1990s.

Keke Rosberg's V6-engined Calibras, complete with four-wheel-drive, had to compete against expensively-financed Alfa Romeo and Mercedes-Benz cars. Three cars were powered by 450bhp 2.5-litre engines, which had been built and developed at Northampton, but there was only one race win to report in the original season; Opel was hoping for more in 1995 and beyond.

By 1995, however, the balance of Cosworth's activities was already changing – rapidly. There was never any let-up, in the design offices, on the test beds, or in the production factories. For the future, still to come, and already planned, were new 10-cylinder F1 engines, new generation Indy units, and further upheaval at Wellingborough and Worcester.

Could any of us have foreseen Cosworth producing Rolls-Royce engines, cylinder head castings for Jaguar, or engine balancer-shaft kits for Ford? Could any of us have foreseen Cosworth being sold off by Vickers, that the business would then be split into two, and that companies bearing 'Cosworth' names would come to be owned by Audi of Germany, and Ford?

All this would occur in the mid-1990s, such that Cosworth in the year 2000 would be very different from that of 1995.

When Ford began development of the front-wheel-drive Mondeo for saloon car racing in the 1990s, Cosworth was tasked with producing race-winning power from the Ford-USA-based V6 which powered the car. This was the FC type of 1993, which produced a rev-limited (by regulation) 300bhp at 8500rpm.

Cosworth race car engines appeared in the most amazing places! In 1995, Ford produced Transit Supervan 3, basing it on a redundant mid-engined C100 rolling chassis, but using a 650bhp version of the HB F1 engine for motive power. It was quite phenomenally fast and spectacular, but when asked why they had done it, Ford spokesmen merely smiled sweetly and said "because we can ..."

15: TURBO V8s AND V10s – THE PACE QUICKENS

> **"Using the standards by which CART teams test themselves – outright qualifying pace on Superspeedways – the XD was rated the best of all the competitive power units ..."**

In the mid and late-1990s, Cosworth not only produced an impressive number of new engine designs, but under Vickers' direction it gradually reshaped its business. Not only that, but links with Rolls-Royce (another Vickers company) got closer, a series of new F1 V10s were developed – but then, to crown it all, in 1998 Vickers sold the Cosworth business.

Even then the upheaval was not yet over, and, in the process, all celebration of Cosworth's 40th Anniversary (in that very same year) was completely missed. Audi (VW's prestige-marque division) bought the business for £117 million, then immediately split it into two halves. Cosworth Racing was sold on to Ford in September 1998 for an undisclosed sum, while Audi retained a new company, Cosworth Technology, which was spearheaded to run production, engineering, and casting, as well as the consultancy side. Because both companies – 'Racing' and 'Technology' – originally had their head offices in Northampton, a flurry of building then began (to quote one wag – "real walls replaced 'Chinese walls' ..."), so that by 1999 it was hoped that there would be no confusion between the two businesses, nor who did what, and for whom.

In recent years, in any case, the Cosworth business had changed considerably, and to outsiders it had definitely begun to evolve from one type of company (individual, and proud of the fact) to another (broader-based, and more obviously a Vickers subsidiary). Slowly, but definitely, Vickers had encouraged it to become more of a true corporate body, rather than an exciting, high-tech engine design business, where enthusiasm was first, next and always the most important aspect.

This was not always popular with the staff. In a way, this was signalled by the steady turnover of top personalities, some of whom had been linked with Cosworth for a considerable time, and some of whom did not like what they saw. To some of us, this was a signal that the late-1990s Cosworth company was then meant to look even less like the can-do/will-do team which Keith Duckworth and Mike Costin had founded all those years ago. The arrival of a new managing director and a new chairman in 1996, both ex-Rolls-Royce, seemed to back this up.

Chris Woodwark, Cosworth's high-profile Chairman in the mid-1990s, moved on to Rolls-Royce, then moved up to Vickers' head office, apparently destined for the very top job, but resigned when it became clear that some of his colleagues were determined to sell off two of the companies about which he was so enthusiastic – Cosworth and Rolls-Royce. Charles Matthews (Chief Executive) and Brian Dickie (Managing Director, Cosworth Racing) arrived to take his place.

Dick Scammell, so closely involved at Northampton for a full quarter of a century, latterly as Racing Director, moved into partial retirement in 1996, and although he was then retained on a one-day-a-week consultancy basis, his regular presence was still much missed:

"I left Cosworth in 1996," Dick said later, "because I felt the company was not being taken in the right direction by Vickers. I didn't feel it was being pushed in the correct way to go motor racing successfully."

That, at the time, it seems, was a typical response of long-serving and hitherto enthusiastic staff. Scammell, however, would be back, for when Ford bought Cosworth Racing, Dick was installed as 'interim' Managing Director to oversee the transition. Every enthusiast, whether inside or outside Cosworth, was delighted.

Geoff Goddard, that extrovert engine designer, whose more recent stamp was put on engines as varied as the HB F1 engine and the Mondeo V6 British Touring Car Championship unit, moved to work for Tom Walkinshaw at TWR/Arrows.

John Hancock, one of the 1970s/1980s Cosworth engine design specialists, Steve Miller (latterly a CART racing specialist), Paul Fricker (ex-YB development guru), and several others, all took their leave – and although distinguished young engineers like Nick Hayes then rose to prominence, there no longer seemed to be quite the same bubbling and extrovert air about the place.

Was it coincidence that by this time Cosworth seemed to be taking fewer risks in engine design and development, and was it even fair that it came to be nicknamed, in some motor racing circles, as the 'conservative club?'

Even so, in view of the major achievements that 'went public' in four short years – 1995 to 1998 inclusive – probably it was not. In that time, Cosworth made headlines with:

Jaguar launched its new family of engines – the AJ-V8s – in 1996. These featured complex twin-overhead-camshaft aluminium cylinder heads, whose castings were originally manufactured by Cosworth at its factory in Worcester.

Right: Cutaway showing the layout of the twin-balancer-shaft installation for Ford's I4 four-cylinder engine in the 1990s. Chain and gear-driven from the crankshaft, these balancer shafts were neatly positioned in the sump itself.

As cleverly engineered by Cosworth, the existing Ford I4 power unit was fitted with twin 'Lanchester' balancer shafts, actually under the line of the crankshaft, in the sump of this engine, which was fitted in big numbers to Scorpio and Galaxy models. Its Cosworth project number was HC.

- Series production of cylinder head castings to Jaguar for the new-generation V8 engines, starting with the XK8 sports car, and moving on to saloon cars too. These engines, much developed, and manufactured by Ford in South Wales, would still be being made 20 years later.
- The takeover of manufacture of old-type V8 engines for the Rolls-Royce Silver Spirit and related Bentley model ranges. Previously these had been manufactured at the Rolls-Royce factory at Crewe, where space was at a premium.
- The unveiling of a road-going V10 engine for an unspecified customer. This engine was shown in June 1996. Not only was the new WDA a massive 4.3-litre unit which produced 325bhp, but it was packaged for transverse installation – a very ambitious project. Later – much later – it became clear that Volvo had commissioned it.
- Design and production of a clever twin-balancer-shaft kit for the Ford I4 four-cylinder engine.

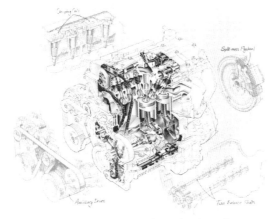

- Design, development and production of a new-generation XD V8 engine for CART/Indycar racing.
- Design, development and production of an all-new V6 engine for Opel to use in the International Touring Car Championship (ITC), where it became dominant.
- Design, development and production of three totally different types of V10 F1 engines for Ford.
- Announcement of a partnership with Ford, to develop a new range of road-car engines for Aston Martin cars. The first evidence of this would be the 6-litre V12 which appeared in March 1999 – and would still be in production as Cosworth approached its own 60th ('Diamond') Anniversary in 2018.

And these, I emphasise, were only the headlines. Much more work was going on behind the scenes, for in the late 1990s, as in previous decades, Cosworth was careful to observe any confidentiality clauses which prestige manufacturers might impose. By the late 1990s, when road-engine assembly work for Ford had been reduced, but had been supplemented by similar activity on behalf of Rolls-Royce, the non-racing side of the business was still active, but not dominant. Race-engine development, however, carried on unabated.

CART/Indycar engines – the XD project

Like every other motor racing specialist, Cosworth had to react quickly to changes in regulations – for it didn't help when the legislators themselves turned about at short notice. The story of how Cosworth came to design the race-winning Ford-badged XD engine was a perfect example.

All this, incidentally, happened in 1994/1995, when the existing CART engine, the XB, was in its fourth racing year, and was still enjoying unprecedented success. Most of the competitive teams were using XBs, the amazing Reynard chassis was the 'new kid on the block,' and the 24-year-old French-Canadian driver, Jacques Villeneuve, swept all before him, to become the youngest-ever CART Champion.

That was the year in which Villeneuve, with four outright wins, and numerous valuable minor placings, took his Team Green/Players cars to a serene and untroubled series win, so capably that he was obviously F1 material – the result being that he joined the Williams F1 team for 1996!

Summing up an exciting year, in which there were 17 races all around the USA, Canada and Australia, in his annual review Gordon Kirby of *Autosport* suggested that:

"… if Reynard was best chassis, the engine war was won even more comprehensively by Ford [Cosworth], its XB taking 10 wins and 13 poles."

But it wasn't all honeyed praise:

"A Series II Ford XB was a major disappointment, proving most unreliable, and a rigorous winter testing programme is planned for the new XD … nevertheless, only one of its top teams, Ganassi, has switched to Honda for 1996 …"

This sums up the influence leading to the design of a new engine, to the standards it would have to match, and to the reasoning behind it all. It was a difficult time, but by 1998 it had all happened long enough ago for Bruce Wood, programme director on these ever-improving CART/Indycar race engines (and, in his own reluctant words, the 'father' of the new XD), to smile about his problems. In 1994, the CART Board in the USA (which was made up of team owners – including Messrs Forsythe and Kalkhoven, who would later buy Cosworth from Ford) announced that CART engines would be limited to 2.2-litres from 1996, and, with that in mind, Cosworth started work on an all-new unit:

"Although the XB was at the height of its powers in 1994, its architecture was not capable of supporting much more, and we had already identified camshaft drive (not valve spring) problems, which meant that we couldn't let those engines run any faster than in the 'high 13,000s.'

"In any case, because we knew that Honda was about to enter CART racing too, there was a real incentive to move forward! By the end of that year, therefore, we'd started work on a new 2.2-litre engine – smaller, lighter, more reliable from the start, and more efficient; by racing standards: we thought we had a lot of time to get it right.

"Then, by the end of 1994, the teams had a change of heart and the CART Board changed its mind – and we were back to the old 2.65-litre requirement! Fortunately, we didn't have to make any huge changes to the new engine's architecture, so the 2.65-litre XD was effectively a 2.2-litre engine with bigger bores and bigger bore centre dimensions."

Logically, one supposes, the new engine should have been coded XC, but Cosworth had already reserved this for another non-racing project – one that has never been identified in public – so XD had to be used instead. To enthusiasts and Cosworth-watchers, such details are important, but Cosworth staff shrugged it off as unimportant, as, I guess, it was to them …

"Fortunately for us, there was no big drama – by the time we came to make detail drawings in January 1995, rather than schemes, the 2.65-litre formula had been reconfirmed, nominally with stability guaranteed until the end of the century."

Which is precisely what happened, for developed versions of the XD, basically a 1995 design, were still competitive, and still ready to win races, in 1999. Compared with the XB, which was itself a very compact engine, the XD was to be entirely new, with a 75-degree instead of an 80-degree angle, about 17lb/8kg lighter, and had a lower centre of gravity than ever.

Commercially, the other important change was that Cosworth decided to build all its XDs to the same specifications. Whereas Newman-Haas's Northampton-built XBs had often been two or more development stages ahead of those prepared at Cosworth Racing Inc in Torrance, California (where a staff of 80 looked after nothing else), this would no longer be the case, as the teams found that it gave them far too many problems in scheduling and controlling the various types.

Interestingly enough, Jacques Villeneuve won the 1995 CART Series using Torrance-built engines, thus proving Cosworth's point about this excellent 'satellite' operation.

As ever, with a modern race engine, performance and specification, details were always publicly scarce, but this new design had much improved cam drive arrangements, which could immediately allow the engine to turn over at more than 14,000rpm. It was the limitations of this feature which had caused so much heartache with the Series II XB of 1994/1995, and which Wood's team was determined to eliminate.

It succeeded. Even after three season's racing, at ever-increasing power outputs, there were no repeats of the problems. Compared with the XB, this was the biggest single step forward in the XD and, even in the 1999 engines, the new drive never gave any problems:

"With the XB, we never reached the limit of valve spring performance, but with the XD, we look on that as the eventual limit …"

The use of F1 type 'air-valve' technology, as pioneered in late-Series HBs for Benetton and McLaren, would have given further scope, but these, and other specific items such as the banning of high-tech material such as titanium (which would be desirable for use in connecting rods, but would need replacing at every engine rebuild), and other details were banned by CART regulations, where the aim was to put a cap on costs, both of purchase, and rebuilds.

"They go around with magnets, scratch surfaces, and all that stuff! We can't afford to step over the limits."

Like its rivals, the XD guzzled methanol fuel at the rate of two gallons per racing minute – that's the same rate as a bath tap at full flow. Initially it was allowed to run at a maximum inlet pressure of 45 inches (of mercury), though the regulations were then tightened, and required that this be reduced to 40 inches for 1997 and beyond.

Like most other Cosworth engineers, Bruce, who had already worked on the HB, DFS and XB V8s, and the

Bruce Wood was the most senior engineer in the USA CART, Champcar and IRL race engine programmes in the 1990s and 2000s, and was then promoted to look after all engine design and development, including that of the ultimate CA F1 engine family. He became Managing Director of Powertrain for the Cosworth Group in 2015.

stillborn VB V12 F1 engine, had masses of experience before coming to concentrate on XD and the next V8 engine (the XF) which would one day replace it, so such frequent, and unwanted, enforcement of rules was accepted as being part of the motor racing game.

To make sure that the teams all got the best out of their XD engines, Cosworth tried to define a complete installation, which therefore included recommended cooling radiator and other heat exchanger sizes, pipe-runs and the location of accessories:

"This was one of the big differences between the XD and the XB. With the XD we tried to repackage all the components, where possible. In previous years we had supplied XBs to many different teams, some of whom were less professional than others, and we failed no end of engines because they had pipe runs trapped by the underfloor.

"It's all very different in F1 where our designers tend to work hand-in-hand with one team, but in CART, which is effectively a customer formula, we realised that, with everyone doing slightly different things, we should take a lot more detail 'in house' – we tried to take complete control of the installation.

"One of the principal design features of the XD was that, in our language, it was much more 'installation friendly' than before. We made the XD ready to plug directly in to the back of the chassis, with no flexible hoses to get trapped or kinked."

Although some CART customers still used old-style XBs in 1996, the new XD immediately made its mark, when Newman-Haas Lolas driven by Michael Andretti won five of the 16 Championship rounds, more than any individual driver had before. The results of the Championship, in fact, were in doubt – and might have gone Newman-Haas's way – until the very last race of the year, which Andretti needed to win, but he was not quite able to make it.

Even so, Cosworth, and its major rival Ilmor/Mercedes-Benz, have both admitted to being shocked by the performance of the new Honda CART engine ("We guessed we were about 75bhp down on them …"), and although the basic XD engine had immediately proved itself to be very sound and reliable, the design team needed to keep pushing ahead in future seasons. Fortunately, well before the end of 1996, Northampton-based development engines were already proving that this deficit had been made up, and that Cosworth hoped it could once again compete on equal terms in 1997.

In spite of its frustration on some 'power' circuits,

for 1997 Newman-Haas, which had been heavily courted by Honda, stayed loyal to Cosworth, and with its engines still being maintained back at Northampton (there was regular air-freight traffic in engines between the USA and the UK), it benefited from even better units than before.

Even though the latest XDs were being prepared and built to the same specification, whether in the UK or in the USA, the engineers were always relieved that part of the effort was still UK-based, so that they could have ready and immediate opportunities to look at engines being torn down after an energetic race.

At the circuits themselves, detail adjustments and diagnosis of a particular engine's performance were always monitored by engineers from Cosworth Racing. By the end of the 1990s, the relationship between Cosworth the engine supplier, and the teams as users, was much closer than ever before. The Newman-Haas cars were supported specifically by two engineers from Northampton, who made well over 20 transatlantic return trips in a season.

Cosworth Inc, at Torrance, near Los Angeles airport, serviced and rebuilt all other XD engines (a task which included fitting a new cylinder block – the old one would have cracked – after every two or three rebuilds) and, incidentally, stored all the old XB units which had been taken out of service. In one corner of the workshops, wall to ceiling racking was erected to store no fewer than 120 obsolete XBs, which would never again be used in serious competition.

In a way this looked like a shameful waste of 100,000bhp – except that there was no obvious racing formula where such engines could still be competitive. Because all such engines were leased to the teams by Cosworth, they had to be returned to Torrance, and since the company was not immediately willing to sell them off (because of the high and secret technology hidden away inside, not for some years had non-Cosworth personnel been allowed to strip, inspect and rebuild a state-of-the-art racing engine), they had to be stored – carefully – until Sales Director Bernard Ferguson could find a use for them. For 1997 there was significant improvement all round, and teams found that the latest XDs were fully competitive.

Although Cosworth was very happy with the performance of the original XD engine, the second version, the reduced-boost XD, was much changed, with a lot of fresh hardware, including new cylinder heads, new induction systems and new fuel installations, for motorsport standards were moving ahead so rapidly that simple retouching would not suffice. Although the opposition was still awesomely reliable, the power deficit was clawed back, though the next two seasons were no less tough than before.

So how did Cosworth know that, although it might be squeaky clean, its rivals might be cheating? Basically because CART has its own technical inspectors, who after every race randomly selected an engine for a complete strip down:

"Twice a year, at least," Bruce Wood told me, "they will seal an engine after a race, follow it back to the workshops, and see it stripped to its component parts."

Purely because of the number of engines out in the field, the problems of making updates to the XDs was more serious. Whereas a Stewart-Ford F1 programme of the day might involve no more than about 30-35 engines (including development units which spend much time on test-beds), by the end of 1996 there were no fewer than 86 XDs in existence.

In 1997, facing fierce competition from Ilmor/Mercedes-Benz and Honda (though not from Toyota, who struggled to get on the pace at first), the latest XDs were fully competitive, though unlucky. XD-equipped cars won two more CART races, with three second and five third places.

For 1998, most of the upgrading went into the bottom end of the engines, while leaving the 1997 'top end' improvements basically unchanged. Using the standards by which CART teams measure themselves – outright qualifying pace on high-speed Superspeedways was one of the most reliable guides, these tracks sometimes being nicknamed 'dynos on wheels' – the XD was rated the best of all the competitive power units, not only at the start but also at the end of the season.

During the season there were four convincing race victories, five practice pole positions, seven seconds (some by only a car's length behind the winner) and seven third place 'podium positions,' even better than in 1997. With more input by drivers fresh to the XD from other makes of engine, it got a reputation for producing the most power, but with a rather 'aggressive' torque delivery, not ideal for twisty road courses.

Even then the XD story was not over, as several areas for improvement were identified, changes were made and tested; 1999-spec engines were expected to produce at least 25bhp extra top end power, and to be much more 'driver friendly' units than before. As ever, the engineers refused, adamantly, to publish a peak horsepower claim, nor would they even admit how fast the engine was expected to rev at. Those days, all they would admit was that they seemed to be at least on a par with 'the opposition,' and the opposition with them. All of which makes recording an engine's development very difficult for an author!

In insiders' language, The Big Number (peak power) was already impressive, but it was the detail of part-throttle delivery, and response, which made an important step forward.

As in all recent years, Cosworth's CART design and racing operation was kept completely separate from the F1 operation – separate designers, separate offices, separate engine build and separate management areas – but at management level it was always possible for one specialist to pay a quick visit to his opposite number, a few doors away, to pool precious knowledge.

By the late 1990s there was much more sharing of new technology, and new component or material development programmes, than before, but both teams took great delight in being first – successfully first, that is – with any particular wrinkle. Healthy internal competition was always encouraged.

As the twentieth century came to an end, CART had still not ended its feud with the breakaway IRL (Indy Racing League), where entirely different sets of engine regulations were applied, in different chassis, on different circuits, but there was real hope that this nonsensical situation could be resolved by the early 2000s.

CART could certainly live without the IRL (and without the Indy 500 race), it seemed, and so could the motor racing public, but it would rather not have to do so. Victory at the Indianapolis 500 race (which until recently was probably North America's most important motor race) would continue to do wonders for Cosworth's (and Ford's) morale – just as it had done so many times in the 1980s.

With or without the merging of these formulae, though, Cosworth Racing and Ford were determined to be major players. Even before the Ford purchase, development engines were already running at Ford-USA's state-of-the-art testing facilities in Dearborn, the two companies coming closer and ever closer together.

From September 1998, Cosworth Racing took on responsibility for future CART engines, which it set out not only to design, but also build, drawing both on its own experience, and on the trends shown up by its rivals. Having used sophisticated listewning devices at trackside, Cosworth now knew how fast the rival engines were revving, and the trend towards smaller units with repositioned auxiliaries looked certain to continue. For the year 2000 an all-new replacement for the XD was already on the way.

F1 – V8s for sale

Once Cosworth's F1 V10s came on stream in the mid-1990s, a change of F1 regulations meant that 3-litre versions of the previously-successful HB and Zetec-R-V8 V8s had to become available as 'customer' engines.

Although the EC/Zetec-R-V8 was never extensively used, ultimate developments of the HB, reworked and given the new Project code of ED (eventually, in their final form, ED5), were supplied to teams such as Minardi, Simtek, Forti, Pacific and Tyrrell, always on a lease basis, and always on the 'black box' principle, which meant that these teams were not given any access to their insides, and had to design their chassis installations around a standard Cosworth package.

By 1997, though, the technology had been overtaken by events, and by F1's rapid advances, so Cosworth was then faced with storing a large number of these V8s – or changing its policy.

But, what goes around, comes around. Although Cosworth had gone through a period of not selling F1 engines, but only leasing them ("It is all a matter of retaining our IPR – Intellectual Property Rights"), as far as the obsolete V8s were concerned, this policy was then reversed in the late 1990s. With the development of V10s taking up all of Cosworth Racing's current and forward attention, it was decided to sell off the stock of slightly earlier HBs, EDs and even Zetec-R-V8s. In some cases, and in the interests of ensuring reliability to new 'private' owners, an element of de-tuning, or the application of rev-limiters, would take place.

With one major proviso, made clear to me by Sales Director Bernard Ferguson at the time:

"We won't sell anything until we are sure that there is nothing unique about the technology included. Technically, we've moved on from HBs, so we now allow other people to rebuild them, but we haven't released them in 'air-valve' form, because that's a technology we are still proud of, and keep to ourselves. Nowadays we're selling them all with a modern wire-spring technology – many of them for hill-climbs, sprint cars and increasingly for historic F1 racing – and

we exercise no further control of where, and how, they are employed.

"The next batch of engines we are likely to ship out will be the early-generation F1-type JD V10s, of the types run by Minardi and Tyrrell in 1998, re-engineered to wire springs instead of air-valves. There's no future for them in F1, everybody's moved on, so now we have to decide what to do with them …"

At that time, Ferguson thought, originally such engines would probably be leased (perhaps to a well-funded historic F1 team) and supported by on-track engineers, with outright sales to follow in future years. Historic F1 racing developed rapidly in the late 1990s, from the 'look what I have bought!' demonstrations, to what looked like fairly serious races by a series of discarded F1 cars.

By no means all of 'Racing's' work was being done for Ford, as a study of worldwide formulae proved. As the 1990s rolled by, Cosworth built and developed engines for a whole variety of customers – and what might once have been called obsolete engines turned up again and again, in entirely different types of cars from those for which they were originally designed.

Although Cosworth's truly major programmes – F1 and CART being the prime examples – took up more and more of the company's time, even at the end of the 1990s, a significant part of Cosworth Racing's sales activities concerned component supply – pistons, older engine pieces, complete cylinder heads for engines as varied as the YB of the 1980s and the BD of the 1970s. Every year between £1 million and £2 million was garnered from supplying historic pieces.

To quote Bernard Ferguson:

"We can supply anything from a cylinder head gasket, to a complete YB engine, to a complete F1 programme. We can go back a long way into our history, but one major constraint, these days, is that because we have constantly updated our machine shop equipment, sometimes the old jigs and fixtures we preserved don't fit the new machines. This means that making new jigs and rewriting CNC programmes would sometimes make resupply far too expensive."

Cosworth in touring car racing

One engine type, the Ford-USA-based 24-valve V6 2.0-litre which Cosworth had been developing since 1993, was a stock of units always owned by Ford, and always confined to use in Mondeo touring car racers,

Bernard Ferguson, sales director at Cosworth from the early 1990s until the 2000s, when he retired, was one of the surviving links between the company and its myriad customers.

not only those competing in the BTCC, but in France, Germany and outside Europe.

Because the regulations were so tight (an electronically-monitored 8500rpm limit was always imposed – "but we learned an awful lot from that" Mark Parish told me), peak power figures of around 300bhp proved difficult to exceed, but there was a great deal of work on installations, on mid-range response, and on reliability.

This engine, it would be fair to say, was often let down by the cars themselves, especially in 1996 and 1997 when they suffered from a serious lack of chassis development. Programmes were decided at the last minute, new cars were ready far too late, too close to the start of the seasons, and for a time no-one had a good word to say about anyone.

The engines, bulky but highly efficient, were as powerful as any other in these formulae, for they had significantly more piston area and lighter moving parts. In Britain, however, the Mondeos were often recalcitrant. In 1995 Andy Rouse's 'works' team achieved two victories and eight other podium positions in the BTCC, while Matthew Neal's privately-financed Mondeo won the Total Cup for independent drivers, though *Autosport*'s reviewer commented that:

"The problem with the Mondeo has been well-recorded – too much of the V6's weight is over the front wheels, leading to excessive tyre wear, plus a rear end more passenger than willing participant ..."

After that, as far as the cars (but not the engines) were concerned, tyre technology changed, and things went from bad to worse. For the next three years West Surrey Racing took over the running of the cars from Andy Rouse. In 1996 the cars were built to a German design, where the engines were laid back at an angle with a complex transmission; in 1997 and 1998 they were more conventional (and engineered by Reynard), but the results were always deeply disappointing.

It was never easy to package this unit into the Mondeo shell, especially when trying to lower it, and push it back into the bulkhead. Individuals looking for something, anything, to blame, suggested that using such a V6 was all very well, but that it got too hot, later in a race. The fact that it had already powered winning cars for two very full seasons was, however, studiously ignored by those critics. In 1998 not even a trio of highly publicised, but ludicrously unsuccessful, British outings by Nigel Mansell could make a difference.

For 1999, Ford's newly-appointed motorsport supremo, Martin Whitaker, therefore decided on a

To meet the latest European Touring Car regulations, Ford evolved the new Mondeo, but fitted with a Mazda/Ford-USA based V6 engine, which Cosworth re-engineered to provide a 300bhp 2-litre power output to the front wheels. Driving cars prepared by Andy Rouse Engineering, Paul Radisich immediately started winning major races ...

... including the World Touring Car Cup event at Monza in both 1993 and 1994.

clear-out, sacking both Reynard and West Surrey Racing, and installing the much-respected Banbury-based Prodrive team in their place. After a brief flirtation with the idea of running a four-cylinder Ford engine, Ford decided to stay faithful to the Cosworth-developed V6, the management of this programme (along with the supply of V10s to the Minardi F1 team) being one of Mark Parish's responsibilities.

Except that the cylinder head and block castings were bought in, direct, from Ford-USA, all the machining, and every one of the moving parts, was now a dedicated Cosworth component, so this was as near to a racing engine as possible. To keep Prodrive's cars on the track, a pool of about 12 engines was needed.

Cosworth's efforts for Opel, in the DTM/ITC (International Touring Cars) touring car series were remarkably successful, though at the time, for contractual reasons Cosworth could reap little publicity benefit. Previously (as constrained by the regulations) Cosworth had prepared engines using a GM road-car V6 block, with two race victories for Klaus

JJ Lehto driving the KC-powered Opel Calibra, which was a race winning combination in the German DTM series in 1995.

For 1996, Cosworth produced the all-new KF V6 race engine for Opel to use in the German DTM 'touring car' series, where it proved to be extremely successful.

KF-equipped Opel Calibras, with four-wheel-drive, won their first event, and in a 26-event series, went on to win nine races, with Manuel Reuter winning the Drivers', and Opel winning the Manufacturers' sections of the ITC Championship. After this the series died suddenly, because both Opel and Alfa Romeo withdrew from it, disappointed by a general lack of TV and media coverage. Cosworth was delighted to prove its point, yet again, though GM/Opel had only scratched the surface of the KF's potential before it was rendered obsolete.

To quote *Autocourse*'s annual review of the season:

"The '96 spec Calibra was a very different beast from the one that had blown hot and cold in the previous two seasons. A new wider-vee 2.5-litre V6 had brought the power the car had hitherto lacked, while the Achilles heel of its fragile four-wheel-drive transmission had finally been cured."

For GM/Opel it must have been an expensive exercise, which may explain why it pulled the plug at the end of the year. As Cosworth's Mark Parish pointed out to me, Opel always ran eight cars, and sometimes nine cars, in every event. As with other unique engines, the units were of no value for future series, so Opel took them into stock, and they were not raced again.

Getting rid of the empties

But for Cosworth, it wasn't all good news. The AC V8, designed specifically for F3000, was dominant by 1995 – yet it was outlawed from the formula at the end of that year. In the 1995 season, where all but one of the eight qualifying events was won by an AC-powered car, there were complaints that costs were getting too high, and the authorities decided to impose a 'one-engine/standard specification' formula in future.

Several companies, Cosworth included, were invited to tender for the privilege of supplying engines, a lower tender was received from a previously-unsuccessful engine-builder, and suddenly there was no further use for the Cosworth ACs. These, therefore, went back into store with companies like Heini Mader and John Nicholson, who would have to find their own ways of selling them on.

As with the stored (but, in fairness) obsolete CART XBs, this seemed to be a criminal waste of horsepower. The authorities' pious hopes of reducing costs, incidentally, were not upheld, so this move was all in vain.

Ludwig's Calibra 4x4 at the end of the season, but for 1996 there was to be an all-new purpose-built KF-type racing V6.

This, although a winner almost from the moment Opel put it on the tracks, was by no means at its peak when the formula died away at the end of the year. With a rev-limit of 12,000rpm this engine presented a different challenge for Cosworth Racing's designers than the Mondeo's V6 had ever done.

For 1995 and 1996, the newly-drafted ITC regulations required a special race-car engine to have the same bore spacing, and the same vee angle as a manufacturer's road car unit (though the same cylinder block did not have to be employed), so the new KF's basic layout was based on that of a corporate GM V6, this time with a 60 degree vee angle, rather than the 54 degrees of the previous year. The latest F1 'air-spring' technology was used in the classic Cosworth four-valve twin-cam top end, and though the programme was completed faster than any previous Cosworth product, it was an immediate winner.

Interestingly enough, even after Ford bought Cosworth Racing, there was no immediate embargo on doing business with other car-makers:

"They actively encourage us to keep doing this," Ferguson commented, "just so long as we will not be competing in the same formula as a Ford, and there is no potential betrayal of IPR in either direction."

Brave words, of course, and one could quite see a smaller independent company or – say – a motorcycle manufacturer, still approaching Cosworth Racing, though one wonders whether a company like GM-Opel would ever again employ Cosworth in the way that it succeeded, so brilliantly, with the ITC V6 units.

The production engine scene

By 1995, Cosworth's factory at Wellingborough was busy with the building of late-model 'small turbo' YB engines for the Ford Escort RS Cosworth, 210bhp FBC V6 engines for the Ford Scorpio, and old-type 150bhp pushrod 'Cologne V6' engines, also for the Ford Scorpio – but all that was about to change.

Before the end of 1996, and as the Escort RS Cosworth had reached the end of its career, series production of YB engines closed down (it had been continuously 'in build' for a decade), while the last of the pushrod-engined V6 units was assembled for Scorpios at about the same time, though engine build for an 'All Time Service' requirement continued. As far as Ford business was concerned, this therefore left the four-cam FBC 2.9-litre V6 on its own – and even this line was due to close down by 1999.

Before then, however, Wellingborough's incredibly flexible facilities had been re-organised to deal with the manufacture of a famous, if ageing, power unit – the light-alloy Rolls-Royce/Bentley V8, a pushrod design which had originally gone into production in 1959. It was all very convenient – as production of Ford road-car engines began to run down, Cosworth was able to build up Rolls-Royce V8 engine assembly, partly to take their place.

Although this venerable old V8 was originally designed and tooled for manufacture at Rolls-Royce's own factory at Crewe, where it had been built for 37 years, this facility had always taken up a lot of factory space at that location. When Rolls-Royce set out to redevelop its premises (with a moving final assembly line for its cars, for the very first time) it needed to vacate one complete block of the factory.

On the basis that the V8 was eventually projected to be replaced by purpose-built BMW power units (though there would be an overlap of at least two to three years), manufacture was then moved to Cosworth's Wellingborough plant, though it was typical of both companies that no high-profile announcement about this was ever made.

By the 1990s this 6.75-litre leviathan was an old-technology engine in almost every sense (Keith Duckworth had once famously commented that: "Using push rods to operate valves is like lying on your back and trying to play a piano with your feet"), yet in turbocharged form it had nevertheless eventually been developed to produce no less than 420bhp.

Although at this time its original-type cylinder head steadfastly refused to breathe properly at much above 4000rpm (if it was not allowed to redesign the heads, not even Cosworth could do anything about that), and its fuel efficiency figures were awful, it had all the torque of an old-fashioned steam engine, and was as refined as only a company like Rolls-Royce could make it. At peak, during 1997, Cosworth produced approximately 2000 complete V8 engines for Rolls-Royce, the numbers then dropping steeply from 1998 (after the new-generation BMW-powered cars came along), but were still expected to proceed steadily thereafter.

In the meantime, Jaguar's new-generation V8 engine, complete with twin-overhead-camshafts per bank, and four-valves-per-cylinder, and made in 3.2-litre and 4.0-litre guise, was launched in March 1996. Manufacture of engines was actually by Ford, at its Bridgend factory in South Wales, Cosworth's part being to supply cylinder head castings from Worcester.

When a new F3000 race series was introduced, Cosworth designed the V8 AC power unit, which was totally unrelated to the old DFV. It became dominant for several years, before effectively being outlawed by a change in regulations.

For a time in the 1990s and early 2000s, Cosworth took over the complete manufacture of Rolls-Royce V8 engines at Wellingborough, for fitment to Bentley and Rolls-Royce road cars. This was the prestigious Bentley Azure DHC of the period.

When Cosworth's chief road car engineering designer, Mike Hall, retired in 1989, Ford gave him great send-off, including this lavish dinner party. Cosworth chairman Mike Costin is presenting the painting to Mike, with Cosworth founder Keith Duckworth grinning in the background.

The fabulously smooth, refined, and powerful 6-litre V12 SG type first went on sale in the Aston Martin DB7 Vantage in 1999, and would then power the majority of Aston Martin road cars for the next 15 years.

There was, perhaps, one major lost opportunity, though I doubt if we will ever know the full story. Rather shyly, in June 1996, the company unveiled an all-new and extremely compact 72-degree V10 engine, the 4.3-litre WDA. As traditionally expected of any modern Cosworth engine, this came complete with twin-cam heads, four-valves-per-cylinder, fuel injection, along with state-of-the-art ignition and emission controls. It was, in every respect, a road-car engine, intended for series production.

This 325bhp/4.3-litre power unit, made its debut at an Open Day at MIRA, when it was claimed to be a road-car project which had been carried out for an 'un-named' manufacturer. The engine, it was stated, had been designed so fast that it had first run only nine months after the job had been commissioned, and ran in one of the client's cars only eight weeks after that. Even in prototype form, it weighed only 441lb/200kg.

Then, and ever afterwards, there were several mysteries and unanswered questions behind its layout. Physically much larger than the contemporary Cosworth V10 F1 engine, it shared only the 72-degree vee angle (chosen for balancing purposes) but had no common components with Cosworth race engines.

Its sponsor was not revealed at the time, yet it was eventually admitted that it could be mounted in a transverse 'East-West' position in the engine bay of a large family car model. Rated at 325bhp, this would no doubt have posed formidable traction and cooling problems for engineering teams to solve ...

Because Volvo was already using transversely-mounted 2.5-litre five-cylinder engines in its cars (which, according to the pundits, meant that a V10 might also be squeezed into a similar space!), the Swedish company then became the target for further rumours in the specialist press, but it was years before this link was ever confirmed. Incidentally, the 325bhp output surely meant that four-wheel-drive would have been needed to harness its torque – and Volvo had a four-wheel-drive system too.

At about the same time, Cosworth also showed an ingenious twin-balancer-shaft kit which it had developed for Ford – a kit which subsequently found its way into the 2.3-litre 16-valve 'I4' power unit which had evolved from the 1990s-type Ford RS2000 engine.

This engine, a Ford rather than a Cosworth design, had originally been rated as a 2.0-litre/150bhp unit, giving the Escort RS2000 sparkling performance. For use in less sporty cars like the Scorpio and the Galaxy models, however, Ford decided to enlarge it to a 2295cc unit, but with a longer cylinder stroke it was no longer thought to be smooth enough for these applications, so it was decided to treat the engine to twin 'Lanchester'-type contra-rotating balance shafts (driven from the crankshaft at twice engine speed) to solve the problem.

Normally this would have meant positioning a shaft along each side of the cylinder block, and hiding them away in unique and expensive-to-tool castings, but Cosworth thought up a better way. Neatly and unobtrusively, the shafts were positioned *under* the crankshaft, in a much-modified sump casting. The sump was only a little deeper than before, and actually added rigidity to the entire assembly.

In 1997, and well before the company was officially put up for sale, Cosworth also announced a long-term deal with Ford, to design, develop and eventually to manufacture a series of new road-car engines for use in Aston Martin cars – a marque also owned by Ford at the time.

The first evidence of this co-operation was made public in March 1999, when Aston Martin introduced the DB7 Vantage, complete with a new Cosworth-designed 60-degree 6-litre V12. Not only did this engine have very complicated beginnings (it stemmed, originally, from a Ford-USA prototype V12 which had been seen at the Detroit Auto Show in the mid-1990s), but in its early production years there was bound to be commercial complication too. Manufacture of this Ford-financed engine would be at Wellingborough, which by 1999 had become part of the Audi-controlled Cosworth Technology concern.

Like many previous Cosworth engines, the new 6-litre V12 – which was, incidentally, the most powerful road car engine so far to be put into production by Cosworth – was a mixture of innovation, pragmatic development, and sheer expertise. Way back in the mid-1990s, the layout of the prototype Ford-USA engine was essentially two Ford Duratec V6s mounted end to end, which explains the 60-degree vee angle. Not only because of the historical reference, but because it gives an ideal balance situation (and keeps the engine commendably slim for mounting in an engine bay) this angle was retained for the production-standard engine.

By 1998, in any case, all this activity had been overshadowed by a corporate upheaval, and by the never-ending drama surrounding the development of new F1 V10 engines. That ever-unfolding saga now deserves a complete chapter to itself.

16: COSWORTH RACING + FORD – A NEW LIFE BECKONS

When Vickers decided to reshape its business in 1997, first of all by putting up the Rolls-Royce company for sale, the rumour-mongers then moved swiftly into action: as far as they were concerned, this immediately then put the Cosworth business 'in play.' If Vickers did not want to keep Rolls-Royce, some pundits reasoned, it would surely not want to keep Cosworth either?

At this point, with Rolls-Royce on the market, and with the brand-new Rolls-Royce Silver Seraph and Bentley Arnage models ready to be launched, it is worth remembering how Cosworth had come steadily closer to that prestige business at Crewe.

First of all, in 1989/1990, and purely as consultants, it had designed a state-of-the-art twin-cam conversion of the existing Rolls-Royce V8 engine: this was the stillborn RB type, and nowadays both Cosworth and Rolls-Royce would rather not talk about it. Next, from 1994, for its new generation of four-door cars, Rolls-Royce elected to buy engines from BMW, deciding that its new 'Bentley' power unit should be a BMW 4.4-litre V8, which would be re-engineered by Cosworth as a twin-turbo assembly (though series manufacture would always be carried out by BMW in Germany).

The equivalent Rolls-Royce, on the other hand, was to use a lightly-modified version of the existing BMW V12 power unit.

Then, because Rolls-Royce needed to free-up a lot of factory space to modernise its facilities, from 1996 Cosworth took over complete manufacture of its famous, but venerable, 6.75-litre pushrod overhead-valve V8 engine (which, by this time, was being produced in normally-aspirated and 420bhp turbocharged form). From that time, those engines were built in the ever-versatile Wellingborough plant.

Even after the new-generation BMW-engined Rolls-Royce and Bentley models had been launched in 1998, however, the more specialised two-door Bentleys (Azures, Continental Rs and Continental Ts), and the hand-built 'stretch' limousines, remained in production, all powered by the old-type pushrod engine. All the signs were that such models would remain on the market until the start of the next century and, as it transpired, the engine would then live on for two more decades.

By the spring of 1998, however, Vickers had already decided to sell Cosworth, and industrial turmoil ensued ...

Since both Cosworth and Bentley were controlled by Vickers in the mid-1990s, it was logical that Cosworth should develop and manufacture the twin-turbo conversion of the BMW V8 engine (Cosworth coded this engine the MD), for use in the new-generation Bentley Arnage of 1998.

Cosworth + Ford – nothing new

Even though BMW and VW (or its Audi subsidiary) immediately became hot favourites to bid for Cosworth, rumours of a counter-bid from Ford surfaced at once. For a few days, financial pundits rubbed their hands at the thought of a juicy 'bidding battle' – until Ford made it clear that it was not in the running for the entire business.

As far as the racing arm was concerned, however, it was a different story, for Ford's motor racing presence, and its future, were by that time so closely linked to Cosworth that a divorce seemed impossible. Ford managers obviously thought the same, as this quote in *Autocar* of 29 April 1998 made clear:

"Ford owns the intellectual rights to the Cosworth-built Zetec-R-V10. 'The trucks would be backed up to the door, and we would be loaded up,' says a Ford insider. 'No way would we deal with another car maker under these circumstances.'"

Yet at this moment there was not, and never had been, any financial link (in terms of shareholdings, that is) between the two companies of Ford and Cosworth. For more than 30 years, from 1965 onwards, Cosworth had merely been a favoured, and much respected, supplier. Even so, from time to time the idea of Ford buying Cosworth, or at least buying a financial stake, had been seriously considered.

In 1987/88, when Ford was making a major commitment to Cosworth, not only with the deal to make YB turbocharged Sierra RS Cosworth power units and 24-valve Scorpio engines at Wellingborough (see Chapter 13), and in new F1 engine design (the DFR, followed by the HB – see Chapter 12), Ford certainly asked UEI if a sale might be possible, but it was turned away.

Then, at the end of 1989, soon after Carlton Communications had absorbed the UEI conglomerate (and therefore the Cosworth part of it), Ford perceived that Cosworth might once again be on the market, and began to worry about a hostile takeover battle, which might come from companies like Fiat, General Motors or Mercedes-Benz. If that had happened, Ford would certainly have withdrawn all of its business from Cosworth ("If we do not acquire Cosworth," a Ford insider commented at the time, "we should probably have to find an alternative manufacturing source ..."), especially in motor racing for, as Director of European Motorsport, Stuart Turner, wrote in a Ford internal memo:

"We should have a contingency plan to give, say,

Brian Hart enough support for him to tempt away the four to six key people [he needs ...] ... If Fiat buy Cosworth we should on no account believe any promises to keep a Ford F1 engine competitive with Ferrari ..."

Although Ford was apparently ready to put in a 'knockout' bid against someone like Fiat, this was never needed. Cannily, it concluded that Carlton might encourage a neutral third party to buy the business instead – which is what happened with Vickers in 1990.

In the spring of 1998, however, the same nightmare scenario surfaced once again, when VW's prestige subsidiary, Audi, finally bought the entire Cosworth business from Vickers. Although wild rumours then began to circulate – that Cosworth had already built an F1 engine for Audi (which was not true), that Audi wanted to get into front-line motorsport via Cosworth (possible, but only an idea), and that Ford would immediately torpedo the deal (as it did) – it was some time before the dust settled.

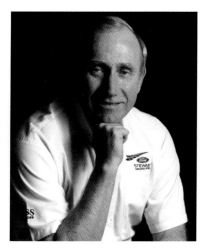

When Ford took control of Cosworth Racing, Neil Ressler (Ford's Vice-president, Research and Vehicle Technology) became chairman.

Corporate upheaval

This is what seems to have happened. Way back in 1996/97 the Board of Vickers set out to redirect its business strategy, the new idea being that it would separately sell off two prestige businesses – Rolls-Royce (which included the Bentley brand) and Cosworth. One-time Cosworth chairman, Chris Woodwark, who by this time had moved up rapidly to be Vickers' chief operating officer, fundamentally disagreed with this – and resigned.

In November 1997, however, Vickers made it clear that Rolls-Royce was to be sold, and although the same was not publicly stated of Cosworth, a load of assumptions were immediately made. By February 1998 BMW and VW were both bidding hard for Rolls-Royce, and Cosworth's name was already being mentioned.

Although the Vickers Board originally favoured a sale to BMW, it later changed its mind, stating that it would sell the business to VW instead, for a cool £430 million. As already detailed above, Audi then agreed to buy Cosworth from Vickers too, paying £120 million for the business.

Common sense then prevailed, for, months before that sale, Ford had made it clear that if this happened, then it would withdraw all its motor racing business (F1, CART/Indycar, and British Touring Car projects) from Northampton. To quote Bernard Ferguson: "the intellectual rights would have marched out of the door …"

Audi really had no alternative. Its deal with Vickers was announced in June 1998, but in a matter of days it also made it clear that a portion of the business, henceforth to be called 'Cosworth Racing' would be split off from the rest of the business (to be called Cosworth Technology) and would be sold on to Ford. Tacitly, it seems, Audi had agreed to this well before the Vickers announcement came, but did not want to confuse an already complex situation by making a premature announcement.

It then took a further three months to finalise the deal, but from mid-September 1998 Cosworth Racing became a wholly owned subsidiary of Ford, a move which some say should have happened 20 or even 30 years earlier!

The split, though professionally achieved in a businesslike manner, was not easy to arrange, especially as there were manufacturing aspects of the operation still being used by both sides.

The modern, versatile, and very high-tech foundry at Worcester was a perfect example, for in 1998 not only was it making major castings in quantity (such as cylinder heads for Jaguar), but it was also producing F1 and Champcar castings for Cosworth Racing.

At that time, however, Cosworth Technology controlled the foundry, and so therefore was supplying castings to Cosworth Racing, as well as castings to Jaguar, which was a Ford subsidiary. Contractual arrangements existed, but for how long would that situation persist into the 2000s?

"At the moment," a Cosworth Racing spokesman said in 1998/99, "we have an agreement with the Worcester foundry to carry on supplying castings. Ford, fortunately, already have a licence for the process in any case, and we already have a strategy to make ourselves self-sufficient in the future."

Ford's intent – to run Cosworth in a benevolent, rather semi-detached, manner – then became clear. Ford-USA's Neil Ressler (vice-president, Research and Vehicle Technology) became Cosworth's chairman (and he also joined the Board of Stewart Grand Prix), while Dick Scammell who, in theory, was already semi-retired and spending some time in his native Bath, was lured back as what Ford called an 'interim managing director.' Ressler, it was clear, wanted to see Stewart Grand Prix brought closer together with Cosworth Racing.

"I had no advance warning, none at all. The phone call came, out of the blue, from Neil Ressler," Dick Scammell told me, with a broad grin, "asking me if I would come back, and help them through the 'gap,' to give the company some direction and stability in the first months, and to help fuse Cosworth Racing and Ford comfortably together."

Why Dick, and not a sporting-minded nominee from Ford's own HQ in Essex?

"I don't know, but I suppose it was because I knew the company, I knew the business, and I think the company needed some stability and some continuity. I'd been doing business with Ford for 30 years, I'd known Neil Ressler for eight years – and I think I understood the philosophy of the company …"

It was, in other words, the 'stick of rock' syndrome, for here was a man with the word 'Cosworth' running right through him, in a pure, rich vein, ideal for a very taxing, and ticklish, job.

For Dick, who had been with Cosworth from 1972 to 1996, then a part-time consultant, this was not only a great honour, but a real pleasure. By all accounts, he was delighted to be given an enviably free hand to reshape the business to Cosworth Racing's, and Ford's, best advantage – and originally expected this to take between six months and a year. Before he returned, Nick Hayes (engineering) and Bernard Ferguson (sales and marketing) had to put in a lot of good work, keeping the show on the road during the disruption attending the sale:

"Cosworth Racing is a different company already," Dick told me after the first three months had passed. "Ford has told us that in the future they want to invest in us, and they want us to go out and win motor races – which is all that Cosworth, all our people, and Dick Scammell, ever wanted to do. It's the best thing that could ever have happened to Cosworth Racing – we're all very comfortable with it."

Life it seemed, was going to be far more straightforward than in the past, and in organisational terms the racing side of the business was no longer going to trip up over production or consultancy projects at every turn.

For Dick, and for Cosworth Racing, this looked like an ideal arrangement, for functionally they reported to an engineering, rather than a finance or marketing centre, where everyone understood one another.

Because it was clearly never going to be an ideal situation for Cosworth Racing (Ford) and Cosworth Technology (Audi) to live side-by-side, cheek-by-jowl, in Northampton, one of the first visible signs of a new commercial reality came when the builders moved in to the Northampton site, and a geographical (and functional) split between 'Technology' and 'Racing' was speedily started. By the spring of 1999, although the two businesses were still able to operate side by side, they had become functionally (and financially!) completely separate. In the long-term, however, it was suggested that Cosworth Racing would eventually move to another site – though 20 years on, this had still not happened.

"But, as I told the workforce," Dick Scammell confirmed, "we would only move to a new site, a new state-of-the-art facility, if we could take all of them with us! That's how much we think of them: they're very important to us."

For traditionalists like the author, it was interesting to see that the Ford-owned 'Racing' had also negotiated to retain almost all its existing archive, and almost all the historic artefacts, including the mouth-watering collection of historic engines, both ancient and modern. Of equal importance was that Racing kept the use of the 'Cosworth' name on vehicles and engines.

From that moment on, Ford not only injected rock-solid back-up, enthusiasm and – always important – good financial backing, but Cosworth could now gain access to Ford's very large and very powerful computers for design purposes, access to test equipment that Cosworth could never have afforded for itself ("In crude terms, they have very big toys!"), and huge purchasing clout.

To keep the workforce informed, Neil Ressler had a video made, including a personal presentation from himself, had it played on the company's internal video screen system on the very day of the purchase, then charged Dick Scammell with holding a series of meetings in every department – including the night shift, in the middle of the night – seeing every one of the 600 workforce in Northampton in the next few days, to explain the new situation.

By the end of 1998 there were smiles on every Cosworth Racing face that I encountered in Northampton, its five-year development and action plan had already been agreed with Ford, and there didn't seem to be a downside in sight. Not only that, but Cosworth Racing had already been given clearance to expand its coverage of world-class motor racing engines. Already famous in F1, in Champcar, and in Touring Car racing, a new strategy was clear:

"Ford have already given us a directive." Scammell confirmed. "They haven't bought Cosworth Racing to put their latest engine work into other companies. Gradually, where we are able to, they would like us to take on their other racing programmes. And when the time is right, in the 2000s we will be able to pick up other Ford projects, all round the world."

Because of the way that the two businesses had been split, however, some oddities were bound to persist for some time – an early, and prime, example being that the new Aston Martin V12 engine, officially unveiled in March 1999, would be assembled by Cosworth Technology in Wellingborough. Ford, however, had already developed an expansion plan for Cosworth Racing, where all its major activities – including limited-series manufacturing – would be brought back 'in-house' during the 2000s.

Formula 1 V10s – the latest technology

In and around all this, Racing's design team had not only designed a series of F1 V10 engines, but rapidly built up its expertise, and raised its achievements considerably. By 1999, in only four years, the team had designed its third-generation 3-litre V10, the new CK (in public it was always known as the CR-1, where CR was Cosworth Racing), and although peak power figures were not revealed, in my own estimation I have no doubt that the CK produced at least an extra 100bhp, and maybe more, than the original JD of 1996.

As Cosworth's F1 design chief, Nick Hayes, confirmed, the V10 story actually began in 1994, when a change in regulations made mid-event refuelling not only possible but advisory. This tipped the philosophical balance between V8 and the (by definition) thirstier and higher-revving V10 layouts. That was the year when the EC (always known as the Zetec-R-V8) Michael Schumacher/Benetton combination swept everything before it in F1, and represented the point at which Cosworth then started working on a 3.5-litre V10. Then came the FIA's abrupt decision to reduce F1 engine sizes to 3.0-litres in 1995 – at which Cosworth's plans were thrown into confusion.

Nick Hayes, who had joined Cosworth in 1984 – via Salford University, a sandwich course with Rolls-Royce Aerospace, post-graduate work for Rolls-Royce, and a phone call from Keith Duckworth – came to the V10 design programmes with a fascinating pedigree. Having originally worked alongside Geoff Goddard and Martin Walters, he then carried out five years of F1 race support with Benetton.

Stand well clear! Keith Duckworth always used to say that if he could only trap the energy that went into making race car exhaust systems so hot, he could gain a lot more power!

By the end of the 1990s, Cosworth was pushing the technical boundaries as far and fast as it could. Caught here in this studio shot are examples of the Champcar XD (left) and the latest F1 engine, the JD (right). One was a V8, one a V10, one had a vee angle of 75 degrees, the other 72 degrees. No chance of any commonality there then!

Many years after it was first launched, Ford contributed to the total restoration of one of surviving Lotus 49/DFV F1 cars. Here, proud and happy to be involved, were (left to right) Dick Scammell, Walter Hayes, Jackie Stewart and Keith Duckworth.

After some time running the evolution of the VB V12 programme (which was cancelled in 1993 without ever getting into a race car), Nick then carried out a new study of F1 V8, V10 and V12 alternatives. Cosworth then consulted Benetton about his findings, the result (already described in Chapter 14) being the design of the EC.

"As you go down in cylinder numbers, everything goes better for you except peak power," Nick said. "10s and 12s can produce more power, but they are longer, heavier, the heat rejection gets worse, and fuel efficiency gets worse. Before refuelling came back, the start-line weight of an 'eight,' plus its smaller fuel load, was a definite advantage."

Under Dick Scammell's direction, Martin Walters, with Nick Hayes as one of his key staff, then led the entire project, which provided winning power for Michael Schumacher in 1994:

"Then, once we were fully committed to the EC and had proved to ourselves that it was the best all-round answer for Benetton, refuelling was re-introduced. Because this meant that F1 cars could then carry less fuel, that tipped the balance to a V10, to be honest. So, as soon as we had done the EC 'eight', and made it reliable, we started designing a new 3.5-litre V10.

"That was what Michael and Benetton both wanted, so we got a long way with it – five or six months of concept, and drawing, as I recall – then the authorities moved the goalposts yet again, reducing the capacity to 3.0-litres. The original QC 3.5-litre V10 was going to be too large, so we stopped that dead – there and then – and developed 3.0-litre versions of the EC instead." Although three different internal versions of the 3.0-litre EC/Zetec-R-V8 (using different bore/stroke

Nick Hayes led the Cosworth design team at the end of the 1990s when three totally different F1 V10s were revealed in only four years – JD, VJ and CK – during which remarkable progress in power delivery was achieved. When it was newly announced, the CK was so special, and so much lighter, than its predecessors, that Hayes would not allow any photographs to be published. He later relented.

ratios) were eventually produced for Sauber to use in 1995, the link-up with the Swiss team came very late in the day, the Sauber C14 was not the best chassis on the track, and mid-field (and some points scoring) finishes were the best that could be achieved.

To quote the authoritative *Autocourse* annual:

"All in all, the engine didn't suit the chassis, the weight distribution was wrong, and the car suffered from inherent understeer ..."

In the meantime, Cosworth (and Ford) started work on the second of their V10 designs, the original 72-degree JD, which was totally different from the stillborn 3.5-litre QC unit. Project work began in January 1995, the first engines were running before the end of the year, by which time Cosworth knew that Ford intended to supply it exclusively to Sauber of Switzerland, whose drivers would be Johnny Herbert and Heinz-Harald Frentzen.

"It was a difficult first year," Nick Hayes admits," because we had to learn all about V10s." As both Nick and his boss Dick Scammell now admit, they had to learn a lot about the best way to optimise the exhaust system:

"By the 1990s we reckon we knew a lot about the tuning and shaping of the exhaust system of a V8," Scammell told me, "but with the V10s we had to learn everything from scratch.

"If we looked at what other people had done, that only told us part of the story. We are still learning!"

Although the V10-engined Sauber was quicker than the Ford V8-powered type had been, the combination of Sauber C15 and Ford-Cosworth JD was not a success. Although Cosworth's F1 team resented being labelled as 'the conservative club' at this time, the JD was not as powerful as some outsiders had expected, and was widely seen as having a 'black hole' in the mid-range

of the power curve at first, and was not at all driver-friendly at that stage.

Although it was actually shorter than the old EC/Zetec-RV8 (which was a real surprise to many observers, though this tells us a lot about the big cylinder bore of the 'eight'), and was a little bit lighter, by other F1 V10 standards it was still too heavy and, in retrospect, slightly too bulky. It did not make friends at first, but weight melted away during the year, peak revs rose, and the engine went through four development phases – Projects 1 to 4 – during the season.

Ford's link-up with Stewart GP

This was the point at which another contractual upheaval, quite outside Cosworth's control, then added complication to the ongoing V10 project. Instead of to Sauber, for the next five years the latest Ford-Cosworth V10s would be supplied to the newly formed Stewart Grand Prix team:

"It all started on 11 June 1995," Jackie Stewart recalls, "on the Ford plane … from Montreal to Detroit after the Canadian GP. Ford bosses … were unhappy with their involvement in F1, and asked me what they should do?

"I said they should get out, because they weren't doing it properly; they weren't spending enough, weren't committed to it. I told them they would never get from F1 what they did in the past without total commitment."

This, apparently, shocked Ford so much that the bosses went into a huddle, thought it through, and eventually invited Stewart to take up the challenge, with a long-term commitment to an F1 team. The

deal was done in October 1995, and was officially launched in January 1996, with the first Stewart-Fords due to be ready to go racing in 1997. Stewart started designing a new car at once, and an incomplete JD V10 engine arrived for installation work to commence on 13 February 1996. Even so, the first Stewart SF-1 car would not turn a wheel until the end of that year.

"This deal made a huge difference," Nick Hayes confirmed, "because we now had a five-year commitment to one team. Anything we had had before was a year-by-year deal. With guaranteed stability in mind, we could be a lot more open with each other, and work on long-term projects. All subsequent engine work was to be done with Stewart in mind, and when it came to doing layout work on the next V10s [the VJ of 1998 and the CK/CR-1 for 1999] we could consult Stewart right from the start."

In 1997 Stewart's major problems, being brand new, included having to play 'catch-up' behind every other established team, and not having the resources to do the private testing which would have helped so much.

Therefore, although the JD V10 entered its second year, further-developed, more powerful, and with a number of packaging differences – and carried on improving, rapidly, during the season – the record shows that Stewart suffered a number of engine failures where new components had to be race-tested in the full glare of publicity.

No-one, however, was complaining about the engine's potential, or its driveability, and in only its fifth GP, at Monaco, Stewart's Rubens Barrichello achieved second place. Jackie Stewart himself was so overcome by this that, when faced by TV crews demanding a comment, he was full of emotion, totally unable to answer.

Jackie Stewart (soon to become Sir Jackie, by the way), three-times F1 World Drivers' Champion in DFV-powered Tyrrells, set up his own F1 team – Stewart Grand Prix – in 1996, and secured an exclusive five-year deal to use Cosworth-designed engines.

The CK V10, introduced in 1999, was one of several F1 V10s Cosworth produced in a hectic development period of the time. At the time it was by far the most powerful and lightweight V10 which the company had so far introduced.

Having bought out Stewart GP in 1999, Ford then rebranded the team as 'Jaguar,' which raced Cosworth-engined cars for the next four years.

COSWORTH – THE SEARCH FOR POWER

Johnny Herbert drove this Stewart-Ford SF3 to victory in the European F1 GP of 1999, this being the first victory for the new-generation CK engine.

Much was expected of the Stewart team in the late 1990s and early 2000s – this was the launch of the 1999 SF3 model in 1999 – but Ford soon bought out the team, and renamed it Jaguar. Left, Rubens Barrichello and right, Johnny Herbert.

One of the great advantages of supplying engines to Stewart instead of Sauber was that the Stewart base was so much closer to Northampton. With the best will in the world, it had not been easy to support Sauber's racing operation in Switzerland, whereas Stewart, with its HQ in Milton Keynes, was less than 20 miles away. By the time the third-generation V10, the new CK/CR-1, came to be designed, there was such close co-operation that the engine was more closely integrated to the single-seater chassis package than ever before.

Stewart used the JD throughout 1997, while Cosworth put it through no fewer than six further development phases – Projects 5 to 9 inclusive:

"We've always been honest about this," Hayes told me. At the start of 1997 we decided that we had fallen too far behind, and with a new commitment from Ford, we elected to go ahead, as fast as we could, to try new things – and as soon as we had anything better, we would stick it in a car. "If that meant we were going to lose an engine, in public, that was tough, but we had to accept the public embarrassment of a cloud of smoke – for we were moving ahead much quicker than by any other method. With each upgrade, we learned from the last one – we made a lot of progress in a single season. In terms of power and capability, we moved a long way up the grid in a short time.

"The Project 6 JD, which we first ran at Silverstone in mid-1997, was really half of a new engine anyway, which we had been working on since February – I don't think Cosworth has ever before moved as far, and as fast, as we did with development of the V10s. If you look at the horsepower-per-litre figures [which I could not ... AAGR!], we've done many years' work in two years.

Even so, all the time that this was going on, the second generation F1 V10, coded VJ, was being designed. Running for the very first time on Christmas Eve 1997, it was ready for installation early in 1998, and powered all Stewart SF-2 cars used in that season. By any standards, it was clearly better than before. It was another significant step away from the 'conservative club' levels of 1995.

Although Cosworth has always refused to provide peak power figures for its modern F1 engines, display units of VJ, built up for show, carried the legend '700bhp when announced.' This, please note, indicates a specific output of 233bhp/litre, which should be compared with the 135bhp/litre achieved by the original DFV of 1967.

Although breathing improvements continued to be made, much of that was due to the amazing way in which engines have been made to spin faster, for peak revs of 16,000rpm and more were now common.

Although some elements of the final JD engines were seen in the new VJ, one major change to the camshaft drive system – gear drive instead of chain drive – seemed to make the high-revving units more reliable than before, and during the year no fewer than six versions – Series 1 to Series 6 – were employed. By this time no fewer than 35 VJ-type V10s were in use, 25 of them permanently allocated to the Stewart cars, another ten being used back at Northampton as development power units.

"Perhaps you wouldn't notice major improvements from one step to the next," says Hayes, "but the difference between the original JD V10 of 1996 and the late-1998 VJ was absolutely massive. The architecture, in some ways, was still similar, but none of the components were 'carryover.'

"We like to think that we are using certain exotic materials, and exotic features, hidden away inside our engines, but the opposition probably have some of these too …

"You can tell a lot by looking at the outside of new engines, you can learn a lot that way. There are things on the 1999 engine, the CR-1, which we would really not like people to see …"

Which explains why no F1 engine design concern has allowed modern cutaway drawings to be published since the 1970s ("I don't mind that, as long as they're not accurate!"), and why photographs of current units were so difficult to find. When was the last time, for instance, that you saw an F1 team changing engines at the circuit, in full view?

"It costs millions of pounds, and a great deal of time, to learn enough to make those improvements, but it takes no time and no money to give it all away …"

Development and innovation had certainly accelerated in the late 1990s, such that the FIA's decision to cut engine sizes from 3.5 litres to 3.0 litres – by 15 per cent – was shrugged off, as engine manufacturers clawed all that back, and more, inside three years. Cosworth Racing, starting from a slightly lower base, did even better than that.

Neither Cosworth, nor Stewart, however, was content with this, so, early in 1998, work on yet another brand-new F1 V10 engine began, the object being not only to leave behind any existing achievements, but to set completely new standards. Although Cosworth would probably not admit it, it was stung by the recent achievements of its rivals; it was determined to make up for any previous deficit at a single bound, and an engineering group of up to 30 people (multi-talented research, design and development people, "and a lot of outside support, too") set out to achieve that.

As with other recent engines, this project moved from 'first thoughts' to first running in about nine or ten months, an established timetable which Cosworth still found difficult to compress. When I talked to Nick Hayes in December 1998, for instance, he told me that he was already thinking about the demands of the year 2000.

The result was the first engine to be introduced by Cosworth Racing under Ford's care, which explains why it was the CK, but in publicity material proudly carried the all-new Cosworth Racing type code, CR-1. Revolutionary in so many ways, or so Cosworth claimed, its layout relied much more on computer aided design (CAD) than ever before – yet, with their own particular needs in mind, Cosworth was still a great believer in drawing lines on paper when assessing all the possibilities.

When Stewart launched the new SF-3 F1 car at the *Autosport* International Show in January 1999, although the new CR-1 engine was praised as being revolutionary and sensational, it stayed firmly out of sight, under the engine cover. Admitting only that it was completely new, lighter, lower, smaller, and with an even lower crankshaft centre line than ever before, neither Cosworth nor Stewart would say any more.

Nor would they say how much lighter it was, though a massive ingot of aluminium, complete with lifting handle, was displayed to denote the weight saving. [That ingot, incidentally, later became a prominent, if quirky, display unit in the museum!] All this secrecy, however, misfired, when a written release confirmed that the CR-1 actually weighed only 221lb/100kg, making it much the lightest Cosworth F1 V10 ever, 66lb/30kg lighter than its VJ predecessor.

Complete with a brand-new Ford-sourced Visteon engine management system, the all-new CR-1 first ran on a Cosworth test-bed at 1.34am on 18 December 1998. The second engine ran the very next day, was rapidly delivered to Stewart Grand Prix at Milton Keynes the following day, and drove the car out on to the track at Silverstone on 23 December. Christmas for an F1 mechanic? Don't be facetious! Even at that point, Cosworth Racing noted, it was significantly more powerful than any previous naturally-aspirated Cosworth F1 engine had been – and that there was a lot more to come.

On behalf of Ford, Cosworth provided V10s to both the Ford-backed teams in this period – Sauber and Stewart – thus setting up a triangular relationship. Where money was concerned, Cosworth dealt direct with Ford, but technically the link was entirely with the teams themselves.

From time to time, Ford motorsport insiders have told me (and I do not think this was always a jocular comment) that in the past Cosworth has been almost as secretive towards them as to the outside world, that they did not know what the true performance of each engine actually was, and they had not actually seen the inside of a V10 engine either.

This unsatisfactory situation was soon resolved, with the sharing both of technical and management information in both directions, greatly to the benefit of the new Ford-Cosworth racing partnership.

Keeping the 'customer' happy

As with Ford-Cosworth V8s, so with its V10s. As soon as one level of V10 technology was surpassed by the next, Cosworth was ready to supply V10s to 'customer' teams, always on lease-hold terms. This explains why Sauber and Stewart were unique 'works' team users in 1996 and 1997, but why Tyrrell and Minardi then joined the ranks of V10 users in 1998.

By that time, Stewart was ready to use the VJ type of V10. It was, in most respects, a very different design from the JD, and, since stocks of those circa-700bhp V10s existed, they were ideal material for credible customers.

Tyrrell, in fact, was a long-time friend of Ford and Cosworth, returning from an unhappy spell of using Yamaha V10s to use final-development EDs in 1997, then moving up to 1997-spec JD V10s in 1998. Hampered to a great extent by a lack of finance for testing and development, this was only a 'marking time' year for the Surrey-based team, which (having been bought by Craig Pollock's BAR enterprise) would disappear at the end of the season.

Minardi, the enthusiastic but always under-financed Italian team, was a different proposition. Knowing that it could probably never rise even to mid-grid 'works' team levels, it persevered for years in a pragmatic and economic way. Having already used DFVs, HBs, and then EDs (all being Cosworth V8s), it then dabbled unsuccessfully with Hart V8s. Minardi also took up a supply of JD V10s for 1998, which did the job, but could do little more for the team.

For 1999, however, both Minardi and Ford-Cosworth reassessed their futures, and discussed a longer-term strategy. Even though there was no question of Minardi using 1999-spec CR-1s, as early as August 1998 it was decided that the team would be able to lease the best possible VJ V10s.

"We are also going to back this engine up," Neil Ressler commented, "with an intensive and ongoing development package."

Stewart's stock of VJ V10s, recognised as good (if not outstanding) engines in 1998, were to be reworked, updated, and improved, and would be used exclusively in F1 by Minardi. Much attention immediately went into the optimum installation in the new chassis, while updates and improvements were planned to follow during the season.

Purely as an example, such a contractual deal might mean leasing the right to use about 15 engines, and perhaps 75 rebuilds during the year – and the presence of three dedicated Cosworth engineers at every event and every race. Even if these engines were not quite the most powerful, or the most modern on the grids, they were certainly seen as honestly supported and professionally maintained.

For the new century, however, Cosworth Racing was already looking ahead to what the sport, the teams and that indefinable body 'the public' might demand. With that in mind it was an active, and influential, member of F1's Engine Rules Group. Smaller engines? Larger engines? Engines with fewer cylinders? The ability to run on low-octane unleaded fuel? A ban on refuelling? Minimum fuel efficiency standards? Cosworth would know what was brewing at the same time as anyone else.

If one lesson, above all, had been learned from its experience in the mid-1990s, it was that the design of motor-racing engines could never again be tackled like that of any other conventional business. To get ahead, to be ahead, and to keep ahead of its rivals, Cosworth Racing, and Ford, had to spend whatever it took.

Enthusiasm and experience was certainly one aspect, but enterprise and technical bravery was another – and Cosworth Racing seemed to have plenty of that. All the signs were that it knew which way to go in the 2000s – and was already on the way.

17: COSWORTH IN THE NEW CENTURY

Dick Scammell, back from semi-retirement, was asked to return to Cosworth by Ford, to become managing director of Cosworth in 1998.

Brendan Connor became Cosworth Racing's CEO between 2001 and 2003.

Racing repeatedly found itself in a state of corporate and managerial change – not upheaval, for sure, but change. Managing director Dick Scammell, who saw his role only as a bridging appointment under Neil Ressler, retired permanently in mid-1999, and was replaced by Trevor Crisp, who had been Jaguar's long-time engine design chief. Soon afterwards, Ressler himself retired and Cosworth moved further under the control of Ford-USA's Premier Performance Division subsidiary, then chaired by Richard Parry-Jones.

It was always going to be uncomfortable, if not inconvenient, it was thought, for the two Cosworth companies (Racing and Technology) to stay in St James Mill Road indefinitely. Cosworth Racing concluded that it was potentially short of space, and it was not long before the search began for alternative sites.

At about the same time – in June 1999 – only nine months after Ford had absorbed Racing into its motorsport empire, it also took over Stewart Grand Prix, renaming that operation Jaguar. Along with the acquisition of the electronics expertise of Pi, these were all swept into the newly formed Premier Performance Division.

Ressler, it seemed, was keen to see the combined concerns providing a 'sea of green' around the circuits of the world, effectively in a head-to-head battle with Ferrari red, which seemed to be everywhere at the time.

It was not long before there was some talk of moving both the Jaguar F1 and Cosworth Racing factories onto a new, common, greenfield site, and for a short period Wolfgang Rietzle headed up the Division. Even so, this was not to Ressler's long-term satisfaction, so he asked Sales Chief Bernard Ferguson to approach Bobby Rahal of the USA, who duly took over from Ressler in 2001.

Rahal did not last long, and eventually ex-World F1 Champion Niki Lauda was drafted in to be the boss of the Jaguar F1 team *and* of the PPG (Premier Performance Group). Lauda, effectively, therefore ruled the roost at Cosworth for a short time.

For a time, it looked as if an ambitious new base might be set up at Silverstone, next to the famous motor racing track (a move far away from Northampton was never considered, due to the company's desire not to lose any of the unmatchable expertise which existed at St James Mill Road), but high and ever-escalating investment costs got in the way, and all proposals for relocation were eventually abandoned. To this day there has never been a publicly-known attempt to revive that strategy, and although there is still a shortage of elbow room, miracles of space-utilisation continue to be achieved with 730 employees.

Trevor Crisp's appointment as CEO came to an end in 2001. He was later seen as a somewhat remote figure by the Cosworth workforce, especially by comparison with Dick Scammell who he had replaced. Trevor was then replaced by Brendan Connor in 2001 (Brendan was later described as more of a businessman than a motoring enthusiast – probably the first such character to have occupied the MD's chair at Northampton – and certainly, when interviewed soon after his arrival, succinctly described the possible move to Silverstone 'dead issue' and: "In any case, persuading our staff to relocate to Silverstone would have been a worry ..." Even so, after coming in from the multi-national TRW engineering group in 2001, Connor might not have been a racing 'petrol-head', but was already a great admirer of Cosworth's traditions and successes.

Facing up to a totally different type of business than he had previously known, his task, as he saw it, was not only to preserve Cosworth's mighty motor-racing reputation, but to bring more general automotive business into the company, and drive down costs along the way:

"Ford want to set Cosworth Racing onto an even more solid, commercial, base." Connor told me: "Partly because of previous changes of ownership, it had been a rather volatile business. But it is a business, never forget that, with an annual turnover of more than £80 million. Only about 10 per cent of what we actually do here is different from any type of engineering business, because of motor racing."

In the meantime, separation from the road-car programmes, which had overhung the sell-off and de-merger processes of 1998, went surprisingly well. The most pressing problem was that the two companies – Racing and Technology – had to share the same high-tech foundry facilities in Worcester, which had ended up as Cosworth Technology property.

Co-existence there (and, indeed in Northampton) was remarkably peaceful, but Racing then set up a joint venture agreement with a company of foundry experts called Grainger & Worrall, in a new dedicated facility near Shrewsbury. This gave much scope for expansion in the future, perhaps even into road-car engines?

Once Brendan Connor had settled in, Nick Hayes took responsibility for all engineering projects, and found himself travelling even more than usual. "In 2002," he told me, "I went on as many rallies as Grands Prix, and more CART events too ..."

F1 V10s – more power; more secrecy

When Cosworth Racing introduced the radical new Formula One CK V10 engine in 1999 (for promotional purposes it was always called CR-1 [CR = Cosworth Racing]), the company never showed it off in public, did not issue drawings, and only revealed the barest of details. Formula One, it seems, had become so competitive, and so 'dog-eat-dog,' that Nick Hayes' team was not willing to show its latest technology to Cosworth's rivals.

In the previous edition of this book, therefore, I was not able to show pictures of the latest F1 engines, (now shown in Appendix 1) and, as far as I know, these never appeared in the world's press until they were rendered obsolete by the all-new CA V8 2.4-litre engine of 2006. When, for instance, did you ever see a Stewart, Jaguar or Arrows V10-engined F1 car stripped out, with its engine cover removed?

Even so, in four years, the CK family (it reached CR-4 in public, but was actually coded LK, from mid-2002) built a fine reputation: the original CR-1 was a massive leap ahead of the VJ V10 which Stewart had been using in 1998, and regular improvements followed, not least in race-long reliability, which was impressive.

Although there was only one outright win to boast about (Johnny Herbert's European GP victory in 1999), F1 watchers frequently measured these V10s among the top three F1 power units. By 2002, peak power was thought to be well over 800bhp, and more than 18,000rpm was regularly seen on the digital telemetry read-outs shown on F1's TV screens. This was all done while keeping the operation entirely separate from Bruce Wood's CART/Champcar projects, although technical breakthroughs were shared.

"There is very little magic in the F1 world," Hayes insisted, "it all comes down to hard work and the quality of the people working on the projects." Rob White confirms this when he says: "There's nothing in these engines which would horrify our forebears ..."

From 1999 to 2001, the CK-series V10s were used exclusively by Stewart (which became Jaguar F1), and then, for 2002, such engines were also supplied, on a lease basis, to the Arrows team. Arrows, however, ran into serious financial problems in the summer, missed several races, and ended up owing Cosworth a great deal of money. At the same time the previous generation VJ V10 was used by Minardi from 1999 to 2001, although ongoing development had been hived off. Minardi then defected, to spend an unhappy 2002 season using the Asiatech (ex-Peugeot) V10, learnt the error of its ways, then returned to the Ford fold in 2003.

In that time, development and evolution never faltered, with different engine 'steps' introduced as soon as they had been devised, and proven in testing. The so-called CR-1 variety gave way to CR-2 in 2000, CR-3 followed in 2001, and the much-improved CR-4 (actually coded as LK) came along in mid-2002. It was only after another brand-new layout – the 90-degree CR-5 type (internal coding TJ) from ex-CART engine specialist Rob White's design team – was finalised at the end of 2002, that this 72-degree family finally reached maturity. In all this, the pace of change, and improvement, actually seemed to accelerate. "To do a typical F1 engine takes nine to ten months now," Hayes pointed out, "quicker if we cut corners. As a company, if the desire is there, we can now move very quickly, and our processes are improving all the time. The CR-1 was the first engine we designed completely using 3D CAD aids: we saved an enormous amount of weight, by being smart in the engineering."

In this move, incidentally, Cosworth's V10 became the lightest of all contemporary F1 engines.

"From CR-1 to CR-4, there were many intermediate steps, but the concept of the engines remained the same. Over the years, many of the major pieces were changed.

"Certainly the CR-4 (LK), which first appeared in Canada in June 2002, was longer, and had a bigger cylinder bore, which automatically meant using many new pieces. We are certainly adequately funded to remain competitive."

All this, allied to the release of the new-generation TJ/CR-5, and of the allocation of CR-4s to the Jordan F1 team for 2003 (Jordan, in fact, signed a two-year deal for the supply of Ford-badged F1 engines), meant that Cosworth seemed to be more determined on F1 success than ever before. With the company committed to developing a brand-new engine (TJ/CR-5) and a near-new engine (LK/CR-4) at the same time, this meant that the effort at Northampton was going to be more intense than ever before. At least 25 TJ/CR-5s would be in use by Jaguar in 2003 – to cover racing and testing – with between 140 and 160 rebuilds taking place during the year.

At Cosworth Racing, every change has a reason. The choice of 90-degrees for the 2003 CR-5 was governed by the need to lower the centre of gravity still further. According to Nick Hayes, this would be a major step forward: "We'd already explored ultra-wide angles." Hayes grinned. "I could show you a 120-degree V10 which we designed and built …" [the one-off VK power unit: AAGR].

F1 engine evolution at Cosworth Racing, in other words, was as intense as ever.

CART – back to 'Formula Ford'

As the new century unfolded, North America's CART series seemed to be in constant turmoil. Not only were engine regulations changed regularly, but a brand-new engine formula was discussed at length, and it was not until mid-2002 that an agreement was finally reached.

"Changes had been discussed for years," American Racing Programme Director Bruce Wood told me, "which were partly responsible for the foundation of IRL …"

In the meantime, and against all the financial odds, Cosworth's turbocharged V8 engines had always been CART's most reliable source of power. Mercedes-Benz (for which, read Ilmor) finally gave up the struggle in 2000, while two Japanese concerns – Honda and Toyota – spent truckloads of yen on their own engines for this high-profile formula.

In its fourth and final year, 1999, the Cosworth XD won five races, at a time when an all-new power unit, the XF, was already being prepared. Everything ever learned about the XD, along with information gleaned from the ongoing F1 programme, went into the XF for 2000. Still a 75-degree turbo-V8, it was lighter, smaller, higher-revving – and blisteringly competitive. Somehow or other, by 2002, Cosworth had persuaded it to rev up to more than 16,000rpm, still with steel valve springs – a previously unheard-of figure for restrictor-limited CART engines. The fact that regulation changes had gradually reduced the

Using the Cosworth XF power unit, Team Rahal's Shell-sponsored machines were among Champcar's most successful teams in 2002. This as a scheduled pit-stop, for fuel and tyres, at Fontana.

allowable boost (as ever, by supplying calibrated pop-off valves which had to be positioned in the inlet plenum – to no more than 34in of mercury in 2002), could not blunt its edge.

In spite of increased competition from the Japanese manufacturers, new XFs won seven races in 2000, seven more in 2001, and a creditable four in 2002. In the last year, there is no doubt that a squabble over pop-off valve positioning (which was precipitated by Toyota) harmed the XF's performance.

In the meantime, arguments about a new CART engine formula intensified, usually with a view to limiting power, and thus speeds, on the high-speed ovals. First there was to have been a proposed 2.2-litre, then 1.8-litre V8s or even 1.6-litre V6 types with 50in boost, along with a gradual reduction in turbocharger boost levels – and a constant urge to reduce costs.

Cosworth, however, found that it could not reduce its leasing costs to the teams, without losing money on the entire programme. It is not generally known that CART imposed a limit on rebuild charges – which Cosworth eventually found almost impossible to support. Parent company Ford was uneasy about this. A complete withdrawal was actively considered, which would have reduced Cosworth's annual business by more than £19 million/$30 million.

"In the end," Bruce Wood commented, "the costs were being driven by the competition – because our rivals didn't seem to have limits on what they would be spending …"

Obvious solutions, CART thought, were to limit revs, and get rid of turbocharging. Yet Honda was keen on retaining the turbos, and on the high-tech nature of the series, while Toyota decided to transfer to the newly-founded IRL (Indy Racing League), whose pride and joy was the world-famous Indianapolis 500 race.

Late in 2001, CART finally made a decision, and announced that for 2003 its new engine formula should be for a naturally-aspirated 3.5-litre V8, which just happened to be the same basic engine as used by the rival IRL series, so Cosworth started work on such a concept. Looking to have a new 90-degree XG power unit running within a year, Wood's team started by building an XF Hybrid, where the proposed XG's 3.5-litre crank, pistons and cylinder head were somehow inserted and grafted into a much-carved-about 75-degree XF.

Amazingly, when it was fired up in May 2002, it ran so well that it was power-tested on the first day, and found to be well ahead of expectations.

Typically of Cosworth, an extra 20bhp was found in the following weeks, although Wood agrees that "… the wall thicknesses and clearances were well outside our normal envelope. We could dyno test it, but we wouldn't have dared put it into a car …"

Within weeks, however, all bets were off. Well before the definitive XG had been properly designed, and put on the test bed – it was months away from being run for the first time – CART had changed its mind yet again, concluding that its proposed 3.5-litre formula would push up the costs too far.

Instead, CART switched its requirements to what was called a 'spec engine' – where all entrants would be obliged to use the same power unit. To Cosworth's delight, a proposal that it had first made in mid-2001 (when it was decisively rejected) was finally adopted in mid-2002. At Cosworth's suggestion, CART chose to use a controlled, 750bhp derivative of the well-known XF power unit, (Cosworth dubbed it XFE – where 'E' stood for Endurance), this power reduction being assured by dropping peak revs to 12,000rpm, and putting up the boost to 41.5in.

The new formula was adopted for 2003 and 2004 (and if successful, this could be extended further, which eventually it was), and effectively made CART into a high-output 'Formula Ford'. At a stroke, CART's future was secured, Cos Inc at Torrance then found itself forging ahead with the 'Birthday Build' of all 100 XF engines in the existing 'float'. ('Birthday Build' meant that all engines received new cylinder blocks, heads, cranks, rods, and pistons, with much new detail.)

Yet it wasn't all good news, for this put the all-new XG project on to the back burner, a competitive engine for which there was no exact formula that it could meet at that time. Knowing Cosworth, though, everyone was sure that a use would be found for it, one day. And it was – as a description of the Chevrolet IRL engine (in the next chapter) will confirm.

Nevertheless, by the end of 2002, the often-frenetic atmosphere in the CART project offices had settled down:

"It's been an interesting year," Nick Hayes commented, "for this went on for more than 12 months. We were convinced that we had to support CART, so we carried out design work on the XG normally-aspirated engine. In the end, though, it was Bernard Ferguson and Bruce Wood who came up with the spec engine idea which was finally adopted. Without that, CART might have found it too difficult to continue: it could

For 2002, Cosworth collaborated with the Italian motorcycle firm Aprilia to develop Superbike engines, then the GK MotoGP power unit. This was Noriyuga Haga with the successful 2002 Superbike.

Malcolm Wilson took on the running of the Ford 'works' Escort rally team in the late 1990s, using BD-powered Escort World Rally Cars, then from 1999 began campaigning new-generation Ford Focus WRCs, using Cosworth-developed Zetec-M power units.

have imploded. CART can control their own destiny now, and keep the costs down."

The XFE engine then carried on, and allowed the Champcar series to carry on, until 2008, and it was no fault of the engine when that series eventually closed down. Company statistics later confirmed that the XF/XFE had enjoyed a nine-year front-line career, and the fleet had completed more than two million racing miles.

In amongst all this excitement, it is easy to forget that Cosworth had also got involved, in a very modest way, in the building of 5.8-litre V8 NASCAR engines for use in Ford Taurus cars. These engines, used in the Busch series, were also based at Torrance.

Within a year the team had evolved an AK power unit which was equally as powerful as anything provided by the long-established NASCAR engine builders.

Although inter-team politics (and long-term contracts) meant that there was initially no chance of these engines being used on front-running cars, these activities proved just how versatile, and experienced, the company had become.

Cosworth on two wheels

Once links with Cosworth Technology had been unscrambled, 'Racing' began to seek out a number of diverse projects. Some of these, probably connected with road-car engine work, looked set to remain confidential for some years. Surprisingly, however, the company found itself drawn into the brash and spectacular field of motorcycle racing.

It was first approached in 1999 by the high-profile Italian motorcycle manufacturer Aprilia, which had become dominant in the small-capacity 125cc and 250cc divisions of the MotoGP World Championships, and had ambitions to go higher. Cosworth originally provided much advice on the development and power-tuning of the 1.0-litre V-twin Aprilia 'road bike' engine used in Superbike racing, and lately in machines ridden by Noriyuki Haga.

Aprilia, however, had even bigger ambitions, and for 2002 the two companies co-operated in the evolution of a magnificent little 1.0-litre, in-line, three-cylinder watercooled power unit, which was used in Regis Laconi's Aprilia in the recently-updated MotoGP World Championships.

Internally known in Cosworth parlance as the GK engine, in many ways this engine used contemporary F1 cylinder head engine technology, including four valves per cylinder, and air springs.

This joint project progressed from 'good idea' to a running engine in a mere seven months, and by the end of the first season there was a float of 15 such engines in existence, and under intensive development. In a formula which had been historically dominated by Japanese bikes and engines, great things were expected of this high-revving 'three' in the years that were to follow. Unhappily, and even though these jewel-like little engines produced a least 250bhp, the Aprilia effort failed, due to deficiencies elsewhere in the machine, and to a serious financial burden that the Italian concern could not accept, so the project was duly wound down.

World Rally

Only a year after Cosworth Racing had been absorbed by Ford, it took on all development and long-term design of the turbocharged 2-litre Zetec-type engines used in the Ford Focus World Rally Car. Although Mountune (the tuning house based at Maldon, in

Essex) had originally developed these engines, Ford decided to bring the operation 'in house' for 2000 and beyond. Cosworth readily admits what a great job had been done at Mountune, but Ford clearly decided that the Northampton company's vast experience could add value to that engine programme.

Mountune, long-term supplier of rally engines to the Ford 'works' team, had built its first prototype Focus engines in mid-1998, and the Focus WRC first ran in October of that year. Two-litre turbocharged units were transversely mounted in the nose, and laid back in the engine bay to get the weight down and back as far as the regulations would allow. Malcolm Wilson's Cumbrian-based M-Sport business, which ran the cars, chalked up two early World victories in 1999, but was looking for more power, more torque and better reliability in the future.

Although Cosworth Racing had long experience of supplying rally engine parts to customers, it had never before run a complete develop/build/service operation for a major rally team. Happily, factory space once used to build 'customer' engines such as F1 V10s for Tyrrell and Opel DTMs, among others, had become available, and the very experienced Malcolm Tyrrell (who had joined Cosworth in the late 1960s) was tasked with running the department. In a matter of weeks what became known as the Zetec-M programme was rolling.

"We started from scratch in October 1999. Up to that point," Malcolm told me, "we had not been involved in that programme, not even supplying pieces to Mountune. It was a brand-new effort, for all of us."

The changeover, in effect, was very gradual, for in 2000 much of the basic engineering was carried over from Mountune, which had done a successful job with more limited resources. Because peak power outputs were limited by the compulsory 34mm diameter inlet passage restrictor, which had to be mounted upstream of the turbocharger, change and improvement had to be concentrated on torque delivery in the low-speed and mid-range of the power curve.

Reliability, on the other hand, improved significantly, the peak power was eventually nudged up by about 20bhp at 6000rpm, and the engine's driveability was improved considerably. Because the regulations also stated that mass-production cylinder blocks, heads and valve sizes had to be retained, the trick was to reduce weight by removing metal, and to raise mid-range engine performance, by the typical Cosworth attention to breathing, camshaft designs and valve gear. There was no such thing as a 'closed season'

in World rallying (and there were 14 events during that season), so there could be no separate 'winter development' period. In fact, some of the engineers seemed to spend more time away from base than in the factory.

In the first three seasons, the Cosworth magic worked well, and M-Sport's Focus WRCs were always potential winners. First with Colin McRae, and from 2000 with Carlos Sainz too, the team was always competitive, always likely to win, and often on the podium. Before McRae moved on at the end of 2002, in those three seasons with 'Cosworth power' the team had notched up no fewer than nine victories and 24 other podium positions, while the Ford cars had been robbed of at least one Manufacturers' Championship by outrageous mechanical misfortune.

Cosworth always sent two engineers to every World Championship event where, sometimes, they could keep sick cars in the events – cars which had been crashed, or whose cooling systems were suffering.

During the same three years, the engine programme evolved from the Zetec-M to the new-type Duratec-R. Along the way there were changes which included new turbochargers (later versions had ceramic components), the use of drive-by-wire throttle control, and a gradual reduction in weight – more than 20 per cent compared with the Mountune versions.

Compared with pure race engines, of course, these rally units had to be rugged and relatively long-lived. Flat-out use in adverse conditions (sometimes in heat and dust, sometimes in snow and ice) of up to 1500km was needed, but much more was achieved in endurance testing.

For use in the Focus WRC rally car, and as first seen in 1999, the turbocharged Zetec-E engine (coded YC by Cosworth) was transversely mounted, and the exhaust manifold was swept across the front of the engine to meet the turbocharger.

The Ford Zetec M engine, for the Focus WRC car, was a neatly packaged 2-litre power unit, which produced more than 300bhp, in spite of having to use a 34mm inlet restrictor.

To celebrate Cosworth Racing's success in winning the Ford Focus WRC engine development contract, Dick Scammell (left) got together with Ford's Martin Whitaker to make the announcement.

company where many advances were shared. Although the use of a cast iron block might look archaic to them, this was a function of the regulations, and as Ford was planning to change over to alloy block engines in the Focus road car, this was also due to disappear in the future. Well before it was revealed, Cosworth admitted that it was already working on WRC derivatives of that design.

By this time, in any case, the World Rally programme had become one of the cornerstones of Cosworth Racing's activities, and looked likely to become even more significant in the future.

And then ...?

Yet again, at Cosworth Racing it seemed that more change might be on the way. Brendan Connor confirmed that he would like to get the company more closely involved with the development of road-car engines.

Although certain emissions and climatic test cell facilities had been ceded to Technology in the de-merger, the two companies continued to trade with each other as the new century developed. ("In any case, one of Technology's biggest customers," Connor confirmed in 2002, "is still Ford ...")

"We have space, and talent, to look for new opportunities," Nick Hayes insisted. "We are totally used to making big changes, ramping up and down our activity on various programmes."

Connor confirmed that since the de-merger, only Cosworth Racing had the rights to see the word "Cosworth" on the cam covers of road-car engines, and that he intended to see such power units in the future: "This business has an enormous iconic brand potential, an under-utilised asset, and I hope we can deal with that in the future. We want Ford to re-establish the Cosworth name as their premier performance brand. We don't have the capacity to make engines here, but we'd certainly like to do all the design and development, then to get an ongoing revenue stream from Ford in royalties on production engines."

In press statements published in late 2002, Ford made a series of very positive comments on such projects. These, however, take much longer to come to fruition than does an F1 engine, so Cosworth-watchers had to be patient, and had to wait.

Starting in 1999, the Cosworth-Ford powered Focus WRC became a World rally winner in the next decade, often with Colin McRae (right) and Nicky Grist in the cabin. This was the Safari victory of 1999.

Although the bodyshell of the new Focus WRC was based on that of the Focus road car, the running gear was very different. The Cosworth-prepared Type YC engine was transversely mounted, and allied to four-wheel-drive.

At any one time, M-Sport could call on a 'float' of around 18 engines to keep the M-Sport 'works' fleet in being, and Cosworth Racing looked after them all. Whenever a complete car was sold off to a private owner (usually at the end of a season) an engine would be sold to M-Sport, who would look after it thereafter.

Hidden away inside these engines, a number of the features, components and materials would look familiar to F1 or CART engineers, for Cosworth was a

18: COSWORTH'S LAST F1 ENGINES

"Williams' biggest asset was its Cosworth CA2006 V8. It was unquestionably the best, most potent, engine of all ..."

It was in 2003 that Cosworth seemed to welcome all manner of changes – both in technical terms, in motor sporting policy, and in their corporate relations with Ford. That was the year, for instance, in which the last of the company's amazing F1 V10s (the TJ) appeared, when the XFE 'endurance' engine took over as the power unit used by all competitors in the revived USA Champcar series, and in which the XG (badged as a Chevrolet, not a Ford) rescued Chevrolet from sporting oblivion in the North American IRL series. The miracle was that all three engines started life successfully, and went on to bolster up what the company was being tasked to do, all over the world.

Because the F1 programme produced the majority of sporting headlines, worldwide, the fortunes of the latest Jaguar (ex-Stewart) car, the R4-Cosworth, were carefully monitored throughout the year. It was no secret that the R3 of 2002, and the management surrounding it, had not been a success, so it was hoped that for the following season a new car, new drivers and a new V10 engine, would make a difference.

This is what Alan Henry had to say about the situation, in the 2003/2004 edition of *Autocourse* at the end of that season:

"After riding a management roller-coaster for the two previous years, which had claimed the scalps of high-profile team principals Bobby Rahal and Niki Lauda, the Jaguar F1 team sailed into more tranquil waters in 2003, under the stewardship of Tony Purnell and his MD, David Pitchforth. Jaguar had been a highly charged political battleground for too long, and the management realised that they might be drinking in the 'Last Chance Saloon' if they didn't do something about achieving hard results. And do it quickly ..."

From the very beginning, though, it was clear that the latest Jaguar would benefit from the latest Cosworth V10, the innovative new TJ type. Not only was this engine totally different from its predecessors – it was, in fact, Cosworth's fifth new V10 F1 engine to appear in seven years (ignoring the 'might-have-been' projects which had also been designed, but never finalised, in that time). For reasons which are made clear in the panel "Vee angles of V10 engines" (see page 190), this was the first of the ten-cylinder Cosworths to be built around a cylinder block with a 90

degree vee angle. Like almost all of the company's F1 rival engine builders, Cosworth had recently concluded that 90 degrees, rather than 72 degrees, was the most efficient way of laying out a block to accommodate the inlet passages, trumpets, fuel-injection and related electronic gear into the vee, and also to help lower the centre of gravity.

Even at the start, in 2003, this was an extremely powerful unit which revved to at least 18,000rpm, and two years later, when the 3-litre formula came to an end, it was able to rev at more than 19,000rpm. The peak power, in maturity, was finally advertised as 915bhp, but this was almost certainly an understatement. Only Cosworth knew (and will still not reveal) what the real figure actually was, but the pit-lane, in general, recognised that it was at least the equal of any other power unit – from Ferrari, BMW or Mercedes-Benz.

To quote Bruce Wood, who became overall technical director soon after the TJ reached its peak, compromises had always had to be made:

"The car designers always wanted to bring the height of the engine cover down, and to have a teardrop-like profile towards the back, which meant a narrower trend in the vee angle. But for us it was getting very hard to install all the stuff into the vee ... though bringing the banks closer together meant that there was a bit more space at the sides for exhausts. However, in the end, because the engines were running faster and faster, and inlet trumpets were getting shorter and shorter, we couldn't fit it all in, so went back up to 90 degrees.

As it turned out, in 2003, the latest Jaguar F1 car was a significant improvement over its hapless predecessor, but even though the gritty and immensely talented Mark Webber had joined the team, and was well able to get the best out of the splendid TJ engine, Jaguar was rarely able to race higher than about sixth in F1 races.

This was the time, too, when Ford once again became embroiled with Jordan, which was going through a difficult patch due to the collapse of a huge potential sponsorship deal with Vodafone. Jordan, who had recently been running with Honda V10 engines, were anxious to jump ship. Using his legendary Irish blarney, Eddie Jordan persuaded Ford's PPG boss, Niki Lauda, that he should recommend that Ford give him near-equal treatment with Jaguar (except that he would have to pay hefty leasing fees), though he never benefited from the use of the new and very effective TJ engine.

Predictably, as sales chief Bernard Ferguson confirmed many years later:

"The relationship with Eddie was just as miserable for us then, as with the previous one, for on the very first day he rang me, and told me that he was never going to pay Cosworth anything. We had to tell him that the contract was between him and Ford, but we were the people who had to build the engines, do the rebuilds and collect the money from Eddie.

"In the end, I had to talk to Bernie, which ended up with Eddie's Jordan money being paid direct from the FOM to Cosworth, out of his FOM earnings, direct to us!"

It may be significant that Niki Lauda was released by Ford just as this deal was being finalised …

One consequence was that Jordan did not benefit from the same development advances as Jaguar, but they still had the gall to complain to the motoring media that their engines were less powerful, without ever admitting why. Amazingly, though, they delivered an outright win for the LK engine in Brazil, when Giancarlo Fisichella, who had been running a strong third, avoided the carnage and debris resulting from a start/finish-line accident, to be awarded the victory when the race was stopped.

In the meantime, the F1 organisers had been moving the goalposts yet again, nominally with a view to reducing costs, by asking the existing engine builders if they were prepared to sign up teams to a 'customer engine budget' of around $10 million, all subject to an engine being able to last a full Grand Prix weekend, so that more 'privateers' would once-again swell the starting grids. During 2003 several of the builders responded positively, or so it seemed at the time, but in the end it was only Cosworth who really seriously carried on the discussions (and even then the $10 million limit was in doubt …).

Jordan and Minardi were the two most obvious customers if this deal had gone ahead, but with Ford increasing their financial demands on the Cosworth business, the costs might even have to go up again. The result was that, for 2004, Jaguar carried on (as the 'works' team) with updated TJs, Jordan (the team that was always reluctant to pay any bills) also took TJs, while Minardi carried on with the best of the old-model LK types.

VEE-ANGLES OF V10 ENGINES – COSWORTH AND ITS COMPETITORS

THE fashion in choosing specific vee-angles – the angle measured in the cylinder block between the lines of five cylinders used to package a V10 – changed several times during the 1990s and 2000s, and until the very last moment there seemed to be no general consensus among engine builders about the ideal layout.

Although Cosworth was a pioneer when it came to thinking about a V10 F1 engine, it was not until 1996 that their first such power unit was fitted to a Formula One car. As is detailed in Chapter 12, Cosworth's first serious thoughts were evolving in 1988 when Ford asked for a new-generation normally-aspirated engine to replace the turbocharged GB V6. As Mike Kranefuss told the author at the time :

"We looked at a 12, but thought it would be bigger, a bit more thirsty, and would need a bigger car. A V10, well, no-one could really warm to the idea."

Rory Byrne of Benetton, the constructor which would the first to receive such a new engine, agreed that the V12 would probably be too large, and that a V10 was a 'maybe'. The result was that it was decided to develop an all-new V8, which became the HB, this being a 3.5-litre power unit which had a very successful career.

However, when the FIA introduced a new 3-litre limit on F1 engines for the 1995 season, there was an immediate, and universal, swing towards new-generation V10s, which held sway until 2005, after which the engine size limit was further reduced to 2.4-litres, and 90 degree V8s became compulsory.

In the meantime, the first F1 V10s to start winning races had been the Renault RS01 of 1989, which had a 67-degree vee-angle, along with the contemporary Honda RA109E which used a 72 degree installation. In the next decade – 1995 to 2005 inclusive – many and various vee-angles were chosen by such major engine builders as Cosworth, BMW, Ferrari, Honda, Mercedes-Benz, Renault and Toyota.

This was how Cosworth's 3-litre engine dynasty of V10s evolved in the next decade:

Year introduced	Type	Vee-angle	Users
1996	JD	72 degrees	Sauber, Stewart, Minardi, Tyrrell
1998	VJ	72 degrees	Stewart, Minardi
1999	CK	72 degrees	Stewart, Jaguar, Arrows, Minardi
2002	LK	72 degrees	Jaguar, Jordan
2003	TJ	90 degrees	Jaguar, Jordan, Red Bull, Minardi, Toro Rosso

– and, as noted in Chapter 17, a prototype 'wide-angle' Cosworth engine (the VK type) was developed in 1999/2000, in which a 120 degree vee angle was a feature.

A survey of V10 engines of F1 type produced, worldwide, in that period, shows that 67, 71, 72, 75, 80, 88, 90 and 111 degree layouts were all used at one time or another by Cosworth's rivals: the most extreme variations – 67 degrees and 111 degrees – were both used by Renault.

In 2015 Cosworth's Managing Director – Powertrain, Bruce Wood, summarised the rationale behind this wide spread :

"It doesn't make much difference for a race engine, but in road car terms (with balance and Noise-Vibration-Harshness [NVH] in mind, a V10 should be 72 degrees. In a race engine, the elements which are more important are packaging and exhaust tuning.

"The width is critical, really, because F1 designers want to bring the engine cover down, to be as narrow as possible. That drives a narrower and narrower trend in vee-angle. However, the point came when it was getting very hard to install all the stuff into the vee – you've got to allow for inlet trumpets, throttles, injection systems and so on.

"Generally, bringing the banks closer together meant that there was a bit more space for exhausts, and you got a bit more bending stiffness, vertically, for the engine itself. In the end, though, because the engines were running faster and faster, and the inlet trumpets were getting shorter and wider, we had less and less space to fit the hydraulic throttle actuators …"

Which explains, succinctly, why at the end of the V10 period, only Renault (which had reverted to 72 degrees) was no longer a part of the '90-degree club' …

In 2004, Cosworth's F1 effort, therefore, was not about winning, but about survival, for Ford had already made it obvious that it was no longer financially happy with the company as a business subsidiary of 'the empire.' Early in the season, Jaguar-F1 Managing Director David Pitchforth made it clear that the brand's reputation was on the line, and by mid-season Ford was actively threatening to withdraw from F1, there and then. Cosworth insiders had to spend ages pointing out to Ford management that if the team dropped out at that juncture, it would lose its 'entry position,' and FOM money – so who was going to want to buy the 'goodwill,' such as it was, that was left over?

The machinations that took place within Ford, which involved it selling Cosworth – are described in the next chapter. As far as the F1 season was concerned, however, it looked like business as usual on the circuits until September 2004 (by which time the racing was almost over for the year. The latest Jaguar – the R5 – was an improvement on the 2003 example, but, to quote one observer: "The car ran reliably, though it was never fast."

Its best results were sixth in Germany and Belgium, Mark Webber was undoubtedly the star driver, but his best qualifying position was second fastest before the Malaysian GP. Unfortunately, he could only qualify tenth, and finish eighth, in front of top hierarchy of 'the client' at the British GP.

Jordan, running slightly less up-to-the-minute TJs for the first time, had an awful season, getting no further than it deserved, for its whingeing standards were well in excess of their performance on the track. Claiming that 'its' engines were 70bhp down on those provided to Jaguar, and that things got worse towards the end of the season, it was therefore a relief to all concerned that the so-called 'partnership' was dissolved at the end of the year.

The change, however, did nothing for Jordan's performance, nor its reputation. In 2005, Eddie Jordan sold out to the team which became Midland; the Toyota-engined cars were significantly slower than Toyota's own machinery, and not a single credible result was achieved …

At the end of 2004, as detailed in the next chapter, Ford announced that it was to pull out of F1, and that the Jaguar F1 team would close down. Within weeks the corporate sale of Cosworth (to Kevin Kalkhoven and Jerry Forsythe) went ahead, and the sale of the Jaguar F1 operation to Dietrich Mateschitz of Red Bull was formalised in November 2004. At the same time, Red Bull turned its gaze to Minardi and would rename it Toro Rosso for 2006.

Suddenly, for 2005, Cosworth found itself owned by a new management team, and also found that it was obliged to supply two F1 teams with the same TJ V10 engine – a daunting prospect, even though many of the personnel were well-known to them. Red Bull took over the design of the 2005 R6 Jaguar, calling it the Red Bull RB1 – and had the first complete car running within days – while Minardi was a few weeks behind them.

What turned out to be the last of the state-of-the-art TJ V10s was a remarkable power unit, with ample power and torque to make it the equal of the Ferrari and Mercedes-Benz machinery, but neither car quite did it justice. Minardi, as expected, was never truly among the front runners, though team-owner Paul Stoddart had the grace to say: "Cosworth was fantastic, as always. Minardi's relationship with it is one of the best that I've ever had in business, never mind in F1. Minardi has had total reliability, and a damn powerful engine." All of which made a nice change from the negative complaints which sometimes came from previous customers …

Red Bull, whose ambitions were as high as the ego of its team owners, was not quite as fulsome, though with David Coulthard leading the driving strength, and Christian Horner as Sporting Director, it was rapidly building to new levels. Two fourth places for Coulthard (in Australia and Europe) were a good start, though by mid-season it was already known that the team would take its business to Ferrari in 2006. By the end of the year, the performance of Coulthard's Red-Bull-Cosworth was on a par with that of Ferrari, so it can only have been money which persuaded Red Bull to jump ship.

F1 – back to V8s in 2006

Then, at the end of 2005, came a big change in F1 regulations, when the compulsory engine size was arbitrarily cut from 3.0-litres to 2.4-litres, V10s to V8s and peak power from – an estimate only – 900/950bhp to about 750bhp. Was F1 going to be less exciting? The teams themselves were determined that this should not happen – and there is no doubt that the new breed of engines which resulted, and which could rev up to 20,000rpm, sounded magnificent?

20,000rpm? Indeed yes. Even at an early stage, in the autumn of 2005, an unofficial video of a 2.4-litre Cosworth F1 engine (internally it was a V8, but actually used a speedily-modified V10 block and a special crankshaft) was seen on YouTube, sounding gorgeous, and revving freely up to 20,000rpm, seemingly eager to do so.

Yet again, however, at the end of 2006 the demand for Cosworth's truly excellent F1 engines was hard-hit by the economic facts of life. Although all the signs were that Cosworth, who probably knew more about developing high-revving V8s than any other specialist engine designer in the world, was developing an excellent 2.4-litre V8 to meet the new regulations, it went on to suffer one huge disadvantage compared with its rivals – that Cosworth did not have a major sponsor, or parent company, with bottomless pockets who could provide 'Free Issue' power units to its clients – and it was therefore obliged to charge considerable sums for the lease of its products.

This, unhappily, was the brutal truth of the contemporary F1 business – for by this time it was a high-spending, high-cost business, not merely a sport. Almost every other rival engine was freely available to selected teams (or, for marketing reasons, at much-reduced leasing rates), and therefore those companies had a strong marketing advantage. Mercedes-Benz, Renault, Ferrari, McLaren, Honda, BMW-Sauber and Toyota were all teams which could benefit from such an arrangement, leaving only a few other two-car teams in the level-playing-field/marketplace.

Of those, for 2006, only two teams – Williams and Toro Rosso (which we had known as Minardi for many years) – were finally able to choose Cosworth power, of two entirely different types. This did not exercise Cosworth too much, as they were thoroughly used to running a number of programmes from the same factory complex in Northampton.

A further explanation is needed. To keep teams in the F1 series for 2006 (where the sport was then struggling for entries to maintain a full grid), as an interim measure the FIA allowed old-type 3-litre V10s to be used alongside the newfangled V8s, though the V10s were subjected to using a 77mm diameter inlet passage restrictor (placed immediately behind the driver's headrest in the engine air-scoop), and a strictly-policed electronically-controlled 16,700rpm rev limit. This, it was thought, would make a throttled V10 more or less equivalent to a new-type V8, though the weight and size penalty of the larger engine would remain.

Toro Rosso, therefore, kept its TJ-type V10s, which were rumoured to be producing about 725bhp. This put the engine more or less on a par with some of the rival new V8s at first, but as neither Cosworth nor Toro Rosso were able (or allowed by regulation) to carry out any development work on the V10s throughout the season, those cars and engines nevertheless gradually fell further and further towards the back of the field.

The story regarding the new 2.4-litre CA-type V8, where Alex Hitzinger was currently design chief at Cosworth, and where the team reverted to the classic (and compulsory, in this case) 90-degree vee angle for such an engine, was completely different. When design studies began in the summer of 2004, Cosworth had no guaranteed customers for it, but plenty of hopeful prospects. Even after Ford sold Cosworth to Kevin Kalkhoven and Jerry Forsythe in November 2004, much detailed design work on the engineering of this power unit had not yet begun. To their credit, however, the new owners realised that if they were to stay in the F1 business it would have to be approved – and it was.

During 2005, Cosworth originally hoped that their links with Red Bull Racing (ex-Jaguar, of course) would continue – it seemed logical that they should – but they were speedily rebuffed. Negotiations were well advanced when Cosworth directors flew to the Imola GP to meet Red Bull, but (to quote Bernard Ferguson): "As we were coming in to land, my mobile phone suddenly lit up. I got text after text, and even as we landed we discovered that Red Bull had just announced that they

The original version of the high-revving 2.4-litre CA V8, as supplied to Williams for the 2006 F1 season.

were going to Ferrari for the following year ..." A year later, insiders at, or observers of, Red Bull were still noting that the change had been a big technical error, as the Ferrari engines were by no means as effective as claimed ...

On the other hand, Cosworth discovered that Williams, which had been using BMW engines since 2000, had decided to break this long-term partnership (there had been a growing mutual distrust between the teams at Grove and Munich), and found themselves looking for new power in 2006. Even so, it would need a successful demonstration of the new engine to convince Williams to do a deal, this eventually being arranged so that Frank Williams himself was taken to Northampton, to see the 'mule' V8/V10 2.4-litre (already described) singing away at 20,000rpm.

A one-year deal was soon concluded, and after that decision was made public in June 2005, it was clear that Williams had apparently already talked to at least three different engine suppliers (most notably Toyota) – yet it was Cosworth's Bernard Ferguson who finally clinched a prestigious lease deal in August. By this time, engineering work on the new V8 had been going on for some months, the first test bed runs followed in October 2005, and stocks of the definitive power unit were made ready early in 2006.

As it transpired, the original CA-type 2.4-litre V8 – which made its racing debut at Bahrain in March 2006, where the two new Williams FW28s took sixth (Mark Webber) and seventh (Rosberg) – was a real jewel, even though it was neither as light, nor as small, as Cosworth would have wished.

Simply, the latest set of F1 engine regulations were so strict that they specified a 90-degree vee angle, a maximum cylinder bore of 98mm, cylinder bore spacings of 106.5mm, and a dry weight of 95kg/209lb, plus the requirement that an engine had to run for at least two races without a rebuild. By combining the 98mm bore with an ultra-short stroke of 39.77mm, the capacity lined up as 2399.875cc.

This was all well and good, though the specification was by no means as extreme as Cosworth could have wished, for Bruce Wood (who would soon became overall Technical Director) reckons it could have got down to 85kg/187lb without affecting the demands for longer-term reliability, and the unit could also have been made dimensionally smaller.

As expected, it had a (by Cosworth standards) conventional four-valves/cylinder layout, with a compression ratio of 13.3:1, and, because of the minimum (not maximum, please note) weight requirement, the team also had the luxury of being able to add some material to sections which might otherwise have developed some cracking issues.

Until the company came up against the rigid freeze on development, imposed by the governing body, the CA's early improvements were remarkable. Although the initial test bed run of a CA demonstrated 'only' 684bhp at 20,000rpm, by the start of the 2006 season this had risen to 720bhp, and to a remarkable 756bhp by mid-year. It is worth noting that this final figure equated to 315bhp/litre, which compared very favourably with the 135bhp/litre achieved by the ground-breaking, and legendary, DFV of 1967. In less than 40 years, therefore, Cosworth had pushed up its boundaries by no less than 230 per cent!

Even so, in its 'first life,' the excellent little CA would only have a one-season career as a front-line power unit, even though the otherwise mediocre Williams FW28 car had already started scoring points, and driver Mark Webber had briefly led in Australia, and in Monaco. After the V8s became all but compulsory, the first race was held in Bahrain in March, the 18th and last in Brazil in October – and at that point (and as expected) Williams was tempted away by Japanese yen, to use Toyota power for the next three seasons. It was not, the story goes, that the 2.4-litre Toyota engine was even a match for the latest Cosworth, but that it came in a financially-free package, and Williams' accountants could see a bargain when they sensed one. Even during 2007, when Williams came to carry out back-to-back tests of the first Toyota V8 against a Cosworth CA, they discovered that the Japanese power unit was still at least 25bhp down on the CA's standards.

In almost every way, therefore – technically, financially, and in marketing terms – this was a sporting tragedy for Cosworth, as the new V8 was demonstrably competitive, and would have been more so if development cash had been there to back it. To quote Mark Hughes' survey in *Autosport* at the close of the season:

"[The Williams' ...] biggest asset was its Cosworth CA2006 V8. In its very first test it was running comfortably at 20,000rpm, a figure the others didn't catch up with until well into the season. It was unquestionably the best, most potent, engine of all at the start of the year, giving Williams a clear 15bhp advantage over the best of the rest. It helped that, even prior to the 2006 ban on variable inlet systems,

Cosworth had not run one. Nor had it been running the very high fuel pressures of some of the others, prior to this year's limitation of 100 bar ... but, lack of a development budget [at Williams] meant that it was only average by the end of the season."

Even so, it was costs, and packaging inadequacies of the engine in the chassis, rather than engine power and availability, which damaged the short-lived arrangement. Williams' campaign, in truth, was disappointing because of the failings in its latest car, though there was one scintillating display at Monaco, where driver Mark Webber took the lead and looked sure to win, only for his car to suffer an engine bay fire, unconnected with any Cosworth part of the installation.

Well before the end of the year, Williams was known to be unhappy with Cosworth's engine leasing costs (these were rumoured to be about £12 million for a two-car season), so they did a free-supply deal with Toyota for future seasons. That move, like so many others carried out by F1 teams looking for financial gain rather than the best performance, turned out to be a big mistake – but it was also a great disappointment to Cosworth itself.

Prospects for 2007, however, still looked good in September 2006, when both Spyker-Midland and Toro Rosso looked likely to take up CA options, which had been under discussion for some time. Both, in the end, opted to go for Ferrari V8s instead (neither of them with any success, as it transpired ...). Spyker actually pulled out of what Cosworth thought was a done deal at the very last moment, for when Bernard Ferguson arrived at the Chinese GP, in Shanghai, with drafts of the engine contract in his baggage, it was only then that Spyker admitted that Ferrari had made them a better (ie 'cheaper') offer.

The end, when it came in Brazil, was a very emotional occasion, for (temporarily at least, as it transpired for 2010), it brought Cosworth's F1 involvement to a close after 40 turbulent seasons. As Commercial Director Bernard Ferguson was quoted at the time:

"To have done such a good job this year, on an extremely limited budget, and to come away with nothing, is a bit of a kick in the teeth ..."

Driver Mark Webber put it equally bluntly: "There's no doubt about it, what Cosworth has done with the budget they had is totally embarrassing for the others. The Cosworth engine is one of the most amazing pieces of technology in F1 this year, I think. They were doing 20,000rpm back in January/February, and we had more power and better reliability than most other teams ...

"The only thing they don't have is the big girlfriend on the arm in terms of a manufacturer's name. They don't get the credibility they deserve. For me they are the unsung heroes of the year."

And so they were. The bad news, though, was that no sooner had Cosworth re-possessed all its leased engines from Williams, and put them in store, than the cull of staff had to begin, and a number of key personalities began to drift away to what had always been rival concerns. Alex Hitzinger, for instance, moved off to join Toro Rosso as technical director of the plucky little 'Red Bull junior' team. Not only that, but Bernard Ferguson, who had become such a pivotal figure on the Cosworth racing scene since the 1990s, also chose to take retirement at this time.

As far as Toro Rosso was concerned, in 2006 the use of the rev-limited/air-restricted versions of the TJ V10 engines was a dismal failure, although the team had hoped to struggle up towards mid-field status as the year progressed. This did not happen, as *Autocourse* confirmed in its end of season review:

"Immediate rivals came up with scare stories – that its torque would be a massive advantage around tight circuits such as Monaco and the Hungaroring – that

COSWORTH AND F1 IN 2006 – IMPOSSIBLE ODDS

AS most observers acknowledged, Cosworth first dropped out of F1 at the end of 2006, even though their new 2.4-litre CA V8 engine was seen to be the most powerful of the field. The reason? This was simple – it was not due to technical failings, but to commercial and financial realities.

This was the line-up of F1 engine builders in 2006:

Cosworth	An independent company
BMW	Owned by the BMW car and motorcycle giant
Ferrari	Owned by Fiat, Italy's largest industrial concern
Honda	Owned by the extremely large Japanese car and motorcycle concern
Mercedes-Benz	Owned by the billion-Euro German concern
Renault	Owned by the large French car-maker
Toyota	Owned by the huge Japanese car-making colossus

FACED with such big-hitting competition, it was no wonder that Cosworth had to drop out of the marketplace, due to the relatively high leasing costs they had to charge for their CA power units to make the project viable, and at the end of 2006 no-one should blame Williams for turning to Toyota, even though the Japanese engines were apparently not as effective.

Ten years on, incidentally, BMW and Toyota had also dropped out of F1, the others carrying on supporting the ever-increasing burden of F1 involvement.

turned out to be rubbish, even though the team was allowed another 300rpm for qualifying, as continued development had allowed V8 manufacturers to raise their revs to 20,000 ..."

The fact is that Toro Rosso finished dead last in the 2006 series, their failings not merely being technical, but financial, and in not having the best of drivers, or car details either.

Clearly there was no obvious future or alternative use for the last of the 3-litre TJ V10s, which went into retirement, or became display units, but what of the modern and extremely effective V8s? Working on the 'never say never' basis, Cosworth made sure that the CAs were all returned to Northampton, all being carefully preserved, and kept a watching brief on what F1, and the FIA, were doing or proposing, and waited ...

In the next three years – 2007, 2008 and 2009 – while Cosworth was watching from the side-lines, the F1 regulations changed gradually, but persistently, not only by limiting the peak of the electronically-controlled engine revs – first back to 19,000rpm, then to 18,000rpm – but also by insisting that teams made their engines last for longer and longer before a rebuild could be authorised. Although this was exactly the sort of changing scene which Cosworth thought was in their favour, they could still not do anything to break the 'big girlfriend on the arm' (to quote Mark Webber) syndrome. Until, that is, early in 2009, when the controversial president of the FIA, Max Mosley, made an important announcement.

CA V8 from 2010 to 2013

In recent months, F1 had found itself to be in a growing crisis, as manufacturers such as BMW, Honda and Toyota began to announce their withdrawal from the sport. With grids forecast to be down to 20 cars in 2009, and perhaps to 18 or below in the 2010 season, FIA boss Max Mosley made determined efforts to change that trend.

Before the end of 2008, F1 grids were beginning to look sparse, and 'ringmaster' Bernie Ecclestone's oft-quoted assurance – that there would 'always' be 24 cars on the start lines – was looking unattainable in the future. At that point Max Mosley then persuaded Bernie Ecclestone to make it financially possible for a number of new teams to take part (as ever, the details were never spelt out in public – this being normal for the twilight period that was F1 financing for many such

years), but only if they could have the same 'spec' engines and transmissions.

This was Mosley's last fling – and very successful it was, too – before he stepped down from the Presidency of the FIA at the end of 2009 After several engine builders had been contacted, and invited to tender, Cosworth was successful, not only in gaining what commercially, was a very profitable leasing deal for them, but in setting up a busy period when new teams and new customers were involved, and would use a thoroughly updated version of the CA engine which had performed so well in 2006.

When the dust had settled, three new two-car teams (Lotus, HRT and Virgin) took the FIA's deal, and appeared on the start line in Australia in March 2010, though a fourth team called US F1 (to be based in the USA, and effectively run, but not financed, by ex-Williams team manager Peter Windsor), withdrew at a late stage, before any Cosworth CA engines could be delivered to them, even though they had already been built and allocated. Even so, they got as far as having cars partly built, and having ex-Cosworth director Bernard Ferguson advise them on the acquisition of the CA engines from 'his' old business!

Although the new 'customer cars' were by no means competitive with the 'big hitters' like Red Bull, Ferrari and McLaren, Cosworth was suddenly, well and truly back in the limelight. The reason for this was that it also welcomed back the Williams F1 operation as a prestigious customer. Williams, it should be recalled, had used the 2.4-litre CA throughout 2006, when the F1 'family' seemed to agree that this engine was the best of a tightly-specified bunch, but that their car had not been up to scratch. Williams had then defected to Toyota (the reason was financial, with a lot of money – all flowing in Williams' direction – involved), but it soon became clear that the Toyota engine was not as effective as promised.

Except that, for 2010, the CA engines supplied to Williams had certain external components, and systems (including a unique gearbox/hydraulics installation) relocated to suit the layout of their FW32 car, all the new generation power units (coded CA2010 within the Cosworth factory), were the same. At a stroke, Cosworth was back on the scene for, having supplied V8 power to just two F1 entries in 2006, and none at all in the next three seasons, it was now happily involved in supplying engines for eight cars (if the American team had made it to the grid, as forecast, it would have been ten cars!) in 2010.

Not that the 2006-specification engines would have been right for 2010, if only because there were two important technical changes which now had to be embraced. One was the compulsory (and electronically controlled) 18,000rpm limit; the other was that each driver, in each team, was only allowed to use eight engines in the 19-event season (and that included all the practice/qualification sessions), after which grid position penalties for enforced changes would be imposed.

After an extremely busy summer and winter in 2009/2010, so that the CA2010 power unit would be ready for the new season, Cosworth produced an homologated and approved power unit which produced 772bhp at 17,500rpm, a touch better than had been expected before work began (and, in fairness, quite phenomenal when compared with the specific output of other normally-aspirated F1 engines of ten years earlier). In spite of the limitation on engine changes, and a ban on mid-season testing, by the time this engine was finally phased out in 2013, no fewer than 220 engines of all types – test, development, display and race – had been built, and used in no fewer than 22 cars: a complete strip-and-rebuild programme for each engine took 240 man hours!

Matthew Grant, who was project manager for the 'rebirth,' recalled that, even though the CA project had not been abandoned, a lot of activity went into getting it race-ready for 2010:

"People think that we just updated the original 2006 Williams stock, but it wasn't like that. There was little in those engines which was useful, so we had to start again. Because of the rule changes, we had to ensure that the engines had to be able to do three or four races each before being stripped, and the peak revs limit came down from the 20,000rpm, which the original had done, to 18,000rpm – this was good for us.

"Working with four different teams [five, if US GP had actually raced their cars: AAGR], means that we had to make them 'installation friendly' – we moved the engine mounts, and more or less said to the new teams 'This is what you can have' ... Originally we had the same engine/all-teams strategy in mind, but then Williams, a very experienced F1 team, came along, and were very specific, and very demanding.

"We built ten endurance/test engines in 2009, all with the aim of proving to ourselves and the teams that we could guarantee 3000 kilometres without failures, Williams then took three or four new engines for the pre-season winter test in Barcelona, and there

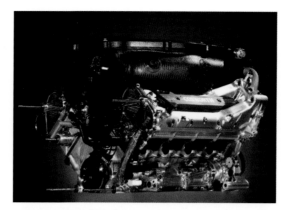

would be about six others for the new teams. Even at the very start of the season, in Bahrain, we had to produce six engines for each team. All in all, during that winter, we had to build or rebuild up to 50 engines in that three month period."

[This is a far cry from the early days of the DFV, and of course of the HB in 1989, which, in retrospect, seemed to be altogether more relaxed.]

As will become clear in the summary below of all activities that took place at this time, the ever-changing Cosworth company, which was being evolved by the Kalkhoven/Forsythe management team, covered a whole range of engineering activities at the same time, and although the CA2010 engine was seen as completely competitive when launched (and 'homologated' according to F1's increasingly strict regulations), it was only the Williams team that did it justice at the time. The reason, in every other case, was the inexperience and lack of finance of the new teams, which, typically, lacked the skills to get the 'aero' packages of their cars right.

Throughout the 2010 season, the CA V8-powered Williams FW32 (whose star driver was Rubens

Barrichello, though his team-mate Nico Hülkenberg was clearly a rising talent) was regularly in or around one of the ten fastest cars in the sport. The highlight of the season was undoubtedly Nico Hülkenberg's Pole Position before the Brazilian GP, yet the team's best finishing performance was fourth in Spain, at Valencia. Williams agreed that their car lacked development (because the design could not be settled until the deal was done to switch from Toyota to Cosworth at the end of 2009), to which Cosworth could only signal agreement, and hope for better in 2011.

In 2011, Cosworth had already lost Lotus (not to be confused with Team Lotus, a different team entirely, with which Lotus had been involved in a seedy legal battle over the use of the name – and both teams were to run with cheaper-to-hire Renault power), so only six CA-powered F1 cars took to the tracks. For Cosworth, the season was marred by the poor Williams performances (even Williams admitted to this), because of the failings of the FW33 car, particularly in the thinking behind its new and radically small transmission, and the poor aero package which resulted around it, while the HRT and Marussia-Virgin teams were, frankly, no-hopers.

Williams, who was fast gaining a reputation in the F1 scene for the regular number of changes it made to its engine line up (BMW, Cosworth, Toyota, Cosworth, and, for 2012 it seemed, Renault – all since 2000), was soon written out of Cosworth's affections for that policy. The other two teams were supplied regularly, honestly and efficiently, but did not look likely to win any major awards in the near future.

The end for the superb CA came swiftly and brutally, for 2013 was no more productive than the previous season had been, and a proposed total change in F1 engine regulations for 2014 meant that there was no obvious place for a normally-aspirated 2.4-litre V8 in future seasons. Because a number of CA engines had been carefully brought towards the end of their competitive lives by that time, these were scrapped; others went into store, and a number became show exhibits, with at least one later becoming a permanent display in the reception area of Cosworth at Northampton. With a specific output of more than 320bhp/litre, the CA was the most efficient race engine so far produced by Cosworth – though there was sure to be an improvement on that figure in the company's future history.

SPECIFIC OUTPUTS

- The first Cosworth engine to produce more than 100bhp/litre was the Ford 105E-based Mk XI of 1963, which produced 110bhp from 1098cc.
- The first DFV V8 of 1967 produced approx 135bhp/litre – yet by 1983 when the final 3-litre version (the DFY) appeared, it had approx 176bhp/litre.
- The original Cosworth DFX, a turbocharged V8 for Indycar racing in the USA, produced 317bhp/litre. This discouraged the opposition so much – for they could not match these figures – that they successfully brought pressure to have the regulations changed to impose a lower boost limit. Later DFXs, therefore, were less powerful – but just as successful.
- The first BDA of 1970 produced a normally-aspirated 120bhp, but the turbocharged 2.1-litre BDT-E of 1987 produced 234bhp/litre, and up to 310bhp/litre in rallycross trim.
- For the original Sierra RS Cosworth of 1986, the turbocharged YBB produced 102bhp/litre in road car form – but by 1988 a race-tuned Sierra RS500/YBD derivative could produce no less than 275bhp/litre, and could race, flat out, for 24 hours without faltering.
- Cosworth's only dedicated turbocharged F1 engine to go into service was the 1.5-litre V6 GB of 1985-1987. The original version aimed for 500bhp/litre, and attained it almost at once when testing began. By 1987 the engine was already rated at 668bhp/litre, and was impressively reliable.
- Cosworth developed a whole series of 3.5-litre, later 3.0-litre, normally-aspirated V10 F1 engines in the 1990s and early 2000s. Early types produced over 220bhp/litre, but by 2003 the final TJ, as used by Jaguar, was (conservatively) rated at 305bhp/litre.
- For F1, where increasingly strict regulations were being imposed, The normally-aspirated 2.4-litre V8 CA type eventually produced up to 320bhp/litre, which could certainly have been improved if some of the regulations had been eased.

FROM 1963 to 2006, therefore, Cosworth had increased the peak output of its finest race engines by more than 300 per cent. Even when comparing like with like – the original DFV of 1967 against the final CA of 2010, for example – that improvement had been 237 per cent!

Not forgetting the North American scene

It was in the same period that the XG engine, produced for use in the USA, suddenly turned from 'good idea' to 'active project.' As already noted in Chapter 17, Bruce Wood summarised what came next:

"We had seen the writing on the wall: the manufacturers' interests were waning in CART/Champcar, and were gathering around the Indy 500 race (which was IRL dominated), which left Champcar with no serious engine suppliers except ourselves.

"So we started thinking, again, about the XG. We did it without any customers in view, we did the design, but not at first the expensive part which have been to start making engines. Because we were part of Ford's Premier Performance Group, under Niki Lauda, we had got to the point with the XG where we would need to spend some money if we were go from designs to some solid hardware – and we had to see him.

"Nick Hayes and I then went down to London, and

met Niki in his very plush offices, and had a cup of coffee with him. We put it to him that if we wanted to stay in American racing, then we would have to spend some money on this XG engine. Incidentally, we wouldn't then be able to enter the engines as Cosworth, because Champcar rules said your engine had to be 'owned' by a car manufacturer. Since Ford had not expressed much interest at this time, we didn't have an idea of what the end game was ..."

Lauda approved the design and building of half-a-dozen prototypes of the XG, but with the decision on Champcar rules still not made, Cosworth kept a foot in both camps by casting an eye on the new (and, at that time, still barely settled) IRL series, and thought it would like to be involved, especially since the IRL now included the prestigious Indianapolis 500 race.

Cosworth, however, still under Ford control in 2002 and following its corporate guidance on making money, was cautious. Much time was spent in North America, in looking for a car manufacturer to 'badge' the engine, and at one time it was close to making an agreement with Hyundai North America. That, in the end, came to nought at the pre-contracting stage, for although the American network was keen, the parent company in South Korea was not, and negotiations finally ground to a halt. The fact that Cosworth had designed and was testing a new XG engine was becoming known – as was the fact that it was, in effect, an 'orphan.'

At which point, and quite out of the blue, came a transatlantic phone call from John Barnes, whose Panther team had dominated the IRL in 2001 and 2002 with the series' control engine, a so-called General Motors unit. This engine, in which TWR apparently had had some input, was suddenly being overwhelmed by new IRL engines produced by Toyota and Honda, and Barnes wanted to do something about it.

Soon after this, Bruce Wood was persuaded to visit the Panther operation, meet the GM management, and discuss ways and means. After much negotiation (which could, alternatively, have involved Cosworth working on the suddenly-uncompetitive GM V8 engine, as GM was reluctant to lose face by abandoning it ...):

"We showed them some power curves," Bruce Wood revealed, "and came up with a plan of how we would make the engines last longer. We had to develop a plan to make about 100 engines, for there were eight GM-engined users in the IRL."

In the end, GM (the paymasters, after all ...) demanded a back-to-back test, to be completed in one day, on the Chicagoland 1.5-mile oval circuit, using the same car into which an XG and a GM engine would alternately be bolted. The story of how there was trouble in building up that car, how there was ignition trouble with the XG which took hours to sort out, and the stratagems needed to meet General Motors' deadline would fill a complete chapter – but the 'end game' (to quote from modern USA usage) was that:

"... in the morning we did 212mph in the GM-engined car, and in the afternoon we did 217mph with the XG ... which was the equivalent, we thought, of about 50 horsepower. We shook hands with the GM bosses there and then, and that was it."

The fairytale then continued to unfold, as *Autocourse* 2003 tells us:

"Sam Hornish, who had won the 2001 and 2002 IRL titles ... appeared to be a non-contender during the first part of the season, his Chevrolet engine soundly dominated by Toyota and Honda. Then came the 'Gen IV' engine, which was in fact a Cosworth. The engine was competitive right off the bat, and Hornish was able to win three races with it ..."

He also took two second places, and fifth overall in the Championship.

Cosworth eventually manufactured about 80 XG engines, looked after the entire fleet at Torrance, in the USA, rebuilt each of them every 500 miles, and threw them away after 1500 miles. Success, however, was short-lived, for Toyota and Honda both then threw millions of Yen at improving their own products for 2004, when the regulations changed to limit engine sizes to 3-litres, which GM was not prepared to match, and there were fewer victories to chalk up. Politics, the changeover of company ownership (Ford sold out to the Kalkoven/Forsythe consortium at the end of 2004), and the decision to concentrate on the XFE programme in the rival Champcar series were all factors.

For a company the size of Cosworth, the 'Noughties' (the 2000s), it seemed, were going to be turbulent, both financially and commercially. New management, and new strategies, would be needed to ensure that all was well.

19: NEW PRODUCTS AND NEW HORIZONS

"Let's be clear – this company is expanding, not contracting, for we are supplying engines, electronics and expertise to companies all over the world ..."

In 2006 Cosworth was still at the peak of the F1 business, building and developing the very best of the world's F1 engines then in existence. So how could it be that ten years later the company was no longer in the F1 business, and showed no signs of re-entering it? The reasons, in fact, were many and various, and it all took time to evolve, so the explanation of what happened, when, and why, must begin in 2004.

At that time, Cosworth's owner, Ford-Worldwide, was going through an agonising time of business appraisal, where the need to simplify its corporate structure, and hopefully to restore higher profits to the global operation, was seen as paramount. At the centre of this change of corporate heart was the decision to hive off several of the smaller concerns which had been absorbed in recent years and – this being vitally important as far as Cosworth was concerned – at the same time to dissolve the Premier Automotive Group (PAG).

Since Cosworth Racing, absorbed by Ford in 1998, had always been a part of this grouping – more specifically a part of the Premier Performance Division, which Ford had set up at the start of 2001, succinctly describing it as "the motorsport arm of the PAG," this gradual, piecemeal, but ruthless disposal of the assets was important.

Although the dismantling of the PAG officially began in 2006 – immediately after Alan Mulally became Ford-Worldwide's President and CEO – the unravelling had already begun, for Lincoln had been returned to the mainstream umbrella of Ford in 2002. Then, in mid-2004, Ford announced that it was to sell off the Jaguar F1 team (based at Milton Keynes), and to sell off Cosworth.

Almost at once, a large number of suitors (some of them financial no-hopers, it must be admitted) made themselves known, but it was not until November 2004 that the sale of the two companies (both being part of the PPG) was formalised. As already spelt out in the previous chapter, the Jaguar F1 business was acquired by Red Bull Racing (who carried on using Cosworth F1 engines until the end of 2005), while Cosworth was acquired by a small group of American investors, led by Kevin Kalkhoven and Jerry Forsythe.

"The reality is that when Jerry and I bought the Champcar series in 2003, our engine supplier was solely Cosworth," Kevin commented. "So as the engine supplier to the series, they were obviously very close to us. Without Cosworth, we obviously wouldn't have an engine for the Series!

"Subsequently, of course, when we ascertained that Ford might be interested in selling the business, we leapt at the chance."

Bernard Ferguson still shows pride in his initial part of bringing this 'marriage' about:

"From my office in 2004, which was in the front of the HQ building at Northampton, I could see various people coming and going. In the end, Ford didn't seem to be getting anywhere, so one day I sat down with managing director Tim Routsis and said 'Look, wouldn't it be wonderful synergy if we could bring Kevin Kalkhoven and Jerry Forsythe together, and get them to buy Cosworth ...'

"Anyway, it was decided that I should speak to them – initially it was with Jerry Forsythe. Jerry eventually said: 'Well, yes, I'm interested, but you'd better ring

JERRY FORSYTHE

ALTHOUGH Jerry Forsythe became a major shareholder in Cosworth in 2004, he did not take up an executive position within the company. Then, as later, he was a great motor racing enthusiast, and had been closely involved in USA sport since 1993. One of his successful 1990s-type Cosworth-engined CART race cars was a prominent exhibit in the reception area of the company in Northampton.

Already established as a successful businessman in North America, he set up a racing team, Forsythe Racing, in 1983, seeing Teo Fabi win four races, and taking six pole positions, before the team was sold so that he could concentrate, once again, on his business interests. Over the years, these have involved the development of the Indeck Companies, and in more modern times he added resort ownership, cattle ranching and farming to a very wide range of activities.

Returning to motor sport in 1993, he joined with Barry Green in founding the Forsythe/Green Racing team, which was backed by the Canadian Players tobacco company, and contested the Toyota Atlantic Championship. The team, with drivers Claude Bourbonnais and Jacques Villeneuve, graduated to the CART/Indy Car series in 1994, when Villeneuve became Rookie of the Year.

From 1995 Forsythe took complete control of his CART team, which used XB and (late) XD and XF engines, its most successful season being 2003, when Paul Tracy won seven races and the last-ever CART Championship. Thereafter, however, Forsythe refused the offer of joining the nascent IRL series, choosing instead to join Kevin Kalkhoven and Paul Gentilozzi to buy up the CART series, rename it the Champcar World Series, and to arrange for this to use Cosworth 'spec' XFE engines in all competing cars until 2008.

Although he withdrew his team from motor racing after the Champcar series merged with the IRL series in 2008, he maintained his interests in various circuits, and continued to be an active shareholder in the Cosworth business.

By the 2010s, Cosworth's main reception building put a glossy and forward looking face to the world, and was almost unrecognisable from the modest little factory that Keith Duckworth had financed more than 40 years earlier. Part of that building, however, can still be seen, immediately to the left of the Octagon itself.

FORD: DISMANTLING THE EMPIRE

IT is now a well-documented part of Cosworth's history that although the Cosworth Racing business was bought by Ford of Europe with great pride in September 1998, it was sold with great reluctance to Kevin Kalkhoven and Jerry Forsythe in November 2004. This, it should be emphasised, is not because Ford was unhappy with Cosworth's business performance, but was really caused by its growing tendency to hive off parts of the worldwide Ford empire that were not closely connected with the group's core activity.

The Premier Automotive Group, within the Ford orbit, was originally founded in 1999 to take responsibility for the Lincoln, Mercury, Aston Martin, Jaguar, Land Rover and Volvo brands, and since its initial CEO was Jacques Nasser, who was a real sporting enthusiast, Cosworth Racing was also swept into its control. In the next few years, a huge amount of money (some say it was as much as $17 billion) was spent in attempting to integrate this sub-empire, even though it rapidly became clear that most of those brands had their own unique markets, and requirements, to satisfy.

By 2004 it was becoming clear to Ford's top executives that this strategy was not working, as Lincoln and Mercury had been returned to the mainstream Ford operation, and the only true signs of technical integration were that Jaguar and Lincoln were sharing a chassis platform, while Volvo was leaning more and more heavily on the use of Ford of Europe platforms and hardware.

After the sale of Cosworth to Kevin Kalkhoven and Jerry Forsythe, the major components of the PAG were also sold off before the end of the 2000s. Cosworth's only important links with other companies in the PAG were the supply of the Aston Martin V12 engine design, and continuing advice on the evolution of the current Jaguar V8 engine.

Kalkhoven, because he's the one with more of the money ...'"

Initially, it was Routsis who visited Kevin Kalkhoven in California, and eventually a deal was done, after which the hard-bargaining began.

It then took a month of discussions, not only on matters of engineering, intellectual rights, and the complications of dealing with Cosworth Electronics (which had originally been Pi research, based near Cambridge):

"It was never going to be simple," Kalkhoven later admitted, "but Ford-Worldwide is a very large company, so it has all those departments we had to deal with. There were times when 'simple' became 'miserable,' but not for long ..."

At that moment – November 2004 – Kalkhoven insists that there was no such thing as a 'Master Plan' in his, or Jerry Forsythe's head, but:

"The logic went something like this. First of all, we (my associates and I) needed Cosworth for the race series, but the reality was that we immediately realised that Cosworth was such an incredible company, an incredible brand, with some incredibly bright people on the staff. It wasn't just a case of acquiring a company, but of acquiring a company with a brand, and a quality of stuff and reputation, which was a pretty unique situation."

No sooner had the Kalkhoven/Forsythe team taken control of Cosworth (leaving Tim Routsis as the CEO in Northampton), than they gradually came to realise that the survival and development of the business was to allow the 'racing' side – engines and electronics – to carry on as the flag-waving side of the operation, while looking around for more commercial (ie non-motorsport-orientated) opportunities to develop.

This is now the moment, perhaps, to flag up the ever-growing importance of a little-known activity of a Cosworth subsidiary – that of the electronics concern, centred on anonymous premises outside the high-tech city of Cambridge, and one which became the first Cosworth activity to break through into the OEM (Original Equipment Manufacturing) business, to supply major motoring manufacturers.

Way back in 1989, a young man called Tony Purnell, who was working on his own PhD studies at Cambridge, spotted that the trend towards electronic miniaturisation was swelling. That trend, and the explosion of a need for data acquisition and capture in motor racing, led him to create Pi Research, and a data system small enough to go inside a model race car that was going into a wind-tunnel.

Moving from successful wind-tunnel work on one car led to contracts with several other F1 manufacturers, and a dominant position in motorsport, such that most of the F1 'circus' came to be satisfied customers and have remained so. From this point, installation in complete cars was a logical trend, taken up by several prominent manufacturers both in F1, and in Champcar racing. Pi Research was later absorbed by Cosworth, and was, therefore, part of the group bought by Ford in 1998, and sold off to the Kalkhoven/Forsythe group of investors in 2004.

From 2005, however, Cosworth's mode of operation gradually evolved (and has remained so), for it soon became clear that two major motor racing activities were likely to change considerably. Firstly, in the USA, Champcar racing, though a source of great publicity for the XFE 'spec' engine, found itself under increasing pressure from the higher-profile IRL series (which included the world-famous Indianapolis 500 race); and secondly, Formula 1 was becoming more and more dominated by rival companies determined to succeed by providing very cheap, or even free-issue, power units, to teams who might otherwise have done business with a still-competitive Cosworth operation.

In contrast, the electronics business managed to retain its activities across an impressive variety of customer bases – not only in the F1, Champcar and IRL series, but with Honda in the Far East, with M-Sport in the World Rally Championship and – on a strictly confidential basis – with several OEM companies too. Even so, from the end of 2006 Cosworth found itself out of F1 for the first time in 40 years, and in 2008 (after a series of wearying and increasingly personality-dominated merger proposals with the IRL had failed), the Champcar series closed down in 2008.

Inevitably, job losses had to be sustained at this point, though the key personalities stayed on board, and the company's individual project reputations were not submerged. Although there was still much for the Powertrain side of the business to do, within the company its standing was slowly, if honourably, declining. To quote one (anonymous) senior personality at Cosworth:

"As the revenues from F1, and the revenues from Champcar slowed, the question was thrown up by management of the day: 'What else are we going to do?' or 'What else can we do?' The company recognised that the clock was always ticking, and that now, not later, was the time to think again about many other activities."

This phase of the company's development, which occupied the early years following Ford's sell-off, lasted for much of the second part of the 2000s, and resulted in an amazing number of 'Why don't we' projects being aired. It did not help that in 2008 the world's economy had a major financial shock, which caused several businesses to close in upon themselves, and not consult outside suppliers as much as they would hitherto have been willing to do.

The company's diversification started out as an expansion, and continuation, of projects (often private projects) that Cosworth engineers already found interesting, sometimes including aerospace and defence activities. Always encouraged by the Kalkhoven/Forsythe axis, who were incredibly brave and supportive at a time when profits were hard to come by and confidence sometimes sagged, and administered by CEO Tim Routsis, the need was seen as aggressive diversification, and the finding of opportunities in adjacent, not automotive, markets, which was aimed at transforming Cosworth. It would change from a motorsport business to a diversified engineering group – the model arguably set up by Vickers 20 years earlier being seen as a historic inspiration.

At one stage, diversification into the aerospace

Electronics expert Thomas Buckler directed the fortunes of Cosworth's electronic speciality division, based in the Cambridge area, this company having grown from the original Pi operation.

industry seemed to be a promising strategic move, for Cosworth was ideally placed to supply high quality components in small volumes – 50 to 500 units. Much investment was put into people, systems, and procedures, with the company seeking, and achieving, AS900 certification.

The defence industry, too, was seen as a possible partner to aerospace work. Cosworth considered that another, near-unique, feature of what it could offer the clientele was that it was (and still is) very quick in moving from problem to solution, bringing it to the marketplace, and making it available to put into service.

[At the time the defence industry had a well-chronicled reputation for moving slightly faster than a glacier, if all things went well, but this was not the way that Cosworth wanted to do business ...]

In the end, it was Cosworth's very own fleet-of-foot approach which made it difficult to deal with such ponderous, long-established, standards. As one company insider remarked:

"If your competitive advantage is that you are faster than the incumbent suppliers, that's a great thing. One of the things that Cosworth wasn't very successful at was, effectively, that it did not enjoy 'disengaging the clutch.' The company had a clock speed which is extremely fast – it comes from the motorsport history of being a motorsport-orientated company, with the ability to make decisions extremely quickly.

"But when you want to engage with one of these behemoth industries, it has much bigger cogs which turn much more slowly – and sometimes trying to engage our faster-spinning cog wheels with the behemoth wheels meant that teeth came off."

At the time, this growing realisation was a big disappointment. Thoughts had gone into work on drone aircraft (via single-cylinder heavy-fuel diesel engines), but the possible demand (even worldwide) didn't add up. Work on the mitigation of vehicles to the effects of IED explosions (in the Middle East, and Afghanistan, for instance) seemed promising, and there were many other top-secret initiatives that came to nothing, mainly because top management simply could not see ways in which they could become profitable enterprises.

In the meantime, other more traditional engine-based projects were tackled, and came to profitable (sometimes still-secret) conclusions. As detailed in Appendix A, therefore, further use was found for the seemingly indestructible XG (ex-General Motors IRL engine) power unit, the concept of 'crate engines' was formalised – and there was an amazingly capable

rescue-job around the legendary, but old-fashioned, Napier Deltic engine.

These two projects alone, show just how versatile, innovative and light-on-its-feet Cosworth could be. On the one hand, one particular type of road car engine – in this case a modern mass-production Ford unit (the Duratec) – was chosen and modified in a whole series of ways, to make it attractive to limited-production car-makers, while on the other, the massive Deltic power plant was effectively brought back from the dead!

The two projects could not have been more different. On the first, Cosworth started to weave its well-known and much-respected magic on an already fine Ford-Europe 2-litre engine, which would normally be rated at 145bhp; while on the Deltic this was a massive job based on Cosworth's legendary reputation for what is known as 'reverse-engineering.'

The Ford-based engine project – coded 'YD' in Cosworth-speak, a definite and knowing nod back into history, when the company had produced more than 30,000 YB/Sierra units, and had then moved on to the Duratec's predecessor, the YC, for World Rally Car use – was produced in an entirely logical manner, by adding a steel crankshaft, high-performance camshaft profile, a modified cylinder head and dry sump lubrication: turbocharging was not needed.

After this, the company produced several different states of tune, before a 2.3-litre version went out to the limited-production car industry, as typified by Caterham, asking the theoretical question: "Well, just how much power would you like?" With the engines quietly being assembled in what had been the F1 build shop, this provided steady business for the next several years.

Work on the Deltic project, however, was a real tour de force, the like of which Cosworth had never tackled before. The contract came from Rolls-Royce, which had previously had corporate links with Cosworth in the 1990s. Given a definitely symptomatic code name (DC = Deltic, no question), the project involved an unheralded rescue job of the once famous power plant. The Deltic engine was a 44-litre two-stroke diesel power unit, with a unique 18-cylinder layout involving three geared-together crankshafts and an opposed-piston way of operation; the engine weight could be measured in tonnes rather than kilograms! It was immediately clear that this was no ordinary job.

The Deltic story began way back in the 1940s, when the London-based Napier concern conceived it for use in military ships, including motor torpedo boats, mine-sweepers, and other fast patrol boats. Napier, in business since the end of the 19th century, had produced a series of fine aero-engines during World War Two, but had then been taken over by English Electric, who eventually sold off the diesel engine division to Rolls-Royce.

In cross-sectional profile, the original Deltic engine featured a triangular layout, with three crankshafts all geared together, and was rated at no less than 1650bhp at 1500rpm. The layout, and its detailing, was so complex (though successful, by the way!), that it can only really be understood by referring to drawings of its actuation.

Some years into its life, the Deltic engine was then 'courageously' (meaning financially brave – as Sir Humphrey would have had it in the BBC sitcom *Yes Prime Minister*) adapted as power for British Railways' Type 55 express locomotive, which took two such engines per unit (giving a power output of 3300bhp). The locomotive's job was to haul passenger trains up and down the East Coast main lines between London, Leeds, Newcastle and Edinburgh: a job that was done with real honours during the 1960s and 1970s. The Class 55's 100mph cruising speed was quite unsurpassed on British rail tracks until the HS125 fleet began to arrive at the end of the 1970s.

But that was then, and Cosworth's involvement did not eventuate until the mid-2000s. At that time the Deltic was no longer in railway service, although it was still in use in ships of various types. Rolls-Royce could see a continuing market, and kept Deltics in stock, but that stock was afflicted by a fire which did serious damage.

Searching around for repairs to be made, and new component parts to be produced, Rolls-Royce soon settled on Cosworth, which was not only famous for its ability to work miracles, but also at this time known to be actively looking for work. The story of how this project was completed by a lot of 'reverse engineering' and sheer 'can-do' ability would make a complete chapter on its own.

In the meantime, there had been something of an upheaval in Cosworth's North American activities, first because the XG (the engine which had rescued General Motors from oblivion in the IRL series) had been dropped from IRL racing when GM decided to withdraw entirely from open-wheel racing); and then in 2008, when Champcar racing came to a sudden halt, putting the long-running XFE out of business. Neither engine, it seemed, had a future, so the

Just imagine this beast lining up on the front row of a race car grid! The Cosworth connection is that, in the 2000s, the company undertook the rescue, remanufacture and reverse-engineering of major parts of the complex Napier Deltic engines, so that they could keep running in modern times. The British Rail locomotive is a Type 55, which was the premier East Coast (London-York-Edinburgh) power unit of the 1960s-1980s, and powered by two 1650bhp Napier Deltic engines.,

North American racing operation was closed down completely.

This was the point at which the XFE's career came to a graceful end (the XF family, after all, had been around for eight very profitable years), but when the stock of XGs were brought back to Northampton, it was decided to put them to whatever further use could be found. This, however, was not the end of Cosworth's activities in the USA, for, as the remainder of this chapter makes clear, more and more healthy co-operation with mainstream road-car manufacturers in this vast continent was to follow. For that purpose, Cosworth maintained a base in Indianapolis.

Within months, in any case, two 'sub-projects' connected with the XG evolved – one eventually proving worthwhile, the other something of a damp squib. First of all, an approach from Japan caused the XG to be a useful cornerstone for road cars to be entered in the Super GT50 Championship. The regulations for this series were very specific, and restricted the use of engines of not more than 3.4-litres in a compulsory 90-degree V8 configuration. This, of course, was a meat-and-drink requirement for a company like Cosworth, which just so happened to have a basic engine – the XG – sitting on its shelves. The only major change was that the now-obsolete XG engines, which had been reduced to 3.0-litres towards the end of their life as 'General Motors' power units, could now be enlarged once again, and the use of a compulsory inlet passage restrictor (to limit the actual peak power output to only 500bhp) was no hardship either.

Because this engine was to be supplied to several different (Japanese) customers, Cosworth used a positive blizzard of 'alphabet-soup' project codes – specifically XJ, NR, VR and (as an evolution of NR), the XK.

The damp squib was at one and the same time intriguing and pathetic. In one of its many frenetic attempts to widen and modernise its product base, Lotus of Norfolk (inspired by new CEO Dany Bahar) decided to produce a specifically-designed 'track day' single-seater, the Lotus T125, one which would not comply to any Formula 1 requirements, and was intended to provide F1-like performance and sensations to wealthy enthusiasts who might otherwise have struggled to purchase or campaign a real F1 car for 'classic' events. The specification, in general, would be simplified compared with that of an F1 car. Lotus concluded that it might be able to sell 25 such machines, and set out to do just that in 2010. Initially, when the car was first shown at Pebble Beach, in California, in August 2010, the sale price was set at £650,000, and it was delicately suggested that the cockpit would be made more roomy than usual on such single-seaters 'to cater for' the high and mighty.

Cosworth was approached, to see if it was interested in providing power (as an obvious connection, the company had sold off many 1990s-type HBs, ECs, and even some earlier specification JD V10s to enthusiasts aiming to compete in 'classic' F1 racing series), and chose to satisfy this by modifying a small number of otherwise redundant ex-IRL XGs. Because the company saw this as an indulgence for Lotus, but a profitable diversion for itself, never gave it a two-digit recognisable Cosworth project code, calling it GBV8 instead. Once again, the generic XG engine was further modified, enlarged to 3.8-litres by using the largest possible bore and stroke that the cylinder block could accommodate, and, by applying an electronic engine limiter set to 11,000rpm, was able to guarantee an output of 640bhp at 10,000rpm.

Although the T125 got a sympathetic reception by the British specialist press, sales did not follow, and, in spite of more recent vigorous discussions on motor sporting forums, no-one seems to know of any such cars being delivered, or ever being seen in public. Cosworth officials, when quizzed, merely shrug politely and say that it was yesterday's news, and of totally minor interest.

In the meantime, the most astonishing turn of events (a development not generally made known for years to come) was evolving behind the scenes. As the 2010 decade progressed, although Cosworth recognised that economic pressures meant it would eventually have to withdraw from Formula 1 (as detailed in the previous chapter), it was by no means out of the picture, and was still amazingly well-thought-of by every team.

The project, which linked Formula 1, an F1 team, a previous sponsor/co-owner, and a move towards modern hybrid technology, took shape, flared, and went into honourable retirement in no more than three years. Even though Cosworth knew that it would lose its contract to supply 2.4-litre CA V8 engines to the Williams F1 team at the end of 2011, it had already picked up an alternative, and equally lucrative, deal from Williams to supply engines for a new Jaguar supercar which Williams Advanced Engineering was to develop.

As usually happens at this stratospheric level of the industry, Cosworth's involvement in the project was not originally planned by Jaguar, was only undertaken to get the project out of a big 'hole' – and was then achieved remarkably quickly! The story goes something like this:

In 2010, Jaguar, having recently been absorbed by the Indian industrial giant, Tata, was already tackling a massive engineering programme, and to emphasise how far-reaching this commitment was to be, had commissioned its UK-based team to develop a proposed supercar. This fabulous mid-engined machine, coded C-X75, first went public in October 2010, as a sleek two-seater model with a potential top speed of more than 220mph.

So far, so believable, but when its proposed (though totally unproven) hybrid drive line was revealed, observers' doubts soon began to surface. The single prototype had not even been completed when the details were published: not only was the car to be driven by four 194bhp electric motors, but power for these (with a massive 408lb/185kg lithium-ion battery pack backup) was to be provided by tiny twin Bladon Jets gas turbines (weighing just 77lb/35kg each), each of which was placarded as producing up to 188bhp at 80,000rpm, and could run on a variety of fuels. It can have been no coincidence that Bladon Jets's HQ was less than a mile away from the Jaguar engineering centre in Coventry.

All this, frankly, sounded too good to be true, even in May 2011 when Jaguar unveiled plans to build up to 250 such cars, provisionally priced at £700,000 each, after development had been completed on its behalf by Williams, whose research arm was separate from, but adjacent to, the F1 operation at Grove in Oxfordshire. In theory, production would begin in 2013.

By this time, however, the plan to use micro-turbines had already been abandoned, and Cosworth – like the cavalry in every good US movie – had been called in, just in time, to save the day. Bruce Wood now takes up the story:

"When the new F1 engine formula (1.6-litre and hybrid power) was first announced, we invested some of our own money, and studied a 1.6-litre four-cylinder unit – originally as a paper study, then with a lot of design, and we did a lot of simulation. At which point, Williams, who knew what we were doing, turned up and said 'We've got this Jaguar contract, and now what we want for it is to use a Formula 1-type engine for the road …'"

Jaguar, having abandoned the micro gas turbines almost immediately after the launch, was looking round for a more conventional high-output power plant, and was ready to consider a piston engine of some sort, but had neither the time, nor the particular type of engineering team, to tackle the job itself. Williams, who had already been contracted to start building a batch of prototypes, was consulted, and immediately recommended that Cosworth should get the contract. It needed little beyond the initial meeting (and Williams, make no mistake, already knew that Cosworth had by that time schemed up a new-generation four-cylinder F1 engine, the HK project) for the deal to be done.

As Bruce Wood confirmed:

"Basically, this was a fabulous contract for us. Right from the start, of course, we made it clear that we thought they really did not exactly need a Formula 1 engine, which would have been hideously difficult and unpleasant to drive in a road car. However, an engine built around those regulations, and influenced by F1 thinking, was what they needed."

The result was that the new Cosworth 1.6-litre HK engine design was modified, somewhat de-

tuned, and matured around a layout with an Eaton supercharger which 'handed over' at about 5000rpm to a turbocharger. Not only was this always designed to be a dry-sumped power unit with gear-drive to the twin camshafts, but it had both direct and port-fed fuel-injection – the result being a sweetly-revving engine which produced 500bhp at 10,000rpm.

All this was revealed to the public in the summer of 2012 (but at this stage never, please note, was the 'Cosworth connection' made clear – for the engine was described as 'Gaydon designed and built,' which it most assuredly was not), when the car's projected price had risen to £900,000. Cosworth pressed on with great vigour, but after the first dozen engines had been completed, tested, and delivered to Grove for assembly into ten prototypes, Jaguar suddenly announced the cancellation of the entire project and put the complete fleet into secure storage. The result is that the Cosworth-designed HK engine has not been seen in public.

[The use of what were claimed to be C-X75 cars in the James Bond film *Spectre*, is something of a 'red herring,' as the cars used were mere look-alikes, with different space-frame chassis, and using supercharged Jaguar V8 engines …]

There is an interesting 'might-have-been' to this story. No sooner had the FIA changed its mind about F1's future – specifying the use of 1.6-litre V6 engines instead of 4-cylinder engines (this rule change was finalised in 2012) – Williams immediately made contact with Cosworth to ask if it would consider producing an F1-type V6 for use in the C-X75 in place of the suddenly-obsolete 4-cylinder HK? Cosworth apparently thought about this, ran the financial figures through its computers, was horrified by the risks, and turned it all down!

In the meantime, Cosworth had experienced what, in some light-hearted corporate terms, might be described as a 'light-bulb' moment, when it became clear that the company needed to a long, hard, look at itself, perhaps change its strategy, and spend more money on that future.

In 2008, or thereabouts, the view was taken that the time might now be ripe for an approach to the stock market for investment – to make what is known as an 'Initial Public Offering' – which would raise new capital and make further investment easier to tackle. At this point, one should remember, is that in all its 50 years of existence, this was the very first time that Cosworth had proposed to raise funds in this way.

HK: THE STILL-BORN 2014 F1 ENGINE

IN 2011 F1 found itself contemplating yet another change in engine regulations for 2014 and beyond. To replace the existing 2.4-litre V8 formula (from which Cosworth had just, reluctantly, withdrawn), a new 'hybrid' package was proposed, the 'old-fashioned' engine side of this new combo to be a turbocharged 1.6-litre unit.

At first (and without finalising this, nor even getting the tacit approval of engine manufacturers such as Cosworth), it was proposed that the 1.6-litre engines would have to be straight four-cylinder units. Although it still had no committed customer for such an engine, Cosworth's design team, led by Bruce Wood, started work on such a new unit, which appears in the company's official Projects List as a Type HK, and was also linked to Jaguar's C-X75 hypercar project, a road-car whose prototypes were built and developed on its behalf by Williams Grand Prix.

Although no such engine was completed by Cosworth as an F1 engine in 2011/2012, this was perhaps wise, as the FIA abruptly changed its mind, and then opted for a compulsory V6 layout instead. As far as is known, no dedicated hardware for the proposed HK F1 engine was ever produced. Sickened by this upheaval, Cosworth abruptly ceased further work and apparently did no more than carry out some investigative studies of what a new type of Cosworth F1 V6 engine should be.

An illustration shown on page 233 tells us more about the abilities of 3D computer software, and a short-lived (but expert and lively …) technical study, than it does about the actual engineering, for I am assured that no actual engineering of HK features actually took place, and no hardware ever existed. Unlike the examples of other Cosworth engines which still exist, this one only every existed as a computer file.

Along with the equally un-finalised BB, VB, QC and VK F1 engine projects, the HK was therefore committed to the 'Might Have Been' archive. As is made clear in this chapter, the economic facts of life in the mid-2010s made it unlikely that any further Cosworth F1 engines would be produced. One day, perhaps, there may be more to relate …

Hal Reisiger became Cosworth's CEO in 2013, and, although based in Northampton, has to oversee, and direct, a company with other plants, not only in Cambridge, but also in the USA.

All this was well and good, and preparations were going ahead, until the world's economy wobbled very seriously, the world's financial markets tucked their heads under their wings and hoped for the best – which encouraged Kevin Kalkhoven and his advisors to stop the proposed float.

Wisely, it was therefore decided that if this was not the right time to look for further financial capital for expansion, then it was surely time for experienced heads to sit down, look around them, and decide what could and should be done instead, using the company's avowedly expert and world-beating experience as 'capital' instead.

While this rather unsettling, and worrying, period was going on, Kevin Kalkhoven had already cast around for the very best advice on what should – and could – now be done to revive Cosworth's fortunes. Following the advice of an individual corporate advisor, his quest eventually ended when he approached a Californian-based engineer, Hal Reisiger, who had already enjoyed a stellar career in the engineering companies of North America. After securing a prestigious management qualification at the UCLA of Los Angeles, California, he had started his business career as an applications engineer, and progressed upwards. His first contact with UK business came in 1983, and, after stints as CEO of companies in the USA, he was approached by Kevin.

"I was approached in 2009," he told the author, "to have a look at Cosworth's financial standing, and comment on possible policies. Now I'm definitely a car fan, and have rebuilt some 1960s and 1970s musclecars, and my recognition and respect for the Cosworth brands was already obvious, but at first I told them that they were approaching the wrong guy.

"They shrugged that off, and I took the assignment. I think they recognised that motorsport was becoming very challenging. When I looked at the economics of F1, an independent engine manufacturer like Cosworth now found it difficult to compete. It was, in my humble opinion, even then, that I thought that Cosworth couldn't retain its existing DNA and survive, so suggested that the company should develop the motorsport-inspired innovation, for which it was famous, into what I call the field of limited-production, high-end, road cars."

Among his several and various recommendations was that the company should reluctantly draw a line under its Formula 1 activities – and, since then, more than one prominent Cosworth personality has confirmed that the company could not get back into this highly-expensive 'sport' [for 'sport,' read 'marketing exercise': AAGR] until and unless a new client arrived with a colossal financial guarantee, and a confirmed place for the product to be used.

Clearly, Reisiger's incisive report was well-received by his North American clients, for it was not long before he joined the company as President of the group's North American companies, his main

COSWORTH – NO FUTURE IN FORMULA 1, OR INDYCAR RACING?

WHEN questioned in 2016, everyone at Cosworth agreed that they would love to see the company once again supplying engines to F1 teams – but that for them it simply was no longer practical.

As Chairman Kevin Kalkhoven commented:

"Frankly, as you can see from the decline in TV audience figures, Formula 1 is no big deal in many parts of the world. When you look at major markets around the world – Japan, China, the United States and so on – Formula 1 is not the ultimate sport any more.

"Emotionally, of course, I would love to have an engine in Formula 1 – I would love to have an engine at Le Mans too (as we did in 2015) – but motor racing is now a wealth destruction machine …"

CEO Hal Reisiger was equally persuasive, and analytical on the same subject:

"We have often made it clear that we would love to be in Indycar again, Chevrolet and Honda would like us to be in Indycar too, because they would lose less money if we were there. They lose money on every Indycar engine they sell. But we are not an OEM – and we are not willing to fund these things from a Marketing Budget.

"We were recently invited to bid on a Formula 1 'second engine' project – you will recall that there was this alternative engine idea – but we 'No Bidded' and the whole idea apparently flopped. Bernie [Ecclestone] had not specified much. He had provided an engine specification, and asked us to provide a quote. Depending on the type of engine involved, there would be engine development costs which would be in tens of millions of pounds, but that was only the design and development. Then we would have to manufacture, to support them at the tracks, and would also have to have continuing sustained engineering …

"If we had bid, and won, this deal, we would certainly have had to get rid of some existing part of our current business, and I would have had to go to Kevin and Jerry to ask for a lot more capital.

"As with our interest in Indycar racing, although it would foster innovation within the company, of course it mustn't lose money. Certainly it would have to cover itself – and I think we are now past the point where we can accept otherwise …"

Miracles, however, do sometimes happen – but it would need a major, and financially very generous client – to walk in through the doors to persuade this totally practical management to change its mind.

recommendations for the future were accepted, and he became Chief Executive Officer of the entire operation in October 2013.

By this time Cosworth had changed its entire operating 'balance,' one which was gradually to move it from being a motor racing concern with other interests and various 'maybe' projects in hand, to one which had identified its strengths, and would aim to build on them in the future.

Once again, to quote a privileged insider:

"Rather than continuing to look at the possibility of expanding eight or nine diverse little business units, with a smaller-than-expected availability of investment, we would need to 'pick a winner' here and there. As you might expect, the world saw Cosworth as a business with at least half a century of expertise, at brand improvement of things with wheels on them. On the other hand, the same contacts politely suggested that this did not give Cosworth the right to get involved with an unlimited number of things that fly, things that float, and things that go 'Bang!'"

One of the first moves was to push hard at the expansion of the company's electronics activities, where an already well-deserved reputation for making what the layman might call 'data acquisition' could be in great demand. Smart moves, all backed by the company's illustrious reputation in the North American continent, meant that suitable road car units were soon adopted by General Motors, for production cars like the Corvette, the Cadillac CTS-V and the Camaro. Other contracts, some still confidential, were secured, and it was not long before the hitherto unheralded operation in Cambridge became even better known, as did the work being done, in parallel, in Cosworth's Indianapolis-based operation in the USA.

"We were not, and still are not, a large company," Hal Reisiger commented, "but these OEM contracts are for four- to six-year model cycles. By some standards, these would not be considered as mass production cars, but in our chosen market segment, which is the limited-production performance road car, people buy them to enjoy driving."

Although Kevin Kalkhoven, as Chairman, was not always on the premises – either in the UK, or in the USA – his aim was to miss nothing, and to be ever-present when big projects and decisions were brewing. As an entrepreneur with a multitude of interests, he reckoned to spend about a third of his time on Cosworth affairs, but (using Silicon-valley slang)

"A-Players hire A-Players, which is what I did with Hal. We are a team, we talk almost every day, whether it's about money, whether it's about the new facilities, there's always something going on …"

Following the motor industry's recovery, worldwide, from the financial turbulence of 2008, Cosworth found that the non-motor-racing opportunities open to it were even more substantial than had been hoped. Within months, it seemed, the company began to look again at the need to return to high-tech, limited-volume, manufacture of engines – not just working on other companies' products, but manufacturing them, in toto, on their behalf.

This was the time at which the original Ben Rood wisdom ["Any fool can make two, any fool with a lot of money can make a million – it's making the hundreds and small thousands that is difficult, and Cosworth is good at that …"] became relevant once again. Cosworth concluded – rightly, triumphantly rightly as it transpired – that it should return to high-tech, limited-volume, manufacture, originally of machined cylinder head and cylinder block assemblies but eventually (if contracts could be gained) to undertake high-tech complete engine manufacture once again.

As Kevin Kalkhoven then commented, Cosworth was seen as an increasingly 'International' business, rather than merely a marvellous little Northampton-based operation, and both he and Hal Reisiger as determined to make that even more obvious in the future. Starting in 2013, two strategic manufacturing programmes were initiated – one to expand and modernise the premises in Northampton, the other to set up a modern facility (almost a twin of what was to be developed in the UK) in Michigan, USA.

First of all, at Cosworth's Northampton HQ, work began on the biggest expansion and upheaval of premises which had been tackled for decades. Construction work on the 38,000ft^2 building – one soon to become known as the AMC (Advanced Manufacturing Centre) – started in the winter of 2013/2014, and was ready to be opened, formally, by the Prime Minister, David Cameron, in February 2015. Although names were not named at the time, it was claimed that over £75 million of new business had already been secured to keep it busy – and that more, much more, was in the offing.

Inside the walls was what looked like a vast, but single multi-function computer-controlled machine tool, but this was one which could undertake a multitude of tasks, and was capable of taking in raw

In the mid-2010s, the latest addition to Cosworth's business at Northampton was the new AMC block, where a multi-million machine tool complex can look after a series of different machining operations on cylinder heads, blocks, other castings and forgings, both for its own purposes, and for (usually unrevealed) other prestige customers.

light-alloy castings at one end, delivering completely machined, ready-to-assemble components at the other, and could rapidly be reprogrammed to work on cylinder heads, cylinder blocks, sump pans, and engine front covers.

More than 70 new jobs were advertised for this new £22 million investment in 2015/2016 and work began on major contracts for two prestigious concerns (both of whom were introducing new high-performance models). Those of us who observed the new AMC, and the work-in-process, from a raised walkway in 2016 asked politely who those contractors were, and were equally politely told that this was classified information for the time being. Later in the year, it became public knowledge that one of those clients was Honda-USA, which was ramping up production of a new-generation Acura (the North American name for Honda), but the identity of the other customer was still known only to a mere handful of insiders.

In parallel to this, the company's growing prestige reputation for designing, developing and manufacturing high-performance power trains, and for the closely related production of electronic data acquisition devices encouraged a move to build new premises in North America.

To quote Kevin Kalkhoven: "We have made a decision to go into the United States, a decision to start manufacturing over there, because of our experience with engine design, and our subsequent manufacturing of them. One of the largest companies in the world is developing a new engine for a new car – in fact for a whole range of cars – and asked us if we want to be involved in the manufacture of it? It's a good start to get this company on board: between the electronics and the hardware side, we are looking at a lot of business."

Officially announced in May 2016, Cosworth chose to develop its new USA premises in Shelby Township, in Michigan, which is about 35 miles due north of the manufacturing centre of this city. At first the claim was that 'only' $30 million was to be invested, and that there would be a minimum of 50 new jobs, but this was thought to be only the beginning.

Hal Reisiger, Cosworth's much-travelled CEO, was quite clear about the future:

"What's happening now is that we have facilities selected in Michigan, whether it is the data acquisition kit we already supply to GM, which is contracted to at least 2023 on an exclusive basis, or the power train programmes on which we are currently contracturally engaged. There are also a couple of large programmes

that we are bidding on, so that the new Michigan headquarters are vitally important."

These mid-2010s manufacturing developments – and the suggestion that an AMC facility could also be set up in other parts of the world in the foreseeable future – virtually laid to rest the snide rumours some ill-informed observers made about the company, that it was not busy enough, and would eventually have to seek a takeover rescue. Quite the opposite, in fact, for at that time top management was even admitting that "it was looking very full." To quote Hal Reisiger:

"I think that being independent allows us to work with all the OEMs, for being owned by any single automotive OEM would close other doors to us. We now see ourselves offering consultancy at all levels, and seeing it all the way through to manufacture. That makes complete sense. What I have tried to do from the strategy and capability aspect is to ensure that we can consult, prove a concept, prototype, set up engine pieces manufacture – and now we are adding engine assembly. We are quite busy at Northampton, at the moment, but there is square footage available – you'll see us using it soon."

Cosworth's offices in Northampton have famous race-engine types on display stands in strategic positions, and the meeting rooms are decorated with images of high-performance engines – which rather conflicted with the company's present and future policy regarding motor racing. Was it likely, one wondered, that there was likely to be less and less motorsport activity in future years. Reisiger retorted that he simply would not allow that to happen, for it was, and still is, an important part of the brands, and of the DNA:

As far as LMP1 and F1 are concerned, Chairman Kevin Kalkhoven reacted sturdily to that inference:

"Hang on, no. Let's be clear, this company is expanding, not contracting, for we are supplying engines, electronics and expertise to companies all over the world. We may not have the lustre that goes with being in Formula 1, but I'd rather have the existing hard economics and the hard projects which companies are now giving us …"

In the midst of all this discussion of Cosworth's present and near-future expansion strategy, it would be easy to forget what other projects had more recently been revealed (and there were others, the like of which will one day raise collective eyebrows at their scope and reach, which are still on the 'Wow,' or top-secret list).

There was the much-publicised (but not originally

publicised by Cosworth) project to resurrect the TVR sports car brand, where the engine was to be a Cosworth-rework of the latest USA-based Ford Mustang V8 (once begun, Cosworth's original efforts with this engine were apparently so outstanding that when TVR was informed it asked if the tune could be toned down a bit ...).

Then there was the special twin-turbo 3-litre 60-degree V6 power unit – the NV in Cosworth-speak – which was especially designed for Nissan (in great secrecy) to use in its futuristic GT-R LM race car, and was intended to be an ultimate-specification LMP1 hybrid machine which should have been competitive against Porsche, Toyota and Audi, at Le Mans in 2015. The engine was fine – with approximately 500bhp, allied to a hybrid power train with which Cosworth was not involved – but its parentage was kept secret until after the event, when the car itself proved to be totally uncompetitive. The fact that it put most of its power down through the front wheels (there was a four-wheel-drive system too ...) didn't help, but once the front tyres were gripping, the NV's power and torque delivery proved to be remarkably effective. It was just that the wait for traction to be assured was unacceptable ...

These, of course, were examples, but by no means the full story, of what had been achieved in the recent past. As the company then moved closer to a celebration of the 50th anniversary of the birth of the now-legendary DFV F1 engine, it was clear that it had changed completely in that time. Hal Reisiger, however, emphasised that there were elements of the company's 'DNA' which would never disappear:

"One benefit to our clientele, of working with Cosworth, is our speed to market. We can go from engine concept to engine running on the dyno in 11 to 12 months. Few OEMs are that nimble, nor can they move that fast.

"I think that one reason for this is that we still have a motorsport culture, which says 'speed' – speed to market, speed to the track, speed on the track, speed of innovation. The second element – and I think this is where the value stream really is – we can design, prototype, develop, prepare to produce, and manufacture, all under our own roof.

"There are very few in the world who can emulate what we do ... it is our USP [Unique Selling Proposition], which explains the very high-calibre road car development programme we have recently acquired from an Asian OEM. If I had a two-minute 'after dinner' sales sentence, it would be: 'We aim to complete our

UK centre of excellence programme by adding engine assembly, so that our value stream – for both power train and electronics – can go all the way from design to assembled product.' We will then replicate that UK centre of excellence to the USA, and then to Asia."

Until now, though, Cosworth's in-built failing has always been a reluctance to boast about what it was doing, and what was going on in the business. Confidentiality, of course, counts for a lot in the way it does business, but Kevin Kalkhoven admitted that he would like to see changes made:

"We already have OEM contracts which now go out until 2025, but there are still people who don't appreciate how much we have changed the Cosworth business in recent years. Maybe that's my fault, for I have frequently argued with Hal and other members of the management that what is going on in this company is as much of a secret as a covert operation inside MI6! There is still this reticence, this British reticence, of not talking about how good we are ..."

All this, though, might be due to change in the near future, but in true Cosworth style, the news will only be revealed after a project has gone public, not beforehand when it falls into the 'delicious rumours' category. The Cosworth story is by no means yet complete.

One of Cosworth's most prestigious contracts of the 2010s was to supply completely machined cylinder blocks and heads for the new-generation Honda NSX (badged Acura NSX in the USA).

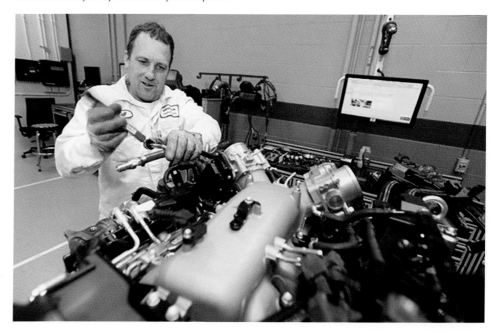

Buried under all the complex installation is the engine of the new-generation Honda (Acura) NSX supercar, with cylinder blocks and heads courtesy of the latest Cosworth AMC transfer machine in Northampton.

APPENDIX 1: COSWORTH ENGINES FROM THE VERY BEGINNING

Although this Appendix is based on that originally provided by Cosworth Engineering Ltd, it is much more than a bald list of types and dates. However, some engine projects never progressed beyond the design concept stage, and have not been listed.

On this occasion, in many instances, I have tried to collect the various engines into groups, and to indicate the chronology and relation of one engine to the other. A handful of company projects remain secret (especially those still being developed for modern clients).

Wherever possible, authentic peak power ratings are quoted – though in later years in F1 this information was rarely revealed.

MODIFIED FORD 105E OHV, AND LOTUS-FORD 2OHC ENGINE FAMILY

Year	Type	Size (cc)	Bhp	Comment
1959	Mk I	997	–	Purely experimental, and never put on sale. The original Cosworth-Ford, on which Keith's radically new ideas of camshaft design were developed. The first Cosworth production engine, designed specifically for Formula Junior. This was the first Cosworth engine to start winning races, and it also established the Lotus-Ford-Cosworth connection.
1960	Mk II	997	75	The first Cosworth production engine, designed specifically for Formula Junior. This was the first Cosworth engine to start winning races, and it also established the Lotus-Ford-Cosworth connection.
1960	Mk III	997	85/90	A developed version of the Mk II, with a different (A3 instead of A2) camshaft profile, a stronger bottom end, and with optional dry sump lubrication.
1961	Mk IV	1098	90/95	A bored-out version of the Mk III, for use in Formula Junior cars.
1962	Mk V	1340	80	The first-ever Cosworth engine for a road car, a lightly-modified (109E) Ford Classic unit for use in the Lotus Seven of the period. Three-bearing camshaft retained.
1962	Mk VI	1340	105	The most powerful Cosworth engine so far, a racing version of the Mk V. Very few made.
1962	Mk VII	1475	120	A yet more powerful unit, a bored-out version of the Mk VI, to take it nearer to the 1.5-litre class limit for sports cars. Still a 3-main-bearing engine.
1963	Mk VIII	1498	90	Like the Mk V, a simply-specified engine based on the new 5-main-bearing 116E unit, as used in the Ford Cortina. Also for road-car use in the Lotus 7. A large number were built.
1963	Mk IX	1498	125	A racing version of the Mk VIII.
1963	Mk X/TA	1498	–	A one-off experimental development version of the original Lotus-Ford twin-cam engine, with cylinder head designed by Harry Mundy (not by Cosworth), later used bored out to 1558cc for use in road cars such as the Lotus Elan, Plus 2, Europa, Ford Lotus-Cortina and Escort Twin-Cam. Also see Mks XII/XIII/XV and XVI below. (This engine was unveiled by Lotus in 1962 – many thousands were built, but not by Cosworth.)
1963	Mk XI	1098	110	An updated version of the Mk IV Formula Junior engine, the first-ever Cosworth unit to produce 100bhp/litre. Very successful, and sold in large numbers.
1963	Mk XII/TA	1594	140	Racing version of the Lotus-Ford twin-cam engine, enlarged to the 1.6-litre class capacity limit. Dry sump lubrication, but standard rods and crankshaft.

The Lotus-Ford Twin-Cam engine was internally coded as the TA.

COSWORTH – THE SEARCH FOR POWER

1963	Mk XIII/TA	1594	140	Developed version of the Mk XII, this time with steel rods and crankshaft, to allow for (eventually) higher rpm, and higher power outputs.
1963	Mk XIV	1498	100	A developed version of the Mk VIII, for road car use in the Lotus 7.
1963	Mk XV/TA	1594	140	A racing version of the Lotus-Ford (TA) twin-cam engine, this time with a wet sump (as required by some regulations), for use in the Lotus-Cortina. Closely related to the Mk XIII/TA.
1963	Mk XVI/TAI	1498	140	Lotus-Ford twin-cam based (with 81mm cylinder bore), with tune like that of the Mk XIII. Specifically developed for use in Australasian racing of the day, where a 1.5-litre capacity limit applied.
1964	Mk XVII	1098	120	A special development of the Mk XI Formula Junior engine, with specially-modified cylinder heads incorporating downdraught inlet ports. Only a few engines made, due to difficulty (and expense) of brazing inlet passages into modified cast iron Ford cylinder heads.
1965	MAE	997	100	A very successful further development of this Ford-based family, for use in the new 1-litre Formula 3 of the mid-1960s. Formula 3 replaced Formula Junior, with regulations requiring one single-choke carburettor. Many MAEs were sold as kits, rather than as complete engines.

SINGLE-OVERHEAD-CAMSHAFT SCA FAMILY

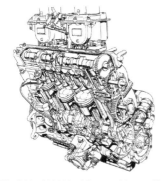

The SCA of 1964 had Cosworth's very first 'own-design' cylinder head, featuring a single-overhead-camshaft layout, in line valves, and the combustion chambers in the top of the pistons.

Year	Type	Size (cc)	Bhp	Comment
1964	SCA	997	115	The first Cosworth engine to use a Cosworth-designed cylinder head, in aluminium alloy, with vertical valves, and a single overhead camshaft. Based on the Ford Cortina-type 116E cylinder block, with five main bearings, and with bowl-in-piston combustion chamber. Designed for the new 1-litre Formula 2 of 1964-1966. Power output eventually pushed up to nearly 140bhp.
1964	SCB	1498	175	A 1.5-litre derivative of the SCA, made only for experimental purposes.
1965	SCC	1098	135	An increased-bore SCA, designed for use in a North American sports car racing Formula. Many SCAs, redundant from F2, were later converted to SCC by new bore, pistons, and other details. The camshaft was chain-driven.

TWIN-CAM/16-VALVE FVA FAMILY

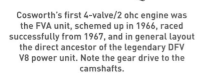

Cosworth's first 4-valve/2 ohc engine was the FVA unit, schemed up in 1966, raced successfully from 1967, and in general layout the direct ancestor of the legendary DFV V8 power unit. Note the gear drive to the camshafts.

Year	Type	Size (cc)	Bhp	Comment
1966	FVA	1598	218	The first Cosworth-designed twin-cam engine to go into production, establishing the successful twin-cam/narrow opposed-valve-angle, four-valves-per-cylinder, pent-roof combustion chamber. Based on the 5-bearing Ford 116E cylinder block, and with gear drive to cams. The dominant engine in the 1.6-litre Formula 2 of 1967-1971, and the direct ancestor of the legendary DFV V8.
1967	FVB	1500	200	A purely experimental version of the FVA, made to speed development, and to examine the problems and possibilities for the DFV V8 before that F1 engine actually ran.
1969	FVC	1790	235	A long-stroke version of the FVA, produced for use in current European 2-litre sports car racing, a series which it won twice. Nevertheless, an 'interim' engine.
1973	FVD	1975	275	An experimental version of the FVA family, using the enlarged bore/stroke dimensions of the BDG of the day.

V8 DFV FAMILY – ALL TYPES

Year	Type	Size (cc)	Bhp	Comment
1967	DFV	2993	405	All previous Cosworth engines had used a proprietary (Ford) block, so this was the first engine to be designed totally by Cosworth. The legendary and enormously successful Formula 1 engine, which won 155 World Championship GPs between 1967 and 1983. A 90 degree V8, with four valves per cylinder, twin overhead camshafts per bank, and fuel-injection. DFV power output eventually pushed up to circa 510/520bhp.
1968	DFW	2491	358	A short-stroke version of the DFV, used by Lotus in Australasian Tasman Series racing. Engines were converted from DFV, later re-converted to DFV spec.
1975	DFX	2645	840	A short-stroke turbocharged version of the DFV, for use in CART/Indy racing in the USA. Limited by regulations to a maximum turbo boost (in USA measure) of 80in of mercury.
(1986			700	Regulations were later changed, and a maximum of 48in of boost pressure was imposed: 700bhp was available. This was still an enormously successful 'Indy' engine.)
1981	DFL	3955	540	Much-enlarged 'endurance' normally-aspirated version of the DFV, developed for use in Group C sports cars, with larger bore and stroke dimensions. Originally intended for Ford's own C100 project. A turbocharged derivative was developed in 1982/1983 (but not raced).
(1981	DFL	3298	490	A short-stroke version of the 3.9-litre DFL was also produced for Group C2 racing.)
1982	DFV short stroke	2993	500	Combining the larger bore of the DFL, with a short stroke crankshaft, to give a higher revving, slightly more powerful, version of the DFV for F1 racing.
1982	DFY	2993	520/530	Further derivation of the short-stroke DFV, with new and narrower-valve included-angle cylinder heads. For use only in F1 racing.
1986	DFV (F3000)	2993	420	Specially developed for F3000 single-seater racing, rev-limited (by regulation) to 9000rpm.
1987	DFZ	3495	560	An enlarged version of the definitive DFV/DFY, for use in F1 racing from 1987, where normally-aspirated engines could be enlarged to 3.5-litres.
1988	DFR	3495	595+	A thoroughly modernised version of the DFZ, for use in Formula 1, with new cylinder heads and four valves per cylinder. Five-valve cylinder heads (initially designed by Yamaha) tested in 1987/1988, but never raced. Used only by Benetton F1 team in 1988, but widely available in 1989. Up to 620bhp finally available.
1988/9	DFS	2645	not quoted	A modernised version of the turbocharged DFX, for CART/Indy racing in the USA, drawing on DFR experience. This time with max boost pressure of 45in. Replaced by the XB in 1991.

This Theo Page cutaway drawing shows all the hidden details of Keith Duckworth's magnificent DFV design. How times change – for when the HB was introduced in 1989, no cutaway drawing, no bore/stroke dimensions, no valve angles, and virtually no technical information was ever made available.

By turbocharging the DFV, and redeveloping every aspect of its design, Cosworth produced the DFX engine for Indy racing in the 1970s. It went on to dominate that branch of the sport for more than a decade.

Although the turbocharged DFX was clearly based on the design of the DFV, it was different in many important features, not only by reduction of the capacity to 2.65 litres, and by turbocharging, but by many unheralded changes to the breathing arrangements, and to the cylinder heads.

COSWORTH – THE SEARCH FOR POWER

Towards the end of its career, the DA series was redeveloped as the DFL (L = Long Distance), for use in long-distance 'Endurance' sports car racing. This studio shot was of the 1982 DFL type. A turbocharged version was also proposed, but not finalised before the programme came to an end.

Produced in a tearing hurry, by Cosworth, as an interim solution to the demand for a 3.5-litre normally-aspirated F1 engine in 1987, the DFZ was a great success of its type, though outgunned by the turbocharged engines then being developed by its rivals.

The 16-valve BDA was launched in 1970, based on a cast iron cylinder block, but from 1972 (this type) it was re-engineered around an aluminium block. BDs were in production until the late 1980s, when the last of the turbocharged RS200s was manufactured.

Right: The original DFV of 1967/1968 was a miracle of compact packaging, and every one of the 3-litre power units produced more than 400bhp.

Far right: The DFY of 1983, complete with new narrow-angle cylinder head, and short-stroke internal dimensions, was the final flowering of the 3-litre F1 engine. Many further evolutions would follow, however.

Right: For 1988, and working under extreme time pressure, Geoff Goddard's tiny team produced the DFR F1 engine, which was the ultimate redesign of the original DFV engine layout.

Far right: The DFS was a redesign of the long-time successful DFX, was used exclusively in Indy car racing, but was only truly competitive in 1988 and 1989.

TWIN-CAM/16-VALVE BDA FAMILY

Year	Type	Size (cc)	Bhp	Comment
1969	BDA	1601	120	Same basic cylinder head breathing layout as four-cylinder FVA, and V8 DFV, but based on taller Ford 'Kent' block, and with toothed-belt drive to twin overhead camshafts. As with other engines, four valves per cylinder.
1970	BDB	1700	200	An engine developed for Ford for use in the Escort RS1600 in rallying (where engine enlargement was allowed). Used an enlarged cylinder bore, different pistons, cam profiles, etc. All but one engine sold in kit form.
1970	BDC	1700	230	A fuel-injected racing version of the BDB (see above), developed with Group 2 saloon car racing in mind, for the Escort RS1600. As with BDB, all but one sold in kit form.
1971	BDD	1600	210	Developed specifically for use in Formula Atlantic single-seater race cars. All but one sold as kits.
1972	BDE	1790	245, later 255	For use in the 2-litre Formula 2, which came into force in 1972 (but not yet close to that class limit). With larger cylinder bore and fuel-injection.
1972	BDF	1927	270	An improved development of the BDE, with larger cylinder bore, and oversize liners brazed into the standard (cast iron) cylinder block. Also for the 2-litre F2, and very successful in 1972 itself.
1973	BDG	1975	275	A further enlarged, and improved, version of the BDF, used in F2 in 1973, but later used by many Ford Escort RS cars in rallying. Originally with a cast iron block, later with an aluminium block.

1973	BDH	1300	190	A 1.3-litre version of the BDA design, using a short-stroke crankshaft, and using the shallower 1.3-litre version of the Ford 'Kent' cylinder block. For Group 2 saloon car or sports car racing. Considered by Ford for use in an Escort RS1300 road car, but the project was cancelled.
1974	BDJ	1098	150	Another ultra-short-stroke version of the BDA design, using a shallow Ford block. For use in American SCCA Formula C single seaters.
1974–	BDL	1425	–	An experimental turbocharging evaluation. Never put on sale.
1975	BDM	1599	225	A further-developed version of the 1.6-litre BDD (Formula Atlantic) engine, with larger valves, and fuel-injection.
1977	BDN	1600	210	A serialised version of the BDD Formula Atlantic engine, for the Canadian FA Series. The series organisers sold all engines and components.
1984	BDP	1975	245	Specially developed by Cosworth's USA subsidiary (from original 1979 1845cc prototype), for use in USA 'Midget' single-seater racing, combining the latest light alloy block/crankcase, the 1975cc size of the BDG, fuel-injection, and the use of methanol fuel.
1983	BDR	1601	120	Closely based on the BDA road car engine, but sold as kits, for building of engines for the Caterham (one-time Lotus) Super Seven sports cars. Also built in 1.7-litre form, in 150bhp and 170bhp tune.
1975	BDS	1975	235	Brazed-block version of BDB rally engine kits, with BDE head. Up to 285bhp on some versions.
1981	BDT	1778	200 (RS1700T) 1803cc 250bhp (RS200)	Turbocharged version of light-alloy block BD engine, evolved by Ford for the Escort RS1700T project. 200 engine kits built by Cosworth, assembled by JQF; same engines redesigned, rebuilt, and slightly enlarged for use in Ford RS200.
1986	BDT-E	2137	530 (finally to 650bhp)	Enlarged, 'evolution' version of BDT engine, developed by Brian Hart Ltd, for use in RS200 'E' models. 25 engines built, and many more parts.
1981	BDU	1975	235	Gasoline-fuelled version of BDP for racing in North America.
1976	BDX	1975	285	1976-type BDGs, supplied as kits to Swindon Racing Engines, for sale.

This final version of the basic BD design – the BDT-E – was a turbocharged engine designed and manufactured by Brian Hart Ltd, for Ford Motor Co Ltd usage. In standard 'road car' form, it was a 2.1-litre unit, but as a rally-cross racer it could be tuned to more than 650bhp.

CHEVROLET VEGA ENGINE FAMILY

Year	Type	Size (cc)	Bhp	Comment
1972	EAA	1995	275	Based on the USA Chevrolet Vega light-alloy cylinder block – the first Cosworth 'stock-block' engine not to be based on a Ford cylinder block: 16-valve cylinder head of similar layout to current BD-series, also with belt-driven twin overhead camshafts. Designed for F2 and Sports Car racing, but only successfully used in Sports Cars. Limited by a lack of cylinder block strength. Later productionised, producing 122bhp, built by Chevrolet, for use in the Chevrolet Cosworth Vega of mid-1970s.

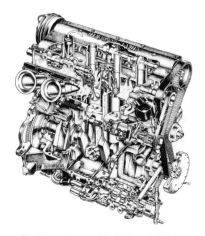

The Cosworth-modified Chevrolet Vega – coded EAA – was originally developed with 2-litre racing sports car use in mind, but was eventually taken up by GM of the USA, who turned it into a limited production power unit.

Specifically designed by Cosworth as a racing-sports car engine, the Ford 'Essex'-based GA was an amazingly powerful 3.4-litre power unit. The Ford road-car engine had been an overhead-valve, 136bhp 3.0-litre V6 power unit, but Cosworth's magic, allied to the use of twin-cam cylinder heads, liberated 440bhp. Used in the 'works' Capri RS3100s of 1974 and 1975, it was a phenomenally successful unit.

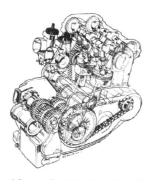

A real Cosworth rarity – the twin-cylinder Type JA motorcycle engine, designed personally by Keith Duckworth, for Norton to use in racing, and also in a proposed road machine. Norton's recurrent financial problems killed it off before it could conclusively prove itself.

Cosworth carried out redesign and development work for GM on a 16-valve twin-cam engine, eventually producing the successful 2.4-litre KA-Series Opel Ascona/Manta unit of the early 1980s. This was a 'road car' engine, with inlet passages swept up and over the cam cover.

FORD-UK 'ESSEX' V6 RACING ENGINE

Year	Type	Size (cc)	Bhp	Comment
1973	GAA	3412	440	Based on the existing Ford Capri/Granada V6 block, but with light-alloy 4-valve, twin-cam cylinder heads, and cogged belt drive to the camshafts. The original engine was a 2994cc unit: the GA was a bored out version. For use in Group 2 touring car racing in the Ford Capri 3100 from 1974, and later used in F5000 single seaters. 100 kits produced, and sold through Ford Motorsport.

JA-TYPE TWIN-CYLINDER MOTORCYCLE ENGINE

Year	Type	Size (cc)	Bhp	Comment
1974	JAA	750	65	A parallel-twin water-cooled motorcycle engine, with twin balancer shafts, designed for Dennis Poore of Norton Villiers. Effectively using the 'top end' of the DFV engine, with two camshafts and eight valves. For projected use in a production motorcycle. Norton Villiers struck financial trouble, and the project was cancelled after about 30 engine/transmission units were built.
1975	JAB	750	95/110	A racing version of the JAA, at first with carburettors, later with fuel-injection.

KA-TYPE OPEL ASCONA 400/MANTA 400 ENGINE

Year	Type	Size (cc)	Bhp	Comment
1978	KAA	2410	240	Based on the existing Opel diesel cylinder block, and an existing Opel design, this 16-valve, twin-cam unit was developed for the Group 4 Opel Ascona 400 'homologation special.' In road-car tune, with injection, it produced 140bhp, but for rallying, twin dual-choke Weber carbs were used, and 240hp was available. From 1982 it was also used in the Manta 400 which replaced the Ascona 400, and up to 275bhp was finally available.

VW FORMULA SUPERVEE ENGINE

Year	Type	Size (cc)	Bhp	Comment
1979	OAA	1600	170	This design was based on the single overhead camshaft four-cylinder VW Golf design, and was developed purely for the one-engine Formula Supervee racing formula.

The OA-Series Formula Super Vee engine for VW, which produced 170bhp, was partially successful, but was soon sidelined in favour of more important projects.

OVERHEAD-CAM CHEVROLET V8 CONVERSION

Year	Type	Size (cc)	Bhp	Comment
1983	AB	–	Not quoted	Early in the 1980s, with racing in North America in mind, Cosworth completed the redesign and conversion of the 'Big Block' Chevrolet V8 engine, using that company's cylinder block, but providing single-overhead-camshaft cylinder heads. This block, which had already been raced very successfully over many years in overhead-valve 'pushrod' form, could have been built in sizes up to 7.5 litres, and would have been immensely powerful. By the time the engine was being tested, more important priorities had intervened at Cosworth, and the engine was never put into production.

MERCEDES-BENZ 16-VALVE ENGINE

Year	Type	Size (cc)	Bhp	Comment
1984	WAA	2297	187	Like several Ford engines, a twin-overhead camshaft conversion of an existing engine, this time for Mercedes-Benz on the M102 four-cylinder unit. Originally conceived (in 1981) as a competition engine, then redeveloped for use in a road car, the 190E 2.3-16 model. This was Cosworth's largest-quantity project to that point, with completely assembled heads supplied to West Germany at the rate of 5000+ units per year.
1988	'WAB'	2498	195	The 16-valve Mercedes engine was enlarged to 2.5-litres for the start-up of 1989 Model-Year production.
1989	WAC	2463	201/330	An 'Evolution' short-stroke version of the 'WAB' engine, for Group A racing use in 2.5-16 model in German touring car racing.
1990	WAC	2463	235/330	

The Mercedes-Benz 190E 2.3 16 saloon of the 1980s was powered by the WA engine. Cosworth built several thousand cylinder head assemblies for this engine before Mercedes-Benz took over manufacture themselves.

THE FORD SIERRA ROAD-CAR ENGINE

Year	Type	Size (cc)	Bhp	Comment
1983	YAA	1993	Undisclosed	Originally a privately-financed Cosworth project, with 16-valve, twin-overhead-cam, cogged-belt camshaft drive, on a cast iron Ford T88/'Pinto' block. Intended to be normally-aspirated, for sale to small specialist manufacturers. Three engines built.
1990	YAC	1993	Undisclosed	(Original use of this code, for prototypes in 1983/1984). For 1990, a normally-aspirated version of the YBG (see below).
1984	YBA	1993	200	Prototype version of later YBB production engine. Ten engines built.
1985	YBB	1993	204	The turbocharged version of YAA, as commissioned by Ford for use in the Sierra RS Cosworth road car 'homologation special.' The first-ever Cosworth road car engine to be totally built at the new Wellingborough factory. More than 5000 engines were made in 1986 so that Group A/Group N homologation of the Sierra could be achieved for 1987. From 1988, used in the Sierra (Sapphire) RS Cosworth four-door saloon.
1986	YBC	1993	280/300	Original Group A Rally engine, based on the YBB, gradually with more power extracted.
1987	YBD	1993	225	The uprated 'Evolution' version of the YBB, used in the 500-off Sierra RS500 Cosworth hatchback model. Compared to the YBB, there was a larger turbocharger, eight instead of four fuel injectors, and the car itself used an enlarged intercooler and inlet passages. Capable of more than 500/550bhp in racing tune, making the Sierra the dominant Group A race car of the late 1980s (see YBF, below).
1987	YBE	1993	–	Engine for Ford Industrial Power Products to sell, identified by black 'non-Cosworth' cam covers. Built to purchasers' specification, but only fitted in Ford-approved installations. The Panther Solo used a YBE derivative.

The YB-Series (or 'Sierra' engine as it was always known at Cosworth) was commercially the most successful engine ever produced by Cosworth, with a 16-valve/twin-cam head and turbocharging, all on the basis of the Ford T88 ('Pinto') cylinder block.

1987	YBF	1993	400+ -550bhp	Race version of YBD 'Evolution' engine, with 400+bhp nominal, though much more regularly obtained.
1989	YBG	1993	207	Later version of YBB, certified for 83US emissions, and capable of running on 95 octane unleaded fuel.
1989	YBJ	1993	207	Similar to YBG, this time certified for 15.04 emissions, and 95 octane unleaded fuel.
1990	YBM	1993	300+	Motorsport derivative of the YB series. Rally use for Escort RS Cosworth, etc.
1992	YBT	1993	227	Escort RS Cosworth road-car engine, with T35 turbocharger, Weber-Marelli engine management and 'blue top' cam covers.
1994	YBP	1993	227	For revised Escort RS Cosworth road car, with T25 turbocharger, Ford EEC IV engine management, and reshaped 'silver top' cam covers.
1992	YBV	2295	Not disclosed	A 2.3-litre version of the YBM, for use with Methanol fuel, sold by Cos Inc in the USA.

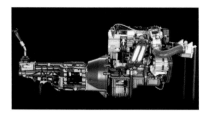

This glossy display unit shows how the YB engine of the Sierra Cosworth was initially integrated with the Borg Warner five-speed transmission.

Late-model Escort RS Cosworths used the YBP derivative of the basic YB series, complete with a T25 turbocharger, Ford EEC IV engine management, and reshaped 'silver-top' camshaft covers.

BUICK-OLDSMOBILE-PONTIAC V6 POWER UNIT

Year	Type	Size (cc)	Bhp	Comment
1987	EB	3340	Not quoted	A commission from GM-USA (Buick-Oldsmobile-Pontiac division) to produce a 24-valve four-cam road-car version of an existing 3.3-litre V6 engine which had originated with Chevrolet. This engine had a 90-degree vee, and was to have been compatible with front engine/rear drive, or transverse-mounting/front engine front-wheel-drive models. This was taken all the way to the 'oven-ready' and prototype-tested stage at Cosworth, and assessed by GM, but after a bout of corporate in-fighting within GM, was cancelled.

THE TURBOCHARGED BD DERIVATIVE, FOR F1 USE IN THE 1980S

Year	Type	Size (cc)	Bhp	Comment
1984	BA	1.5-litre	Not disclosed	A project to produce a 750bhp+ evolution of the BDA, with complex turbocharging + supercharging installation. One prototype engine was built and tested, but the project was then abandoned.

THE TURBOCHARGED V6 FORD F1 ENGINE

Year	Type	Size (cc)	Bhp	Comment
1986	GBA	1497	750 (later 1000+)	A 120-degree V6 twin turbocharger engine developed for Ford, for use in F1 racing in 1986 and 1987. 1000bhp available, with 'rocket fuel,' for Benetton, in 1987.

The Buick-Oldsmobile-Pontiac EB V6 of 1987 was intended for road car use in GM-USA models, but the project was cancelled at the prototype stage.

Cosworth's most powerful engine – so far, and still not surpassed – was the 120-degree V6 1.5-litre twin turbo Type GB F1 engine, used by Benetton-Ford in 1986 and 1987. In final form, it produced more than 1000bhp in race (as opposed to short-life) tune.

GM-PONTIAC ENGINE

Year	Type	Size (cc)	Bhp	Comment
1987	DBA	3000	370	Typical Cosworth twin-cam 16-valve conversion for GM (Pontiac division) Super Duty four-cylinder engine, for use in the USA. Fuel injected, and normally-aspirated, with chain drive to the camshafts. To be sold in kit form.

VAUXHALL-OPEL 2-LITRE 16-VALVE ENGINE

Year	Type	Size (cc)	Bhp	Comment
1987	KBA	1998	156	16-valve twin-cam conversion of Vauxhall-Opel 'Family 2' 2-litre engine, later fitted to GM Astra, Kadett, Vectra, Cavalier models. Cylinder head casting and complete head assembly by Cosworth at Worcester/Wellingborough at first.

NORMALLY-ASPIRATED FORD F1 ENGINE

Year	Type	Size (cc)	Bhp	Comment
1989	HB	3500	650+	An all-new 75-degree V8 Formula 1 engine, originally for Ford for use in the Benetton cars in 1989 and beyond. Though equipped with twin cams per bank, and four valves per cylinder, no carry-over parts from the famous DFV series. First win in Japanese GP, October 1989, two more victories by 13,000rpm Series IV types in 1990. Peak power then approached 680bhp. Used in the successful Jaguar racing sports cars of 1991 (and known as the HBC), its development continued. At least 700bhp was available for Benetton in 1992: Benetton and McLaren both used 700bhp-plus 'air-valve' Series VII and Series VIII types in 1993, when there were six GP victories. By this time the engines revved to 13,500rpm. When the Zetec-R V8 arrived, the HB then became available as a 'customer' engine for other F1 teams: four F1 teams used HBs throughout 1994, and the 1995 F1 3-litre 'customer' engine was effectively a further redesign.

COSWORTH MBA V6 PROJECT ENGINE

Year	Type	Size (cc)	Bhp	Comment
1991	MBA	2497	226	The MBA design was a concept engine, to demonstrate and evaluate many novel features. Although it appeared to be a conventional four-valves/cylinder, twin-camshafts-per-bank road-car unit, there were many advanced details. Cosworth also revealed that this could be the basis of a modular range, which may explain the 90-degree vee angle and the very compact dimensions. A possible V12 was mentioned, and even three-cylinder derivatives would have been possible. When revealed in 1991, development was at a very early stage, and although engines were tested (and demonstrated) in a four-wheel-drive Audi 80 quattro (where it fitted the engine bay very easily), the project did not find a customer, though many features may be used in later Cosworth designs. Innovative design details included the use of a contra-rotating balance shaft which doubled as an oil separator, and two throttles per cylinder, the second being inside the head casting itself.

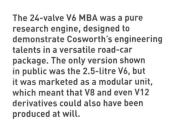

The 24-valve V6 MBA was a pure research engine, designed to demonstrate Cosworth's engineering talents in a versatile road-car package. The only version shown in public was the 2.5-litre V6, but it was marketed as a modular unit, which meant that V8 and even V12 derivatives could also have been produced at will.

Cosworth produced a high-performance 16-valve engine for GM-USA, labelled 'Pontiac Super Duty 16-valve,' but known internally as DBA.

The Cosworth KB engine was produced on the basis of GM-Europe's Family 2 2-litre cylinder block, and was later fitted to whole range of Opel and Vauxhall passenger cars.

New for 1989 was the normally-aspirated 3.5-litre V8 engine, the HB, which had a 75-degree cylinder bank angle. It was lighter and more compact that the ageing DFV/DFR/DFZ series. Originally it produced at least 650bhp, but by the time the last was built in 1994, it had been further improved to produce approximately 750bhp.

The FB was the productionised version of a 24-valve 4-cam V6 originally conceived by Brian Hart Ltd. Based on the long-established Ford-Cologne V6 block and bottom end, it went into the Ford Scorpio 24V range in 1992.

Designed at the same time as the 24-valve FB, a 12-valve single-overhead-camshaft version was also developed. Years later, in the 1990s, having been redesigned by Ford, it found use as a 208bhp/4.0-litre V6 to power the Ford-USA Explorer 4x4, and was manufactured at Ford-Cologne.

FORD SCORPIO 24-VALVE ENGINE

Year	Type	Size (cc)	Bhp	Comment
1991	FBA	2935	195	Having absorbed Brian Hart Ltd in 1987, Cosworth acquired the rights to a conversion on the Ford-Cologne 60-degree V6 road-car engine, to a twin-cam 24-valve unit with new cylinder heads. This became a full Cosworth/Ford mainstream engineering programme, and was installed in the Scorpio 24V model.
1992	FBE	2935	300	
1994	FBC	2935	210	

Manufactured at Wellingborough, the original FBA was a refined and flexible road-car unit, with 'only' 195bhp. Fitted with chain drive to the camshafts, with Ford EECIV engine management, and designed to pass every standard Ford test, this engine was always mated to automatic transmission.

Thus equipped, the Scorpio was much more refined than before, and Cosworth also offered a race-tuned version (the FBE), producing a reliable 300bhp. For the revised 1995-model Scorpio, Cosworth and Ford then produced the 210bhp FBC, and development continued.

In 1994, Cosworth also took over manufacture of the existing overhead-valve Ford-Cologne V6 engine. Later they also developed a single-overhead-camshaft-per-bank version of this V6 engine for Ford, coded JB. Much-changed by Ford, a 208bhp/3996cc derivative was fitted to Ford-USA Explorers from late 1996. Engine manufacture of that type was at Ford-Germany, in Cologne.

FORD-COSWORTH XB TURBOCHARGED INDY CAR ENGINE

Year	Type	Size (cc)	Bhp	Comment
1991	XB	2650	750-800	Although it had resembled the HB F1 engine of the period in some ways, the XB was a totally new turbocharged V8 engine with different cylinder block, head and other major castings and forgings. It was specifically designed for Indycar racing, where there was a strict limit on boost pressure, and where the engines were fuelled by an alcohol-based blend.

Like the HB, it had four-valves per cylinder and twin-camshaft cylinder heads. Virtually no other information was ever issued, with rebuilds always carried out by Cosworth itself, either at Northampton (for Newman-Haas) or at Cosworth's USA base at Torrance, California.

First used in 1992, the XB won six of that year's 16 races (Michael Andretti's Newman-Haas Lola was second in the Championship), while in 1993 it powered Nigel Mansell's Newman-Haas Lolas to his sensational 'rookie' victory in the Indycar Championship, there being six race victories in all. More victories were gained in 1994 and 1995, before the new XD engine replaced it.

Designed to replace the long-running DFX/DFS CART/Indycar engine, the 2.65-litre XB was launched in 1991. Although there were a few similarities to the HB F1 engine of the period, the XB was totally different in detail. Instantly competitive, it provided race-winning power in the next few seasons, most noticeably for Nigel Mansell to become Indycar Champion in 1993.

FORD V12 F1 RACE ENGINE

Year	Type	Size (cc)	Bhp	Comment
1991/ 1992	VB	3500	Not quoted	Intending to replace the successful HB F1 engine in the Benetton, Ford asked Cosworth to design a 3.5-litre 70-degree V12 unit. Extensively bench tested, but never installed in a car, the V12 eventually produced more power than the HB, which was an ever-improving V8 during this period.
				Cosworth persevered with a modified V12 design, the final version being slightly longer and less cramped in its detailing than the original, but because the architecture of the Benetton changed so much to meet changing regulations, the VB was abandoned.
				In the meantime, the Series VI/Series VII/Series VIII HB V8s were so effective that no VB V12 was ever seen in public, or installed in an F1 car, before cancellation.
				In its place, Cosworth therefore developed the very successful Zetec-R V8 F1 unit (coded EC), which took over at Benetton in 1994.

COSWORTH F3000 V8 RACE ENGINE

Year	Type	Size (cc)	Bhp	Comment
1993	AC	3000	Not officially quoted (approx 450bhp)	To follow the famous DFV engine, the legendary ex-F1 unit which was still successful in much-modified form in F3000 in the early 1990s, the AC was an all-new purpose-built 3-litre V8 for this formula.
				Except that this was a 90-degree V8 engine with twin-cam cylinder heads and four valves per cylinder, limited by regulation to 9000rpm, very little was ever revealed about its character – not even the horsepower developed! Cosworth's customers were expected to accept that it would be competitive – and it was!
				The AC dominated F3000 from 1993 to 1995, providing winning power for almost every race, usually in Reynard chassis. Olivier Panis won the International series in 1993, Jules Boullion in 1994 and Vincenzo Sospiri in 1995. A change of F3000 regulations then outlawed the super-successful AC for 1996 and beyond.

FORD ZETEC-R V8 F1 RACE ENGINE

Year	Type	Size (cc)	Bhp	Comment
1994	Zetec-R (originally coded EC)	3500	750+ (est'd by author)	Once the F1 VB V12 engine programme was abandoned, Cosworth designed yet another compact, 75-degree, four-valve engine for Ford. The new Zetec-R engine (so named for publicity purposes, to align with Ford's latest road-car engines, though its original Cosworth project code was EC) took over from the HB at Benetton in 1994. Though with a similar V8 layout to the HBs, the Zetec-R was different in every detail. Compared with the HB, it was longer, with larger cylinder bores and shorter strokes, and more sophisticated detailing. *(Continued on next page)*

The 3.5-litre VB V12 race engine was developed in 1991 and 1992 as an F1 engine for Benetton to use as a successor to its HB power unit. Although development was protracted, and competitive power was achieved, the VB was never fitted to a car, and the programme was abandoned in favour of the new EC unit of 1994.

The AC was a 90-degree 3-litre race engine, especially designed for use in European F3000 racing, to take over from the venerable (rev-limited) DFV. Introduced in 1993, it immediately became the most successful power unit in that category.

No sooner had work on the VB V12 F1 project been suspended, than work began on a brand-new F1 V8, which was internally coded as EC, though known in public as the Zetec-R V8. For Benetton, it was phenomenally successful in its only season as a 3.5-litre engine, when Michael Schumacher became World Champion in 1994 ...

... though it was not as successful in 1995, when it had to be reduced in capacity to 3.0-litres to meet new F1 regulations. Sauber used the engine in 1995 only, and customer supplies were then made available for 1996.

Last used in F1 in 1997, the ED was effectively the final, much-modified and improved evolution of the long-running HB, which has first raced in 1989, but reduced to 3.0-litres to meet new regulations. Cosworth has never issued authentic power figures for this, but the author estimates that EDs could ultimately produce up to 650bhp.

The Ford-USA based race engine for Ford Mondeos to be used in the Super Touring Category in the mid and late 1990s produced more than 300bhp in strictly rev-limited (to 8500rpm ...) 2-litre form. Cosworth listed this as a QG, though Ford publicity images were always captioned 'Zetec V6-R.'

Year	Type	Size (cc)	Bhp	Comment
1995		3000	670 (est'd by author)	Particularly when driven by Michael Schumacher, Zetec-R powered Benetton B194s were incredibly successful in 1994, winning the majority of F1 races. On-screen TV telemetry relayed from Benetton confirmed that the engines revved to 14,500rpm, and rumours of 750bhp and more (at least 214bhp/litre) were not denied, before FIA rule changes reduced top-end outputs during the season. A new 3-litre F1 formula was abruptly imposed for 1995. A total internal redesign of the Zetec-R V8 (this engine was then coded ECA) was then used as Ford's 'works' engine by Sauber in 1995, and by customer teams in 1996 and 1997.

FORD ED F1 RACE ENGINE

Year	Type	Size (cc)	Bhp	Comment
1995	ED	3000	650 (est'd by author)	When the FIA imposed new regulations for F1 in 1995, the engine size limit was reduced from 3.5 to 3.0 litres. This immediately rendered the successful HB obsolete. Teams which had previously used the HB, or other 3.5-litre F1 engines, needed a new 3-litre F1 engine to allow them to stay in racing. Cosworth therefore designed a new 'customer' 3-litre, the 75-degree V8 ED unit, which had evolved from the successful and proven layout of the HB. This was used by five F1 teams until 1997, by which time it had progressed to ED5, and was significantly more powerful than the first of its type.

FORD-USA BASED RACE ENGINE FOR MONDEO RACE CARS

Year	Type	Size (cc)	Bhp	Comment
1993	FC	2000	300+	For its new racing series of Mondeo touring cars, which allowed the use of any type of current corporate engine, Ford and Cosworth chose a Ford-USA V6, which had a light alloy block and cylinder heads, four-valves-per-cylinder and twin-overhead-camshafts per cylinder head. Race-engine development was carried out by Cosworth Racing. The regulations required the use of standard cylinder block and head castings, though these could be re-machined and modified, while there was a mandatory rev limit (electronically enforced) of 8500rpm. Early engines produced nearly 300bhp and, with development, this peak figure was slightly improved, with a considerable increase in mid-range torque. First raced in 1993, when Paul Radisich's Andy Rouse-built Mondeo won the World Touring Car Cup, it repeated this trick in 1994, and was a competitive touring car unit for the rest of the decade, after which straight-four-cylinder engines became compulsory.
1997	QG	2000	300+	

OPEL RACE ENGINE FOR THE GERMAN TOURING CAR CHAMPIONSHIP

Year	Type	Size (cc)	Bhp	Comment
1993	KC	2498	400 (est'd)	The KC project was carried out by Cosworth on the existing GM V6 engine, which had a 54-degree cylinder angle in a cast iron block, allied to four-valve twin-cam cylinder heads. As prepared for Opel to campaign Calibras in the German DTM series, they were race winners, but for 1996/7, when the DTM evolved into the ITC series, new rules allowed a new KF power unit to be developed around the 'bones' of a corporate GM-USA V6, with a 60-degree vee angle, and a new light-alloy block.
1996	KF	2498	500 (est'd by author)	With the object of winning the ITCC, GM/Opel commissioned Cosworth to build an all-new 2.5-litre V6 race engine which merely retained the same cylinder bore centres and vee angle as the GM engine. Cosworth then, in a very rapid programme, produced the successful KF design. When fitted to cars which looked like Opel/Vauxhall Calibras, but were entirely different except in outline, and were fitted with four-wheel-drive, the KF was a great success. In a 26-race season, Opel recorded nine victories, nine seconds and ten third places. This remarkable engine was then rendered obsolete when Opel withdrew from the ITC, this precipitating the collapse of the series, and turning the KF into a one-season wonder.

Far left: In the mid-1990s, Opel commissioned Cosworth to develop a DTM race engine for their Calibras, this being a 2.5-litre 54-degree vee unit, the KC, which was based on the current GM-Europe road engine.

Left: To meet new rules in the German TM-type series, for 1996 Cosworth designed an all-new 2.5-litre/60-deg V6 power unit for Opel, the KF, which was a dominant success, producing 500bhp. Four-wheel-drive Calibras with this engine won nine of the 26 races in the season.

V10 ROAD CAR ENGINE, TYPE WDA, FOR TRANSVERSE MOUNTING IN VOLVO CARS

Year	Type	Size (cc)	Bhp	Comment
1996	WDA	4300	325	This power unit was unveiled in June 1996 with typical Cosworth reticence, being placarded as a road-car engine, for transverse positioning, and had been designed for an 'unnamed' manufacturer. Except that 325bhp at 7000rpm was claimed for it, and it was announced as having a 72-degree vee angle (this is a popular angle for V10s, as it gives the best solution to various balancing problems), no further details were ever provided. Visually this was a typically complex modern Cosworth design with (in the show engine) an impressive collection of cogged drive belts and pulleys. Except that this was a very compact engine, the purpose of this V10 was not further explained. Suitable for transverse mounting in the engine bay of a large passenger car, it was unbadged at the time, and was not seen again after its initial showing. Years later, Volvo admitted that it had been designed for them, but the car intended to use it was abandoned.

Considering its size and potential – it was rated at 325bhp/4.3-litres – the WDA V10 was an amazingly compact design. Intended to fit in a road-car in a transverse position (and to integrate with front-wheel-drive or four-wheel-drive transmissions, it could take the place of an existing transversely-mounted straight-five cylinder engine. Although anonymous at first, it was later credited to Volvo, who later cancelled the car or cars intended to be powered by it.

FORD XD TURBOCHARGED CART/INDYCAR ENGINE

Year	Type	Size (cc)	Bhp	Comment
1996	XD	2650	Not revealed	The turbocharged XD V8, first seen in 1996, was a direct replacement for the XB. It was purpose-built for use only in CART racing, where tight limits on boost pressure and methanol fuel consumption were imposed. Compared with the XB, the XD was entirely new, with a 75-degree vee angle, being smaller, lighter and with a lower centre of gravity than before. Even initially, it produced more power than the XB, could rev to 14,000rpm, and gulped methanol fuel at the rate of two gallons a racing minute. XD-powered cars won five events in 1996, then (with maximum boost further reduced, by regulation, from 45in of mercury to 40in), two more races in 1997, and a further four victories followed in 1998. It was competitive, often the most powerful on the tracks, and in great demand throughout the period. Even then the engine was not at its limit, with more powerful and versatile XDs being prepared for 1999, when there were five wins and four pole positions. As before, Newman-Haas engines were maintained at Northampton, all other XDs being rebuilt at Cos-Inc in Torrance, California.

Originally schemed up as a 2.2-litre for a proposed new CART/Indycar formula, the XD finally appeared as a direct 2.65-litre replacement for the existing XB unit. A very tight new set of regulations meant that it was obliged to run with steel-valve-spring and steel-connecting-rod technology, allied to severe boost limitations. A race winner from the very start, it was progressively improved between 1996 and 2000.

FORD JD ZETEC-R V10 F1 RACE ENGINE

Year	Type	Size (cc)	Bhp	Comment
1996	JD	2998	Not revealed	In 1994 a 3.5-litre V10 design project (the QC) was abandoned when F1 regulations changed, imposing a lower, 3.0-litre, capacity limit. For 1996, an all-new and more compact 3.0-litre V10 was designed to replace the EC Zetec-R V8 unit. Like earlier Cosworth F1 engines, it featured twin-cam cylinder heads, with four-valves-per-cylinder, and featured a 72-degree cylinder vee angle. In 1996 it was supplied exclusively to Sauber. As with other F1 engines of the period, power and torque figures were never revealed. During the first season it went through four improvement phases – Project 1 to Project 4 – each being more powerful/more torquey than before. In further-developed form, and running through Projects 5 to 9, the JD was used exclusively by the new Stewart-Ford F1 team in 1997. When Stewart advanced to using the new VJ V10 engine, JD V10s were supplied for Minardi and Tyrrell to use in 1998.

Cosworth's first V10 was a 3.5-litre design, but was abandoned in 1994, as new regulations demanded a 3.0-litre in 1995. The JD which followed was raced exclusively by Sauber in 1996, and Stewart Grand Prix in 1997, with Tyrrell and Minardi taking 'customer' supplies in 1998.

FORD VJ ZETEC-R V10 F1 RACE ENGINE

Year	Type	Size (cc)	Bhp	Comment
1998	VJ	2998	Not revealed	For 1998, Cosworth racing designed a second-generation V10 F1 engine, the VJ, which was a much-modified version of the later JD units. Fitted with gear drive to its camshafts instead of chain drive, the VJ was at once a more powerful and a higher-revving engine than the JD, weighing only 265lb/120kg in race-ready condition. Even in its first season, the VJ went through Series 1 to Series 6 stages of tune, the final version being considerably more powerful than the original JD types had ever been. Because technology moved so fast in late-1990s F1 racing, Cosworth and Ford developed yet another V10 engine for Stewart's use in 1999. Further-improved versions of the VJ, therefore, were supplied to Minardi.

The VJ V10 F1 engine was used exclusively by Stewart GP in 1998, and was (unofficially) thought to have produced at least 50bhp more than the JD had done a year earlier. More powerful and more reliable than that earlier engine, it was nevertheless an interim V10 design, for the radically different CK series was to follow in 1999.

FORD CK V10 F1 RACE ENGINE

Year	Type	Size (cc)	Bhp	Comment
1999	CK	2998	Not revealed	For 1999, Cosworth and Ford designed a brand-new V10 F1 engine, usually known in public as the CR (Cosworth Racing) series. Except that it shared the same 72-degree vee angle, it had virtually no carryover components from any previous Cosworth engine. In almost every way it was claimed to contain more innovative and radical features than any previous Cosworth F1 engine. Cosworth had already made a tremendous effort to produce its fourth brand-new F1 engine in five years – Zetec-R V8, JD V10, VJ V10, and now the CK V10. This, the third-generation F1 V10, was significantly smaller – shorter, lower and lighter – than any previous Cosworth V10s, and was claimed to be considerably more powerful than ever before. It had the lowest crankshaft line and centre of gravity of any Cosworth F1 engine, and weighed little more than 221lb/100kg.

For 1999 the Type CK (always marketed by Ford as the CR-1 family) was an all-new F1 V10 power unit – lighter, smaller and more powerful than any of the previous F1 V10s, with which it shared no carry-over components. Later, updated, versions were known as LK types.

ASTON MARTIN V12 ENGINE FOR ROAD-CAR USE

Year	Type	Size (cc)	Bhp	Comment
1999	SGA	5935	420	As part of its long-term strategy for developing new models at Aston Martin, Ford commissioned Cosworth to develop a new-range of power units. Although the deal 'went public' in mid-1997, work on the first of these engines, a 5.9-litre V12 unit, was already well advanced.
				Based on the layout of the prototype Ford-USA V12 shown at the Detroit Motor Show (and even more loosely based on the concept of two Duratec V6 engines mounted end-to-end), the new Cosworth SGA engine had lightweight aluminium alloy castings for cylinder block and heads, the castings being sourced from Worcester, and with manufacturing and final assembly at Wellingborough.
				The new engine had a 60-degree vee angle, twin-overhead camshafts per cylinder head, four-valves-per-cylinder and a Visteon EEC V engine management system. Although this engine was only at the beginning of its development, it was already the most powerful road-car power unit ever manufactured by Cosworth.
				A further-developed version, rated at 450bhp, was introduced in 2001, for use in the new Aston Martin Vanquish model. Series manufacture of this engine was later located in a Ford-Germany factory close to Cologne.
2002/date	JK, JM, JN		Up to 565	Development of this engine, later used in several new Aston-Martin models, always with the same 5935cc capacity, continued until the mid-2010s, with power outputs of up to 565bhp.
2009/2012	AR	7300	760	In 2008 Aston Martin previewed the very special 'limited edition' One-77, of which only 77 examples were ever built, from 2009 to 2012. The existing V12 engine was enlarged to 7.3-litres, and was rated at no less than 760bhp.
				To keep up with the demand for deliveries, Ford (the current owners of Cosworth), put the SG engine series into production in a dedicated section of the Ford-Cologne engine plant, where it remained, even after Ford sold control of Cosworth in 2004.

Much modified, and further developed, from an original Ford-USA V12 project, the SGA was developed for Ford, by Cosworth, to power a whole series of Aston Martin road cars, starting with the DB7 Vantage of 1999. It was a complex, but silkily smooth and immensely powerful 6.0-litre engine which, even in original form, produced 420bhp. Series production was originally carried out by Aston Martin, but later in a dedicated part of a Ford-Germany factory near Cologne.

CK AND LK V10 F1 RACE ENGINES, 2000-2004

Year	Type	Size (cc)	Bhp	Comment
2000	CR-2	2998	Not revealed	The later (CR-2 to CR-4, and evolutions) F1 engines were directly developed from the original CK which had been launched in 1999. Because of F1 secrecy which surrounded the sport at this time, Cosworth never described the technical and evolutionary changes made to this engine family during its life, and rarely published any photographs.
2001	CR-3	2998 (CK-Type)	Not revealed	In 2000, the CR-2 was produced exclusively for use by Jaguar, as was the CR-3 in 2001. Then in 2002, the updated CR-3 was supplied both to Jaguar and to Arrows.
2002	CR-4	2998 (LK-Type)	Not revealed	The LK (publicly known as the CR-4) was then introduced from the Canadian F1 GP (June 2002), solely for the use of the Jaguar team. This engine used many carry-over parts from the CK, and had a 95mm cylinder bore.
2003-2004		2998 (LK Type)	Not revealed	For 2003, CKs (CR-3s) were supplied to Minardi, and LKs (CR-4s) to Jordan, while a new generation V10-engine (the TJ, or familiarly CR-5, described separately) was supplied to Jaguar.
				Cosworth never revealed any peak power output figures, and would never comment on any estimates suggested by observers. Original CR-1 types were thought to produce up to 800bhp. By 2002, indeed, the CR-series was seen as one of the most effective in F1, and was thought to be producing in the region of 850bhp at approximately 18,300rpm: these were independent estimates, unconfirmed by the company itself.
				Weight continued to be pared away, and for 2002, Cosworth claimed a ready-to-run figure of only 212lb/96kg – an amazing 30 per cent reduction compared with the 300lb/136kg figure quoted for the last of the early-1990s HBs. The CR-series was small too – even though it was a V10, it was only 22.6in/579mm long.
				For 2003, the LK engine became the LK2003 (though still known as CR-4 to the public); it was provided to Jordan, and used in the car that won the Brazilian F1 GP. In the meantime, it had been supplanted at Jaguar by the TJ, which is described separately.
				Minardi also used late-model LKs in 2004, but with no success.

XF TURBOCHARGED CART/CHAMPCAR RACE ENGINE

Year	Type	Size (cc)	Bhp	Comment
2000	XF	2650	850/870	After a very successful four-season CART/Champcar career, the XD power unit was replaced by a new-generation of turbocharged engine, the XF. Like its predecessors, the XF was developed specifically to meet CART/Champcar regulations. These limited the size to 2.65-litres, specified the use of methanol-based fuel, and initially imposed a maximum overall inlet manifold pressure of 40in of mercury (the organisers provided sealed and pre-set pop-off valves to be inserted into the inlet plenum chamber to enforce this).
2003	XFE	2650	750	

The XF CART engine was a winner from the very start, but later, in 'spec' form as XFE, it had a long and illustrious career in Champcar racing. From 2003 the XF was re-engineered to become XFE – E for 'Endurance' – the spec engine for the long-running Champcar series in the USA.

Although the XF shared its 75-degree cylinder vee angle with the XD, it was new in almost every detail. Bore and stroke dimensions were not revealed, but the XF was 2in/50mm shorter than the XD, it was apparent that the cylinder bore dimensions (and therefore the bulk of the cylinder block around them) had been reduced, and the stroke increased.

Up to 200 engines were manufactured to service all the XF users in 2000 and 2001, with the 'works' supported team having engines built in Northampton, the balance being assembled and maintained at Torrance, in California. Although fewer teams used XFs in 2002, with all engines being assembled or rebuilt at Torrance, the 'float' of 100 power units was retained.

At first, in 2000, Cosworth agreed that with a 40lb boost limit, the XF was producing well over 850bhp, at around 15,000rpm. New regulations reduced the maximum boost limit to 37in mercury in 2001, and to 34in mercury in 2002, by which time it was thought that peak power had slipped back a little, but that the engine was now revving to more than 16,000rpm – quite remarkable for a turbocharged power unit.

The XF, in fact, won the CART engine Manufacturers' Championship in the year of its introduction, 2000, and also powered Jimmy Vasser's car when it won the Fontana 500 'oval' race at a world record speed, at the end of the 2002 season.

Although the XF was intended to be replaced by a new-type normally-aspirated XG 3.5-litre V8 for 2003, there was a late change to the regulations. From 2003 to 2008, CART/Champcar racing became a 'one-engine' (a 'spec' engine) formula, with that engine being a revised, rev-limited version of the XF, titled XFE. With revs limited to 12,500rpm, but with boost back up to 41.5in mercury, peak power was 750bhp.

By this time the Champcar 'circus' had split with the IRL (Indy Racing League organisation, the two then promoting separate series thereafter. From 2003 onwards, therefore, Champcar racing was exclusively for cars powered by the XFE engine, of which the entire fleet was maintained in California. The same business group which had taken over the Champcar series also bought the Cosworth concern at the end of 2004, and from 2005 the power of the XFE was increased to more than 800bhp.

To keep costs to a minimum, no significant developments were allowed in the 2003/2007 seasons, and when the Champcar series finally folded in the winter of 2007/2008, this brought the XF/XFE's long and successful career to a close.

AK FORD-USA-BASED RACE ENGINE FOR TAURUS CARS IN NASCAR

Year	Type	Size (cc)	Bhp	Comment
2000/01	AK	5865	575	Cosworth finally became involved in North American NASCAR (and related) saloon car racing in 1999/2000, when it began working on the preparation and development of Ford pushrod V8 engines for use in Taurus cars.
2002		5865	710	

NASCAR (and related) racing has always been closely controlled. The only Ford-based cars authorised for use in the late 1990s/early 2000s were tubular-framed saloons, with bodyshell shapes based on that of the Ford Taurus car, and powered by a derivative of the long-established Ford-USA 5.8-litre/358CID V8 engine.

This was a final evolution of an engine that had been used in many different Ford-USA and Ford-Australia cars from the 1960s, although for NASCAR/Busch use, it was completely special. In standard 'road-car' form it had a cast iron block with a 90-degree vee, cast iron cylinder heads, and two overhead valves operated by push rods and rockers from a centrally mounted camshaft. Race car derivatives used specially cast iron cylinder blocks and aluminium cylinder heads.

Cosworth's improvement of these engines was limited by Championship regulations, development being concentrated on better cylinder head breathing, camshaft redesign, and on better control of the valve gear. For 2002, the regulations limited the compression ratio to 12.0:1, and with a single, four-barrel Holley 4150 carburettor the power output was limited to no more than 710bhp. Earlier examples, with a lower compression ratio, had reached 575bhp.

A developed version, coded BK, was subjected to test bed work, but was never put into production.

YC (ZETEC-E-TYPE) FORD-BASED ENGINE FOR FOCUS WORLD RALLY CARS

Year	Type	Size (cc)	Bhp	Comment
2000	YC (Zetec-E)	1998	300	For use in World Rally Championship events, the all-new Focus World Rally Car was unveiled in time to start the 1999 season. This car featured a transversely mounted engine and four-wheel-drive, the engine being a turbocharged derivative of the 16-valve Ford Zetec power unit (which had a cast iron cylinder block), where a compulsory, 34mm diameter, restrictor was fixed upstream of the turbocharger itself.
				Original cars were powered by a Mountune-developed power unit, for which 300bhp at 5500rpm was claimed, after which Cosworth Racing took on the development/build of all engines before the end of 1999. From then until the end of 2001, the Focus WRC used Cosworth developed Zetec-E power units which eventually developed 300bhp at 5500rpm, along with a massive 56kg/m peak torque at 4000rpm. Such engines powered Focus WRC cars to many World, and International championship victories in 2000 and 2001. All such engines were supplied to M-Sport of Cumbria, the official contractor/builder/developer of all the Focus WRC cars for which this engine and the Duratec-R was manufactured.

The YC was publicly described as the Zetec-E, and was a much-modified Ford engine, redeveloped for use in the Focus in World Rally events from 1998 on.

YC (DURATEC-R-TYPE) FORD-BASED ENGINE FOR FOCUS WORLD RALLY CARS

Year	Type	Size (cc)	Bhp	Comment
2001 2006	Duratec-R	1998	300	The Duratec-R engine took over directly from the Zetec-M four-cylinder turbocharged engine at the end of 2001, for use in the latest Ford Focus WRC rally car. Although the name was new, the Duratec-R power unit was a direct descendant of the Zetec-M, and was lighter with improved peak power and torque figures. It was thought to be one of the most powerful World Rally engines, all of which were limited by the same technical regulations, and by the 34mm diameter inlet restrictor mounted upstream of the turbocharger.
				In its first season, 2002, the Duratec-R powered Ford to second place in the World Manufacturers' Championship, and provided the driving team with three outright victories, including two for Colin McRae.
				One other advance, made between 2000 and 2002, was that the latest engines were more than 20 per cent lighter than the 1999-type Zetec-Ms had been originally, although an actual weight-reduction figure was not revealed.

VK WIDE-VEE ANGLE F1 ENGINE

Year	Type	Size (cc)	Bhp	Comment
2002	VK	3000	Not revealed	In an effort to lower the centre of gravity of the V10 F1 engine as much as possible, this project, which was never seen in a car in public, featured a 120-degree vee cylinder block, with a 95mm cylinder bore. Three engines were completed, and tested. The power output was competitive, but the project was abandoned after further study of the packaging implications within the car. Much was learned, though, and Cosworth filed away all the knowledge against some, unspecified, future requirement.

COSWORTH – THE SEARCH FOR POWER

XG NORMALLY-ASPIRATED CHAMPCAR/INDYCAR ENGINE

This engine started life as a possible power unit for Champcar racing, but was finalised as a Chevrolet-badged power unit for use in the parallel IRL series, where it was immediately a winner.

Year	Type	Size (cc)	Bhp	Comment
2002/2003	XG	3500	Not revealed	This engine was designed in 2001/2002 to meet new CART/Champcar regulations that were projected to come into force in 2003. These would have specified a normally-aspirated, 90-degree, V8 power unit, a type of engine which could also have been adapted for the other US-based formula, the IRL, and was always intended to run on methanol fuel. However, no sooner had an interim test engine – the 'XF Hybrid' – been designed, developed, and run in mid-2002, than these projected regulations were abandoned. The 'XF Hybrid' was a normally-aspirated, bored and stroked version of the XF (which was, itself, a turbocharged 2.65-litre), and was a 75-degree V8 without the structural endurance safety margins which would have been necessary in a finalised design. The XF Hybrid first ran in May 2002, immediately exceeding its target power output figures. In mid-2003, however, the XF Hybrid was redeveloped, and enlarged, to 3.5-litres, to be supplied to Chevrolet as a 'Chevrolet Gen 4' for use by IRL teams. The XG finished second in its very first race (Michigan, USA, in July 2003) and there were three race victories before the end of that season.
2004/2005				To meet a change in IRL regulations, the XG was then reduced in size, to 3-litres, for 2004, and there was a final race victory in 2005, before Chevrolet withdrew all its support to the engine, and the IRL series.

GK APRILIA THREE-CYLINDER MOTORCYCLE RACING ENGINE

The three-cylinder Aprilia MotoGP motorcycle engine, Cosworth Type GK, used much contemporary F1 engine thinking in its valve gear and breathing arrangements.

Year	Type	Size (cc)	Bhp	Comment
1996	BG	997	Not revealed	In the mid-1990s, Cosworth was approached by the Italian motorcycle manufacturer, Aprilia to help develop that company's existing V-Twin engine for use in World Superbike racing. Cosworth designed new top ends for these successful engines, Aprilia/Rotax retaining work on the rest of the engine.
2002	GK	990	Not revealed	This modest liaison then led to a more ambitious project – the GK of 2002. For 2002, a new engine formula came into force in the motorcycle MotoGP racing formula (the equivalent of Formula 1 for cars), which specified the use of 1.0-litre four-stroke power units. To meet this new formula, Cosworth Racing was asked by Aprilia to advise on the design and development of a new engine, the GK. Working together, the two companies evolved an in-line, 12-valve, three-cylinder water-cooled power unit. This was mounted across the frame of the motorcycle, but leaning forward towards the cooling radiator, with a separate transmission mounted to one side (the back, as installed in the frame) of the cylinder block. In some ways the cylinder head architecture and air-spring valve gear of this GK motorcycle engine was related to the contemporary family of Cosworth CR-type F1 V10 engines, being based on a CK1999, and was certainly capable of revving up to similar speeds. No power output figures were released, although it was strongly rumoured that this was in excess of 250bhp.

TJ V10 F1 RACE ENGINE

Year	Type	Size (cc)	Bhp	Comment
2003	TJ	3000	Not revealed, but finally 915bhp+	The TJ replaced the LK, and was an all-new-generation V10 engine for use in Formula 1. It used a vee angle of 90 degrees (the LK and earlier Cosworth V10s had used a 72 degree angle). Like the LK it retained a 95mm cylinder bore. As first used in 2003 it was the TJ2003 (CR-5 in public) and was supplied only to Jaguar. Then, upgraded for 2004, it became TJ2004 (CR-6 for Jaguar) and RS2 for Jordan); in 2005 it became TJ2005, and was supplied to Red Bull (which had purchased the Jaguar F1 operation) as RB1, and to Minardi as the PS05. In later years Cosworth revealed that the TJ2005 derivative had revved to 19,000rpm, with peak power outputs of at least 915bhp. This was almost certainly a conservative claim.

(Continued on next page)

			725bhp	When F1 regulations were changed for 2006, in which 2.4-litre V8s became near-mandatory (hence Cosworth designed the CA, described below), the FIA also allowed existing-type V10s to be used, these being electronically restricted to 16,700rpm, and to run with a 77mm diameter air inlet restrictor. Such engines were supplied to Toro Rosso (ex-Minardi), as TJ2006.
2006				

All new for Jaguar's use in 2003, the TJ 3-litre V10 was Cosworth's ultimate V10 race engine – with a 90 degree vee it was lighter, more compact, and considerably more powerful than any previous Cosworth V10. By 2005, its final year in front-line use, it was rated at a minimum of 915bhp, though Cosworth insiders suggest that some engines were significantly more powerful than that.

YD (MODIFIED FORD DURATEC ENGINE) FOR SALE TO OTHER MANUFACTURERS

Year	Type	Size (cc)	Bhp	Comment
2004	YD	2000 2300	205/225 250/255 220/250/280	Based on the existing series-production four-cylinder Ford Duratec four-cylinder engine, which featured aluminium cylinder block and head castings, with twin overhead camshafts and four-valves per cylinder, the Cosworth version featured a steel crankshaft, performance camshafts, a modified cylinder head and a dry sump.
	YDD			The original version was a 2.0-litre/250bhp unit, marketed by Caterham in the Super Seven, known as the CSR260.
	YDE			The YDE was supplied to several customers, in 2.0-litre and 2.3-litre form. It was also supplied to BAC Mono in 280bhp form, for this road/track car.
	YDF	2300	200	The YDF and YDG derivatives were supplied to Caterham as the CSR200, in 2.3-litre/200bhp form.
	YDG			
	YDJ		225	YDJs were 2-litre/225bhp race engines for Caterham C400 use, along with 205bhp YDK.
	YDK		205	

This was the original version of the high-revving 2.4-litre CA V8, as supplied to Williams for the 2006 F1 season. Later it was improved to ...

CA 2.4-LITRE V8 F1 RACE ENGINE

Year	Type	Size (cc)	Bhp	Comment
2006	CA	2400	756/770	The CA F1 engine was tested in 2005, then unveiled in 2006, to comply with new FIA regulations, which specified engines of 2.4-litres in a 90-degree V8 layout. The same rules made a minimum weight of 209lb/95kg compulsory, though Cosworth estimated that 187lb/85kg would have been possible. Development was speeded up by the use of much experience, and some components, from the TJ V10. The first race engines produced 720bhp at 20,000rpm, but 756bhp was available from mid-season in 2006. In 2006 the new CA was provided to Williams, whose cars led several races, but the engine was more effective than the cars themselves, which had a disappointing season. Williams then moved its allegiance to another engine manufacturer, which proved to be a major error for that company, but this left the CA without a customer.
2010	CA2010 CA2011 CA2012 CA2013			During 2007, 2008 and 2009, the CA was side-lined, but not abandoned, so development continued. This was in a period when F1 regulations were compulsorily changed the peak rev limit was compulsorily lowered to require electronically ' policed)' peak speeds, first to 19,000rpm, and then to 18,000rpm. Then, for 2010, the FIA launched a complex financial deal to increase the number of F1 cars on the grid. Not only did Williams return to use the Series 16 version of the CA, but three new teams – HRT, Lotus and Virgin Racing (later to be renamed Marussia) – all took supplies. Unhappily, although the revised 18,000rpm CAs were competitive and reliable throughout, there were no outright victories to celebrate, and because they were only ever leased (not provided on 'free issue' like some rival engines), Williams withdrew at the end of 2011, and at the end of 2013 the last F1 team released its hold on the still-competitive CA.

... the CA2010 type, to meet the latest F1 regulations, which included a compulsory rev limit of 18,000rpm, and the ability to go through four Grands Prix without a rebuild. With upwards of 770bhp, this was a remarkable power unit. There were many detail differences, but nothing basic, compared with the original 2006 type.

Cosworth's last F1 engine, the 2.4-litre CA type, featured a 90 degree V8 layout, and was subject to several 'long life' limitations to meet the latest limitations. Cosworth insists that without these limitations the engine could have been small, a little lower, and lighter too.

This is not a view seen often in learned articles about F1 engines – this being the worm's eye view of the sump and underside of the final 2.4-litre CA of 2013.

XG-BASED V8 FOR JAPANESE SUPER GT500 RACE SERIES

Year	Type	Size (cc)	Bhp	Comment
2007	XJ NR VR XK	3400	Approx 500	The specific Japanese Super GT50 Championship was restricted to much-modified road cars (which were mainly Japanese-manufactured). The regulations were carefully policed, and restricted engines to 3.4-litres in 90 degree V8 configuration, with peak power limited to approximately 500bhp by the use of an inlet passage restrictor. Based on the original XG ('Chevrolet'/IRL)unit, this engine was supplied in XJ, NR or VR sub-derivative, this depending purely on the customer who bought the engine. The XK engine, which followed in 2008, was specifically developed for use in worldwide LMP2 events, and was an evolution of the NR.

REMANUFACTURING OF EX-NAPIER DELTIC ENGINES, FOR ROLLS-ROYCE

Year	Type	Size (cc)	Bhp	Comment
2008	DC	44,115	1650	Strictly speaking, the 18-cylinder Napier Deltic two-stroke diesel engine was not a Cosworth-designed power unit, though the company's unrivalled experience allowed it to remanufacture a number of major units for Rolls-Royce (who owned the Napier business), to replenish stocks which had been depleted in a fire. Dating from a 1940s design, the Deltic was a massive high-power diesel engine, originally intended for use in small ships. Its layout featured a triangular layout, with three geared crankshafts and eighteen cylinders – six to each cylinder head – turbochargers and fuel-injection, which produced a thunderous 1650bhp. A smaller, half-sized nine-cylinder 'baby Deltic' engine was also developed, with a mere three cylinders per bank. After an extremely successful career in Royal Navy vessels, the Deltic engine was then adapted for use in the Class 55 express British Rail locomotive, where two engines in the one 'chassis' produced 3300bhp, and the train's high-speed cruising speed of 100mph was easily achieved. This, incidentally, is one of the engines on which Cosworth's founder, Keith Duckworth, might have worked if he had accepted a job offer from Napier when he graduated from Imperial College in London in 1957.

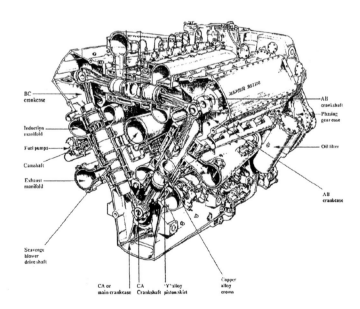

Much of this amazingly large, heavy and complex, Napier Deltic marine/railway engine was re-engineered by Cosworth under Project DC in 2008.

RACE ENGINE FOR LOTUS, FOR THE EVORA GT4 MODEL

Year	Type	Size (cc)	Bhp	Comment
2010	GL	3456	360	The two-seater Lotus Elise sports model, the original rear-drive Elise, was launched in 1995, and progressively improved and developed in the years which followed. The Evora of 2009, a 2+2 coupé derivative, had a longer wheelbase and was powered by a mid-mounted transversely-positioned Toyota V8 engine, as used in various contemporary Lexus and Toyota models. In initial standard form, the normally-aspirated Evora-spec engine produced 280bhp, and a supercharged version with 350bhp was set to follow. This was a state-of-the-art series-production power plant, with twin overhead camshafts, and four-valves per cylinder. In 2010, under Code GL, Cosworth developed the normally-aspirated engine to produce 360bhp (and 445Nm of torque), complete with a dry sump layout. Later derivatives pushed up the peak power to 470bhp.

DEDICATED ENGINE FOR THE LOTUS T125 SINGLE-SEATER

Year	Type	Size (cc)	Bhp	Comment
2010	GPV8	3800	640	Lotus of Norfolk produced a single-seater track car, superficially like a contemporary F1 car, but not complying with those restricted regulations. Lotus proposed to built 25 such cars, intending to give (wealthy) enthusiasts access to F1 performance and driving conditions, though with a simpler mechanical package. Cosworth provided a specially-developed normally-aspirated 3.8-litre V8 engine, coded GPV8, which had all the expected features of twin overhead camshafts, four-valves per cylinder, and in layout was closely related to current F1 engines which were still being built at Northampton. It was, in fact, an evolution of the XG power unit (already described above), though 3.8-litre rather than 3.0-litre, with peak power developed at 10,000rpm, and was electronically limited to 11,000rpm.

SPECIAL ENGINE DEVELOPMENT FOR THE SUBARU FACTORY IN JAPAN

Year	Type	Size (cc)	Bhp	Comment
2010	SB	2457	395	A special vehicle programme for Subaru of Japan, for which Cosworth provided a comprehensive re-work of the company's 2.5-litre flat-four engine as fitted to the STi CS400 saloon model, which already had turbocharging, twin overhead camshafts, and four valves per cylinder. Improvements included high-performance pistons, connecting rods, bearings along with a new turbo compressor and wastegate details. Peak power was increased from 300bhp to 395bhp.

At the time of writing, a 'security blanket' was still being applied over some of the latest projects on which Cosworth was diligently working, and which would not be unveiled before 2016/2017. Cosworth, however, has authorised mention of the following projects, if not their complete details:

Year	Type	Size (cc)	Bhp	Comment
2012	AL			A generator set/compact diesel generator for military use.
2013	HK			A straight-four 1.6-litre cylinder engine which would have been suitable for the then-proposed (but ultimately new/still-born F1 regulations of 2013, though design began in 2009. It would also have been used in the still-born Jaguar C-X75 high-performance hybrid project, where prototypes were built by the Williams F1 organisation, in which application it was rated at 502bhp at 10,000rpm. The design included direct injection, and turbocharging and, as fitted to the C-X75 was very conservatively rated. It was likely that, if the project had gone further ahead, it would have been integrated into a hybrid package and used by Williams in a new-generation F1 car. Unhappily, the C-X75 project was cancelled by Jaguar on cost and 'political' grounds. By then, too, the proposed/revised F1 formula had been changed, to specify a V6, rather than a straight-four-cylinder layout, which rendered Cosworth's HK design immediately obsolete.

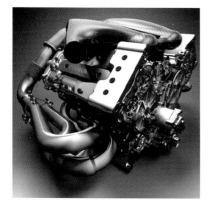

This very detailed artist's impression shows how Cosworth might have built a 1.6-litre V6 turbo engine to meet the proposed F1 regulations which came into force in 2014 – except that the finance was not available to carry out detailed work. To emphasise, this image is of a purely 'pipe-dream' project.

Year	Type	cc		Description
2013	RV			A single-cylinder research engine connected with a 1.6-litre V6 F1 power unit. Tested on the dynamometer.
2013	SV	1600		A planned turbocharged 1.6-litre V6 for F1 use in the new-for-2014 F1 series [See also, the HK project, above]. The design never progressed beyond computer studies, general layouts, and some component manufacture, and was not completed or power tested. 'Just for fun,' as one Cosworth insider later commented, a mock-up of what an SV might (repeat 'might') have looked like was generated in the extremely capable bowels of an engineer's computer, as seen to the left.
2013	NV			An LMP1 'hybrid' engine was completed for an (at the time) unstated customer. Later it became known that it had been designed for the ultra-unconventional Nissan GT-R LM Nismo, for use in World Championship Endurance sports car races in 2015. This car had its engine fitted up front, ahead of the cabin, and basically driving the front wheels, though there was provision for a proportion of the torque and power also to be fed to the rear wheels. At this point, one should emphasise that Cosworth was not at all involved in the layout and engineering of the transmission. The NV engine itself (which Nissan publicly called the VRX 30A) was a 60-degree V6 of 3-litres, with twin turbochargers and direct fuel-injection. With fuel economy in mind, it was rated at 500bhp at an unstated rpm peak. In 2015, the radical new Nissan was problematic in pre-season testing, and although three cars appeared at the Le Mans 24 Hours race they were embarrassingly slow, a failing which was not blamed on Cosworth, but on the general concept, layout, traction and aerodynamic failings of the car. The project was abandoned before the end of 2015.
2013	FX	1994		An aftermarket equipment package for performance upgrades of the FA20 power unit used in Toyota GT86, Subaru BRZ and Scion FR-Z road-going sports cars.
2014	-	4951		TVR, the Blackpool-based sports car manufacturer, lapsed into receivership in 2004, but was rescued by businessman Les Edgar in 2013, who set about the design of a new car. Cosworth was commissioned to develop a special version of the latest Ford-USA 5.0-litre 'Boss 302' V8 engine, which had twin-overhead camshafts per bank and four-valves per cylinder, along with alloy cylinder block and heads. Forecast to commence in production in 2017, Cosworth would produce engines in Northampton, and the peak power output was forecast to be between 450bhp and 470bhp.

Note: At the time of writing this edition (2016), but subject to strict confidentiality clauses, Cosworth was also producing fully machined cylinder heads and blocks, in quantity, for at least one make of well-respected Hypercar, and for a new-technology sports coupé. More such projects get under way all the time, and their identity will eventually be revealed.

Developed in strict secrecy for Nissan in 2013 and 2014, the Cosworth NV engine was designed to power the company's new Le Mans prototype of 2015. It was the car, strange in much of its detailing, and not the engine, which let this project down.

APPENDIX 2:
COSWORTH-ENGINED
ROAD CARS

No engine, not even a Cosworth engine, can prove itself unless it powers the right sort of car. Over the years, Cosworth-designed, developed, or manufactured engines have been used in a fascinating variety of road cars. Here, in summary, is the road car story:

Caterham Super Seven (introduced: 1974)

Caterham Sevens (developments of the Lotus 7) went on sale in the 1970s, using a whole variety of Cosworth-influenced engines.

This two-seater sports car, the direct descendant of the famous Lotus Seven model, has been built with a whole variety of Ford-based four-cylinder engines (and, in fairness, many others, including Vauxhall and Rover Group types). Like the Lotus Sevens themselves, Caterhams have used many different units – Lotus-Ford twin cams, Vegantune VIA twin-cams, and modified Ford 'Kent' units. The most powerful option of all, however, in the 1980s, was the Cosworth BDR unit, offered either as a 155bhp/1598cc or a 170bhp/1698cc size.
Basic layout: Two-seater open sports car, front engine/rear drive.
Performance: (170bhp version) Top speed 120mph, 0-60mph 5.0sec, typical fuel consumption 27mpg.

Chevrolet Cosworth Vega (produced: 1975 and 1976)

The Cosworth-engined Chevrolet Vega of 1975 showed great promise, though its engine output was severely hampered by the USA exhaust emission regulations of the day.

As detailed in the text, the Chevrolet Cosworth Vega used a productionised version of the EAA 16-valve engine, of which special versions had originally been designed for F2 and sports car racing.

Development of the road car was protracted, and although it was mentioned in 1973 and 1974, it did not go on sale until the spring of 1975. It was built in the USA, and sold almost entirely in that continent. It was a limited-edition, top-of-the-line derivative of the mass-production Chevrolet Vega car. At this stage, normal Vegas had 2.3-litre single overhead-camshaft engines producing 78 or 87bhp. The productionised EAA unit was a 2.0-litre twin-cam producing 122bhp. In 16 months, 3507 Cosworth Vega production cars were built.
Basic layout: Three-door four-seater hatchback, front engine/rear drive.
Performance: Top speed approximately 112mph, 0-60mph 9.0sec.

Ford Escort RS1600 (produced: 1970-1974)

RS1600 was a very significant RS road car, and a world-beating race and rally car.

Ford's first 'hot' Escort was the Twin-Cam of 1968-1971, which used the Lotus-Ford twin-cam for which Cosworth had provided development and racer-tuning expertise.

To replace the Twin-Cam, Ford produced the RS1600, which was effectively a Twin-Cam model, re-engined with the first of the 16-valve BDA engines. Cosworth manufactured some of the pieces, but never assembled the production car's engines, which were originally sourced from Harper Engineering of Letchworth. All road-car engines were 1.6-litre units, with twin horizontal twin-choke Weber carburettors, rated at 120bhp (DIN), with cast iron blocks at first, but light-alloy blocks from the autumn of 1972. The RS1600 road car was assembled at the AVO plant at Aveley, but many RS1600 competition cars were 'created' from parts, or by the re-engining of tired Twin-Cams. The RS1600, in 1.6-litre, 1.8-litre and eventually in light-alloy 2.0-litre form, was an incredibly successful competition car. Ford has never revealed accurate production figures for this car, though total output exceeded 1000.
Basic layout: Two-door four-seater saloon, front engine/rear drive.
Performance: Top speed 113mph, 0-60mph 8.9sec, typical fuel consumption 22mpg.

Ford Escort RS1800 (produced: 1975-1977)

Ford's mainstream Escort was restyled for 1975, which meant that the RS1600 was rendered obsolete. After a short interval, a new BD-engined car, the RS1800, took over.

Like its predecessor, the RS1800 was very closely related to other Escort RS models of the day, having the new and rather more angular body style. The engine was no longer 'pure' Cosworth, for it was an enlarged BD type (with a 1835cc/86.75mm bore x 77.62mm stroke layout), and a single downdraught dual-choke Weber carb, producing 115bhp (DIN).

Very few of these cars were produced as road cars, the engines being assembled by a variety of specialists, including Brian Hart Ltd. The first few cars were built at Ford's Halewood factory, but most RS1800s were sent over from West Germany as near-complete RS Mexicos, where they were re-engined and re-badged at the Aveley plant. Accurate production figures are not known. As with the RS1600s, many RS1800s were 'created' for motorsport purposes, some by the reshelling of old RS1600s.

Basic layout: Two-door four-seater saloon, front engine/rear drive.

Performance: Top speed 111mph, 0-60mph, 9.0sec; typical fuel consumption 27mpg.

The RS1800 of 1975 took over from the RS1600, using a 1.8-litre derivative of the BDA engine. It used the same platform as the original Escort, but had a newly-styled body. Between 1975 and 1981 it was developed into the world's most successful rally car – this being exemplified by victory on the 1977 East African Safari by this 'works' car, driven by Björn Waldegård and Hans Thorzelius.

Ford Escort RS1700T (announced: 1981, cancelled 1983)

For the 1980s, and for the new 'Group B' category, Ford proposed to build a new 'homologation special' called the Escort RS1700T. Although it looked superficially like the newly-announced transverse-engine, front-wheel-drive Escort Mk 3, it had a different floorpan/running gear layout – with an in-line engine driving the rear wheels through a rear transaxle. To take advantage of new regulations, the engine was a 1.78-litre turbocharged and fuel-injected version of the famous BD family (which, according to FIA regulations, with the 'equivalency factor' built in, made it equal to a 2.5-litre normally-aspirated unit); this was basically a Ford-developed unit, dubbed BDT (T = Turbocharged).

200 cars were slated to be built in 1983, with road cars producing 200bhp, and full-house rally cars up to 350bhp or more.

200 engine kits were manufactured by Cosworth, but JQF Engineering carried out assembly. The engines were fine, but the rise of four-wheel-drive in rallying rendered the car itself obsolete before sales could begin. In March 1983, just as production-build preparations were well-advanced, the new motorsport supremo, Stuart Turner, cancelled the project. The engines went back into store – to be used in the RS200 project which followed.

Basic layout: Three-door, two-seater hatchback, front-engine/rear drive.

Performance: No authentic figures recorded.

This was the striking side-view of the Ford Escort RS1700T, which was developed at Ford's Motorsport centre at Boreham, having a front-engine/rear-drive layout, with a turbocharged BDT engine up front, and a rear-mounted gearbox/rear axle assembly. Unhappily it was cancelled in 1983 before full production could take place.

Ford Escort Twin-Cam (produced 1968-1971)

The Twin-Cam was the very first Cosworth-engined Escort – if, that is, one credits the Lotus-Ford (Type TA) engine as being 'rescued' by Cosworth before it could be turned into a satisfactory road car. Like later Escort RS types, it was an 'homologation special,' produced in sufficient numbers to reach acceptance by the motorsporting authorities, so that Ford, its contractors and – eventually – many private owners, could go racing and rallying up to World level.

Although Cosworth never produced TA twin-cam engines in quantity, they take credit for the capability of those which were built, originally by JAP for Lotus, and later by Lotus itself. Production of the Twin-Cam was concentrated at Ford's factory at Halewood, on Merseyside, and in three years a total of 1263 cars were built. In the meantime, many more such cars were built for motorsport, by effecting the transformation of originally more humble Escorts.

Basic layout: Two-door four-seater saloon, front-engine/rear-drive.

Performance: Top speed 113mph, 0-60mph 9.9sec, typical fuel consumption 22mpg.

Although it did not carry a Cosworth-designed engine, the Ford Escort Twin-Cam used the Lotus-Ford engine which had been productionised by Cosworth, and which was coded Type TA. More than 1000 Twin-cams were produced between 1968 and 1971. Competition versions of this machine were race and rally winners throughout, and were only supplanted at Ford when the Escort RS1600 came along.

COSWORTH – THE SEARCH FOR POWER

Ford RS200 (produced: 1985-1986)

To replace the cancelled Escort RS1700T project, Ford Motorsport developed the Group B RS200 coupé, which bore no relation to any existing Ford. This was a mid-engined two-seater coupé, with permanent four-wheel-drive, a steel/Kevlar/carbon-fibre chassis 'tub,' and glass-fibre bodywork.

The chosen engine was a slightly enlarged and improved version of that developed for the stillborn RS1700T, with a larger cylinder bore, different manifolding/turbo layout, and Ford fuel-injection and EECIV engine electronics. The 1803cc unit was 'equivalent' to a normally-aspirated 2524cc engine – as, with motorsport strategy in mind, Ford intended to enlarge it to the full 3-litre class limit in due course. For road use 250bhp was offered (300bhp and 350bhp packages were also available), and the 1986 'works' rally cars had 420bhp, rising to 450bhp before the end of the season.

A total of 200 cars were assembled (at an ex-Reliant factory) in 1985/86, but following cancellation of Group B by the sporting authorities, many cars were then disassembled. The balance were further developed as road cars, and all were sold off by the end of 1989. 25 Evolution cars were produced, almost all for use in motorsport. Not only were 300bhp and 350bhp conversion kits of the 1.8-litre version offered by Ford, but Brian Hart Ltd developed the 2.1-litre BDT-E (E = Evolution) engine for motorsport purposes. In 'standard' form this produced more than 500bhp, and in 'sprint' configuration, for rally cross, approximately 650bhp was available.

Basic layout: Two-seater sports coupé, mid-engine/four-wheel-drive.

Performance: (250bhp version) Top speed 140mph, 0-60mph 6.0sec, typical fuel consumption 18mpg.

Ford produced 200 mid-engined/four-wheel-drive RS200s in 1985/1986, using turbocharged BDT engines rebuilt from those originally designed for the Escort RS1700T. Standard road cars produced 250bhp, but double that was available for full-blooded competition use.

Ford Escort RS Cosworth (produced: 1992-1996)

As the ultimate in YB-engined 'homologation specials,' Ford developed a new car using a shortened/modified Sierra Cosworth 4x4 platform and running gear, clothed in a much-modified three-door Escort superstructure, with ambitious and extrovert aerodynamic aids, including a vast rear spoiler.

For rallying in 1997 and 1998, Ford Motorsport produced a limited number (about 50, all in all) of the Escort World Rally Car, which was really an Escort Cosworth with a modified YB-type engine, and a much-changed rear suspension. World rally success was achieved, but none of these machines were truly road cars.

Compared with the Sierra Cosworth 4x4, the Escort used an uprated YB-type engine, with larger turbocharger, and was rated at 227bhp at first. More than 2500 cars were built before the end of 1992: this ensuring sporting homologation into FIA Groups A and N. From mid-1994 a new version (with unchanged styling) took over, with a smaller (Type T25) turbocharger and Ford ECU electronics.

Using much-modified Group A machines, with seven-speed transmissions, the 'works' rally team won numerous World Championship rallies in the first two seasons, including the prestigious Monte Carlo Rally of 1994.

Basic layout: Three-door four-seater hatchback, front engine/four-wheel-drive.

Performance: Top speed 137mph, 0-60mph 6.2sec, typical fuel consumption 21/22mpg.

Conceived by John Wheeler at Ford's Motorsport department, the Escort RS Cosworth was always seen as the ultimate Ford 'homologation special' for World Championship rallying. A modified Escort bodyshell hid a shortened Sierra Cosworth 4x4 chassis platform, with YB power to provide the performance. Production cars first went on sale in 1992, and victories in rallying began the following year.

The Ford Scorpio 24V (available as saloon, hatchback or estate car) used the FB V6 engine, and as Ford's early 1990s flagship. Surprisingly, it was only ever available with automatic transmission.

Ford Scorpio 24V (produced: 1991-1998)

Having developed Brian Hart's original four-cam V6 engine concept to the production stage as the FB type, Cosworth then supplied it to Ford for use in a Scorpio 'flagship' model. Intended purely to be a top-of-the-range car, rather than a sports saloon, Ford asked for the new 195bhp FB-Type Cosworth engine to be 'green' and totally flexible, offering it only with automatic transmission in a large (187in/4744mm long) car which weighed about 3280lb/1488kg.

This was definitely the least sporting of all cars powered by Cosworth engines which had been released up to that time. When the Granada/Scorpio range was extensively revised for 1995, the 24-valve engine was itself upgraded, to 210bhp.

Basic layout: Four-door saloon, five-door hatchback, five-door estate car, full five-seater, front engine/rear-wheel-drive.

Performance: Top speed 136mph, 0-60mph 8.5sec, typical fuel consumption 22mpg.

Ford designed the Ford Sierra RS Cosworth as a competition car, but were obliged to produce 5000 YBB-engined examples in 1986 to achieve Group A sporting homologation.

Ford Sierra RS Cosworth (produced: 1986)

With Group A motor racing in mind, Ford developed a very special version of the Sierra, which became a 'cult' car as soon as it went on sale, and also became a very effective rally car in the late 1980s. Using a three-door version of the Sierra structure, but graced by a massive 'whale tail' type of rear spoiler, it was powered by Cosworth's turbocharged YB-type 16-valve two-litre engine, and backed by a Borg Warner 5-speed gearbox. In standard form (YBB) this engine produced 204bhp, but for rally use around 300bhp was available, and up to 340bhp was eventually produced for Group A racing.

More than 5500 examples were produced at Genk, in Belgium, mainly in the second half of 1986. Later developments included the 500-off RS500 Cosworth, the four-door saloon Sapphire RS Cosworth, and the Cosworth 4x4.

Basic layout: Three-door four-seater hatchback, front-engine/rear drive.

Performance: Top speed 145mph, 0-60mph 6.0sec, typical fuel consumption 21mpg.

Ford Sierra RS500 Cosworth (produced: 1987)

To take advantage of the 'Evolution' clauses in Group A Regulations, Ford arranged to build exactly 500 derivatives of the Sierra RS Cosworth, calling them RS500 Cosworths. Partly-built at Genk as Sierra RS Cosworths, these cars were then completed by Aston Martin Tickford at Bedworth, near Coventry, the 'conversion' work including the installation of an 8-injector 224bhp version of the Cosworth YB engine, the YBD, which had a larger turbocharger, and further improvements to the car's aerodynamics. Road cars were little faster than the 'standard' RS Cosworth, but race-tuned engines were capable of more than 500/550bhp. Such cars won the World Touring Car Championship in 1987, the European Touring Car Championship in 1988, and countless other touring car races all round the world. They were so dominant that several Championships had to have their regulations rewritten to give the opposition a fighting chance.

Basic layout: Three-door four-seater hatchback, front engine/rear drive.

Performance: Top speed 154mph, 0-60mph 6.0sec, typical fuel consumption 20mpg.

Left: The Ford Sierra RS500 Cosworth was the 500-off 'Evolution' version of the original Sierra RS Cosworth, with the more powerful (224bhp) YBD-type engine, and refined aerodynamic aids ...
Above: The 500 Sierra RS Cosworths, lined up in a storage compound in Essex in 1987, ready for speedy conversion into RS500 Cosworths.

Ford Sierra Sapphire RS Cosworth (produced: 1988-1990)

From the beginning of 1988, Ford took the Sierra + Cosworth theme a stage further, marrying the original (204bhp) Sierra engine and drive-line package to the four-door 'Sapphire' saloon version of the Sierra structure, and making

Ford's second-generation Sierra RS Cosworth was the four-door 'Sapphire' model, more of a 'businessman's express' than an homologation special. Gwyndaf Evans at speed in the 1990 Scottish rally.

COSWORTH – THE SEARCH FOR POWER

The Sierra Cosworth 4x4 combined the four-body style of the 'Sapphire' RS Cosworth with a developed version of the YB engine, and the established Ford type of four-wheel-drive transmission and chassis/platform. More than 10,000 such cars were produced. The 'works' rally cars of 1991 and 1992 carried this striking Mobil livery.

When it was originally launched, the Cosworth connection with GM's 16-valve engine was not publicised, but later was generally known. The first British car to use this engine was the Vauxhall Astra 2.0i 16V of 1987.

When the new-generation Vauxhall Vectra was launched in 1988, one of the extensive range of engines was the Cosworth KB power unit.

this a mainstream production car. The three-door machine had been a 'homologation special,' built only for a short time, but the Sapphire was a refined, regular-production, 'businessman's express.' It was never intended for use in front-line motorsport, though it proved to be very competitive in Group N 'showroom' form. A four-wheel-drive version was launched in 1990.

Basic layout: Four-door four-seater saloon, front engine/rear drive.

Performance: Top speed 142mph, 0-60mph 6.0sec, typical fuel consumption 20mpg.

Ford Sierra Cosworth 4x4 (produced: 1990-1992)

The final development of the Sierra Cosworth theme came in 1990, when Ford replaced the rear-drive Sapphire RS Cosworth with the Sierra Cosworth 4x4, by adding an updated version of the Sierra XR4x4 four-wheel-drive installation to the existing chassis and structure. This car used the new MT75 five-speed transmission, and according to Ford the uprated YB-type engine developed 220bhp.

More than 5000 examples were produced quickly in 1990 so that Ford could use it as a World Championship rally car; assembly continued, but at a lower rate, thereafter. The Sierra Cosworth 4x4 was a successful rally car, particularly in Group N categories, but there was no suitable racing category for it.

Basic layout: Four-door four-seater saloon, front engine/four-wheel-drive.

Performance: Top speed 144mph, 0-60mph 6.6sec, typical fuel consumption 22mpg.

General Motors (Opel/Vauxhall) Kadett/Astra 2.0i 16V (introduced: 1987)

GM introduced its front-wheel-drive Kadett/Astra series in 1979, then phased in a completely restyled version in 1984. By the late 1980s there were saloons, hatchbacks, and estate car types. All had transversely-mounted four-cylinder engines driving the front wheels. Most cars were Opels, but British-built/British-market types were badged as Vauxhalls.

GM contracted Cosworth to develop a 16-valve twin-cam version of the 2-litre Family 2 engine for its use; this KBA engine becoming available in 1987. Road-car engines produced 156bhp, but full Group A competition versions produced about 220/240bhp.

By the early 1990s the KB-type engine had become a GM 'mainstream' unit, and was used when the new-shape Astra was launched in 1991.

Basic layout: Three-door four-seater hatchback, front-engine/front drive.

Performance: Top speed 132mph, 0-60mph 7.5sec, typical fuel consumption 28mpg.

General Motors (Opel) Vectra 2.0i 16V (introduced: 1988)

GM produced its second-generation medium-sized front-wheel-drive range in 1988, to replace the successful Opel Ascona/Vauxhall Cavalier range of 1981-1988. The Cavalier name was retained, but the new Opel became 'Vectra.' Its smooth style was available as a four-door saloon or a five-door hatchback, both cars having a wide choice of transversely-mounted engine driving the front wheels. For the first time, too, a four-wheel-drive alternative was also on offer.

GM installed the Cosworth-developed (KBA) 16-valve Family 2 engine in the top-of-the-range Vectra four-door saloon, also giving that car a choice of front-wheel or newly-developed four-wheel-drive. GM manufactured the engines itself, in West Germany.

The sleek Calibra Coupé, introduced in 1991, used the same platform, and the same KB-type engine.

Basic layout: Four-seater, four-door saloon, front engine/front drive or front engine/four-wheel-drive.

Performance: Top speed 135mph, 0-60mph 9.0sec.

General Motors (Opel/Vauxhall) Omega 2.0i 16V (introduced: 1993)

GM introduced a new-generation Omega range in 1993, to replace the older Omega/Senator models. One of the engines used was yet another version of the Cosworth-developed, but now Opel-built, KB four-cylinder unit, this being rated at 136bhp.

Basic layout: Four-door/five-door five-seater saloon/hatchback, front engine, rear drive.

Performance: Top speed 130mph, 0-60mph 9.3sec, typical fuel consumption 26mpg.

GM's new-generation Omega (badged as an Opel, or a Vauxhall) appeared in 1993, with a whole variety of engines, one of which was a development of the Cosworth KB 2-litre. By that time, GM had taken over manufacture of this rugged unit.

Lotus Seven (produced: 1957-1973)

The Lotus Seven was a cheap-and-cheerful two-seater kit car, with a multi-tube frame, old-fashioned styling, but very light and with excellent handling. Lotus always used proprietary engines, including the Ford 'Kent' 105E four-cylinder units. By the early 1960s Cosworth had developed more powerful versions of these engines, with fitment of Cosworth Mk V and Mk VIII units into Lotus Sevens beginning in 1962.

There were four families of Lotus Seven, the third being reborn as the Caterham Super Seven (already described) in the early 1970s.

Basic layout: Two-seater open sports car, front engine/rear drive.

Performance: (95bhp 1.5-litre ohv version): Top speed 103mph, 0-60mph 7.5sec, typical fuel consumption 25mpg.

Lotus road cars (produced 1962 to 1975)

The Cosworth-developed TA twin-cam engine went into use for a whole range of Lotus road cars, starting in 1962. Not only were versions of the TA used in the Lotus-Elan, the Elan Plus 2, the Europa Twin-Cam and the Europa-Special, but were also used as power units for the Ford Lotus-Cortina and Escort Twin-Cam saloons.

As an example, this was the detail of the 1962 Lotus Elan:

Basic Layout: Two-seater open sports car, front engine/rear drive.

Performance: (105bhp version of the Elan): Top speed 114mph, 0-60mph 8.7sec, typical fuel consumption 28mpg.

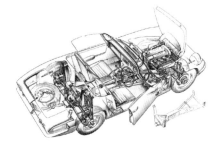

The Cosworth-developed Lotus-Ford twin-cam engine – coded TA at Northampton – was used in several important Lotus road cars of the 1960s and early 1970s. This was the technically advanced Lotus Elan sports car, originally launched in 1962.

Mercedes-Benz 190E 2.3-16 (produced: 1983-1988)

Mercedes-Benz originally approached Cosworth to produce a racing/rallying version of its new M102 four-cylinder engine. In the early 1980s, however, the motorsport project was cancelled, but the 16-valve 2.3-litre WAA engine was refined, and fitted to the 190E 2.3-16 road car from 1983 on.

Although less flamboyant than Ford's Sierra RS Cosworth, this Mercedes-Benz model was definitely an ultra-fast road car, with front and rear spoilers and side skirts all to make the marketing, and aerodynamic, point more emphatically. The standard engine used Bosch injection, and produced 185bhp.

As an 'autobahn-charger' the 190E 2.3-16 was a great success, with more than 20,000 examples produced. It was replaced by the larger-engined 2.5-16 in 1988.

Basic layout: Four-door five-seater saloon, front engine/rear drive.

Performance: Top speed 143mph, 0-60mph 8.0sec, typical fuel consumption 24mpg.

The ultimate technical accolade, for Cosworth, was to be asked to produce an engine for Mercedes-Benz. The result was the 190E 2.3-16, a plushy and very fast four-door saloon car, which was produced from 1983 to 1988.

In 1988, Mercedes-Benz fitted an enlarged engine to its 16-valve saloon car, the result being the 190E 2.5-16, seen here with the more conventional version of the revised 190E, introduced at the same time.

Mercedes-Benz 190E 2.5-16 (produced: 1988-1993)

The developed version of the 190E 2.3-16 appeared in 1988, with 197bhp/2498cc instead of 185bhp/2299cc, and with a new type of limited-slip differential. Mercedes-Benz had lengthened the stroke, leaving the bore alone, and made other minor changes to the layout of the cylinder head, but in essence the car was unchanged.

Basic layout: Four-door five-seater saloon, front engine/rear drive.
Performance: Top speed 142mph, 0-60mph 7.0sec, typical fuel consumption 22mpg.

Mercedes-Benz 190E 2.5-16 'Evolution' (produced: 1989-1990)

To extract the ultimate from its four-door saloon with German Touring Car racing in mind, Mercedes-Benz built two 'evolution' batches of the 2.5-16 model in 1989 and 1980. 502 cars were built each year, with improved aerodynamic aids, and a shorter-stroke/larger-bore version of the engine – 2463cc instead of 2498cc. Both types, therefore, were 'homologation specials,' the 1989 model being rated at 201bhp, the 1990 'Evolution II' model at 235bhp, though up to 350bhp was available in Group A racing tune.

Basic layout: Four-door five-seater saloon, front engine/rear drive.
Performance: No authentic figures available.

With motor racing in mind, Mercedes-Benz produced a limited number of 190E 2.5-16 Evolution models in 1989, with a 201bhp engine, and an enlarged rear spoiler ... which for 1990 became the Evo II model (right), with a 235bhp engine, and even more extreme changes to the body styling.

Opel Ascona 400 (produced: 1979-1980)

To provide GM with a potential rally winner, Opel produced the Ascona 400 model, the '400' referring to the number of cars which had to be manufactured to ensure homologation into the top, Group 4, category.

The basic Ascona was a conventional front-engine/rear-drive range of family cars. The Ascona 400, however, used a two-door saloon version of the range, with a Cosworth-developed 16-valve twin-cam (KAA) 2.4-litre engine. In road-going trim, this engine had 140bhp and fuel-injection, but for rally use it had 240bhp (a figure later raised to 275bhp).

Basic layout: Two-door four-seater saloon, front engine/rear drive.
Performance: Top speed 124mph, 0-6mph 8.0sec.

The Ascona 400 of 1979-1980 was powered by the KA engine.

Opel Manta 400 (produced: 1981-1983)

As a development of the Ascona 400, Opel later produced 400 examples of the Manta 400, this being the two-door coupé version of the same basic 'chassis' and running gear. It was a lighter car than the Ascona, with somewhat more sophisticated rear suspension, but was otherwise mechanically the same.

Basic layout: Two-door four-seater coupé, front engine/rear drive.

Performance: Top speed approx 125mph, 0-60mph 8.0sec.

The Opel Manta 400 was a limited-production 'homologation special,' powered by a 2.4-litre Cosworth KA engine. Here is Russell Brookes driving this particular car in a British rally.

Panther Solo (1989-1990)

The original Panther Solo of 1984 was a mid-engined, rear-driven car, but that prototype design was soon discarded in favour of a new mid-engined machine, which used the YB version of the Sierra RS Cosworth engine. The revised car featured four-wheel-drive, and the YBE engine was mounted 'back to front', driving forward to the main gearbox which was ahead of it in the chassis.

The Sierra-engined Panther was revealed in September 1987, but deliveries from the Harlow New Town factory did not begin until the end of 1989. In spite of a very high price, the project was not profitable, and only 12 production cars were built.

Basic layout: Two-door two-seater coupé, mid-engine/four-wheel-drive.

Performance: Top speed 144mph, 0-60mph 6.8sec, typical fuel consumption 26mpg.

Although fitted with a mid-mounted Ford Sierra-type YB engine, and four-wheel-drive, the Panther Solo was a commercial failure.

Vauxhall Chevette HS (produced: 1977-1979)

This was Vauxhall's very successful late-1970s 'homologation special,' targeted at Group 4 competition in rallies, where 400 cars had to be built to gain approval.

The Chevette HS was built around the basis of the standard three-door hatchback shell, but in production form it was fitted with a Vauxhall-designed 16-valve/twin-cam 2.3-litre engine, developing 135bhp, aided by two Stromberg carburettors, and mated to a five-speed Getrag gearbox. In rally trim, with twin dual-choke Dellorto carbs, 240bhp was produced.

The original 'works' rally cars ran with Lotus 907-type 16-valve cylinder heads (in which Cosworth played no part), and used ZF gearboxes. Homologation was achieved in November 1976, well before the 400 cars had been produced, in fact well before the cylinder heads had been manufactured, but this was even before Cosworth became involved.

From the spring of 1978 the car's homologation was changed, by order of FISA, and after that the Vauxhall-designed/Cosworth-made head was used in motorsport as well as in the rally cars. Peak power was 245bhp.

Basic layout: Three-door four-seater hatchback, front engine/rear drive.

Performance: Top speed 115mph, 0-60mph 8.5sec, typical fuel consumption 21mpg.

The Vauxhall Chevette HS, which went on sale in 1977/1978, used twin-cam cylinder-head assemblies produced by Cosworth. The fully-tuned Group 4 car, in 'works' rally guise, produced 240bhp, and was a match for the latest BDG-fitted Ford Escort RS1800s.

Vauxhall Chevette HSR (produced: 1980)

In 1980, to keep the Chevette rally car competitive, Vauxhall produced the 50-off Chevette HSR. Visually these cars had flared front and rear wings, plastic sills under the doors, and a deeper front spoiler. Most of these cars were completed (converted) from near-finished Chevette HS types, and had tuned-up engines of 150bhp (by Blydenstein).

Twin dual-choke Dellorto carburettors (offering even more power) were optional.

Basic layout: three-door four-seat hatch, front engine/rear drive.

Performance: No authentic figures recorded.

Aston Martin DB7 Vantage (produced 1999-2003)

Introduced in 1999, the Vantage version of the Aston Martin DB7 used Cosworth's newly-developed SGA 6-litre V12 power unit. The original DB7, with a supercharged Jaguar six-cylinder engine, had 340bhp, so with an extra 80bhp, this version was ensured of a colossal performance. The Volante, or convertible version, followed in the early 2000s.

As part of its long-term plan for developing the Aston Martin marque, Ford commissioned Cosworth to develop and manufacture a new family of high-performance road-car engines. The first result of this partnership seen in public was the DB7 Vantage, announced in March 1999.

Already a masterpiece of inter-company co-operation, for the later DB7 the Vantage development took that a stage further. Financed by Ford, based on the Jaguar XK8 platform and suspensions (and with the 'base' car powered by a supercharged version of a Jaguar straight-six engine), the Vantage version was now to be powered by a Cosworth-designed/Ford-USA-based Type SGA V12 engine.

The Vantage had an all-independent suspension chassis, and the engine was backed by a choice of six-speed manual or five-speed automatic transmissions. Available in closed coupé or drophead convertible body styles, the Vantage immediately became the flagship of the DB7 range.

Basic layout: Two-door 2+2-seater drophead convertible or hatchback, front-engine/rear-drive.
Performance: Top speed 185mph, 0-60mph 5.2sec.

Aston Martin Vanquish (introduced 2001)

The second new car to use the Cosworth SGA V12 engine was the Aston Martin Vanquish, which was effectively a replacement for the venerable old V8 engined models which had been in production at Newport Pagnell for 30 years.

This was the first new Aston Martin chassis to be linked to the modern SGA V12 engine (the DB7 had used a modified Jaguar XJS/XK8 platform), and was aimed fairly and squarely at the top of the 'Ferrari market.' The chassis was based on a high-tech structure including many bonded and riveted sections of extruded aluminium, with much stiffening from carbon-fibre mouldings.

The original Aston Martin Vanquish appeared in 2001, and used a 460bhp version of the Cosworth V12 SGA power unit. Even though it was a very large car, the company claimed that it could reach 196mph.

Not only did this car use all-independent suspension and a six-speed manual transmission, but the 6-litre Cosworth engine was up-rated to 460bhp (when used in the DB7 Vantage it was rated at 420bhp). This immediately became the flagship of the marque – a title which the DB7 Vantage ceded after only two years.

Basic layout: Two-door 2+2-seater coupé, front-engine/rear-drive.
Performance: Top speed 196mph, 0-60mph 4.4sec.

V12-engined Aston Martin models (revealed since 2002)

Several different Aston Martin models, all using the same chassis/platform architecture, were put on sale in the 2000s and 2010s, all of them fitted with one or other derivative of the 5.9-litre SG V12 engine, which had first been seen in 1999.

Originally this engine had developed 420bhp in the DB7 Vantage, and 466bhp in the original Vanquish of 2001. The following new models appeared thereafter:

2003: DB9 (2+2 seater coupé, and Volante convertible) – with 450bhp. From 2008 the peak power as increased to 477bhp.

The second-generation Aston Martin Vanquish was introduced in 2012, one of its features being that the Cosworth-developed 6-litre SGA V12 engine had been further modified, to produce up to 573bhp.

2004: Vanquish S (2+2 coupé), developed from original Vanquish, but with 528bhp.
2007: DBS (two-seater coupé), replacing the Vanquish, with 517bhp.
2009: Rapide (four-door/four-seater saloon), with 477bhp.
2011: Vantage (two-door/two-seater coupé or convertible), with 517bhp.
2012: V12 Zagato (two-door/two-seater coupé), based on Vantage V12 engineering, with 517bhp.
2012: New type DB9, with 517bhp.
2012: New type Vanquish, with 573bhp.
2013: Rapide S, evolved from the Rapide, with 558bhp.
In addition, the special limited-edition One-77 of 2010-2013 had a 7.3-litre version of the engine, with 760bhp.

APPENDIX 3: VICTORIES BY COSWORTH-FORD-ENGINED CARS IN WORLD CHAMPIONSHIP F1 RACES

1967

Dutch GP (Zandvoort)	Jim Clark	Lotus 49
British GP (Silverstone)	Jim Clark	Lotus 49
US Grand Prix (Watkins Glen)	Jim Clark	Lotus 49
Mexican GP (Mexico City)	Jim Clark	Lotus 49

1968

South African GP (Kyalami)	Jim Clark	Lotus 49
Spanish GP (Jarama)	Graham Hill	Lotus 49
Monaco GP (Monte Carlo Rally)	Graham Hill	Lotus 49B
Belgian GP (Spa)	Bruce McLaren	McLaren M7A
Dutch Grand Prix (Zandvoort)	Jackie Stewart	Matra MS10
British GP (Brands Hatch)	Jo Siffert	Lotus 49B
German GP (Nürburgring)	Jackie Stewart	Matra MS10
Italian GP (Monza)	Denny Hulme	McLaren M7A
Canadian GP (St Jovite)	Denny Hulme	McLaren M7A
US GP (Watkins Glen)	Jackie Stewart	Matra MS10
Mexican GP (Mexico City)	Graham Hill	Lotus 49B

1969

South African GP (Kyalami)	Jackie Stewart	Matra MS10
Spanish GP (Montjuich)	Jackie Stewart	Matra MS80
Monaco GP (Monte Carlo)	Graham Hill	Lotus 49B
Dutch GP (Zandvoort)	Jackie Stewart	Matra MS80
French GP (Clermont-Ferrand)	Jackie Stewart	Matra MS80
British GP (Silverstone)	Jackie Stewart	Matra MS80
German GP (Nürburgring)	Jacky Ickx	Brabham BT26A
Italian GP (Monza)	Jackie Stewart	Matra MS80
Canadian GP (Mosport)	Jacky Ickx	Brabham BT26A
US GP (Watkins Glen)	Jochen Rindt	Lotus 49B
Mexican GP (Mexico City)	Denny Hulme	McLaren M7A

1970

South African GP (Kyalami)	Jack Brabham	Brabham BT33
Spanish GP (Jarama)	Jackie Stewart	March 701
Monaco GP (Monte Carlo)	Jochen Rindt	Lotus 49C
Dutch GP (Zandvoort)	Jochen Rindt	Lotus 72
French GP (Clermont-Ferrand)	Jochen Rindt	Lotus 72
British GP (Brands Hatch)	Jochen Rindt	Lotus 72
German GP (Hockenheim)	Jochen Rindt	Lotus 72
US GP (Watkins Glen)	Emerson Fittipaldi	Lotus 72

1971

Spanish GP (Montjuich)	Jackie Stewart	Tyrrell 003
Monaco GP (Monte Carlo)	Jackie Stewart	Tyrrell 003
French GP (Paul Ricard)	Jackie Stewart	Tyrrell 003
British GP (Silverstone)	Jackie Stewart	Tyrrell 003
German GP (Nürburgring)	Jackie Stewart	Tyrrell 003
Canadian GP (Mosport)	Jackie Stewart	Tyrrell 003
US GP (Watkins Glen)	François Cevert	Tyrrell 002

1972

Argentine GP (Buenos Aires)	Jackie Stewart	Tyrrell 003
South African GP (Kyalami)	Denny Hulme	McLaren M19A
Spanish GP (Jarama)	Emerson Fittipaldi	Lotus 72
Belgian GP (Nivelles)	Emerson Fittipaldi	Lotus 72
French GP (Clermont-Ferrand)	Jackie Stewart	Tyrrell 003
British GP (Brands Hatch)	Emerson Fittipaldi	Lotus 72
Austrian GP (Zeltweg)	Emerson Fittipaldi	Lotus 72
Italian GP (Monza)	Emerson Fittipaldi	Lotus 72
Canadian GP (Mosport)	Jackie Stewart	Tyrrell 005
US GP (Watkins Glen)	Jackie Stewart	Tyrrell 005

1973

Argentine CP (Buenos Aires)	Emerson Fittipaldi	Lotus 72
Brazilian GP (Interlagos)	Emerson Fittipaldi	Lotus 72
South African GP (Kyalami)	Jackie Stewart	Tyrrell 006
Spanish GP (Montjuich)	Emerson Fittipaldi	Lotus 72
Belgian GP (Zolder)	Jackie Stewart	Tyrrell 006/2
Monaco GP (Monte Carlo)	Jackie Stewart	Tyrrell 006/2
Swedish GP (Anderstorp)	Denny Hulme	McLaren M23
French GP (Paul Ricard)	Ronnie Peterson	Lotus 72
British GP (Silverstone)	Peter Revson	McLaren M23
Dutch GP (Zandvoort)	Jackie Stewart	Tyrrell 006/2
German GP (Nürburgring)	Jackie Stewart	Tyrrell 006/2
Austrian GP (Zeltweg)	Ronnie Peterson	Lotus 72
Italian GP (Monza)	Ronnie Peterson	Lotus 72
Canadian GP (Mosport)	Peter Revson	McLaren M23
US GP (Watkins Glen)	Ronnie Peterson	Lotus 72

1974

Argentine GP (Buenos Aires)	Denny Hulme	McLaren M23
Brazilian GP (Interlagos)	Emerson Fittipaldi	McLaren M23
South African GP (Kyalami)	Carlos Reutemann	Brabham BT44
Belgian GP (Nivelles)	Emerson Fittipaldi	McLaren M23
Monaco GP (Monte Carlo)	Ronnie Peterson	Lotus 72
Swedish GP (Anderstorp)	Jody Scheckter	Tyrrell 007
French GP (Dijon)	Ronnie Peterson	Lotus 72
British GP (Brands Hatch)	Jody Scheckter	Tyrrell 007
Austrian GP (Zeltweg)	Carlos Reutemann	Brabham BT44
Italian GP (Monza)	Ronnie Peterson	Lotus 72
Canadian GP (Mosport)	Emerson Fittipaldi	McLaren M23
US GP (Watkins Glen)	Carlos Reutemann	Brabham BT44

1975

Argentine GP (Buenos Aires)	Emerson Fittipaldi	McLaren M23
Brazilian GP (Interlagos)	Carlos Pace	Brabham BT44B
South African GP (Kyalami)	Jody Scheckter	Tyrrell 007
Spanish GP (Montjuich)	Jochen Mass	McLaren M23
Dutch GP (Zandvoort)	James Hunt	Hesketh 308
British GP (Silverstone)	Emerson Fittipaldi	McLaren M23
German GP (Nürburgring)	Carlos Reutemann	Brabham BT44B
Austrian GP (Zeltweg)	Vittorio Brambilla	March 751

1976

Spanish GP (Jarama)	James Hunt	McLaren M23
Swedish GP (Anderstorp)	Jody Scheckter	Tyrrell P34
French GP (Paul Ricard)	James Hunt	McLaren M23
German GP (Nürburgring)	James Hunt	Mclaren M23
Austrian GP (Zeltweg)	John Watson	Penske PC4
Dutch GP (Zandvoort)	James Hunt	McLaren M23
Italian GP (Monza)	Ronnie Peterson	March 761
Canadian GP (Mosport)	James Hunt	McLaren M23
US GP (Watkins Glen)	James Hunt	McLaren M23
Japanese GP (Fuji)	Mario Andretti	Lotus 77

1977

Argentine GP (Buenos Aires)	Jody Scheckter	Wolf WR1
US GP West (Long Beach)	Mario Andretti	Lotus 78
Spanish GP (Jarama)	Mario Andretti	Lotus 78
Monaco GP (Monte Carlo)	Jody Scheckter	Wolf WR1
Belgian GP (Zolder)	Gunnar Nilsson	Lotus 78
French GP (Dijon)	Mario Andretti	Lotus 78
British GP (Silverstone)	James Hunt	McLaren M26
Austrian GP (Zeltweg)	Alan Jones	Shadow DN8
Italian GP (Monza)	Mario Andretti	Lotus 78
US GP (Watkins Glen)	James Hunt	McLaren M26
Canadian GP (Mosport)	Jody Scheckter	Wolf WR1
Japanese GP (Fuji)	James Hunt	McLaren M26

1978

Argentine GP (Buenos Aires)	Mario Andretti	Lotus 78
South African GP (Kyalami)	Ronnie Peterson	Lotus 78
Monaco GP (Monte Carlo)	Patrick Depailler	Tyrrell 008
Belgian GP (Zolder)	Mario Andretti	Lotus 79
Spanish GP (Jarama)	Mario Andretti	Lotus 79
French GP (Paul Ricard)	Mario Andretti	Lotus 79
German GP (Hockenheim)	Mario Andretti	Lotus 79
Austrian GP (Zeltweg)	Ronnie Peterson	Lotus 79
Dutch GP (Zandvoort)	Mario Andretti	Lotus 79

1979

Argentine GP (Buenos Aires)	Jacques Laffite	Ligier JS11
Brazilian GP (Interlagos)	Jacques Laffite	Ligier JS11
Spanish GP (Jarama)	Jacques Laffite	Ligier JS11
British GP (Silverstone)	Carlos Reutemann	Williams FW07
German GP (Hockenheim)	Alan Jones	Williams FW07
Austrian GP (Zeltweg)	Alan Jones	Williams FW07
Dutch GP (Zandvoort)	Alan Jones	Williams FW07
Canadian GP (Montreal)	Alan Jones	Williams FW07

1980

Argentine GP (Buenos Aires)	Alan Jones	Williams FW07
US GP West (Long Beach)	Nelson Piquet	Brabham BT49
Belgian GP (Zolder)	Didier Pironi	Ligier JS11
Monaco GP (Monte Carlo)	Carlos Reutemann	Williams FW07B
French GP (Paul Ricard)	Alan Jones	Williams FW07B
British GP (Brands Hatch)	Alan Jones	Williams FW07B
German GP (Hockenheim)	Jacques Laffite	Ligier JS11
Dutch GP (Zandvoort)	Nelson Piquet	Brabham BT49
Italian CP (Monza)	Nelson Piquet	Brabham BT49
Canadian GP (Montreal)	Alan Jones	Williams FW07B
US GP (Watkins Glen)	Alan Jones	Williams FW07B

1981

US GP West (Long Beach)	Alan Jones	Williams FW07C
Brazilian GP (Jacarepagua)	Carlos Reutemann	Williams FW07C
Argentine GP (Buenos Aires)	Nelson Piquet	Brabham BT49C
San Marino GP (Imola)	Nelson Piquet	Brabham BT49C
Belgian GP (Zolder)	Carlos Reutemann	Williams FW07C
British GP (Silverstone)	John Watson	McLaren MP411
German GP (Hockenheim)	Nelson Piquet	Brabham BT49C
Las Vegas GP	Alan Jones	Williams FW07C

1982

US GP West (Long Beach)	Niki Lauda	McLaren MP4/1
Belgian GP (Zolder)	John Watson	McLaren MP4/1
Monaco GP (Monte Carlo)	Riccardo Patrese	Brabham BT49D
Detroit GP (Detroit, USA)	John Watson	McLaren MP4/1
British GP (Brands Hatch)	Niki Lauda	McLaren MP4/1
Austrian GP (Zeltweg)	Elio de Angelis	Lotus 91
Swiss GP (Dijon, France)	Keke Rosberg	Williams FW08
Las Vegas GP (Las Vegas, USA)	Michele Alboreto	Tyrrell 011

1983

US GP West (Long Beach)	John Watson	McLaren MP4/1
Monaco GP (Monte Carlo)	Keke Rosberg	Williams FW08C
Detroit GP (Detroit, USA)	Michele Alboreto	Tyrrell 011-DFY

154 victories by cars fitted with DFVs, one victory for a car fitted with the DFY engine.

Victories achieved by HB-engined cars:

1989
Japanese GP (Suzuka)	Alessandro Nannini	Benetton B189

1990
Japanese GP (Suzuka)	Nelson Piquet	Benetton B190
Australian GP (Adelaide)	Nelson Piquet	Benetton B190

1991
Canadian GP (Montreal)	Nelson Piquet	Benetton B191

1992
Belgian GP (Spa)	Michael Schumacher	Benetton B192

1993
Brazilian GP (Interlagos)	Ayrton Senna	McLaren MP4/8
European GP (Donington Park)	Ayrton Senna	McLaren MP4/8
Monaco GP (Monte Carlo)	Ayrton Senna	McLaren MP4/8
Portuguese GP (Estoril)	Michael Schumacher	Benetton B193
Japanese GP (Suzuka)	Ayrton Senna	McLaren MP4/8
Australian GP (Adelaide)	Ayrton Senna	McLaren MP4/8

Victories achieved by Zetec-R V8 (EC) engined cars:

1994
Brazilian GP (Interlagos)	Michael Schumacher	Benetton B194
Pacific GP (TI, Aida, Japan)	Michael Schumacher	Benetton B194
San Marino GP (Imola)	Michael Schumacher	Benetton B194
Monaco GP (Monte Carlo)	Michael Schumacher	Benetton B194
Canadian GP (Montreal)	Michael Schumacher	Benetton B194
French GP (Magny Cours)	Michael Schumacher	Benetton B194
Hungarian GP (Budapest)	Michael Schumacher	Benetton B194
Belgian GP (Spa)**	Michael Schumacher	Benetton B194
European GP	Michael Schumacher	Benetton B194

** Later disqualified due to a chassis infringement, after post-race scrutineering.

Victories achieved by V10 engined cars:

1999
European GP (Nürburgring)	Johnny Herbert	Stewart SF-3

2003
Brazilian GP	Giancarlo Fisichella	Jordan EJ13

At the end of 2003, Cosworth-Ford engined cars had officially won 176 World Championship F1 races.

APPENDIX 4:
THE LIST OF F1 MAKES THAT USED COSWORTH-FORD ENGINES – 1967-2013

In 1967 the DFV was only available to Lotus, and in 1968 the engine was only used by Lotus, Matra and McLaren. After that, the number of users increased rapidly. This, I think, is a complete list of all the makes of F1 car that started World Championship events between 1967 and 2013, while powered by Cosworth-Ford engines. Several other projects, using DFV engines, were initiated, but failed to start F1 World Championship races.

Unless stated, engines used were DFV or DFV-derived, though additional types are indicated.

AGS
Amon
Apollon
Arrows (see also Footwork) (CK-V10)
ATS
Beatrice-Lola (GBA turbo V6 1.5-litre)
Bellasi
Benetton (DFR, plus GBA turbo V6 1.5-litre, plus HB V8, plus Zetec-R V8)
Boro (see Ensign)
Brabham
Coloni
Connew
Copersucar (see Fittipaldi)
Dallara
De Tomaso
Eifelland
Ensign
Eurobrun
Fittipaldi
Fomet
Fondmetal (HB)
Footwork (once the Arrows team, DFR, HB)
Forti (ED, Zetec-R VS)
Hesketh
Hill
HRT (CA V8)
Jaguar (CK-V10, LK-V10, TJ V10 types)
Jordan (HB, LK-V10, TJ-V10)
Kauhsen
Kojima
Larrousse (HB)
LEC
Ligier
Lola (DFV, Zetec-RV8)
Lotus (DFV, HB, CA V8)
Lyncar

Maki
March
Martini
Marussia (CA V8)
Matra
McLaren (DFV, HB)
Merzario
Minardi (DFV, HB, ED, JD-V10, VJ-V10, CK-V10, TJ-V10)
Onyx (later renamed Monteverdi)
Osella
Pacific (ED)
Parnelli
Penske
Pilbeam (see LEC)
RAM
Rebaque
Red Bull (TJ-V10)
Rial
Safir (see Token)
Sauber (Zetec-R V8, JD-V10)
Shadow
Simtek (HB, ED)
Stewart (JD-V10, VJ-V10)
Surtees
Theodore
Token
Toro Rosso (TJ-V10)
Trojan
Tyrrell (DFV, ED, JD-V10)
Virgin (CA V8)
Williams (CA V8)
Wolf

Of these teams, by far the most successful have been Lotus, McLaren, Tyrrell, Williams, Brabham and Benetton.

The thoughts of Chairman Duckworth ...

For 30 years, any conversation with Keith Duckworth has been spattered with well-rounded aphorisms. As with Winston Churchill, such sayings took time to evolve, and were by no means as spontaneous as they might appear.

At the risk of boring some experienced Duckworth-watchers, here is a selection of the 'Thoughts of Chairman Duckworth' ...

- It is better to be un-informed than ill-informed.
- Development is only necessary to rectify the ignorance of designers.
- Very few straight answers are ever possible. The decisive man is a simple-minded man.
- If you are telling the truth, it's simple. If you're lying, you have to remember what yesterday's lie was. It's safer to be honest.
- Academics are seldom any use at engineering. One must have a mistrust of theorists.
- First ideas usually turn out to be complicated.
- There seem to be two categories of racing drivers – those who can drive by natural ability, and those who actually gain competence by experience.
- If someone says something to me which has no meaning, it jars my mind. I worry about it, and I lose the next ten sentences.
- It must be possible to make an interesting living, messing about with racing cars and engines.
- We (Cosworth) are the only people who expect a prototype to go together straight away, without fitting ...
- In engineering there is an answer to everything, it's just that we're usually too ignorant, or too dim, to see it.
- I always seemed to have enough nous to realise that unless your regular income exceeded your outgoings, then bankruptcy was certain.
- I think we (Cosworth) always managed to under-employ people. We achieved higher standards than the others – it comes from not promoting people to the level at which they're making a lot of mistakes. It's the reverse of the Peter Principle!
- It costs you very little to scrub out drawings on paper, and to start again. As soon as you have things in the metal, where you are fighting to make a silk purse out of a sow's ear, that is hopeless.
- A genius can make, for a penny, what a good engineer can only make for 10p.
- Inherently, by nature, I'm one of those people who would rather do a few things very well, than what I see as the other extreme, which is to make a nonsense of lots of things.
- Harry Mundy was stubborn, but I wouldn't like to say that I was other than that.
- I think that borrowing money is the biggest immorality that there is.
- The only substitute for money is genius – if you can make your steps by thinking about them, rather than by trial and error, the end result is the same, and in general it costs less.

- My problem is that when I look at all the kind of people who have made quite a lot of money, I don't think that it is a great criterion of life ...
- I have a vast natural curiosity, so I'm always inventing things.
- We must be the only outfit, ever, to make money from making racing engines – as a commercial venture.
- It is the years of socialism, and the high taxation that went with it, that was the death of all the morals and ethics of the City of London.
- The problems that have developed by suggesting that we are born equal! It just isn't so. It is absolutely paramount to appreciate that our chances in life are accidentally governed by our birth – 80 per cent of our possibilities in life are due to whether we have a lot between our ears, or very little between the ears.
- As far as I can see, in a large company the last thing you can afford to do is not to start replying immediately a question is asked.
- As I inscribed on the side of Mike's '25 Year Clock': "From the Idealist to the Realist. Together, at Cosworth, we beat the world."
- One of the things I have often done wrong was to stop projects at stages of development, because we couldn't afford to produce triumphs of development over design.
- To my thinking, turbochargers in Formula 1 engines were always expressly against the rules.
- I still don't want to be seriously rich. Neither am I interested in external honours.
- Having had a go at beating the world at building racing engines – I do like that. That's a reasonable accolade.
- I am gifted with a small amount of foresight, my problem being that I see problems arising, and that is inhuman. The human being doesn't realise he is in the mire until it's above his head – I can actually recognise that there is a pile of mire over there, and that if I'm not careful, I'm going to arrive in it, so I take avoiding action for some considerable time ...
- The important thing, with racing cars, is to make maximum utilisation of rubber.
- It's better to keep your mouth shut and be thought a fool, than to open your mouth and prove it.
- I used to think that thinking ability is the important factor in life, rather than having a good memory. It wasn't until later that I realised that I had also been gifted with what appears to be a very good memory too – and I hadn't realised the advantages of that. How can people ever learn from their experiences if they've already forgotten what they were!
- One of my principles is that young fools go on to become old fools.

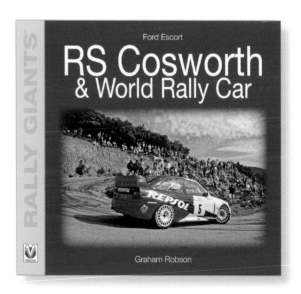

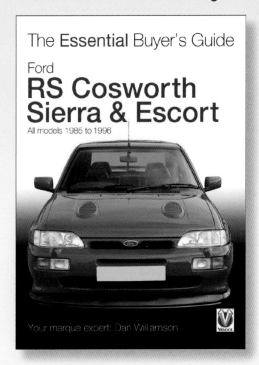

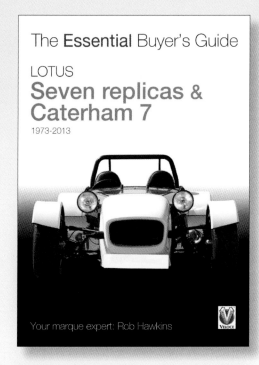

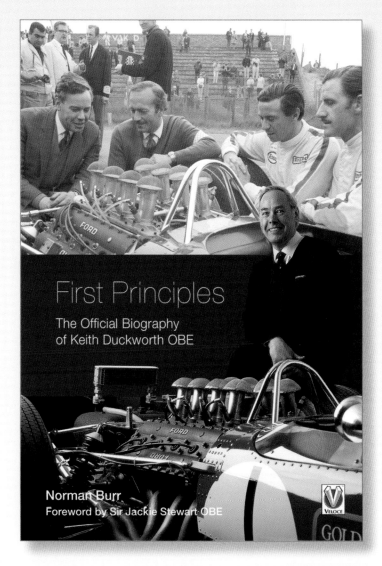

First Principles chronicles the life of Keith Duckworth OBE, the remarkable engineer famous for being co-founder of Cosworth Engineering and creating the most successful F1 engine of all time, the DFV. Although the company's engines are given due prominence, this isn't an intricate technical examination of their design, but a more rounded look at the life and work of their designer – work which included significant contributions to aviation, motorcycling, and powerboating.

ISBN: 978-1-845845-28-5
Hardback • 23.2x15.5cm • £35* UK/$59.95* USA/$64.95
• 352 pages • 200 pictures

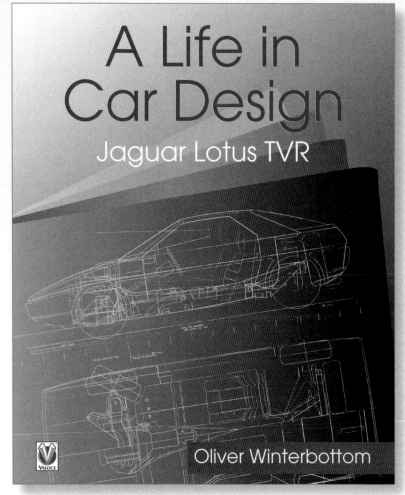

A Life in Car Design gives a unique insight into design and project work for a number of companies in the motor industry. It is aimed at both automobile enthusiasts and to encourage upcoming generations to consider a career in the creative field. Written in historical order, it traces the changes in the car design process over nearly 50 years.

ISBN: 978-1-787110-35-9
Hardback • 25x20.7cm • £37.5* UK/$55* USA • 176 pages • 200 pictures

• email: info@veloce.co.uk • Tel: +44(0)1305 260068
* prices subject to change, p&p extra

INDEX

Note: Keith Duckworth, Mike Costin, the DFV engine (from page 45 onwards), and Ford have been so important to the story of Cosworth that their names crop up on almost every page. In addition, since 1967, Cosworth was involved continuously in Formula 1, and in CART/Indycar/Champcar racing, so those, too, are ubiquitous. For these reasons alone, there is no attempt to include references to these in this index.